A MUGGLE'S GUIDE TO THE WIZARDING WORLD

♥Christina Gallo♥

A MUGGLE'S GUIDE TO THE WIZARDING WORLD

Exploring the
HARRY POTTER
Universe

FIONNA BOYLE

ECW Press

Copyright © Fionna Boyle, 2004

Published by ECW PRESS
2120 Queen Street East, Suite 200, Toronto, Ontario, Canada M4E 1E2

LIBRARY AND ARCHIVES CANADA CATALOGUING IN PUBLICATION

Boyle, Fionna
A Muggle's guide to the wizarding world: exploring the Harry Potter universe / Fionna Boyle.

Includes index.
ISBN 1-55022-655-X

1. Rowling, J. K.—Characters—Harry Potter—Handbooks, manuals, etc. 2. Potter, Harry (Fictitious character)—Handbooks, manuals, etc. 3. Rowling, J. K,—Stories, plots, etc.—Handbooks, manuals, etc. I. Title.

PR6068.094Z54 2004   823'.914   C2004-902554-6

Editor: Jennifer Hale
Cover and Text Design: Tania Craan
Typesetting: Gail Nina
Cover Photo: Fionna Boyle
Cover sky image: Masterfile
All photos on pages 424–435 courtesy Britta Peterson, except page 428, by Fionna Boyle

Printing: St. Joseph's

The publication of *A Muggle's guide to the wizarding world* has been generously supported by the Canada Council, the Ontario Arts Council, and the Government of Canada through the Book Publishing Industry Development Program. **Canada**

DISTRIBUTION

CANADA: Jaguar Book Group, 100 Armstrong Avenue, Georgetown, ON, L7G 5S4
UNITED STATES: Independent Publishers Group, 814 North Franklin Street, Chicago, Illinois 60610

PRINTED AND BOUND IN CANADA

ECW PRESS
ecwpress.com

TABLE OF CONTENTS

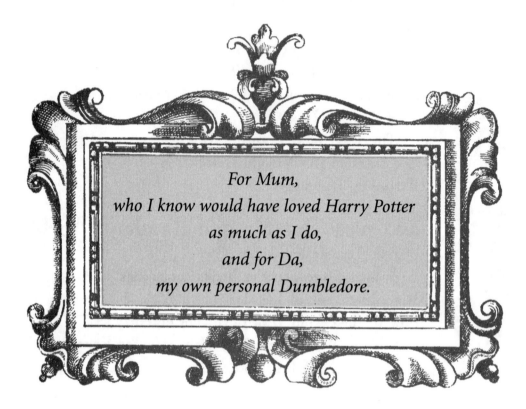

For Mum,
who I know would have loved Harry Potter
as much as I do,
and for Da,
my own personal Dumbledore.

Note to Muggles: *In an effort to stay as authentic and true to J. K. Rowling's vision of the Harry Potter series as possible,* A Muggle's Guide to the Wizarding World *uses British spellings, grammar, and style throughout the book. The first book in the series will be referred to as* Harry Potter and the Philosopher's Stone, *which was J. K. Rowling's original title, and not* Harry Potter and the Sorcerer's Stone, *to which it was changed in the American edition.*

ACKNOWLEDGEMENTS

I am blessed to be surrounded by a multitude of wonderful people, all of whom have contributed not only to the creation of this book but the enrichment of my life.

Much admiration, appreciation, and gratitude to Jen Hale for her infinite patience and magical editing skills, and to Jack David for giving me the opportunity to make a dream come true.

Endless thanks to my father Norman, for bottomless cups of tea and a lifetime of encouragement and support. Thanks also to my aunts, uncles, and cousins for their trans-Atlantic cheerleading.

For proofreading, fact-checking, suggestions, advice, and, most of all, friendship above and beyond the call, I cannot thank Michelle Woolley and Margo Bowling enough.

Kristi Bergman, Nadine Brown, Melanie Chandler, Krizia de Verdier, Keith Follett, Sean Freese, Dottie Lawrence, Stephanie Maiuri, Jyotika Malhotra, Sharlene Moustaf, Chris Mrakas, Armita Rahmani, Vigie Ramos Rios, Krista Stodola, Nephele Tempest, Laurie Travis, Michael Varga, Cindy White, and so many others . . . thank you for your enduring friendship, unconditional support, and endless faith in me.

A debt of thanks to my co-workers (who probably now know as much about Harry Potter as I do) for their indulgence and enthusiasm, especially Joe Varnell and Claudine Quinn for their expertise, Neil Andrade and Angela Ricci for their understanding, Jesse Michaels for his thoughtfulness, and Nadine Brown for her constant encouragement.

Thanks to all my friends at mediablvd.com and fanforum.com, where it all began, and to Robyn Burnett, without whom I would never have been able to write this book in the first place.

Thank you to Britta Peterson, fan extraordinaire, for her assistance and brilliantly creative ideas.

Finally, a special thanks to my goddaughter Maureen, my faerie goddaughter Jazmine, and my "nieces and nephews" — Aaron, Dylan, Trinity, and Luca, the next generation of Harry Potter fans — for their inspiration and for reminding me that magic is present in the world every day.

INTRODUCTION

"He'll be famous — a legend — I wouldn't be surprised if today was known as Harry Potter day in the future — there will be books written about Harry — every child in our world will know his name!"
— Professor McGonagall, *Harry Potter and the Philosopher's Stone*

The adventures of Harry Potter have won the hearts of children and adults everywhere, thanks to the wonderfully complex world J. K. Rowling has created and the minutiae she has developed within it. Rowling spent five years researching and gathering information for the series, and her painstaking attention to detail is evident from the very first page.

Readers lose themselves in Harry's world, but they can sometimes get lost in it, too. Keeping track of all the minor details for every character, creature, object, location, and type of magic can sometimes present a major challenge — yet it is often the seemingly "throwaway" descriptions and information that turn out to be crucial later in the series.

Whether you've forgotten the name of a magical creature, can't remember the effects of a spell, or have trouble keeping all the characters straight, *A Muggle's Guide to the Wizarding World* is an ideal reference tool and companion piece for the Harry Potter series. It contains a comprehensive, at-a-glance glossary covering everything from Azkaban to Zonko's, plus lots of fun, interesting, and useful extras to enrich your reading experience.

How to Use This Guide

A Muggle's Guide to the Wizarding World is not intended as a substitute for the Harry Potter series, nor is it meant to offer clues, opinions, or theories, or tell you how to interpret what you read (after all, that's half the fun of reading!). Instead, think of it as a study aide, a resource you can keep at your fingertips to refresh your memory as you read through the books for the first or the hundredth time.

The guide is arranged by theme (characters, creatures, academics, etc.) with subsections under each topic where applicable. The major themes are listed in the table of contents, but if you are looking for a specific entry, you can quickly consult the alphabetical index at the back.

Like the Harry Potter series, *A Muggle's Guide to the Wizarding World* is "Harry-centric." This means all references to "first year" pertain to Harry's first year, "second year" pertains to his second year, and so on (unless specifically noted otherwise).

In order not to spoil things for those who haven't read the entire Harry Potter series, the guide intentionally refrains from giving away key points of the plot as much as possible. In some sections, information is broken down year-by-year so you can use your own judgement to decide how much you want to read. In a few other sections, certain information is marked with a spoiler warning, so read with caution!

All quotations are from the Bloomsbury (British) and Raincoast (Canadian) editions of the Harry Potter series, copyright J. K. Rowling, Bloomsbury Publishing Plc, Raincoast Books, and Warner Bros.

Ready to begin? Then repeat after me: *"I solemnly swear I am up to no good . . ."*

—Fionna Boyle
June 2004

 Did you know . . . the Harry Potter books have sold almost three hundred million copies in over two hundred countries, and have been translated into sixty languages including Latin, Gaelic, Welsh, and Ancient Greek?

BIRTH OF A BOY WIZARD

THE STORY OF HOW HARRY POTTER CAME TO BE

Born in 1965 in Gloucestershire, England, Joanne Rowling (Kathleen, her grandmother's name, was added when her agent suggested she publish under her initials because little boys were less likely to read books by women authors) wrote her first story around age six, about a rabbit who had measles. Although she would later work as a secretary and a teacher of English and French, Rowling's lifelong love of writing was never far from her mind.

Rowling (pronounced "Ro-ling," to rhyme with bowling) envisioned Harry Potter in 1990, when she was on a train from Manchester to London, although she doesn't quite know where the idea came from: "I just thought, 'boy doesn't know he's a wizard (and) goes off to wizard school.' The idea was just floating along the train and looking for someone, and my mind was vacant enough and so it decided to zoom in there. From that moment I thought, 'Why doesn't he know he's a wizard?' It was as though the story was just there for me to discover."

Excited and inspired, she spent the remainder of the journey forming some of the characters and concepts of Harry's world, and by the time she reached London, Hogwarts School of Witchcraft and Wizardry had been born. Rowling decided it would take the shape of a seven-book series, with each book following a year of Harry's life at Hogwarts. Details began to emerge at a dizzying rate and in the most unusual places — she invented Quidditch whilst in a pub, and came up with the Hogwarts house names on the back of an aeroplane motion sickness bag.

The following year, Rowling moved to Portugal, where she took a job teaching English. She also continued to work on her writing, and returned to the United Kingdom in 1993 with a suitcase full of papers crammed with details and information about the complex magical universe she had created.

The influences and ideas for the Harry Potter series came from a combination of mythology, folklore, and sheer imagination, as well as inspiration from Rowling's own life. For example, she took the surname Potter from childhood friends. King's Cross station was where her parents first met on a train from London to Scotland. Gilderoy Lockhart is the only character in the series who is completely based on someone Rowling knows. And, of course, Harry shares Rowling's birthday — July 31. It is personal touches such as these that make such a whimsical, otherworldly series seem so utterly believable and grounded in reality.

Rowling's attention to detail is painstaking. For five years, she collected unusual names and Latin words, drew fantastic sketches, outlined complex histories for groups like the Death Eaters and Dementors, and created detailed background information for every character, including each of the students at Hogwarts, right down to their magical ability and heritage. Although many of these details won't make it into the books, they are all written up in Rowling's notebooks, which the author has said she will likely never publish. She has also completed the last chapter of the seventh book, which is stored away in a vault. Naturally, she will not reveal anything about it other than the tiniest of hints — apparently, the last word of the entire series is "scar."

On returning from Portugal, Rowling settled in Edinburgh, Scotland, and threw herself into finishing what would become *Harry Potter and the Philosopher's Stone*, as well as planning and writing parts of the six sequels. She wrote for hours, in longhand, at a cosy café called Nicolson's, her infant daughter in a pushchair (stroller) by her side.

After finally finishing the manuscript in 1995, Rowling needed an agent. She chose Christopher Little out of a directory because she liked the sound of his name. Although he didn't handle children's authors, Little liked what Rowling had written and agreed to take her on. The following year saw multiple rejections from different publishing companies, until Bloomsbury agreed to buy the book for £2,500. Rowling was overjoyed, and remembers seeing *Harry Potter and the Philosopher's Stone* for the first time in Waterstones, a large book shop in Edinburgh's Princes Street. "I was there on the R shelf, just like the other authors. It was incredible."

If Rowling thought that was incredible, she was completely overwhelmed by what would happen several months later, when Scholastic Press bought the American rights to the book for $105,000 — the most money ever paid for a first work of fiction by an unknown children's author.

The rest, as they say, was magic. Over the next several years, the popularity of the Harry Potter series soared amongst children and adults the world over, and Rowling won awards and broke records at an astounding rate. With two books left in the series, Pottermania shows no signs of slowing. Indeed, Rowling has created a much-beloved legacy that will endure as one of the great classics of literature for decades to come.

 **Did you know** . . . J. K. Rowling is in the Guinness Book of Records for the largest reading by an author? In October 2000, she read excerpts from *Harry Potter and the Goblet of Fire* to an audience of 20,264 at Toronto's SkyDome, as part of the Harbourfront Centre International Festival of Authors.

PART ONE:

The Characters

THE POTTERS

"Never wondered how you got that mark on yer forehead? That was no ordinary cut. That's what yeh get when a powerful, evil curse touches yeh — took care of yer mum an' dad an' yer house, even — but it didn't work on you, an' that's why yer famous, Harry. No one ever lived after he decided ter kill 'em, no one except you, an' he'd killed some o' the best witches an' wizards of the age . . . an' you was only a baby, an' you lived."

— Rubeus Hagrid, *Harry Potter and the Philosopher's Stone*

Potter, Harry James (The Boy Who Lived): Harry is small and skinny for his age, with knobbly knees and a thin face. He bears a striking resemblance to his father James, who had the same round glasses and jet black hair that sticks up all over, but he has his mother Lily's piercing emerald green eyes.

Born on July 31 (making him a Leo), Harry is an only child and orphan. When Harry was a year old, his parents were murdered by Voldemort on Hallowe'en night (see page 307). As a baby, Harry is given the nickname "the boy who lived" by the wizarding world because he is the only person to have survived a Killing Curse.

A true Gryffindor, Harry is daring, resourceful, quick-thinking, and courageous. Though he is not exceptionally gifted when it comes to academics (except for Defence Against the Dark Arts), he is proving to be a very powerful wizard and can even perform wandless magic under certain circumstances. Over the years, Harry has bravely taken on trolls, giant snakes, criminals, dragons, Death Eaters, and, of course, Voldemort. He has been accused of "acting the hero" and having a "saving people thing," but it is his innate sense of duty and responsibility that defines who he really is.

Harry is deeply loyal to Dumbledore, Hagrid, and his friends. He has a generous nature, especially towards the Weasleys, whom he comes to consider as family. He doesn't hold grudges (except, perhaps, when it comes to his nemesis, Draco Malfoy) and has a strong sense of integrity and fairness.

Although Harry may be the hero of the wizarding world, in some ways he is just a typical teenage boy, particularly when it comes to girls. He doesn't know how to react around the love-struck Ginny, and stammers and blushes around his own crush, Cho. He awkwardly seeks a date for the Yule Ball, where, to his great surprise, he discovers a different side of Hermione. As he gets older and begins his first relationship of sorts, Harry becomes increasingly bemused and frustrated by the inner workings of the female mind.

Harry can be very strong-minded and stubborn. When he becomes fixated on an idea it can be difficult to persuade him to think otherwise, even if it is in his own best interest to do so. He has a tendency to be secretive, especially about things he would be better off sharing with friends.

For such a kind and gentle person, Harry can have quite a temper. He is prone to acting rashly, without much thought for consequences. However, he has a hard time following through when given the opportunity to retaliate against those who have seriously wronged him.

Did you know . . . Harry is J. K. Rowling's favourite name for a boy? It is the medieval English form of Henry, which is taken from the Germanic Heimerich, meaning "home" (*heim*) and "power" or "ruler" (*ric*). Since writing the series, J. K. Rowling has also heard from a number of real-life Harry Potters, including a London barrister, a grandfather (who was delighted his name made him seem cool to his grandchildren), relatives of a soldier who died in World War II, and parents who named their son Harry James Potter.

The Trio

Although Harry is the hero, his adventures always involve his two best friends Hermione and Ron. At first, the boys couldn't stand bossy, know-it-all Hermione. It took a well-placed spell, troll bogeys, and an admission of guilt where none rightly existed to seal their friendship on Hallowe'en in first year — not coincidentally, ten years to the day after Voldemort killed Harry's parents. From that point on, Harry, Hermione, and Ron — the trio — became almost inseparable. Their friendship goes through several rifts over the years, but no lasting damage is ever done.

Although the three are thought of as one unit, each has a unique strength within the friendship. Harry represents the physical, full of drive, motivation, and determination, who takes action and executes plans. Hermione represents the intellectual, full of reasoning, logic, and analysis, who thinks and understands. Ron represents the emotional, full of deep feeling and love, who is capable of great loyalty and sacrifice. Their sum is much greater than their individual parts.

 **Did you know** . . . J .K. Rowling's editors wanted to remove the scene in *Harry Potter and the Philosopher's Stone* where Harry and Ron rescue Hermione from the troll? The author maintained the scene was key to the foundation of the trio's friendship and fought to keep it in.

Harry's Childhood

Immediately following Lily and James's murders, Dumbledore chooses to protect Harry by delivering him to the Dursleys' doorstep. Though Aunt Petunia is a poor surrogate for her sister Lily, Dumbledore knows Harry will be safest with his mother's only living blood relative and her family.

Living with the Dursleys is a necessary evil for Harry, and for the next ten years he leads a horrible, oppressive existence under their roof. At best, he is regarded as a gross inconvenience; at worst, he is frequently mistreated. Harry must earn his keep by performing all sorts of chores and manual labour. He is forbidden to speak to the neighbours and wears his cousin Dudley's oversized hand-me-downs. Harry sleeps in a small, cramped cupboard under the stairs.

The Dursleys consider Harry a freak, and are both afraid and ashamed of his magical ability. They do everything in their power to keep the truth hidden from him. After it is revealed Harry is a wizard, his Aunt Petunia and Uncle Vernon become increasingly paranoid and abusive. While they grudgingly let Harry move into Dudley's smaller bedroom (he has two, to house all his possessions), they confiscate all his Hogwarts things in an attempt to purge the magic from him.

Harry's conflict with his aunt and uncle gets worse as the years go on, but the older he gets, the bolder he becomes and the more he stands up for himself. At the end of fifth year, the Dursleys are warned by a group of Harry's supporters to treat him properly or suffer the consequences.

First Year

According to the Sorting Hat, Harry has plenty of courage, not a bad mind, talent, and a thirst to prove himself. The Hat almost sorted Harry into Slytherin, telling him that house could help him become great, but he willed it not to and became a Gryffindor instead.

Harry is excellent at flying and knows how to do it almost instinctively. His natural talent and skill earn him the position of Seeker on the Gryffindor Quidditch team — he is the youngest Quidditch player at Hogwarts in a century.

Second Year

An over-eager new ally attempts to protect Harry from a secret enemy, but almost kills him with kindness in the process. When Harry discovers a new and disturbing side effect from his scar, it leads many, including Harry himself, to second-guess Harry and his allegiance. He finds the pen is not mightier than the sword after a ghost from the past leads him into danger.

Third Year

After a blow-up at the Dursleys, Harry finds himself in a grim situation. He also learns appearances can be deceiving when faces from the past return, while a new friend helps him tackle the latest horror at Hogwarts. After discovering there is more to flying than broomsticks, Harry and Hermione take a timely trip to rescue a couple of friends in need.

Fourth Year

Once again, Harry finds himself thrust into a spotlight he neither asks for nor wants. To make matters worse, many of his fellow students turn against him, including one of his best friends. Typically, Harry handles himself with composure and calm nobility.

Harry faces a number of challenging tasks throughout the year, but none is as deadly or as dangerous as what he encounters in the graveyard. With his head held high, he bravely faces evil personified with some unexpected help from the last couple of people he ever expected to see. Dumbledore expresses great pride in Harry, and Hagrid offers the highest praise he can by saying Harry behaved much like his own father would have done.

Fifth Year

Harry grows the most during fifth year, both physically and metaphorically. He is faced with new responsibilities, new relationships, new challenges, new disappointments, and new heartache — rather enough to be going on with, as Dumbledore puts it.

Harry's year starts out badly and gets much worse. During the summer, Harry's wizarding and Muggle worlds collide in one of the worst possible ways, and he is left to suffer the consequences. He feels neglected by Dumbledore and treated like a child by the adults around him, who don't tell him anything about what is going on. At Hogwarts things are not much better, and Harry begins to resent the school for the first time ever. He must suffer through Umbridge (whom he comes to hate about as much as Voldemort), disturbing visions, special lessons with Snape, and recurring dreams — not to mention his first awkward and confusing attempt at romance.

Harry blames himself for what happened in the graveyard, special lessons with Snape, and it affects him deeply. He alternates between apathy at what lies ahead and resentment that he has been left alone to deal with it. Harry feels tremendously alienated from his friends, peers, and mentor, and frequently lashes out in self-righteous anger or frustration. He is the subject of much gossip and even ridicule, and feels hurt and betrayed by those whom he thought were friends. Harry has a lot of anger and restless energy bubbling up inside and seems to be constantly looking for a fight.

His attitude also affects the trio's friendship. Harry feels left behind and cut off from Hermione and Ron during the summer, and emotionally isolated from them during the school year. Harry feels particularly snubbed when Ron is chosen for an honour he feels he deserves. Although they suffer the brunt of Harry's mood swings, Hermione and Ron are very patient and mostly understand his reaction. Hermione in particular masterminds a couple of brilliant ideas designed to help Harry regain support and credibility, including the DA (see page 132). Harry finds a part of his mind often speaks in Hermione's voice during fifth year, almost like a conscience.

About the only bright spot in Harry's life is his relationship with Sirius, whom he has come to think of as a cross between father and brother. Harry and Sirius are in a similar predicament — they are locked up in their respective homes, everyone believes the lies about them, and they are powerless to do much to really change things.

Harry's rage comes to a boiling point following the battle at the Department of Mysteries. He finally gets to ask some of the questions that have been haunting him a lifetime, but the answers are not what he wants to hear. Numb with shock, Harry feels more alienated than ever before. It is as if his life has been fractured into two universes, and everything he previously wanted now belongs to a past that is no longer quite connected to him.

 Did you know . . . J. K. Rowling had a cameo on an episode of *The Simpsons* in November 2003, where she jokingly told Lisa Simpson that at the end of the Harry Potter series, Harry would grow up and marry her?

HARRY'S BIRTHDAY PRESENTS

tenth birthday: coat-hanger and a pair of Vernon's old socks (the Dursleys)

eleventh birthday: cake, Hedwig (Hagrid)

twelfth birthday: none mentioned

thirteenth birthday: pocket Sneakoscope and first-ever birthday card (Ron), card and Broomstick Servicing Kit (Hermione), *The Monster Book of Monsters* and card (Hagrid)

fourteenth birthday: cards (Hermione and Ron), cakes (Hermione, Ron, Hagrid, and Sirius). Harry also receives a sack full of rock cakes (Hagrid), a fruitcake and pastries (Mrs. Weasley), and a large box of sugar-free snacks (Hermione) earlier in the summer after the Dursleys force him to go on Dudley's diet.

fifteenth birthday: cards and boxes of Honeydukes chocolates (Hermione and Ron)

Harry's Scar

Growing up, Harry's Aunt Petunia told him the thin lightning-bolt shaped scar on his forehead came from the car crash that killed his parents. In reality, the scar is the only mark that remained after Voldemort attempted to use the Killing Curse on Harry as a baby.

Dumbledore tells Harry it is no ordinary scar — it connects Harry to Voldemort (and vice-versa) in numerous ways. From time to time, Harry feels a sharp pain in his scar, which becomes more frequent and intense as he gets older. Most people in the wizarding world recognise Harry by his scar, something that makes him uncomfortable as it is a symbol of the tragedy of his life, while also drawing unwanted attention his way.

First Year

* After being Sorted, Harry's scar burns with a sharp, hot pain.
* Whilst serving detention in the Forbidden Forest, Harry's scar hurts so badly he falls down. He continues to feel stabbing pain in his forehead for the remainder of the year, even during exams.
* A searing pain courses through Harry's scar when he is touched by someone in the chamber containing the Mirror of Erised.

Fourth year

* The burning pain from Harry's scar wakes him up with a start the exact moment someone two hundred miles away is murdered.
* When Harry dreams of Voldemort performing the Cruciatus Curse, his scar hurts so badly it wakes him up.
* In the graveyard, Harry's scar explodes with a pain so agonising he feels like his head is going to split open, and he drops to the ground, retching.

Fifth Year

* Harry's scar prickles on and off during the summer and throughout the year when he has a recurring dream of a long dark windowless corridor ending in a locked door.
* Harry's scar burns badly when he thinks about Dumbledore not speaking to him.
* When Harry thinks of Mrs. Weasley's Boggart, his scar shoots with pain.
* Harry's scar burns when Umbridge inspects his hand during detention.
* After Quidditch practice in the rain, Harry's scar hurts more than it has in weeks.
* Harry's scar feels like it has been struck by a poker when he has a vision of a snake attacking someone.
* When Harry looks at Dumbledore, his scar burns and he feels a surge of intense emotion.
* After Harry's first Occlumency lesson, the pain from his scar is so intense he falls to the ground, and he is possessed by a fit of insane laughter.

* Harry feels his scar burn when Avery is punished.
* Harry's scar hurts and he feels another surge of intense emotion when Dumbledore urges him to continue with his Occlumency lessons.
* Harry's scar aches when he has a vision of someone close to him being tortured.
* Harry feels searing pain in his scar when he reveals what happened to the prophecy.
* At the Ministry, Harry's scar burns with a pain more intense than he has ever felt before.

HARRY'S DREAMS, NIGHTMARES, AND VISIONS

First Year

* **at the Dursleys:** Recurring dreams of a flying motorbike.
* **first night at Hogwarts:** Dreams he is wearing Quirrell's turban, which tells him it is his destiny to transfer to Slytherin. Harry says he doesn't want to and tries to pull the turban off, but it becomes tighter. Malfoy watches, laughing, then turns into Snape, whose laugh is high and cold. The dream ends with a burst of green light.
* **over Christmas holidays:** Recurring nightmares about his parents disappearing in a flash of green light while a high voice cackles with laughter.
* **after his adventure in the Forbidden Forest:** Recurring nightmare about his parents disappearing, featuring a hooded figure dripping blood.

Second Year

* **at the Dursleys:** Dreams he is on exhibit as an "Underage Wizard" at the zoo. Harry sees Dobby in the crowd and begs for help, but Dobby vanishes and is replaced by the Dursleys. Dudley laughs at Harry and shakes his cage.

Third Year

* **after the Gryffindor v Ravenclaw match:** Dreams he is carrying his broom and following a silvery shape in a forest. The faster he chases the shape, the faster it runs. Harry hears the sound of hooves and the shape starts to gallop, but he is woken up before he can catch up to it.

* **night before the Gryffindor v Slytherin match:** Dreams he overslept and Oliver substitutes Neville for him in the match. Then Harry dreams he forgot his broom, and the Slytherins fly on dragons instead of broomsticks.

Fourth Year

* **at the Dursleys:** Dreams of a small dark room containing a snake, an old man, Wormtail, and Voldemort. Harry hears Wormtail and Voldemort discuss someone they have murdered, and their plan to murder someone else. He then sees the old man die as Voldemort's face is revealed.

* **just before the second task of the Triwizard Tournament:** Dreams he is inside the mermaid's painting in the Prefects' bathroom. She holds Harry's broom over his head, laughing at him, and pokes him in the side with it . . . just as he wakes up to someone poking him in the side with a finger.

* **during Divination:** Dreams he rides an owl to a house atop a hill, and enters a dark room containing a snake, Wormtail, and Voldemort. He hears Voldemort tell Wormtail someone is dead, and that Wormtail's mistake has not ruined everything. Voldemort says he will feed Harry to the snake instead of Wormtail. As Voldemort performs the Cruciatus Curse on Wormtail, Harry wakes up writhing on the floor.

Fifth Year

* **throughout the year:** Recurring dreams of a long dark windowless corridor ending in a locked door.

✷ **at the Dursleys:** Recurring nightmares about his encounter in the graveyard.

✷ **at Grimmauld Place:** Dreams of cannon-faced creatures galloping up and down the corridor outside his bedroom. Harry then hears Hagrid's voice telling him these "weapons" would be studied in class.

✷ **night before school begins:** Dreams of Mrs. Weasley crying over Kreacher's body, watched by a crown-wearing Hermione and Ron. Harry's parents flit in and out, and he sees himself walking down the corridor with the locked door.

✷ **just before Christmas:** Dreams he is in the Room of Requirement with Cho. She accuses Harry of promising her Chocolate Frog Cards but not delivering, and shows him the cards Cedric gave her. Cho turns into Hermione, who suggests Harry give Cho his broom, but he says his broom is confiscated and that he only went to Room of Requirement to hang up Dobby-shaped ornaments . . . the dream changes, and Harry has a vision of a snake biting a sleeping man in front of a door at the end of a corridor.

✷ **after the Gryffindor v Hufflepuff match:** Dreams of McGonagall playing the bagpipes as Neville and Professor Sprout waltz around the Room of Requirement. When Harry leaves, the corridor outside the room is not Hogwarts — it is the same corridor he has been dreaming of all year, only the door at the end is slightly open.

✷ **after *The Quibbler* interview is published:** Has a vision of Voldemort and Avery discussing Bode.

✷ **night the Weasleys' Wildfire Whiz-bangs are set off:** Recurring dream of the corridor, only this time he goes through the door at the end and enters a series of rooms. Harry has the dream again later, and goes a little further than he did the first time before waking up.

✷ **during his History of Magic OWL:** Recurring dream of the corridor and going through the door at the end into a series of rooms, only this time Harry has a vision of Voldemort performing the Cruciatus Curse on someone close to him.

 **Did you know** . . . J. K. Rowling said if she could spend a day with one of the characters in the series, she would choose Harry? In an online chat for World Book Day in March 2004, the author said she would like to take Harry out for a meal and apologise for everything she has put him through!

Potter, James: Harry's father. Thin, with messy black hair and glasses, James looks exactly like his son but with "deliberate mistakes" — his eyes were hazel and his nose was longer. However, they share the same hands, eyebrows, and mouth, and at age fifteen, both were the same height. James was a Gryffindor and made Head Boy at Hogwarts, although he was not a prefect in his fifth year. He was also an excellent Quidditch player and particularly skilled at Transfiguration.

During his time at Hogwarts, James was best friends with Sirius Black, who was like a brother to him and a second son to James's parents. James and Sirius were the "height of cool" and the cleverest students of their day, but also had a reputation as a pair of troublemakers.

James and Snape despised each other on sight as students, much like Harry and Malfoy a generation later and for similar reasons. Snape was said to be jealous of James's intellect and Quidditch skills; he thought James was so arrogant, criticism bounced off him. James, meanwhile, despised the Dark Arts and found Snape an easy outlet for his hatred. Despite James saving Snape's life during their sixth year, their mutual animosity only got worse. James had a crush on Lily since at least their fifth year, and made a fool of himself whenever she was around. They began dating in seventh year, after his attitude and ego deflated a little, and married not long after leaving Hogwarts.

James and Lily were original members of the Order of the Phoenix, and defied Voldemort three times before Voldemort finally murdered them on

Hallowe'en. James put up a courageous fight before he died. Dumbledore suggests Harry's stag Patronus — an animal particularly symbolic of James — means James's spirit is still alive in Harry and appears when his son needs him most.

Potter, Lily (née Evans): Harry's mother and Petunia Dursley's sister. Lily was very pretty, with long, dark red hair and bright almond-shaped emerald eyes, which Harry inherited. Lily was **Muggle-born**, but her parents were proud of her magical abilities, although Petunia was extremely jealous and considered her a freak.

Lily was very intelligent and seems to have been particularly skilled at Charms. She was Head Girl at Hogwarts, where she met James, a fellow Gryffindor. Lily's sacrifice and love for Harry formed a kind of blood protection deep inside him that shielded him from Voldemort's Killing Curse as a baby, and continued to protect him in years to come.

The name Lily is derived from the flower of the same name, which symbolises purity and resurrection.

 Did you know . . . in an online chat for World Book Day in March 2004, J. K. Rowling said all of Harry's grandparents were dead and not particularly important to the story?

THE GRANGERS

"Nobody in my family's magic at all, it was ever such a surprise when I got my letter, but I was ever so pleased, of course, I mean, it's the very best school of witchcraft there is, I've heard — I've learnt all of our set books off by heart, of course, I just hope it will be enough — I'm Hermione Granger, by the way, who are you?"

— Hermione Granger, *Harry Potter and the Philosopher's Stone*

Granger, Hermione Jane (Hermy-Own-Ninny, Hermy): Muggle-born Hermione has brown eyes, lots of bushy brown hair and large front teeth. Her birthday is the nineteenth of September, making her a Virgo. Precocious and mature for her age, Hermione is never short of an opinion and can come across as a know-it-all. She has a bossy voice and can get a steely glint in her eyes when she is determined about something. The brains of the trio, she is practical, analytical, and logical.

Lupin called Hermione "the cleverest witch of [her] age that [he'd] ever met." She is highly intelligent and consistently at the top of her class. (In fifth year, Hermione reveals the Sorting Hat initially thought about putting her in Ravenclaw, but decided she would be better off in Gryffindor — some fans thought this was J. K. Rowling's subtle way of acknowledging those who wondered why brainy Hermione wasn't made a Ravenclaw!) A very conscientious student, Hermione studies hard during summer holidays, and draws up revision timetables for exams months in advance. She loves to read and do research — her school bag is so crammed with books at one point, it bursts a seam!

Hermione is very caring and compassionate, and always helps the underdog. She has a deep-seated sense of right and wrong and stands up for what and whom she believes in. Over the years, she has bravely spoken her mind against the likes of Malfoy, Rita Skeeter, Umbridge, Snape, members of the Ministry (Crouch in particular), an escaped and allegedly maniacal convict, and perhaps most difficult of all, Harry and Ron.

Hermione is unswervingly loyal to her friends. When a nasty article is written about Hagrid, she seeks him out to show her support. She keeps Ginny's confidences. She attends almost every Quidditch match to support her friends on the team, even though she isn't particularly fond of the sport. She is the only one who stands by Harry in fourth year when most of the school turns on him, including Ron. She looks out for Neville and helps him in Potions. Even when her actions exasperate her friends, Hermione's heart is usually in the right place.

Though things with Hermione frequently seem black-and-white, she is often full of surprises. She can have quite a temper when provoked, and Harry and Ron are shocked (as are Crabbe and Goyle) when she gives Malfoy his just desserts in third year. They are also amazed when she walks out of class after openly criticising a teacher. She is rather prim and not prone to "girly" behaviour or outbursts over trivial things, yet has been known to show signs of spontaneous affection, even developing a bit of a crush on Lockhart (but quickly coming to her senses!). Hermione is some-thing of an enigma — at times, she can be openly emotional, while at other times it is impossible to know what she is really thinking.

Hermione and Harry's friendship is mostly stable and calm. Hermione seems to be mentally attuned to Harry — not only does he hear her voice in his head, like his conscience, but they pick up on things others do not notice, such as Malfoy's veiled references to Sirius. Hermione and Ron's friendship is more volatile. They bicker over everything from their pets to schoolwork to S.P.E.W. (see page 134), but are able to forgive and forget, even if they can't agree. They both worry over Harry's safety and welfare, but in different ways.

Hermione is the voice of reason among the trio, and understands the consequences of taking actions — something neither Harry nor Ron often think about. She looks out for the boys by helping them keep up with their homework (although she will not do it for them) and trying to mend the rift when they fight (although she will not play intermediary).

Hermione's name originally comes from Greek mythology Hermione (pronounced "Her-my-oh-nee") was the daughter of Helen of Troy. In Shakespeare's *The Winter's Tale*, King Leontes's wife's name was Hermione.

Did you know . . . the reason why J. K. Rowling chose the name Hermione? In an interview with the National Press Club in October, 1999, Rowling said, "I wanted quite an unusual name for her because I think there are quite a lot of girls like Hermione . . . and it crossed my mind as I was writing that if I ever was published, I didn't want to give her a common name. You know, just in case somewhere out there, there was a Jane with big front teeth who was really swotty [someone who studies a lot, to the point of being geeky] and annoying!"

Did you also know . . . on her official Web site, J. K. Rowling confirms Hermione's original surname was "Puckle," but Rowling decided to change it to something "less frivolous" instead?

First Year

When Hermione first comes to Hogwarts, Ron describes her as a "nightmare." Meddlesome and interfering, she self-righteously frets over the slightest infraction of the rules, and her over-confident attitude in class does not win her any friends. However, she earns Harry and Ron's (grudging) respect after taking the blame when they rescue her from an ugly situation during the Hallowe'en Feast.

After the boys befriend her, Hermione softens around the edges a little. She becomes much nicer and is a little more relaxed about rule-breaking. She demonstrates great grace under pressure, and earns accolades from Dumbledore for her "cool logic in the face of fire."

Second Year

Hermione spends a significant portion of the year in the hospital wing, due to two separate incidents. Yet even when she is incapacitated, her research and intellect still help save the day.

Hermione has no problem with breaking rules for the greater good — the same girl who chided Harry and Ron a year ago for leaving Gryffindor Tower after curfew now has no qualms about stealing Potions ingredients and drugging fellow students as a means to an end!

Third Year

No longer a timid, deferential schoolgirl, Hermione's rebellious streak continues to flourish when she vehemently disagrees with one of her new teachers. She finds herself in disagreements with both Harry and Ron as well, and begins to crack under the strain of an impossible courseload. But when time is of the essence, Hermione and Harry do a good turn and help give a pair of hopeless cases a new lease on life.

Fourth Year

Hermione's fourth year is one of change and development. Her compassion for the plight of house-elves inspires her to help better their lot in life (whether they want it or not). Hermione means well, but becomes somewhat self-righteous and over-zealous in her efforts.

Hermione makes a new friend (Viktor Krum, who drives Ron buggy) and a new enemy (Rita Skeeter, who drives her buggy), both of whom impact her social life in unexpected ways. Hermione handles herself with grace and dignity during the minor scandal that follows, although Ron worries about her reputation as a "scarlet woman." But Hermione has the last laugh when she turns the tables and exposes a little scandal herself.

Like an ugly duckling transforming into a swan, Hermione goes to great pains to make herself over for the Yule Ball. Her newly-straightened teeth, elegant upswept hair, improved posture, and floaty periwinkle robes elicit different but equally interesting reactions from her two best friends. Harry doesn't recognise the pretty girl in blue at first, but his jaw drops when he realises who she is. Ron, on the other hand, barely contains his jealousy and either ignores her or glares at her when she is nearby. He accuses Hermione of "fraternising with the enemy."

Fifth Year

By fifth year, Hermione is a force to be reckoned with (as Marietta Edgecombe and Rita Skeeter can testify) and is really coming into her own as an independent, powerful witch. She is the brains behind a number of important plans, including the DA and Harry's interview with *The Quibbler*. She can perform NEWT-level magic, and, after Harry, is the first of their peers to say Voldemort's name and produce a corporeal Patronus. Naturally, Hermione is made prefect, and takes her newfound responsibilities very seriously.

Harry seems to have taken the place of Ron as Hermione's sparring partner. For the most part, she is able to calmly defuse his anger and remind him that she and Ron are on his side when he flies off the handle irrationally. Hermione is also strong enough to broach uncomfortable subjects with Harry and withstand his subsequent tirades without losing her own temper. At the same time, Hermione and Ron's friendship seems to have matured and stabilised somewhat after Harry's request for a truce.

Hermione is still in contact with Viktor Krum, but the exact nature of their relationship is unknown. During the year, she offers advice to a bemused Harry about the inner workings of the female mind (although the object of Harry's affections appears to have very little affection for Hermione) and asks him rather blunt questions about his own experiences.

Hermione's powers of intuition and perception are keenly developed in fifth year. She is shrewd enough to pick up on the real message behind Umbridge's speech at the start-of-term feast, and observant enough to notice Harry's not-so-secret admirer, much to his surprise.

Hermione's hatred for Umbridge knows no bounds. When Umbridge attempts to hurt someone close to her, Hermione devises a clever plan to give Umbridge a taste of her own medicine — proving that even bookish Hermione can be cunning and deceitful if need be.

Hermione is involved in the battle at the Department of Mysteries.

 Did you know . . . J. K. Rowling said she based the character of Hermione on an exaggerated version of herself as a schoolgirl?

Granger, Mr. and Mrs.: Hermione's Muggle parents. Little is known about them — J. K. Rowling has indicated this is because the Grangers are not important to the plot, but it seems strange that even basic details, such as their first names or where they live, are unknown.

Although Mr. and Mrs. Granger have no real knowledge or understanding of the wizarding world, they are supportive of Hermione and want her to do well at Hogwarts. Rather than react with fear and shame, like the Dursleys did with Harry, the Grangers encourage their only child to enter this strange new world and develop her talents to her greatest ability. They even accompany Hermione to Diagon Alley in second year to buy her school things, despite feeling somewhat nervous and apprehensive.

For all their support of Hermione, however, the Grangers will not allow their daughter to use magic to shrink her large front teeth and insist she continue with her braces instead (they are dentists, after all!).

 **Did you know** . . . J. K. Rowling always planned for Hermione to have a younger sister? However, the character never made an appearance throughout the course of writing, and J. K. Rowling felt it would be too late to include her now with only two books remaining in the series.

THE WEASLEYS

"My father told me all the Weasleys have red hair, freckles and more children than they can afford."
 — Draco Malfoy, *Harry Potter and the Philosopher's Stone*

Described by Dumbledore as one of the most prominent pure-blood families in the wizarding world, the Weasleys are a large, happy, close-knit bunch, all of whom have brilliant red hair. They are the opposite of many other families of their stature — very kind-hearted but not very well-to-do.

Though the name "Weasley" brings to mind weasels, the family seems to have little in common with the animal. Weasels are associated with cunning, slyness, stealth, suspicion, and revenge; traits generally not associated with the Weasley clan. However, weasels also symbolise keen insight, ingenuity, intrigue, and revenge against evil . . . considering Mrs. Weasley's powers of observation, the twins' creativity, Ron's adventures, and the family's continued fight against the Dark Arts, there may be a connection after all.

Weasley, Ron Bilius (**Ronald**): Youngest son of the Weasley family. Ron is tall and gangly, with big hands and feet. He is freckle-faced and has a long nose. His birthday is the first of March, making him a Pisces.

Ron is typical of teenage boys everywhere, Muggle or wizarding — he has an extremely healthy appetite, could probably apply himself better in school, supports his favourite sports team (the Chudley Cannons), and is fixated on taking a pretty girl to the Ball. He has an easy-going personality, and generally doesn't take things too seriously. Ron likes to joke around a lot, but strangely, many of the things he jokes about often wind up actually happening. A true Gryffindor, Ron is brave and loyal. He is also an excellent chess player, indicating a sharp mind capable of strategy and planning.

Ron is very sensitive about his family's lack of money, and is frustrated that he always receives his brothers' hand-me-downs. He craves his own fame and success, and as a result, relishes the few moments in the spotlight he does experience.

Naturally, Malfoy takes great delight in taunting Ron about the things he knows will upset him the most. He knows exactly what to say to get a reaction, and Ron gives him one almost every time. Malfoy (and, to a lesser extent, Hermione) brings out Ron's argumentative, hot-headed side (watch out when his ears glow red!).

Often tactless and impetuous, Ron is prone to blowing things out of proportion and making snap judgements about people (particularly any males who get too close to Ginny or Hermione). He sometimes wears his heart on his sleeve, though in his typically clueless fashion, he doesn't seem to realise he is doing it. Ron has a love-hate friendship with Hermione. One moment he is annoyed and frustrated by her bossiness and adherence to rules, and the next, he buys her perfume for Christmas and stands up to students and teachers who insult her.

Ron is Harry's first real friend in the wizarding world, and has become both a best friend and brother to him. Although Ron grew up knowing who Harry was, he treats him (mostly) like a normal person and likes him for himself, not his fame. Ron is as curious about Harry's Muggle upbringing as Harry is about Ron's wizarding one (although Ron does not share his father's wild enthusiasm for all things Muggle).

The name Ronald is a Scottish variant of Ragnvald, which in turn is derived from the Germanic Reginold, meaning "advice" (*ragin*) and "rule" (*wald*). This could possibly indicate Ron is Harry's right-hand man (he gives advice to the ruler/leader).

 Did you know . . . J. K. Rowling named Ron after a late friend of her family, Ronald Ridley? He is one of the people named in the dedication of *Harry Potter and the Goblet of Fire*.

First Year

Ron starts at Hogwarts with Bill's old robes, Charlie's old wand and cauldron, and Percy's old rat, Scabbers. There are expectations for him to do as well at the school as his five brothers before him — each of whom has left his own legacy — but even if he does, "ickle Ronnie" will likely receive no special attention or recognition because it has all been done before. This explains Ron's vision in the Mirror of Erised, which indicates a desire for prestige, glory, and recognition of his own achievements.

Ron's chess-playing abilities come into play at the end of the year in what Dumbledore later says is the "best-played game of chess Hogwarts has seen in many years." In this instance, Harry and Hermione look to Ron for guidance and leadership and he does not let them down — he bravely and willingly sacrifices himself for their sakes.

Second Year

Not one of Ron's finer years! Mrs. Weasley is howling mad at her youngest son after a well-intentioned joy ride results in serious repercussions not only for Ron and his wand, but Mr. Weasley. Ron feels sluggish after gallantly attempting to defend Hermione against Malfoy's nasty insults. He has a close encounter with spiders, his biggest fear, and is almost the victim of an avalanche. Finally, near-tragedy strikes a little too close to home.

Third Year

Ron and Hermione's pets seem to fight as much as their owners do. After the worst is feared, Ron is furious with Hermione and stubbornly refuses to forgive her or speak to her. But when the axe falls, Ron sets aside his blame and anger and repairs the rift in their friendship by helping her with a life-or-death situation.

Ron's Gryffindor loyalty and bravery rise to the surface again in the Shrieking Shack, where he stands up (as best he can) to a notorious criminal. He is willing to protect his friends with his own life. Ron has a brush with celebrity and seems to enjoy the attention.

When Snape catches Harry red-handed, Ron covers up for him. But Ron cannot believe it when he is betrayed later by someone familiar to him.

Fourth Year

Ron's jealous, stubborn, and temperamental sides show in separate situations involving Harry and Hermione.

Though Ron has always been a loyal friend to Harry up until now, he reacts very badly when Harry is chosen to enter a prestigious event and refuses to listen to Harry's side of the story. Hermione thinks this is because Ron must compete with his brothers at home, and now at school is shunted to the side because of his famous best friend. Later, Ron gets his own fifteen minutes of fame, and embellishes his version of events more and more with each retelling.

In Hermione's case, Ron's jealousy is misplaced and he doesn't even seem to consciously realise why he is angry with her (although both Harry and Hermione seem to understand very clearly). Poor Hermione bears the brunt of Ron's anger at the Yule Ball, and by the end of the evening is rather angry herself.

Fifth Year

In fifth year, Ron takes the first steps towards realising his long-ago vision in the Mirror of Erised. With his newfound responsibilities, Ron matures considerably and begins to move away from the shadows of his brothers. By now, he also owns a new broom, new dress robes, a new wand, and a new owl.

To Ron's (and everyone else's) complete astonishment, he is made prefect — it is the first time he has ever beaten Harry at anything. He tries to be nonchalant as Fred and George give him a hard time, comparing him to Percy, but secretly, he seems proud and pleased. As a prefect, Ron has a spotty record — although he rightly threatens a friend who is out of order with detention, he has a lack of tact with first years, is unwilling to discipline his brothers, and wants to punish Slytherins every chance he gets (not to mention the Firewhisky he contemplates ordering at the Hog's Head).

Ron's other great accomplishment in fifth year is joining the Quidditch team. He is thrilled to be chosen as Keeper, but lacks the self-esteem and confidence needed to play well (Angelina later confides to Harry that Ron wasn't the best choice she had). Ron becomes defensive and sullen when he makes mistakes, and gets extremely nervous playing in front of an audience. He suffers from a bad panic attack the morning of his first match — which the Slytherins exploit with a taunting rhyme that does not sing his praises but royally aggravates him instead. By year's end, Ron's confidence is given a tremendous boost and he struts around, enjoying the spotlight and retelling his story to anyone who will listen. Harry even catches Ron tousling his hair and looking around to see who is watching, just like Harry's own father used to do.

Ron seems to have an admirer in Luna Lovegood; however, he is bewildered by her interest and doesn't quite know what to make of her. He is suspicious and accusatory when he learns Hermione still keeps in touch with Krum, and has a similarly bad reaction when he discovers his baby sister is dating. Ron finds himself partly amused, partly disgusted, and partly curious when Harry discusses his love life. Later, he tries to subtly play matchmaker but his suggestion falls on deaf ears.

Ron is a member of the DA and is involved in the battle at the Department of Mysteries.

Weasley, Arthur: Thin, tall, and balding, the patriarch of the Weasley clan wears horn-rimmed glasses and dresses in dusty worn green robes. One of three brothers, he is a jovial, good-natured family man, although he can seem mildly eccentric at times. Mr. Weasley despises Lucius Malfoy and all he stands for, and wishes he could find a way to expose him for what he really is.

Mr. Weasley is fascinated with Muggles and takes every opportunity to ask questions and learn about their world (he is delighted to camp Muggle-style during the Quidditch World Cup, where Hermione teaches him how to light a match). Though he works for the Ministry in the Misuse of Muggle Artefacts Office, his garden shed is full of Muggle objects that he takes apart, enchants, and reassembles out of sheer curiosity ("if he raided our house, he'd have to put himself straight under arrest," says Fred). Mr. Weasley is also a lifelong campaigner against Muggle mistreatment and an advocate of strengthening Muggle-wizard relations. The only Muggles Mr. Weasley doesn't care for are the Dursleys — he cannot believe how cold and rude they are to Harry.

Although the exact meaning of the name Arthur is undetermined, the name figures prominently in British mythology in the legend of King Arthur, a sixth century king who presided over the knights of the round table. Interestingly, four of the Weasley sons — Bill (William), Charlie (Charles), Fred (Frederick), and George — are also named after kings.

Weasley, Molly (née Prewett): The matriarch of the Weasley clan is short and plump, with a kind face. Mrs. Weasley's world revolves around her home and family. She glows with motherly pride over her children's accomplishments and despairs over their antics — Fred, George, and Ron (and possibly Ginny) give her far more trouble than Bill, Charlie, and Percy ever did. Though she is mostly very caring and compassionate, Mrs. Weasley can have quite a fiery temper. She is very observant and doesn't seem to miss a thing, much to the twins' great dismay.

Mrs. Weasley's maiden name is Prewett, and she has close family members who were killed by Death Eaters. As such, she is terrified someone she loves is going to die by Voldemort's hand. Determined to shield her children from harm, she often makes the mistake of smothering them or making decisions for them. She is well-suited to her name — to "mollycoddle" means to be overprotective or to fuss over excessively, traits Mrs. Weasley displays towards all her family in varying degrees. When her children rebel against this, she becomes flustered and exerts control over the only person left that she can — Ginny, whom she constantly babies.

Mrs. Weasley is a maternal figure to Harry, hugging him when he needs comfort, and cheering him on when he needs support. She considers him to be as much a part of the family as her own children, only Harry can do no wrong in her eyes. She bristles whenever the Dursleys are mentioned, although her sense of propriety will not let her criticise them in front of him. Mrs. Weasley worries incessantly over Harry's well-being, and fiercely argues over what is best for him. He is touched by her concern, but finds her doting and presumptuous manner a bit suffocating as he gets older.

Weasley, Bill: Eldest of the Weasley children, two years older than Charlie. Tall, cool, and good-looking, Bill dresses like he's going to a Muggle rock concert — he has long hair in a ponytail (which Mrs. Weasley desperately wishes he would cut) and a fang earring (which she desperately wishes he would stop wearing). Bill is not afraid to kindly but firmly stand up to his mother and doesn't particularly care what others think of his appearance, although he seems to attract his fair share of attention from both living and portrait-dwelling witches!

A former Hogwarts Head Boy, Bill now works for Gringotts. He has held positions at the wizarding bank both in Egypt as a curse breaker, and in England at a desk job.

Weasley, Charlie: Second eldest of the Weasley children, two years older than Percy. Charlie is shorter and stockier than most of his brothers. Covered in freckles, he is a muscular, outdoorsy type with a broad, weather-beaten face and easy grin.

Charlie is a former Gryffindor Quidditch Captain and Seeker. He was legendary during his time at Hogwarts and talented enough to have played for England but chose a different (although equally exciting and dangerous) career instead — studying wild dragons in Romania. (He has also taken on the role of dragon-keeper during certain special events in England.) Although Charlie can often be seen sporting a fireproof balaclava, he has suffered quite a few burns, blisters, and calluses as a result of his work.

Did you know . . . it is possible Charlie was a prefect too? Although Charlie is only ever mentioned as Quidditch Captain, Mrs. Weasley remarks, "That's everyone in the family!" when Ron is made prefect (causing Fred and George to huff they mustn't belong to the family, then). She also comments that Ron is the "fourth prefect in the family," which would suggest the others were Percy, Bill . . . and Charlie.

Weasley, Percy Ignatius: Third eldest of the Weasley children, two years older than the twins. Tall and thin, Percy wears horn-rimmed glasses and is tidy in appearance. He is pompous, uptight, and overly formal, even to his own family. Percy has practically no sense of humour, although Penelope

Clearwater might suggest there is something of a hidden side to him at Hogwarts. Full of his own self-importance, Percy is exceedingly proud of being both a prefect and Head Boy (he even wears his badges during summer holidays!) and takes his responsibilities very seriously.

Percy is rule-abiding and ambitious, and according to Ron, aspires to be Minister for Magic one day. Ron also thinks his brother will not let anyone stand in the way of his career. After leaving Hogwarts, Percy lands a position in the Department of International Magical Co-operation and after a year, is promoted to the Junior Assistant to the Minister for Magic himself. Percy considers his bosses in both departments as mentors. He is fervently dedicated to them and wholeheartedly endorses all their decisions. However, this blind devotion comes at the expense of his family and friends.

 Did you know . . . Chris Rankin, who plays Percy in the Harry Potter films, was a prefect when he was at school?

Weasley, Fred and George (**Gred and Forge**): Identical twins who are two years older than Ron (their birthday is, appropriately, April Fool's Day). Like Charlie, Fred and George are shorter and stockier in build than the rest of the Weasleys. They are alike in personality as well as appearance, and are so mentally attuned they frequently finish each other's sentences.

A pair of practical jokers, Fred and George can always be counted on for a laugh or a bit of mischief (they know every secret passageway in and out of Hogwarts, for starters). They can be heard regularly exploding things in their bedroom at The Burrow, but know their share of Muggle tricks, too. No one is immune from their pranks — not even their mother, whom they have fooled on occasion by pretending to be each other. (Their favourite victim, however, is definitely Percy.) In fact, the twins enjoy playing jokes so much, they plan to open their own joke shop, Weasleys' Wizard Wheezes, after leaving Hogwarts — to the complete despair of Mrs. Weasley, who had hoped they would wind up with respectable positions in the Ministry.

Also to their mother's chagrin, Fred and George don't seem to have much time for studies (though they are rather fond of showing off their magic skills, such as Apparation, once they come of age). While the twins did not do very well on their OWLs and even debated coming back for their NEWTs, they are actually much cleverer than they let on. They invent or master all sorts of ingenious spells and potions to use in their products for their joke shop. Savvy, shrewd, and resourceful businessmen, Fred and George procure ingredients from unexpected sources, negotiate shady deals, and successfully fill a supply-and-demand niche market at Hogwarts. They turn a tidy profit from fellow students, who literally eat up their wares. After Hogwarts, the twins continue to do well financially, and are even able to afford matching dragonskin jackets!

At Hogwarts, Fred and George are Beaters on the Quidditch team and members of the DA. The twins are well-known and well-liked, although they frequently exasperate their teachers with their antics. They have little respect for certain kinds of authority — they think prefects are prats and don't take them seriously. The twins make a lasting impression on the castle when they leave Hogwarts. Filch is swamped with work in the wake of their departure, although Peeves salutes them in admiration.

Weasley, Ginevra Molly (Ginny): The only girl and youngest of the Weasley children, she is the first girl to be born into the family in several generations. Short in stature, Ginny has brown eyes and long hair, and, from certain angles, bears a strong resemblance to the twins. Ginny is star-struck by Harry before she even knows him. Her crush on him worsens after Harry and Ron become friends and she comes to Hogwarts — she is accident-prone around him, hides when she sees him and will not speak in front of him (finding it easier to write out her feelings instead).

In her first year at school, Ginny is very lonely, vulnerable, and impressionable. Her one friendship possesses her to open up and pour out her soul, revealing all her deepest fears and darkest secrets. However, Ginny soon finds herself in someone's bad books when the friendship is not all it appears to be.

In fourth year, Ginny attends the Yule Ball as the guest of an older student, and by fifth year, she has blossomed and come into her own. She is a member of the DA and makes the Gryffindor Quidditch team (though her brothers are surprised, it is revealed she has been breaking into the Weasleys' broom shed and taking their brooms out since she was six years old). In Quidditch as in life, Ginny prefers goal-scoring (taking action) to Seeking (waiting patiently).

It seems Ginny has inherited a bit of the twins' mischievous and rebellious streaks — she has no trouble lying with a straight face to cause a diversion, or shifting the blame to someone else when her mother asks nosy questions. (She can also cast a mean Bat Bogey Hex.)

As she gets older, Ginny has also become more outgoing and sociable. She is friendly with Neville and Luna, and confides in Hermione. According to Hermione, Ginny's feelings for Harry seem to have changed, too. She is no longer afraid to talk to him and even reprimands him when he is short with her or feels sorry for himself. Instead, Ginny's attention is focused elsewhere — although she hides the fact she is dating from Ron, who (inevitably) reacts badly when he finds out. It appears no boy is good enough for Ron's baby sister in his eyes . . . except, perhaps, one.

Despite Ginny's newfound maturity, she is still treated like a little girl by Mrs. Weasley and others, who are over-protective towards her and exclude her from things. This makes her furious, as she does not like being thought of as a child or left out of the action. Ginny can be stubborn and determined, and will not take no for an answer when she has made up her mind about something.

 Did you know . . . Ginevra is Italian for Guinevere? From the legend of King Arthur, the name means "fair one."

Uncle Bilius: Either Molly or Arthur's brother, he died the day after seeing a Grim and is the source of Ron's middle name.

Weasley second cousin: According to Ron, the Weasleys never speak of Mrs. Weasley's second cousin, who is a Muggle accountant.

 **Did you know** . . . the Weasleys were meant to have a cousin in *Harry Potter and the Goblet of Fire*, but she never made it into the final edition? In an interview with BBC *Newsround* in April 2001, J. K. Rowling explained that the female character appeared in the original draft but was edited out during the rewriting. When asked if the character would resurface in the future, the author replied, "Possibly. I really like her as a character but it's quite a complex plot

 I'm dealing with so I'm not sure that she'll fit anywhere else. She'll be the 'character that might have been.'" On J. K. Rowling's official Web site, she confirms the character's name was going to be Mafalda and would have been the daughter of the Weasleys' Muggle accountant cousin. Mafalda would have been sorted into Slytherin, and was meant to be a nasty witch with a talent to rival Hermione's.

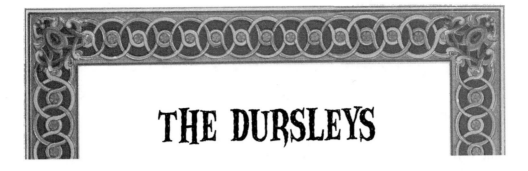

THE DURSLEYS

"Mr. and Mrs. Dursley, of number four, Privet Drive, were proud to say that they were perfectly normal, thank you very much."
— *Harry Potter and the Philosopher's Stone*

Harry's only living relatives are the type of people who give Muggles a bad name. They are insipid, small-minded, reasonably well-to-do people who are pre-occupied with appearances, social climbing, neighbourhood gossip and, above all else, keeping their family skeleton locked firmly in his cupboard.

Dursley, Dudley (**Big D, Diddy, Dinky Duddydums, Ickle Diddykins, Dud, Dudders, Duddy, Popkin**): Harry's cousin *Dudley* certainly lives up to his name — he is a no-good failure in every way (except in the eyes of his relatives, who think he can do no wrong). He has a thick head and a large, pink face, with thick blond hair, small blue eyes, and five (!) chins that wobble when he eats. Porky Dudley waddles along like a pig walking on its hind legs, and at one point, is wider than he is tall.

A cruel, rude, and greedy boy, Dudley has the best of everything but breaks most of it due to carelessness. He is incredibly spoiled, and needs two bedrooms to house all his possessions. He spends most evenings with his gang of thugs, vandalising the neighbourhood. Although he does poorly in school, Dudley excels in his favourite activity — Harry Hunting. He has spent a lifetime terrorising his cousin.

After a forced attempt at dieting and taking up boxing as a new hobby, Dudley becomes the Junior Heavyweight Inter-School Boxing Champion of the Southeast, using the local children for practice. However, the tables are turned the summer before fifth year, when Dudley gets a frightening taste of his own medicine.

Did you know . . . an anagram of the word "Dursley" is "rude, sly"? How appropriate!

Dursley, Marjorie (Aunt Marge): Uncle Vernon's sister. Like him, she is beefy, ruddy-faced, and piggy-eyed, and even has a slight moustache. Aunt Marge is coarse and abrasive, and has a booming voice. She dresses in tweed and owns twelve bulldogs, which she breeds at her home in the country.

Although Aunt Marge doesn't know about Harry's wizarding abilities, she despises him for being a burden to the Dursleys and thinks he should have been raised in an orphanage. She has mistreated Harry his entire life, and constantly compares him negatively to Dudley (whom she spoils rotten). She speaks to him in a malicious, highly critical way and even accuses him of being mentally deficient.

Aunt Marge visits the summer before third year, and enrages Harry with her snide comments and accusations about his parents. When her nasty insults persist, he finally blows up and she suffers the enormous consequences of his wrath (which the Ministry later helps her forget).

Dursley, Petunia (Evans): Harry's mother's sister is a pale, bony woman, with blonde hair, a horse face, and a shrill voice. Aunt Petunia is extremely houseproud and very nosy. She worries what the neighbours think, yet likes to complain about them.

Growing up, she thought her sister Lily was a freak and was jealous of how proud their parents were to have a witch in the family. Although Aunt Petunia has been entrusted with Harry's care as his mother's last remaining blood relative, she has not given him an easy life. She punishes Harry for the slightest perceived infraction (whilst doting on her Ickle Diddykins), never showing him any warmth or compassion.

Aunt Petunia refuses to discuss magic in the house and has kept up an angry pretence of hatred and ignorance towards the wizarding world — but as Harry gets older, he begins to wonder if his aunt knows more than she lets on.

Dursley, Vernon: Aunt Petunia's husband is a big, beefy man with a large, purple face. He has thick, dark hair, a bushy black moustache, and small, mean eyes.

Obsessed with appearing "normal," he hates anything out of the ordinary — especially anything magical. Uncle Vernon is extremely prejudiced against the wizarding world (although he is afraid of some of its members) and deeply ashamed of his nephew, whom he thinks is rotten from the inside out. He has no tolerance for Harry and constantly shouts at him, even threatening to beat him if he lets it slip to Aunt Marge that he is a wizard.

The conflict between Uncle Vernon and Harry gradually worsens and things hit a little too close to home the summer before fifth year, when Uncle Vernon throws Harry's future with the Dursleys into question.

 Did you know . . . J. K. Rowling said the character in the series she dislikes the most is probably Uncle Vernon?

THE BLACKS

"The Noble and Most Ancient House of Black — Toujours pur"
— Black family motto, *Harry Potter and the Order of the Phoenix*

The Blacks are an ancient, aristocratic pure-blood family who practically consider themselves wizarding royalty. They believe in the purification of the wizarding race by keeping pure-bloods in control and getting rid of Muggle-borns. The great majority of the family are involved in the Dark Arts and support Voldemort to various degrees.

Black, Sirius (Snuffles, Stubby Boardman): This mysterious figure from Harry's past re-enters his life in a very dramatic way during third year. Complex and commanding, Sirius has deep, dark grey eyes and long black hair. In his youth, he was very handsome with a relaxed sort of elegance about him, but years of hardship have taken their toll on his features.

Sirius has a quick fiery temper and a bark-like laugh. A dogged, highly intelligent wizard, he has well-developed instincts for survival during adversity. Although the majority of people in the wizarding world believe him to be dangerous and insane, Sirius is also capable of deep affection and loyalty.

 Did you know . . . Sirius is the name of the Dog Star in the constellation of Orion?

Sirius's Background

Black by name if not by nature, Sirius was an exceptionally bright student (and knew it). However, he was also a troublemaker, and had something of a cruel, arrogant streak — at age sixteen he played a near-fatal prank on another student. Sirius was a rebel with a cause, driving a flying motorbike and moving into his own place by age seventeen.

At Hogwarts, Sirius was best friends with James, Lupin, and Pettigrew. He and James were as close as brothers, and James's parents treated him like their second son. Sirius was James's best man at his wedding. James and Lily trusted him with their deepest secrets, even making him godfather to Harry.

Following James and Lily's murders, Sirius was suspected of supporting Voldemort. Witnesses claimed to have seen him blow up a street, killing twelve Muggles and one wizard. After breaking into maniacal laughter, Sirius was led away without a struggle (or a trial) and sent to Azkaban.

Third Year

Twelve years after entering Azkaban and being guarded around the clock by Dementors, Sirius escaped — the only prisoner ever to do so. He is violent and extremely volatile (although when Fudge inspected Azkaban he found Sirius surprisingly normal, and even thought he seemed a little bored). Vampire-like in appearance, he has a gaunt, sunken face with waxy white skin, yellow teeth, and dirty, matted hair.

Sirius plans to avenge the person he considers both responsible for his past and the biggest impediment to his future — a person who is currently residing at Hogwarts. But after a revealing confrontation, it seems as though he has run out of time and will soon be kissing his plans for freedom goodbye.

Fourth Year

Sirius's new life, hidden though it is, initially seems to agree with him. A warmer climate makes him look healthier, cleaner, and younger than he has in years, with shorter hair and a fuller face, although his eyes remain haunted.

In order to preserve his anonymity after he returns north, Sirius is forced to live an alternate existence which has an effect on his appearance. He also gives himself a new code name — Snuffles.

Sirius takes his responsibility as godfather very seriously. He worries about Harry and is very protective over him, and both scolds him and gives him advice as a father would. Dumbledore urges Sirius to put aside his differences with an old enemy in order to fight the future together, something both parties find severely difficult to do.

Fifth Year

Sirius and Harry's bond continues to strengthen and deepen. Harry comes to think of him as a cross between brother and father, while Sirius considers Harry the most important person in his life. At times, it appears Sirius is trying to live vicariously through Harry, egging on his daring behaviour instead of cautioning it. He defends Harry's right to know what has been going on, insisting he is not a child — but others think Sirius forgets Harry is not an adult, either. He seems to consider Harry a substitute for James, and even expresses disappointment in him when he doesn't measure up to his father's standards. Hermione thinks Sirius has been very lonely for a very long time.

Although he is told to stay hidden for his own protection, Sirius becomes increasingly moody and sullen after being cooped up like a caged animal for most of the year. He feels useless and frustrated, as he is not the type to stay behind when others are involved in things. Sirius is known to act rashly on occasion, and there is increasing concern he may take matters into his own hands and do something reckless or foolish. Indeed, on the couple of occasions he does venture outside, there are risks to be taken and consequences to be paid.

Curiously, Harry reads an article in *The Quibbler* that suggests Sirius is innocent of all charges against him — it quotes a witch who says she was with him at the time of the murders, and that he is really Stubby Boardman, lead singer of the Hobgoblins.

number twelve, Grimmauld Place: The Black family house. Sirius inherited it after his mother's death, although he does not have happy memories of living there. It used to be a fine, stately home but has become a "grim old place" after being uninhabited for ten years (except for a creepy, decrepit house-elf). It is located in a small square full of run-down houses with broken windows, peeling paint, and piles of rotting rubbish on the overgrown lawns.

To the eyes of most people, Grimmauld Place appears not to exist — the houses on the street simply jump from eleven to thirteen. However, once its secret is revealed, number twelve seems to magically inflate between its neighbours. Worn stone steps lead up to a front door with peeling black paint and a silver serpent doorknocker. There is no letterbox and no keyhole, but tapping the door with a wand will automatically open the many locks and bolts on its other side. It is Unplottable and protected by numerous wizarding security devices installed by the Black family.

Inside, the house is shabby and run-down, and decorated in varying shades of (Slytherin) green. Damp and dusty, it has a sweet, rotting smell — like entering the house of a dying person. Although traces of wealth from years gone by still remain, Grimmauld Place looks like it belongs to Dark wizards. Among the house's more sinister features are an umbrella stand made from a severed troll's leg, cobwebby serpent-shaped chandeliers and candelabras, and a display of the shrunken heads of house-elves on the wall leading upstairs.

The bedrooms are dark and gloomy-looking, with high ceilings and door-knobs shaped like serpents. On the ground floor, gas lamps light a long, gloomy hallway, which has threadbare carpet and peeling wallpaper, with old portraits of Black ancestors hanging on the walls. The olive-coloured walls of the large drawing-room are full of filthy tapestries and the moss green curtains buzz as though swarming with invisible bees. Narrow stone steps lead down to a cavernous, stone-walled basement kitchen, which features a large fireplace and a long wooden table. Iron pots and pans hang from the ceiling while tableware is stored in an old dresser (Mundungus casts an appraising eye on a fifteenth century goblin-wrought solid silver goblet, engraved with the Black crest).

A great deal of time is spent ridding Grimmauld Place of Dark Arts objects and creatures in order to make it habitable again. This decontamination is a slow, painstaking process, hampered by a certain resident of the house who tries to preserve as many items from the rubbish piles as possible.

THINGS DISCOVERED DURING DECONTAMINATION

* ancient seals
* animated set of robes
* biting silver snuffboxes
* Boggart (in the desk)
* china bearing the family crest and motto
* claws
* coiled snakeskin
* crystal bottle (possibly full of blood)
* dead Puffskeins
* ghoul (in a toilet)
* gold ring engraved with the family crest
* grandfather clock that attacks people
* infestation of Doxys in the drawing room curtains
* musical box
* *Nature's Nobility: A Wizarding Genealogy*
* old silver-framed photographs that scream
* Order of Merlin medal
* rusty daggers
* spider-like instrument
* spiders as big as saucers
* unopenable locket

family tapestry: This enormous tapestry is permanently affixed to the drawing-room wall at Grimmauld Place. It has been in the family seven centuries, and traces the Black ancestry back to the Middle Ages. The top of the tapestry reads, *"The Noble and Most Ancient House of Black — Toujours pur"* (always pure). Faded and threadbare, it is embroidered with golden thread and periodically dotted with small holes like burn marks. Those who brought shame upon the family had their names blasted off the tapestry and were disowned.

Sirius hated his parents and brother, and ran away from home when he was sixteen to escape them. As a result, his name does not appear on the family tapestry.

Mrs. Black: Sirius's mother. A nasty, frightening woman, Mrs. Black has yellowing skin and clawed hands, and wears a black cap. Her drooling, eye-rolling life-size portrait hangs in the hall at Grimmauld Place behind a pair of long, moth-eaten velvet curtains that are always kept drawn. Whenever Mrs. Black is disturbed by the doorbell ringing or noise in the hall, she screeches and shrieks vile names at everyone in sight. Her wrath extends not only to Muggle-borns, half-bloods, and "mutants," but to the pure-bloods who befriend them. She and her husband thought Voldemort had the right idea, although they didn't approve of his methods for gaining power. Sirius claims she kept herself alive out of spite and calls her a "horrible old hag" — the feeling is mutual, as she calls him "the shame of (her) flesh."

Mr. Black: Sirius's father. Not much is known about Mr. Black, although he certainly shared his wife's mentality about pure-bloods and attitudes about their children. He covered Grimmauld Place with numerous protective spells.

Black, Regulus: Sirius's younger brother. Although Sirius considered him soft and thought he was an idiot, their parents considered him heroic. (Indeed, *Regulus* is Latin for "little king.") Regulus was their favourite son because he upheld the family values. Ironically, he died during Voldemort's reign as an indirect result of the beliefs he endorsed so strongly.

Aunt Elladora: Started the family tradition of beheading house-elves when they became too old to carry out their duties.

(unnamed) grandfather: Received an Order of Merlin.

Lestrange, Bellatrix (née Black): Married to Rodolphus Lestrange. Sirius does not consider Bellatrix family (even though she is his cousin) and has only seen her twice since he was fifteen. Bellatrix, Andromeda, and Narcissa are all sisters.

Malfoy, Narcissa (née Black)**:** Married to Lucius Malfoy, she is Sirius's cousin.

Malfoy, Draco: Narcissa's son, Tonks's cousin, and Bellatrix and Andromeda's nephew (see page 53).

Meliflua, Araminta: Sirius's mother's cousin. She tried to force through a Bill at the Ministry that would legalise Muggle-hunting.

Nigellus, Phineas: Sirius's great-great-grandfather. His ornately framed and frequently vacant portrait hangs in a bedroom in Grimmauld Place.

Tonks, Andromeda (née Black)**:** Married to Ted Tonks. Andromeda was Sirius's favourite cousin. She did not subscribe to the Black family values — her name was removed from the tapestry because she married a Muggle-born. Her namesake in Greek mythology, Andromeda, was a beautiful maiden who was chained to a rock at sea and rescued by Perseus.

Tonks, Nymphadora (Tonks)**:** Andromeda's daughter, Malfoy's cousin, and Bellatrix and Narcissa's niece. Tonks's name has also been removed from the tapestry.

Uncle Alphard: His name was removed from the Black family tapestry after he left Sirius some gold. Alphard is a star in the constellation Hydra (Hydra being a multi-headed snake-like monster). Alphard comes from the Arabic phrase "Al Fard al Shuja," which means "the solitary one in the serpent" — appropriate for the only member of the family to help out Sirius!

Weasley, Arthur: Sirius's second cousin, once removed; however, the Blacks consider the Weasleys blood traitors and have disowned them as relatives.

Weasley, Molly: Sirius's cousin by marriage.

THE LONGBOTTOMS

"I'm worth twelve of you, Malfoy."
— Neville Longbottom, *Harry Potter and the Philosopher's Stone*

The Longbottoms are a close-knit pure-blood wizarding family that has suffered great hardships at the hands of Voldemort. Despite their past, they persevere, led by the indomitable matriarch Mrs. Longbottom.

Longbottom, Neville: Gryffindor dorm-mate of Harry. Like Harry, Neville was born at the end of July. Also like Harry, he grew up without parents because of Dark Magic, and was raised by strict relatives (although Neville's Gran is nothing like the Dursleys!). Neville's family was delighted when he got his Hogwarts letter as they didn't think he would be magical enough to be let in — he didn't show any magical abilities until the age of eight, despite his relatives trying to force it out of him.

Neville is pudgy and round-faced, and generally has a kind and gentle nature. He is a loyal friend to Harry and also gets to know Ginny a little better during fourth and fifth year. He thinks highly of Hermione, who frequently helps him in Potions where his perpetually poor performance constantly earns him Snape's wrath.

Awkward, accident-prone, and perpetually forgetful, Neville sometimes wonders if he is a Squib. He doesn't have much self-confidence and rarely does well in anything, so he is secretly pleased to learn Professor Sprout thinks he excels at Herbology, his favourite subject. Neville also gains a newfound determination and confidence after joining the DA and dramatically improving his skills. Although he sometimes wonders if he is brave enough to be in Gryffindor (indeed, the Sorting Hat took a long time to place him), Neville has proved time and again that he is as he stands up to his friends, Slytherins, and even Death Eaters over the years.

Neville is visibly shaken after learning about the Cruciatus Curse, although his friends do not understand why. It is a reminder of a tragic childhood event (and possibly an explanation for his own poor memory, which may be a side-effect from being present when the curse was performed).

Although he keeps it well-hidden from his friends, Neville misses his mother very much, and treasures even the slightest contact with her.

NEVILLE'S MISHAPS AT HOGWARTS

First year

* Melts a cauldron, causing Boil-curing Potion to leak and burn holes in peoples' shoes, then becomes covered in boils himself.
* Breaks his wrist after falling off an out-of-control broom.
* Trips into a suit of armour whilst trying to hide from Filch.
* Locks himself out of Gryffindor Tower after forgetting the password.

Second year

* Strung up by his ears and left dangling from a candelabra.

Third year

* Blamed for losing a list of passwords to Gryffindor Tower.

Fourth year

* Gets his foot caught in a trick step.
* Melts his sixth cauldron.
* Transplants his ears onto a cactus during a Switching Spell.
* Repeatedly Banishes Flitwick (instead of cushions) across the classroom.

Fifth year

* Triggers his Mimbulus mimbletonia plant to squirt Stinksap over himself and others.
* Turns his Draught of Peace into a cement-like substance which must be gouged out of his cauldron.
* Hits Harry with a Disarming Charm at the Department of Mysteries.

Did you know ... J. K. Rowling considers *Harry Potter and the Order of the Phoenix* a "real turning point" for Neville? In an online chat for World Book Day in March 2004, the author said Neville had really changed a lot over the course of the series as he becomes older and more confident.

Longbottom, Alice: Neville's mother is a former Auror and original member of the Order of the Phoenix, who was tortured by Bellatrix Lestrange about Voldemort's whereabouts. She currently resides in a long-term residents' ward at St. Mungo's. Alice Longbottom used to have the same round, smiling face as her son, but is now gaunt and worn-looking, with white wispy hair and eyes that seem too large for her face. She seems to marginally recognise Neville and gives him empty gum wrappers when he visits.

Longbottom, Frank: Neville's father, like his mother, is a former Auror and original member of the Order of the Phoenix, who was also tortured by Bellatrix Lestrange. He currently resides in a long-term residents' ward at St. Mungo's.

Longbottom, Mrs. (Gran): Neville's paternal grandmother is a stern and formidable matriarch with a commanding, almost regal presence (although she cried tears of joy when his magical ability was finally discovered). She raised Neville after his parents were rendered incapable of doing so. Mrs. Longbottom is proud of her son and daughter-in-law, and speaks quite candidly about what happened to them. She frequently tells her grandson he must uphold the family honour.

Although Neville's Gran thinks he is a good boy, she doesn't think he has inherited his father's talent. For the most part, she treats his frequent accidents and bouts of forgetfulness with weary resignation (she even buys him a Remembrall) but has been known to explode at him on occasion, too.

Mrs. Longbottom is friends with Griselda Marchbanks, head of the Wizarding Examinations Authority, and is a staunch supporter of Dumbledore — she cancels her *Daily Prophet* subscription after reading what is written about him in fifth year. Typically, she wears a long lace-trimmed green dress, a moth-eaten fox-fur stole, and a hat with a stuffed vulture, and carries a red handbag in her shrivelled, claw-like hands.

Algie, Great Uncle: He put poor Neville in a number of life-threatening situations as a child to determine if he had magical ability, including a near-drowning and dangling him out a window by the ankles. Great Uncle Algie bought Trevor (the toad) for Neville when Neville got into Hogwarts, and also gave him a Mimbulus mimbletonia plant for his fifteenth birthday.

Enid, Great Auntie: Distracted Great Uncle Algie with the offer of a meringue whilst he was dangling Neville out of an upstairs window.

grandfather: Neville saw him die, although the circumstances are not known.

THE LOVEGOODS

"I think they think I'm a bit odd, you know. Some people call me 'Loony' Lovegood, actually."
— Luna Lovegood, *Harry Potter and the Order of the Phoenix*

Open-minded to the point of being eccentric, the Lovegoods march to the beat of their own drum, regardless of what others may think. They live in the vicinity of Ottery St. Catchpole, near the Weasleys.

Lovegood, Luna (**Loony**): Ravenclaw, one year behind Harry. Luna has long, scraggly, dirty blonde hair, pale eyebrows, and bug-like silvery eyes that make her look perpetually surprised. She is close to her father (her mother died a couple of years before she started Hogwarts) and appears to be an only child. Luna is the name of the Roman goddess of the moon, which is fitting, as the moon is believed to have an impact on behaviour and personality.

Luna seems to believe in things as long as there is no proof of their existence, and wanders along in her own little world most of the time. Her numerous eccentricities include tucking her wand behind her ear for safekeeping, creating animated (and frightening!) hats to show her support for various Quidditch teams, and wearing jewellery made from radishes and Butterbeer corks. She gives the impression of being scatterbrained, but observes and understands much more than others give her credit for. She has a dreamy, sing-song voice and often speaks cryptically, but can be blunt when the occasion calls for it.

A friend of Ginny's, Luna seems to find "Ronald" particularly fascinating and is fond of singing "Weasley is our King" dreamily under her breath, not understanding the irony of the song. She stares at him curiously and laughs far too long at his jokes (poor Ron doesn't quite know what to make of her).

Although Luna seems annoyed by Hermione's dismissive attitude towards *The Quibbler*, the two girls work together to help Harry in fifth year. When Harry worries he is seeing and hearing things no one else can, Luna assures him he is as sane as she is (not a terribly comforting thought!) and that she has the same experiences. Harry feels sorry for her because other students call her names and hide her belongings, but it doesn't seem to trouble her much. Luna is a member of the DA and fights in the battle at the Department of Mysteries.

 Did you know . . . J. K. Rowling described Luna as the "anti-Hermione"? At London's Royal Albert Hall in June 2003, she explained, "Hermione is so logical and so inflexible, whereas Luna is the one who is prepared to believe a thousand mad things before breakfast."

Lovegood, Mr.: Luna's widowed father is the editor of *The Quibbler*. He thinks the *Daily Prophet* is a terrible paper. He is very supportive of any anti-Ministry action, and would believe anything of Fudge. Mr. Lovegood seems to have a good relationship with his daughter, taking her to the Quidditch World Cup and on overseas expeditions to look for mythical creatures.

Lovegood, Mrs.: "Extraordinary witch" who died when Luna was nine after one of the spells she was experimenting with went wrong.

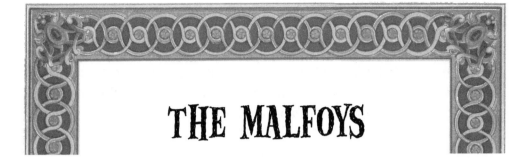

THE MALFOYS

"The name Malfoy still commands a certain respect . . ."
— Lucius Malfoy, *Harry Potter and the Chamber of Secrets*

The name Malfoy is French for "bad faith" (*mal foi*), and in certain circles in the wizarding world, it is held in rather high esteem. However, in most other places, it is associated with cruelty, snobbery, and corruption. The Malfoys are an old and wealthy wizarding family who hold those who are not pure-bloods in complete contempt.

Malfoy, Draco: Slytherin in same year as Harry. Malfoy is Harry's nemesis and opposite in every possible way. He has white-blond hair and a pale, pointy face, with a thin mouth and light grey eyes. He speaks in a bored, cold, drawling voice that conveys arrogance and derision. "Draco" means dragon but it can also mean serpent — both are mean-spirited creatures known for viciously attacking others. Needless to say, Malfoy lives up to his name.

Rich, snobbish, and spoiled, Malfoy is an only child and is used to the best of everything. Never short of a snide or cruel comment, he sneers at those whom he considers beneath him in terms of wealth, intelligence, or wizarding heritage. At Hogwarts, Malfoy thinks he is above the rules and finds ways to manipulate situations to his advantage when things don't go his way. As a prefect in fifth year, he takes great delight in bullying people, although he is really a coward at heart.

Malfoy also enjoys lording his prefect status over Harry, as he has been jealous of Harry's Quidditch skills and fame since first year. The two have an intense rivalry and mutual hatred, sparked by Harry snubbing Malfoy's offer of friendship just before they came to Hogwarts. Malfoy spitefully and maliciously takes every opportunity to cause trouble for Harry and spread lies about him. (Malfoy reminds Harry of Dudley, only he makes Dudley look kind, thoughtful, and sensitive by comparison.)

Malfoy seems to be aware of his father's darker side, and puts great stock in what he says and thinks. He regularly uses his father's stature to his own advantage, whether it is to bribe his Quidditch team; influence the school governors, Ministry committees, and Umbridge; or taunt Harry with sensitive information his father has told him. After the battle at the Department of Mysteries, an enraged Malfoy confronts Harry and threatens revenge for what happened. It will be interesting to see how Malfoy functions when he cannot hide behind or go running to his father.

 Did you know . . . at London's Royal Albert Hall in June 2003, J. K. Rowling said she worried fans were becoming "far too fond of Draco"? Wonder what that could mean for the last two books in the series?

Malfoy, Lucius: Like son, like father. Lucius has the same sleek blond hair, pointed pale face, and light grey eyes as Draco, and speaks in the same drawling voice. Yet despite the similarities, he is a stern, cold, and critical father. In fifth year, the *Daily Prophet* lists his age as forty-one.

The name "Lucius" brings to mind Lucifer, which is an apt comparison — he is a cruel, evil man who delights in corruption, terror, and torture. Fanatical about pure-blood superiority, his hatred for Muggle-borns, Muggles, and the wizards who fraternise with them knows no limits. Lucius has a sadistic streak that is evident in his treatment of everyone from house-elves to children, and thinks nothing of endangering innocent peoples' lives for sport, or as a means to his own end.

Wealthy, well-connected, and intimidating, Lucius is not above using threats or bribes, or making large donations of gold to get what he wants, whether it is a death sentence for an innocent creature or Top Box seats at the Quidditch World Cup. Although he thinks Dumbledore is the worst thing to happen to Hogwarts, he sat on the school's board of governors and has connections at the Ministry reaching as high up as Fudge himself.

Mr. Weasley claims Lucius did not need an excuse to go to the Dark Side. He was in Voldemort's inner circle, but after Voldemort disappeared Lucius was amongst the first to renounce him, claiming to have been bewitched. Ever since then, Lucius has given the appearance of being a law-abiding citizen. He even chides his son for being openly contemptuous of Harry, and warns him to stay out of the trouble at Hogwarts in second year.

Yet behind this mask, Lucius is leading a double life. He has ulterior motives for the things he says, secretly schemes to put Muggle-born lives at risk, keeps Dark Arts objects hidden away at his manor, and covertly associates with like-minded wizards. Eventually Lucius's dark side catches up with him, but no doubt he will find a way to escape the repercussions.

Malfoy, Narcissa (née Black): Draco's mother. Tall, thin, and blonde, she is an attractive woman but wears a permanent expression of displeasure, like she has dung under her nose. Narcissa is the sister of Bellatrix Lestrange and Andromeda Tonks, and Sirius's cousin. Greek mythology tells of Narcissus, a young man who fell in love with his own reflection as seen in a river and remained on the riverbanks, staring at himself, until he died. The narcissus flower bloomed where he died, and has come to be associated with vanity.

HOGWARTS STAFF (PRESENT)

Binns, Professor: The ancient and shrivelled History of Magic professor is the only ghost on staff — he fell asleep in front of the staff room fireplace one evening, and left his body behind the next morning but kept on teaching. His classes are incredibly dull, and he drones on in a dry, wheezing monotonous voice. (No wonder he is named "Binns" — most students think what he teaches is rubbish!) Professor Binns looks like an old tortoise and seems a bit absent-minded, frequently forgetting or mixing up students' names (even referring to Potter as "Perkins").

Dumbledore, Professor Albus Percival Wulfric Brian (Grand Sorcerer; Chief Warlock, Wizengamot; Supreme Mugwump, International Confederation of Wizards): Old in years (one hundred and fifty to be exact) but young at heart, Dumbledore is a modern-day Merlin. He is wise and whimsical, powerful and popular, and considered the greatest Headmaster Hogwarts has ever had. He was once a popular choice for Minister for Magic (even though he had no interest in the job), and is the only wizard Voldemort has ever feared. *Albus* is an old English word for both "white" and "wisdom," indicating Dumbledore is on the side of light in the fight against the Dark Arts. Dumbledore is tall and thin, with a waist-length silvery beard and hair (which were both once auburn). He has a very long, crooked nose, and wears half-moon spectacles. His light blue eyes always seem to twinkle with mischief, but can appear fiery when he is angry and piercing when he is thoughtful. Harry feels Dumbledore's eyes can look straight through him sometimes. Curiously, he has a scar that perfectly replicates a map of the London Underground above his left knee.

Beneath Dumbledore's mildly eccentric and enigmatic exterior is a brilliant mind that seems to know everything that goes on. (He even reads Muggle newspapers on occasion to keep up with their world.) Broad-minded and compassionate, Dumbledore is acutely aware of the injustices and inequities in the wizarding world and treats all creatures with courtesy and kindness. He believes in people and in giving second chances, which inspires tremendous loyalty from others. Unflappable, patient, and calm, he never raises his voice to his detractors, observing them with a serene, almost amused detachment instead.

Dumbledore has said his brain surprises even himself sometimes. He is quick thinking and prone to strokes of genius, but also has the strength of character to plan and execute incredibly difficult decisions. Despite his intelligence, he doesn't take himself too seriously and readily acknowledges his own shortcomings. He can be maddeningly cryptic and secretive, and sometimes lets emotion get in the way of objective thinking. He takes full responsibility for his own errors in judgement, and is deeply humbled by what he terms "an old man's mistakes."

Though Dumbledore is mostly benevolent by nature, he is a force to be reckoned with on the rare occasions he becomes angry. He speaks with a cold fury, and can be threatening without raising his voice. He has an extremely commanding presence and radiates an aura of power and controlled wrath that causes even the darkest of wizards to scatter at the mere sight of him. Although his powers rival Voldemort's, Dumbledore is too noble to use them for evil purposes.

Dumbledore runs Hogwarts according to his own unconventional standards. In the spirit of the school's founders, he welcomes all students from all backgrounds. For the most part, the Ministry gives him free rein to do as he sees fit, even though he doesn't always teach things according to their wishes and outright defies them on other occasions. Dumbledore believes in telling students the truth about things, and treats them with great respect. He empowers students to think and act for themselves, and doesn't mind bending the rules for the greater good.

Harry sees Dumbledore as almost god-like; part mentor, part (grand)father figure and able to solve any problem or situation. Dumbledore cares deeply for Harry as well, and the two share a special connection, much closer than that of Headmaster and student. It dates back to before Harry was even born, and was strengthened when Dumbledore assumed responsibility for Harry's welfare after his parents died. Little is known of Dumbledore's own family (other than a brief mention of his brother, Aberforth).

Dumbledore is highly intelligent and skilled in a number of magical disciplines. He is a Legilimens, a former Transfiguration professor and has experience working in alchemy. He also enjoys chamber music and tenpin bowling.

Did you know . . . *dumbledore* is the old English word for bumblebee? J. K. Rowling chose the name ("dumble" is like bumble, and "dore" is an Old English word for a flying insect that makes a humming sound) because she saw the Headmaster as a benign old wizard, always on the move and humming to himself.

DUMBLEDORISMS (SAGE, OFTEN CRYPTIC, ADVICE)

First year

★ "It does not do to dwell on dreams and forget to live."
★ "To the well-organised mind, death is but the next great adventure."
★ "Humans do have a knack of choosing precisely those things which are worst for them."
★ "Fear of a name increases fear of the thing itself."
★ "The truth is a beautiful and terrible thing, and should therefore be treated with great caution."

Second year

★ "It is our choices that show what we truly are, far more than our abilities."

Fourth year

✶ "Curiosity is not a sin. But we should exercise caution with our curiosity . . . yes, indeed . . ."
✶ "Understanding is the first step to acceptance, and only with acceptance can there be recovery."

Fifth year

✶ "You care so much you feel as though you will bleed to death with the pain of it."
✶ "You cannot know how age thinks and feels. But old men are guilty if they forget what it was to be young . . ."
✶ "Indifference and neglect often do much more damage than outright dislike."

 Did you know . . . in the Italian translation of the series, Professor Dumbledore is known as Professore Silencio? The translator based the translation on the "dumb" part of Dumbledore, meaning mute!

Filch, Argus: Caretaker. Filch is a pasty-faced man with thin grey hair; pale eyes; a bulbous, veined nose; and sunken jowls. He suffers from rheumatism and has a soft, greasy voice. In Greek mythology, Argus was a hundred-eyed servant who guarded Io, who had been transformed into a cow. To "filch" is a slang expression for stealing.

Perpetually mean-tempered, Filch harbours an innate grudge against the young witches and wizards at Hogwarts (he's not particularly fond of Peeves, either). He knows the castle's secret passageways better than almost anyone else and prowls the corridors at night on the lookout for rulebreakers, often aided by Mrs. Norris, his cat and constant companion.

Filch loves to enforce rules and misses the old methods of discipline, such as whipping or hanging students from the ceiling by their wrists or ankles. Naturally, he thinks Umbridge is the best thing to ever happen to

Hogwarts, and is excited at the opportunity to administer more severe forms of punishment.

Firenze: Divination teacher during part of fifth year. The palomino centaur is considered intimidating by most students, although some girls think he is a heartthrob. The other centaurs are extremely upset about Firenze's decision to teach "human foals" and express their disapproval in various ways. Firenze is Italian for Florence, a city noted for its ties to astronomy, architecture, and art during the Renaissance.

Flitwick, Professor: Charms teacher and Ravenclaw head of house. Tiny Flitwick is well-liked amongst students, even though he has to stand on top of books to see them over his desk. Cheery and good-natured, he has thick white hair and a squeaky voice. He is also something of a sensitive soul who has burst into tears after hearing bad news. Flitwick used to be a duelling champion in his younger days, and has been teaching at Hogwarts for many years, at least since Harry's parents and Snape were students.

Grubbly-Plank, Professor Wilhelmina: Temporary Care of Magical Creatures teacher during parts of fourth and fifth year. A gruff older witch with very short grey hair and a prominent chin, she smokes a pipe and wears a monocle on occasion. To Harry's dismay, Grubbly-Plank is an exemplary teacher. Several students prefer her methods of teaching to Hagrid's, and hope she stays on permanently.

Hagrid, Rubeus: Care of Magical Creatures teacher and Keeper of Keys and Grounds. Twice as tall as a normal man and at least three times as wide, Hagrid looks too big to be allowed indoors, with hands the size of dustbin lids and feet like baby dolphins. He has a long, black shaggy mane of hair and a wild, tangled beard, but his smile is kind, and his eyes glint like black beetles below his bushy eyebrows. (Hagrid's name may be a play on the word "haggard," meaning wild or unkempt in appearance.) He is usually dressed in a long black moleskin coat which has all manner of things in its pockets, and enormous beaverskin boots. On special occasions, he wears his "best suit," which is brown and hairy, with a yellow and orange checked tie and a flower in the buttonhole as big as an artichoke.

Though he is physically intimidating and can have quite a temper if provoked, Hagrid is actually a softie with a big heart who simply doesn't know his own strength. He comes across as gruff, but is really quite emotional and has broken down sobbing on more than one occasion. He is occasionally careless and over-enthusiastic, but always means well. Hagrid has an endearing but often troublesome habit of speaking without thinking first, leading him to spill secrets inadvertently, much to his own chagrin and sometimes to his peril. Regardless, Dumbledore would trust him with his life.

Hagrid was raised by his "tiny" wizard father, after his giantess mother left when he was about three years old. Although Hagrid wasn't very good at magic, his father was thrilled he got into Hogwarts. Sadly, he was expelled in third year after being blamed for exposing a secret that, for once, he didn't reveal. Hagrid was forbidden from doing magic and his wand was snapped in half, but a certain pink umbrella of his seems to have served quite nicely as a replacement.

Dumbledore paved the way for Hagrid to stay at Hogwarts as gamekeeper, and later offered him a teaching job. Because of this, Hagrid is deeply loyal to the Headmaster and won't tolerate anything being said against him. He has complete faith in Dumbledore to lead them through any coming storms, and accepts the fight against the Dark Arts with minimal fuss (although, anything must look easy after dealing with Blast-Ended Skrewts!).

Though everyone generally likes Hagrid (except a certain Slytherin, who goes out of his way to wound him), his teaching abilities are thought of less favourably. He has a lot of knowledge about magical beasts, but in his enthusiasm seems to forget how dangerous and frightening some of them can be. In fifth year, Hermione pleads with Hagrid to choose tamer creatures, but he stubbornly dismisses her concerns and suffers the consequences. His stubbornness rears its ugly head again when he refuses to heed a warning about an untameable creature he attempts to domesticate.

Hagrid has a soft spot for Harry, whom he rescued from the Potters' ruined home as a baby. Harry reminds Hagrid of himself as a boy — orphaned and unsure of how he will fit in at Hogwarts. Hagrid also has a soft spot for Madame Maxime, and thinks they have much in common.

Hooch, Madam: Flying instructor and Quidditch referee (she also supervises Quidditch trials). A bit brusque in manner, Madam Hooch has short grey hair and yellow, hawk-like eyes.

Lockhart, Professor Gilderoy (Order of Merlin, Third Class; Honourary Member of the Dark Force Defence League; winner of *Witch Weekly*'s Most-Charming-Smile Award five times in a row): Second year Defence Against the Dark Arts teacher. With his wavy blond hair, constantly winking bright blue eyes, and cheeky, dazzling smile, Lockhart looks every bit the swashbuckling hero. Always immaculately groomed, he wears flashy robes and jaunty matching hats in an array of vibrant colours including, ironically, forget-me-not blue. Witches of all ages are drawn to his dashing, roguish manner (though wizards might call it something else entirely).

Lockhart has a reputation as a global adventurer and conqueror of dangerous beasts and evil creatures. He has written numerous books of (tall) tales bragging about his encounters, and revels in the celebrity they bring him. Vain and pompous, he exploits every opportunity to be in the spotlight — even keeping a stack of autographed photos with him at all times, which he signs with a flourish of his peacock-feather quill (the peacock is, of course, known for its preening and strutting).

Lockhart is so caught up in his own self-importance, he is oblivious to Harry's stature in the wizarding world. Thinking he is doing Harry a favour, Lockhart repeatedly tries to take him under his wing and tutor him on the finer points of managing his fame. This unsolicited and presumptuous attempt at assistance is typical of Lockhart, who has a suggestion or solution for every situation based on his own experiences and skills. Unsurprisingly, when Lockhart is really put to the test, he comes up blank.

After leaving Hogwarts, Lockhart enters a whole new world where no one seems to think much of his former fame and glory, himself included (though he still likes to sign autographs).

 Did you know . . . J. K. Rowling came across the name Gilderoy in the *Dictionary of Phrase and Fable*? Fittingly, it was the name of a handsome Scottish highwayman, but its meaning is fitting, too — to gild something means to cover it in a thin veneer of gold, so it seems more valuable than it really is, while "roy" is derived from the French *roi*, or king.

Lupin, Professor Remus John (Moony): Third year Defence Against the Dark Arts teacher. Although Lupin is fairly young, he looks frail and worn-out. Thin and pale-faced, he has dark shadows under his eyes and his light brown hair is heavily streaked with grey. Malfoy says Lupin dresses like a house-elf, as his robes are extremely shabby and have been patched in numerous places.

Lupin is intelligent, easy-going, and mild-mannered. He treats his students with respect, speaking to them frankly and honestly. Always the voice of reason and responsibility, level-headed Lupin can firmly mediate heated arguments and often acts as a conscience for others. He was a good student when at Hogwarts (although not much of a potion-brewer), and was chosen as prefect to try and exercise some control over his unruly friends. Lupin is kind-natured and full of compassion, but also seems to carry a sense of guilt. There is a quiet, almost noble dignity about him.

A half-blood, Lupin suffered a stigmatising trauma during childhood, the consequences of which would be felt for the rest of his life. As a result he regularly experiences violent side effects, but has taken precautions to try and lead as normal an existence as possible. Because of his condition, Lupin endured great pain as a youth and was often isolated from everyone around him, and had great difficulty trying to find and keep a job later in life.

In Roman mythology, Remus and Romulus were twin brothers who were cast into the River Tiber. They were rescued by a she-wolf, who raised them together with her cubs under a fig tree. "Lupine" means wolf-like, although lupins are also a kind of purplish-blue flower symbolising imagination.

McGonagall, Professor Minerva: Transfiguration teacher, Gryffindor head of house, and Deputy headmistress. McGonagall is in her seventies, and in fifth year, it is revealed she has been teaching at Hogwarts for thirty-nine years. She is tall with black hair, which she wears in a tight bun. McGonagall has a stern face with a thin mouth and piercing stare, and her beady eyes are framed by square spectacles. Similar markings can be seen around her eyes when she turns into her Animagus form, a cat. She wears a tartan dressing-gown at night, and an emerald green cloak during the day.

McGonagall certainly lives up to her namesake — Minerva, the Roman goddess of war and wisdom. She has a reputation for being strict and clever, and is both feared and respected by students (Hermione sees her as a mentor of sorts). McGonagall is someone not to be crossed. She speaks in a brisk, crisp tone that brooks no argument. McGonagall can spot trouble faster than any other teacher, and has a way of always making Harry feel like he has done something wrong.

An excellent judge of character, McGonagall is a sensible sort who does not suffer fools lightly. She is fiercely loyal to Dumbledore, but has little patience for Trelawney and Divination as a whole — practical McGonagall thinks fortune-telling is a very imprecise branch of magic, and true Seers are very rare. However, when the Fates are unkind to Trelawney, she immediately puts aside her irritation and offers genuine compassion. As Head of Gryffindor, McGonagall demonstrates the brave and courageous spirit associated with her house by standing up to Umbridge and refusing to be intimidated by her.

Though McGonagall is considered severe, she also has a softer side, particularly when it comes to Harry. Her eyes tear up when she hears of his parents' murders, and she frets over baby Harry being sent to live with the Dursleys. When Harry comes to Hogwarts, McGonagall continues to look out for him over the years — she buys him a generous gift, is surprisingly gentle when giving him bad news, expresses sympathy towards him when he cannot join his friends in Hogsmeade, is almost in tears when he returns from his encounter in the graveyard, and vows to help him become an Auror if it is the last thing she does. McGonagall also bends the school rules to allow Harry to join the Quidditch team as a first year student — although this could also be because she is desperate to see Gryffindor win the Quidditch Cup!

Moody, Professor Alastor (Mad-Eye): CONSTANT VIGILANCE! The fourth year Defence Against the Dark Arts teacher is an old friend of Dumbledore's who agreed to come out of retirement and take the position just for a year, as a favour. Mr. Weasley also thinks very highly of Moody, who was a great wizard in his day.

Mad-Eye Moody is a fright to be seen. He has long grizzled dark grey hair and a weathered face with scarred skin that looks badly carved — a large chunk of his nose is missing, and his mouth looks like a diagonal gash (his face twists when he smiles). Moody has one dark beady eye and one round electric blue eye that independently moves around in all directions. Moody's mad eye can magically see out of the back of his head and through various substances and barriers, including walls, wood, and Invisibility Cloaks. Moody walks with a limp and has a wooden leg with a clawed foot. He speaks in a low growling voice and doesn't seem to care what people think of his appearance. His personality is gruff and brusque — Moody is an appropriate name for him.

Alastor is a good name for him, too. It is a derivative of Alexander, which means "defender of men" — exactly what Moody used to do. During Voldemort's reign Moody was an Auror, the best the Ministry ever had, but he made lots of enemies amongst the families of the Dark wizards he caught. As a result, Moody doesn't trust anyone and has a reputation for being extremely cautious, to the point of paranoia. He has repeatedly attracted unwanted attention from his Muggle neighbours because of all the magical security precautions around his home. At Hogwarts, his office is covered in Dark detectors, and he prepares his own food and drink at all times. In this case, the concerns Moody has identified are well-founded.

Moody has a bit of a cavalier attitude towards magic — "attack first, ask questions later" seems to be his motto. (McGonagall is horrified when Moody nonchalantly Transfigures Malfoy into a white ferret and bounces him ten feet off the ground after Malfoy attacks Harry.) He believes students need to know the worst in order to be prepared for whatever they may encounter.

In spite of his grim outlook Moody is capable of some compassion, particularly towards those students whose lives have been affected by the Dark Arts. Harry is reacquainted with Moody the summer before fifth year.

MOODY'S MAGICAL EYE

Fourth year

* Catches Lavender showing Parvati her horoscope in class.
* Sees Harry under his Invisibility Cloak at the Three Broomsticks.

* Sees Harry's mismatched socks underneath his dress robes at the Yule Ball.
* Sees Harry stuck on a trick step under his Invisibility Cloak in the middle of the night.
* Ensures the corridor outside his office is empty before letting the trio in to discuss Crouch.
* Sees Harry waiting to speak with Dumbledore outside his office.
* Ensures the corridor outside his office is empty when Harry tells him about his encounter in the graveyard.

Fifth year

* Sees Tonks rolling her eyes at him when they come to pick up Harry.
* Looks from the kitchen up to the drawing room at Grimmauld Place to verify there is a Boggart in the desk.
* Harry feels Moody looking at him through Ron during the party at Grimmauld Place, and again when he leaves and goes up to the drawing room.
* Sees the Dursleys approach from behind him at King's Cross.

Pince, Madam: True to her name, the Hogwarts librarian has a "pinched," shrivelled face, and resembles an underfed vulture. Irritable and stern, she is every bit the stereotypical librarian and prowls the aisles menacingly in her squeaky shoes. A strict disciplinarian, Madam Pince is fond of chasing out rule-breakers, often Banishing objects to hit them over the head as they leave.

Pomfrey, Madam Poppy: As the school matron, Madam Pomfrey has seen it all in the hospital wing, and tends not to ask too many questions about students' mysterious mishaps. She is kind but firm, and not afraid to stand up to anyone — including Dumbledore, Snape, and the Minister for Magic —

whom she thinks is disrupting the welfare of her patients. The poppy flower after which she has been named has long been known for both its medicinal properties, and its association with opium, a powerful narcotic.

Quirrell, Professor: The first year Defence Against the Dark Arts professor is a pale, meek young man who seems to be afraid of his own shadow. He constantly trembles and stammers, and has a nervous twitch in one eye. Professor Quirrell wears a large, funny-smelling purple turban he says was given to him by an African prince for warding off a zombie. During the course of the school year, he becomes paler and thinner, as if something has been draining all his energy.

It seems ironic someone as delicate as Professor Quirrell should teach students how to defend themselves against dark magic. He was said to have had a brilliant mind until he took a year off to travel and experience the Dark Arts first-hand — he ran into trouble in the Black Forest and has never been the same since. All is not as it seems, however, and Professor Quirrell pays the ultimate price for his misadventures.

Sinistra, Professor: Little is known about the witch who teaches Astronomy — perhaps, like Trelawney, she rarely descends from her tower (although Sinistra did attend the Yule Ball, where she danced with Moody). In Italian, *sinistra* is a feminine noun, meaning left-handed. Historically, left-handed people have suffered a bad reputation as being mistrustful or suspicious, hence the word "sinister." (Hmm . . . could this mean we need to keep an eye on Professor Sinistra in the future?)

Snape, Professor Severus (Snivellus): Potions Master and Slytherin head of house. In fifth year, it is revealed Snape began teaching at Hogwarts fourteen years ago. It is common knowledge amongst students that he wants to teach Defence Against the Dark Arts, but Dumbledore turns him down for the position every time he applies. Snape wouldn't mind being Head of Hogwarts one day, either. He is also a highly skilled Legilimens and Occlumens.

Snape is thin with sallow skin and greasy, black, shoulder-length hair. He has a hooked nose, crooked yellowing teeth, and cold empty black eyes. Always dressed in black, he swoops and glides around like an "overgrown bat" and speaks in a low, icy voice.

Snape's name is similar to snipe, which means extremely critical, though J. K. Rowling said she took the name Snape from a English village. His behaviour and the punishments he doles out are severe (Severus). Bitter, vindictive, and malevolent, he is perpetually miserable and burns with a quiet fury. Snape holds all non-Slytherins (especially Harry and to a lesser degree, Neville) in contempt, often provoking, ridiculing, or cruelly insulting them. He considers Harry a "nasty little boy who thinks rules are beneath him" and is extremely resentful that Harry's constant rule-breaking goes unpunished. Snape blames Harry's special treatment on his fame, and always looks for excuses to get him in trouble.

Snape's hatred of Harry stems back to his own schooldays, when he was at Hogwarts with Sirius, Lupin, and Harry's parents. As a teenager, Snape was very unpopular. He was fascinated with the Dark Arts, and knew more curses when he arrived at Hogwarts than many students in upper years. Snape was part of a Slytherin gang whose members almost all later turned out to be Death Eaters. James Potter and Snape mutually despised each other, and Snape has transferred this deep-seated hatred to Harry. Snape also loathes Sirius and Lupin, and holds a lifelong grudge against them that he seeks to avenge at every opportunity.

The period in Snape's life between leaving Hogwarts as a student and returning as a teacher is marked with darkness, mystery, and subterfuge. Moody claims Snape is only at Hogwarts because Dumbledore believes in second chances. Harry, meanwhile, is not entirely convinced Snape is loyal to Dumbledore, but Hermione figures if Dumbledore trusts Snape he must be all right. Still, Dumbledore will not explain why he gave Snape a second chance or why he trusts him. One thing is for certain — there is more to Snape than meets the eye.

Sprout, Professor: As the Herbology teacher, Professor Sprout is aptly named. She perpetually has earth under her nails and on her robes and wears a patched hat over her frizzy hair. She is plump and short but usually very cheery. Also the Hufflepuff head of house, Professor Sprout embodies the spirit of hard work, fairness, and patience associated with her house.

Trelawney, Professor Sybill Patricia: Hogwarts' Divination teacher resembles a large, glittering insect — she is spindly, wears lots of sparkly jewellery and gauzy spangled shawls, and has huge glasses that greatly magnify her eyes. She is ethereal and melodramatic, but also rather creepy. Her soft, misty voice usually appears from out of the shadows of her classroom, where she glides around in a ghost-like way, as if on castors. She has a dewy smile, but usually wears a forlorn, tragic expression.

In fifth year it is revealed Trelawney has been teaching at Hogwarts for sixteen years, although she rarely ventures into the rest of the castle as she believes it clouds her Inner Eye. She considers Divination the most difficult of all branches of magic and believes if students don't have a natural gift for the Gift, there isn't much she can do to teach them. Trelawney is the first in her family to have Second Sight since her great-great-grandmother, a famous Seer named Cassandra Trelawney. (In Greek mythology, Cassandra was a daughter of the king and queen of Troy, whom Apollo tried to seduce after he bestowed her with the gift of Sight. However, when Cassandra refused his advances, Apollo cursed her so no one would believe her prophecies.) Appropriately, the name Sybill is derived from the Greek *Sibylla*, meaning "prophetess."

Although Trelawney takes herself and her talent very seriously, no one else — with the exceptions of Lavender and Parvati — seems to. The majority of her fortune-telling is dismissed as "lucky guesswork and a spooky manner." Her predictions rarely contain good news, and, at best, are vague or self-fulfilling. However, on two separate occasions, Trelawney has entered a trancelike state and used a loud, deep voice to make "real" prophecies — one concerning Voldemort's rise, the other, his potential fall.

Hermione and McGonagall in particular have little time for Trelawney's doom-and-gloom soothsaying. Logical Hermione does not see eye-to-Eye with superstitious Trelawney, and openly thinks she is a fraud who is obsessed with predicting Harry's demise, while McGonagall scoffs that Trelawney has wrongly foretold the death of a student each year since she began teaching. Even Dumbledore didn't initially think Trelawney had much of a Gift when he interviewed her for her position at Hogwarts.

The scepticism surrounding Trelawney's abilities only gets worse in fifth year when she finds herself at a difficult bridge to cross. She feels aggrieved and persecuted by the "Establishment," whom she bitterly insists neither understands nor possesses her knowledge. Her future isn't very bright, but one wonders how she didn't See it coming.

TRELAWNEY'S PREDICTIONS

Students

Harry: Routinely predicts his death. In fourth year, she tells him the thing he fears will come to pass sooner than he thinks, and wrongly deduces he was born in mid-winter. Trelawney temporarily abandons her negative outlook in fifth year, predicting a happy future for Harry instead after he tells his story in *The Quibbler*.

Neville: Tells him his grandmother is unwell. She also warns him he will break a tea cup and be late for his next Divination class.

Lavender: That which she is dreading will happen on Friday the sixteenth of October.

Parvati: Should be wary of a red-haired man.

General

THIRD YEAR

✶ Class will be disrupted in February by a bout of flu (during which Trelawney will lose her voice).

✶ A student will leave "for ever" around Easter.

✶ The crystal ball told her to join the others for Christmas lunch. She was horrified to discover she was the thirteenth diner, as she claims the first to rise from a table of thirteen will be the first to die (apparently either Harry or Ron has this dubious honour).

✶ Lupin "will not be with us for very long."

✶ The "Fates" told Trelawney crystal balls would be on the students' exam — but as Hermione points out, she sets the exam herself!

✷ The Orb tells her that death is circling over Hogwarts.

FIFTH YEAR
✷ Knew all students would return safely as she had been following their fortunes all summer.
✷ After Umbridge urges Trelawney to make an on-the-spot prediction, Trelawney claims to foresee Umbridge in grave danger.

Prophecies

✷ Made a prophecy in the Hog's Head before she began teaching at Hogwarts that described the qualities of the person who would be capable of defeating Voldemort. The prophecy also explained the condition of the outcome of their encounter.
✷ Made a prophecy in third year that concerned a servant assisting Voldemort to return to power.

Umbridge, Dolores Jane: Hem, hem! The fifth year Defence Against the Dark Arts teacher is so evil, she could give Voldemort himself a run for his Galleons. Umbridge is short, squat, and stubby-fingered, and with her wide, flabby face, bulging eyes, and broad, slack mouth, resembles a pale toad. She has pointed teeth fixed in a permanently fake smile, a tinkling laugh, and speaks in a breathy, simpering voice. A wolf in sheep's clothing, Umbridge dresses like an old spinster aunt. She wears a pink cardigan over her floral robes, and usually has a black velvet bow or Alice band in her short, curly, mousy-brown hair.

Ministry-appointed Umbridge wastes no time entrenching herself and her agenda at Hogwarts. She is heavily critical of the teachers and curriculum, and declares the students' knowledge is below OWL standards. In class, she behaves like an old-fashioned schoolmarm, insisting students greet and address her formally and raise their hands when they want to speak (but Merlin forbid they ask questions!). In turn, Umbridge speaks to students (and staff) in a sugary, condescending manner, in tones of poisoned honey. She is fond of interrupting conversations with an annoying false cough when she wants to be heard.

Umbridge gushes that students should think of her as a "friend" and feel free to confide in her, but most are not fooled and can see she has ulterior motives. Her overly polite demeanour is merely a thin cover for her cruel, sadistic nature. Indeed, the name *Dolores* is Spanish for "sorrows," while Umbridge sounds like "umbrage," meaning to take offence or feel resentment (however, it can also mean something shadowy). Umbridge seems to dislike Harry in particular and takes a perverse joy out of provoking and punishing him in ways she knows will hurt the most.

Umbridge proves to be even more of a ruthless tyrant when she is appointed High Inquisitor. She conducts strict inspections of her fellow teachers to try and impose her authority and intimidate them, whilst the slightest perceived infractions amongst students are punished by the passing of severe Educational Decrees. Umbridge will use any means to get what she wants, including physical force, truth potions, dark creatures, threats, spells, and Unforgivable Curses.

Not surprisingly, Umbridge has little tolerance for deviant, non-human, and hybrid creatures, all of whom she considers untrustworthy and beneath her. She is shocked when she finds out the feeling is mutual.

 Did you know . . . during medieval times in Europe, the Grand Inquisitor was appointed by the church and state to persecute those accused of heresy and witchcraft?

UMBRIDGE'S INSPECTION VICTIMS

Flitwick: Doesn't ask many questions of him. He treats Umbridge politely, like a guest.

Hagrid: Twists his words and speaks very slowly and loudly, miming her actions as if he doesn't understand English. Hagrid is confused by the way Umbridge treats him.

Grubbly-Plank: Grills her about Hagrid's absence and the students about what they have learnt. Grubbly-Plank seems indifferent towards her.

McGonagall: Cannot fault her teaching, although McGonagall barely tolerates Umbridge's presence and puts her in her place for interrupting. Umbridge and McGonagall mutually loathe each other beneath a veneer of false civility.

Snape: (Harry hates them both so much, he can't decide which one to root for!) Considers his class advanced for the students' level. Despite this, he has barely hidden contempt for Umbridge, and resents having to answer personal questions in front of students.

Trelawney: Trails her around the room, taking lots of notes. Trelawney is sulky and grumpy when Umbridge asks questions, and becomes flustered when asked to make an impromptu prediction.

Vector, Professor: Very little is known about the witch who teaches Arithmancy, although her name is certainly appropriate — a vector is a mathematical term, and Arithmancy involves predicting the future using numbers.

HOGWARTS STAFF (FORMER)

Paintings of the former Heads of Hogwarts hang in the present Head's office. Although they are bound to serve the current Head, they spend much of their time feigning sleep whenever a visitor is in the office (all the better to eavesdrop!). The former Heads have the ability to travel between their own paintings in the office and other paintings of themselves located outside Hogwarts.

Derwent, Dilys: Esteemed, silver-ringleted Headmistress from 1741 to 1768. She can travel between her paintings in Dumbledore's office and St. Mungo's.

Dippet, Professor Armando: Headmaster prior to Dumbledore. He is frail-looking and mostly bald, with a feeble voice.

Everard: Sallow-complexioned Headmaster with short black fringe. He can travel between his paintings in Dumbledore's office and the Ministry.

Fortescue: Red-nosed Headmaster who accuses the Ministry of corruption from his portrait in Dumbledore's office. (Could he be related to Florean Fortescue, the ice-cream parlour owner in Diagon Alley?)

Kettleburn, Professor: Wizard who retired from teaching Care of Magical Creatures at the end of second year, presumably after one too many close encounters with the beasts in his class.

Nigellus, Phineas: Least popular Headmaster ever. Clever-looking and gruff, with a pointed beard and thin black eyebrows, his portrait depicts him in Slytherin colours. He despised teaching because he couldn't stand the "adolescent agonising" of the students. The name Phineas has several meanings, including the Greek "oracle" or "dark-skinned," and the Biblical "serpent's mouth." According to Greek mythology, Phineas was given the gift of Sight by Apollo; however, when he revealed too much of the gods' plans in his fortune telling, Zeus blinded him. He was confined to an island full of food he could not eat because he was tormented by harpies — beautiful winged women who had been turned into winged hags with sharp talons (sort of like Veela!) — who constantly stole the food from his hands. He was rescued by Jason and the Argonauts.

Ogg: Gamekeeper prior to Hagrid. Ogg is possibly named after the town of St. Ogg in *The Mill on the Floss* by Victorian author George Eliot. Of course, it could also be an abbreviation of "ogre"!

Pringle, Apollyon: Caretaker when Mr. and Mrs. Weasley were students. He caught Mr. Weasley after he and the future Mrs. Weasley had returned from a four o'clock in the morning "stroll" around the castle (Mr. Weasley still has the marks to prove it!). The name Apollyon is taken from Revelations 9:11 in the Bible: "They had as king over them the angel of the Abyss, whose name in Hebrew is Abaddon, and in Greek, Apollyon." In Greek, it means "the Destroyer," and in the Bible, it is commonly interpreted as another name for Satan.

HOGWARTS STUDENTS

Abbott, Hannah: Hufflepuff in the same year as Harry. Pink-faced with blonde pigtails, Hannah is friends with Ernie Macmillan. She is a prefect in fifth year and the first to crack under the strain of preparing for OWLs. Hannah is a member of the DA and always thinks the best of Harry, even when her housemates do not.

Abercrombie, Euan: Gryffindor, four years behind Harry. He has prominent ears and looks perpetually terrified.

Ackerley, Stewart: Ravenclaw, three years behind Harry.

Baddock, Malcolm: Slytherin, three years behind Harry.

Bell, Katie: Gryffindor Chaser, one year ahead of Harry. Katie is a member of the DA.

Bletchley, Miles: Slytherin Keeper from first through fifth years. He jinxes Alicia Spinnet before a match in fifth year.

Bole: Slytherin Beater in third year. Three years ahead of Harry.

Bones, Susan: Hufflepuff, in the same year as Harry. Susan wears her hair in a long plait. A member of the DA, she already knows a thing or two about fighting the Dark Arts — her aunt is the head of the Department of Magical Law Enforcement and her uncle's family was killed by Death Eaters. During fifth year, Susan miserably finds herself the subject of stares and gossip when her family's tragedy makes news again.

Did you know . . . in the Harry Potter films, Susan Bones is played by director Chris Columbus's daughter Eleanor — a huge Harry Potter fan, and one of very few non-Britons in the cast?

Boot, Terry: Ravenclaw, in the same year as Harry. Terry suffers a nosebleed during Duelling Club and is a member of the DA. He is impressed with Hermione's intelligence and wonders why she wasn't put in Ravenclaw.

Bradley: Ravenclaw Chaser in fifth year.

Branstone, Eleanor: Hufflepuff, three years behind Harry.

Brocklehurst, Mandy: Ravenclaw, in the same year as Harry.

Brown, Lavender: Gryffindor, in the same year as Harry. A devotee of Trelawney, Lavender frequently spends her lunch hour in the Divination classroom, and mimics Trelawney's hushed tones when speaking to Harry. She can often be found giggling and gossiping with Parvati. Although Lavender is a member of the DA it is likely she joined purely to hear what Harry had to say in his defence, as she initially believes what the *Daily Prophet* says about him.

Bulstrode, Millicent: Slytherin, in the same year as Harry. A member of the Inquisitorial Squad, she is stocky and much larger than Harry (Ron calls her "no pixie"), with a heavy jaw. Millicent and Hermione have had a number of skirmishes over the years, including a particularly "catty" encounter in second year.

Carmichael, Eddie: Ravenclaw, one year ahead of Harry. Eddie has a corner on the Hogwarts black-market trade in brain boosters and concentration aids for OWL and NEWT students — until Hermione confiscates the pint of Baruffio's Brain Elixir he tries to peddle to Harry and Ron.

Cauldwell, Owen: Hufflepuff, three years behind Harry.

Chambers: Ravenclaw Chaser in fifth year.

Chang, Cho: Ravenclaw Seeker, one year ahead of Harry. Cho is popular and pretty, with long, black hair, and a freckled nose. She is a head shorter than Harry, who has had a crush on her since third year. He is dismayed to learn she is involved with Cedric.

Cho's emotions are on a rollercoaster from fourth year onwards — she goes from giggling far too much for Harry's liking at first, to spending most of fifth year crying like a "human hosepipe," despite growing closer to him. She admires Harry's honesty and bravery, and defies her parents by joining the DA. Cho is a loyal friend of Marietta Edgecombe's but doesn't seem to care much for Hermione. A lifelong supporter of the Tutshill Tornados, Cho eventually abandons her attraction to Quidditch players in favour of a fellow Ravenclaw.

Clearwater, Penelope (Penny): Ravenclaw, three years ahead of Harry. Penelope is Muggle-born, with long curly hair. A prefect, she dates Percy during second year.

Corner, Michael: Ravenclaw of unknown year (however as he went to the Yule Ball and only fourth years and up could attend, he is in Harry's year at least). Michael is dark-haired and a member of the DA. He dates Ginny after meeting her at the Yule Ball (but eventually Seeks another Ravenclaw). Not surprisingly, Ron thinks Michael is a "bit of an idiot."

Crabbe, Vincent: Slytherin, in the same year as Harry. Crabbe joins the Quidditch team in fifth year as a Beater, but he is best known as one of Malfoy's thug sidekicks. Large and "Crabby"-looking, he has long ape-like arms, a thick neck, and a pudding-basin haircut. He is a member of the Inquisitorial Squad, and his father is a Death Eater. Spiteful and stupid, Crabbe lies about being bitten by a Flobberworm in class just to cause trouble for Hagrid. In second year, Ron gets a "taste" of Crabbe and doesn't like it at all.

Creevey, Colin: Gryffindor, one year behind Harry. Small and mousy-haired, Colin is never without his camera — he often takes photographs at the most inopportune moments, mostly to send to his Muggle parents (his father is a milkman). He is a member of the DA and completely star-struck by Harry, whom he overwhelms with his eagerness and trails after like an "extremely talkative shadow."

Creevey, Dennis: Gryffindor, three years behind Harry. Like his brother Colin, Dennis is small and mousy-haired, and a member of the DA. He thinks it is great fun when he falls in the lake during the first years' boat crossing at the beginning of the year.

 Did you know . . . Dennis would have been too young to be allowed into Hogsmeade when he attended the DA meeting at the Hog's Head? Dennis was only in second year, and according to the rules, Hogsmeade visits don't begin until third year, so he shouldn't have been there.

Davies, Roger: Ravenclaw Quidditch Captain from third year onwards (year undetermined, but he is likely a year or two ahead of Harry). Roger is quite a "witches man" — he is completely bewitched by Fleur at the Yule Ball, expresses an interest in Cho in fifth year, and is later seen publicly kissing an attractive blonde girl on Valentine's Day.

Derek: Two years behind Harry (house undetermined). He is flustered when Dumbledore addresses him during Christmas lunch.

Derrick: Slytherin Beater in third year. Three years ahead of Harry.

Diggory, Cedric: Hufflepuff Quidditch Captain and Seeker during Harry's first four years. Cedric is two years ahead of Harry and an all-around nice guy. A prefect and an excellent student, he is tall and very handsome, with dark hair and grey eyes. He is an exemplary Hufflepuff — a loyal friend who values hard work and fair play. Mr. Diggory proudly gloats about how his son is a better flier than Harry, and describes him as gentlemanly and modest (typically, Cedric seems embarrassed by his constant bragging and praise).

After Cedric successfully puts his name in for the Triwizard Tournament, he receives a lot of attention from girls (especially Cho), and even has to fight off autograph seekers. Although he initially is suspicious of Harry, Cedric shows great integrity by believing the best of him, setting an example the rest of his housemates eventually follow. Noble to a fault, Cedric is willing to walk away from the glory Hufflepuff has long been starved for because he feels it is unfair and Harry is more deserving. The two players reach a compromise, but not without huge consequences.

 Did you know . . . the name *Cedric* means "chief" in Celtic, "ruler" in Irish, and "wonderful gift" in Welsh? Appropriately, he is a "chief" of the Triwizard Tournament; "ruler" of his Quidditch team; and a "gift" to his family, house, and school.

Dingle, Harold: House and year undetermined. Harold is quite a huckster — he attempts to sell fake powdered dragon claw (really dried Doxy droppings!) to OWL and NEWT students as a brain stimulant, and peddles Firewhisky to Seamus and Dean after exams are over.

Dobbs, Emma: Three years behind Harry (house undetermined).

Edgecombe, Marietta: Ravenclaw, one year ahead of Harry. Marietta has curly reddish-blonde hair and is described as a "lovely person" by Cho, although others consider her to be a bit of a sneak. She grudgingly joins the DA because of Cho, even though her mother works for the Ministry and has forbidden her from doing anything to upset Umbridge. Marietta is cursed with an unfortunate case of acne during fifth year.

Fawcett: Ravenclaw female of unknown year. She is possibly from the same Fawcett family that lives near Ottery St. Catchpole and could not get tickets for the Quidditch World Cup. Fawcett attends the Duelling Club, and gets into her fair share of trouble at Hogwarts — she tries to put her name in for the Triwizard Tournament by illegally ageing herself, and is caught with Stebbins in the bushes during the Yule Ball.

Finch-Fletchley, Justin: Hufflepuff, in same year as Harry. Curly-haired and Muggle-born, Justin comes from an upper-class family, judging by his manner of speaking and the fact his name was down for Eton. (Justin is another person Ron thinks is "a bit of an idiot.") Justin is almost attacked by a snake during Duelling Club, and turns on Harry when he tries to intervene. After a petrifying experience, he eventually comes around and begins to support Harry, even joining the DA.

Finnigan, Seamus: Gryffindor dorm-mate of Harry. Irish with sandy hair, Seamus describes himself as "half and half" — his mother is a witch, but didn't tell his Muggle father until after they were married. He attends the Quidditch World Cup with his mother and Dean, his best friend. Seamus and Harry's friendship is strained in fifth year after Seamus's mother takes the *Daily Prophet*'s articles to heart. He is a belated member of the DA.

Flint, Marcus: Slytherin Chaser and Captain from first to third year. Flint is large and slow, and Harry reckons he has some troll blood in him. "Marcus" is derived from Mars, the Roman god of war, while "Flint" is a type of hard quartz used to start fires and ignite weapons.

Frobisher, Vicky: Gryffindor of unknown year. She is involved in numerous activities, and tries out for the Quidditch team in fifth year.

Goldstein, Anthony: Ravenclaw, in same year as Harry. Anthony is a prefect in fifth year and a member of the DA.

Goyle, Gregory: Slytherin, in same year as Harry. His surname brings to mind the word "gargoyle," which is fitting — he is big, mean, and ugly, with short, wiry hair, and dull, deep-set eyes. Goyle is one of Malfoy's thug side-kicks and a Beater on the Quidditch team in fifth year. His father is a Death Eater. Almost as thick as he is thick-set, there was hope Goyle would have failed first year and been thrown out. His stupidity extends to his petty thievery — he didn't realise the pocketfuls of gold coins he stole during Care of Magical Creatures class were leprechaun gold. Scabbers bites Goyle after he tries to take one of Harry and Ron's Chocolate Frogs on the Hogwarts Express. Harry has a close encounter with Goyle in second year.

Greengrass, Daphne: Student in same year as Harry (house undetermined).

Higgs, Terence: Slytherin Seeker during first year.

Hooper, Geoffrey: Gryffindor of unknown year. Geoffrey has a reputation for complaining about things. He tries out for the Quidditch team in fifth year.

Johnson, Angelina: Gryffindor Chaser, two years ahead of Harry, and Captain during fifth year. Angelina is a tall black girl with long, braided hair. She is a member of the DA and puts her name in for the Triwizard Tournament (her birthday is the week before Hallowe'en). Angelina has a stressful year as Quidditch Captain, and at times can be almost as ruthless as Oliver Wood was.

Jordan, Lee: Gryffindor two years ahead of Harry. Lee is tall and dread-locked, and has a pet tarantula. He provides commentary during Quidditch matches that he peppers with his largely anti-Slytherin, Gryffindor-biased observations (not to mention his admiration of Angelina), frequently earning him McGonagall's ire. Lee is a member of the DA, and Fred and George's best friend.

Kirke, Andrew: Gryffindor Chaser in fifth year.

Longbottom, Neville: See page 47.

Lovegood, Luna: See page 51.

MacDougal, Morag: Student in same year as Harry (house undetermined).

Macmillan, Ernie: Hufflepuff, in same year as Harry. A pure-blood for nine generations, Ernie is friends with Hannah Abbott and is a prefect in fifth year. He is pudgy and stubborn, and can be pompous on occasion. He worries incessantly about OWLs, but brags about his study schedule. Although Ernie believes the worst of Harry throughout second year, he has come to fully support him by fifth year and is a member of the DA.

 Did you know . . . Ernie was likely named after one of J. K. Rowling's grandfathers?

Madley, Laura: Hufflepuff, three years behind Harry.

Malfoy, Draco: See page 53.

McDonald, Natalie: Gryffindor three years behind Harry.

Did you know . . . Natalie McDonald is the only real person named in the entire Harry Potter series? In the summer of 1999, the books provided an escape from the nine-year-old Toronto girl's struggle with leukaemia. Knowing how much Natalie loved Harry Potter, a friend of the McDonald family contacted J. K. Rowling's publisher, who passed along the message. The author wrote an e-mail to Natalie and her mother, including not-yet-known details about *Harry Potter and the Goblet of Fire*, but sadly, it arrived the day after Natalie died. Her mother wrote back to thank J. K. Rowling for her kindness, and the two struck up a friendship. In the book, J. K. Rowling paid tribute to Natalie by making her a first year and sorting her into Gryffindor.

Midgeon, Eloise: Unknown year and house. Eloise tried to curse her acne off, but wound up removing her own nose instead. Ron dismisses her as a potential partner for the Yule Ball because her nose is off-centre (even though her skin is much better).

Montague: Slytherin Chaser from third year onwards, and Captain in fifth year. A member of the Inquisitorial Squad, he is big and beefy with forearms like hairy hams. When Fred and George shove Montague inside a Vanishing Cabinet, he turns up days later inside a toilet. Interestingly, the coat of arms for the family Montague features griffins!

Moon: Same year as Harry (house undetermined).

Nott, Theodore: Slytherin, in same year as Harry. Scrawny-looking, he is named after his father, a Death Eater.

Parkinson, Pansy: Slytherin, in same year as Harry. Pug-faced Pansy is the leader of a gang of Slytherin girls. She is a member of the Inquisitorial Squad, and takes great delight in the misfortunes of others. An admirer of Malfoy, Pansy shrieks with delight whenever he does something mean-spirited. Despite her horrible nature, she is made prefect in fifth year.

The flower pansy symbolises thoughtful reflection — not terribly appropriate for our Miss Parkinson, unless the reflection involved is for thinking up insults and slurs!

Patil, Padma: Ravenclaw, in same year as Harry. She is a prefect in fifth year and a member of the DA. Padma has long dark hair and is Parvati's identical twin, although she seems to be less flighty than her sister. Padma is conscripted by Parvati to attend the Yule Ball with a certain Gryffindor, but she is not very enthusiastic about it. After being neglected for most of the evening, she finds better company amongst the Beauxbatons boys (see page 201). However, Padma's date gets back into her good books after she hears about his feats of bravery during the Triwizard Tournament.

The name *Padma* is of Sanskrit origin, and means "lotus." Padma was a Hindu goddess of the River Ganges, in India.

Patil, Parvati: Gryffindor, in same year as Harry. Parvati is Padma's identical twin. Although they share the same long dark hair, their personalities are not alike (this may be why they were sorted into different houses) — Parvati seems more interested in gossiping and giggling. Like her best friend Lavender, she is a big fan of Trelawney, especially after Trelawney tells Parvati she has the potential to be a true Seer. She is quite proud to be on display with her date at the Yule Ball, but deserts him in favour of a Beauxbatons boy after he ignores her. Parvati is a member of the DA.

The name *Parvati* is of Sanskrit origin, and means "daughter of the mountains." Parvati was a Hindu goddess married to the god Shiva.

Perks, Sally-Anne: Same year as Harry (house undetermined).

Pritchard, Graham: Slytherin, three years behind Harry.

Pucey, Adrian: Slytherin Chaser in first and second year.

> **Note to Muggles:** *Adrian is not on the team in third year, but there is a Pucey playing Chaser again in fifth year. It is not known whether this is Adrian or a younger brother.*

Quirke, Orla: Ravenclaw, three years behind Harry.

Sloper, Jack: Gryffindor Chaser in fifth year.

Smith, Zacharias: Hufflepuff Chaser of unknown year. Zacharias is like Malfoy "lite" — blond, arrogant, smug, and full of complaints and sneering observations (not to mention most people can't stand him). Tall and skinny with an upturned nose, Zacharias is sceptical about Harry's story and antagonistic about his abilities. He is only a member of the DA because he overheard it being discussed.

Spinnet, Alicia: Gryffindor Chaser two years ahead of Harry. Alicia is a member of the DA.

Stebbins: Hufflepuff male of unknown year. Stebbins was caught with Fawcett in the bushes during the Yule Ball. He may be related to another student named Stebbins who was in the same year as James, Sirius, Lupin, and Pettigrew.

Stimpson, Patricia: Two years ahead of Harry (house undetermined, but likely Gryffindor). She fainted repeatedly as OWLS approached, due to stress.

Summerby: Hufflepuff Seeker in fifth year.

Summers: Hufflepuff male of unknown year. He tries to put his name in for the Triwizard Tournament by illegally ageing himself.

Thomas, Dean: Gryffindor dorm-mate of Harry. Muggle-born Dean is a big fan of West Ham football club, although he supports Quidditch as well, attending the World Cup with Seamus, his best friend. A talented artist, Dean has drawn numerous banners in support of Harry during various events. Dean is a member of the DA. Although he thinks the Patil twins are the best-looking girls in his year, he attracts the attention of a younger housemate at the end of fifth year.

 **Did you know** . . . J. K. Rowling had an elaborate backstory for Dean's character that she decided not to pursue? According to her official Web site, Dean was originally called Gary. He was raised by his Muggle mother and step-father, and had lots of half-siblings. His real father walked out on the family when Dean was young — he was a wizard, but never wanted to tell his wife and son in order to protect them — and was murdered by Death Eaters. Dean was going to discover his father's history during his time at Hogwarts, but J. K. Rowling abandoned the storyline in favour of more development for Neville's character, which she felt was much more central to the plot.

Towler, Kenneth: Two years ahead of Harry (house undetermined, but likely Gryffindor). Kenneth broke out in boils when Fred put Bulbadox powder in his pyjamas.

Turpin, Lisa: Ravenclaw, in same year as Harry.

Warrington: Slytherin Chaser from third year onwards. Warrington is a member of the Inquisitorial Squad. He looks like a large sloth, and is rumoured to have put his name in for the Triwizard Tournament.

Whitby, Kevin: Hufflepuff, three years behind Harry.

Wood, Oliver: Gryffindor Quidditch Captain and Keeper during Harry's first three years. Tall, burly, and broad-shouldered, he is four years ahead of

Harry. Oliver is also Quidditch mad, and desperate to finally win the Quidditch Cup. Known for his pep talks as much as his strictness, he schedules extra practices at all hours and in all weather during the school year and spends his summer holidays devising complicated plays and training regimes. After leaving Hogwarts, he is signed to Puddlemere United's reserve team.

Zabini, Blaise: Slytherin, in same year as Harry.

Did you know . . . until recently, Blaise's gender was a source of much debate amongst fans? In the Russian, Hebrew, Dutch, and German translations of *Harry Potter and the Philosopher's Stone*, Blaise is a female, but the French translation lists Blaise as a male. In addition, the name Blaise is listed under both genders on numerous baby-naming Web sites. However, the issue was settled once and for all when Portuguse translators asked J. K. Rowling for clarification during their revision of *Harry Potter and the Philosopher's Stone* — Blaise is male!

Zeller, Rose: Hufflepuff, four years behind Harry.

MISCELLANEOUS WITCHES AND WIZARDS

Bagman, Otto: Ludo Bagman's brother (see page 277). He was involved in some trouble with a lawnmower that had unnatural powers.

Baruffio: Wizard who mixed up his "s" and "f" when saying "swish and flick," and wound up with a buffalo on his chest. He may be the maker of Baruffio's Brain Elixir, a supposed study aide.

Bashir, Ali: Angry about the Ministry's embargo on flying carpets, he is later caught smuggling them into Britain.

Boardman, Stubby: Lead singer of the Hobgoblins, who retired after being struck by a turnip during a concert at Little Norton Church Hall. However, according to at least one of his fans, the rumours of his retirement have been seriously exaggerated.

Crockford, Doris: Witch who was very excited to meet Harry in the Leaky Cauldron on his first visit to Diagon Alley, and repeatedly shook his hand.

Crouch, Mrs.: Barty Crouch Sr.'s wife (see page 280). She is wispy and frail, and falls critically ill. Mrs. Crouch is very close to her son and would do anything to protect him.

Diggory, Mrs.: Amos Diggory's wife and Cedric's mother. Like her son, she is kind, fair, and noble — she does not blame others for her family's misfortune, and refuses to accept compensation she feels isn't rightfully hers.

Florence: Hogwarts student from the same era as Bertha Jorkins. Bertha saw Florence kissing an unknown male behind the greenhouses.

Fudge, Mrs.: Cornelius Fudge's wife.

Gudgeon, Davey: Hogwarts student from the same era as James, Sirius, Lupin, and Pettigrew, who nearly lost an eye trying to touch the Whomping Willow's trunk. It is not known if he is related to Gladys.

Gudgeon, Gladys: Receives an autographed picture after writing to Lockhart. A few years later, she still continues to write to him faithfully.

Hagrid, Mr.: Hagrid's father, a short wizard who has the same crinkled black eyes as his son. He raised Hagrid alone until his death in Hagrid's second year at Hogwarts.

Harris, Warty: One of Mundungus's crooked friends (see page 299).

Hornby, Olive: Hogwarts student from the same era as Moaning Myrtle. Olive used to tease Myrtle about her glasses and discovered her body after she died. Myrtle blamed Olive for her death and haunted her out of spite for many years. Eventually, Olive went to the Ministry and asked them to make Myrtle stop stalking her.

Jordan, Mr.: Lee Jordan's father ran into trouble recovering money from Ludo Bagman (see page 277) after a bet.

Montague, Mr. and Mrs.: Montague's furious parents come to Hogwarts when their son does not show signs of recuperating after being found inside a toilet.

Mortlake: Questioned after unusual ferrets were discovered in his home during a Ministry raid.

Nettles, Madam Z: Witch who became the pride of her family and friends after taking Kwikspell courses.

Pettigrew, Peter: Pettigrew was a friend of James, Sirius, and Lupin at Hogwarts. He was a chubby, small boy with mousy hair and a pointed nose. Pettigrew was not as skilled a wizard as his friends, and was particularly hopeless at duelling.

Eyewitnesses saw Pettigrew die a heroic but violent death at the hands of a former friend, whom he was arguing with over a betrayal. (His index finger, the biggest part of him found, was returned to his mother in a box.) He was posthumously awarded an Order of Merlin, First Class.

Peter's name has a biblical origin. The Apostle Peter was originally named Simon at birth. Jesus renamed him Peter, meaning "rock" and indicating trust and reliability; however, Peter later denied knowing Jesus three times. Breaking the name Pettigrew apart into "petti" and "grew" indicates something small ("petit" means "small" in French) that grows larger.

Prod, D. J.: Warlock who turned his wife into a yak after taking Kwikspell courses because she belittled his charm work.

Purkiss, Doris: Seemingly delusional witch who insists Sirius is innocent because he is really Stubby Boardman, lead singer of the Hobgoblins, and was with her the night he was accused of committing the murders. She writes a letter to Fudge demanding "Stubby" be granted a pardon, but (surprisingly!) has not heard back.

Riddle Jr., Tom Marvolo: Riddle attended Hogwarts over fifty years before Harry began. Tall, handsome, and charming, he was a Slytherin prefect and later Head Boy who won numerous awards (Ron compares him to Percy). Dumbledore calls Riddle "the most brilliant student Hogwarts has ever seen." Indeed, he sounds almost too good to be true.

Riddle's Muggle father, whom he was named after (Marvolo was his grandfather's name), abandoned his mother when she told him she was a witch and returned to his Muggle parents before his son was born. Riddle's mother died giving birth to him and he was raised in a poor Muggle orphanage, but swore revenge against his father for what he did.

When Riddle encounters Harry, he feels compelled to point out several similarities between them — both are black-haired, both are half-bloods, both are Parseltongues, and both were orphaned and brought up by Muggles.

Tom Marvolo Riddle is a bit mixed-up about certain things, but he is certainly well-suited to his name as there is much more to him than meets the eye.

Smethley, Veronica: Receives an autographed picture after writing to Lockhart.

Widdershins, Willy: Arrested for putting jinxes on Muggle toilets to make them regurgitate their contents. The charge was dropped because Willy turned informant for Umbridge, but he was arrested again for selling biting doorknobs to Muggles. Widdershins refers to a counter-clockwise motion, but is a term also associated with actions being performed in reverse.

Will: Mundungus (see page 299) stole toads from this dim-witted crook, then resold them to him later.

MUGGLES

When J. K. Rowling was searching for a name for non-magical people, she wanted a word that suggested both foolishness and lovability. The word "mug," British slang for a gullible person, came to mind, which she then softened to sound more "cuddly." Indeed, most of the Muggles in the series (with the exception of the Dursleys) seem to be a placid, unassuming bunch who are quite unaware they share the world with witches and wizards, and seem completely bewildered when they stumble across magic by accident.

Bayliss, Hetty: Saw the Ford Anglia flying over Norfolk.

Bryce, Frank: The Riddles' gardener is a war veteran with a stiff leg, who lived alone in a cottage on their estate for over fifty years. He doesn't like crowds and has a reputation for being odd and unfriendly. Arrested for a crime he did not commit, he was later cleared. Ironically, when Frank is seventy-six, he stumbles across the real criminal and falls victim to the same crime he was accused of in his youth.

Colonel Fubster: Retired friend of Aunt Marge who occasionally looks after her dogs and once drowned one of her runts.

Dennis, Gordon and Malcolm: Members of Dudley's gang.

Dorkins, Mary: Newsreader who gave a report on Bungy the water-skiing budgerigar.

Dot: Patron at the Hanged Man pub who thought the worst of Frank Bryce, claiming he had a horrible temper.

Evans, Mark: Ten-year-old boy Dudley's gang beats up.

Fleet, Angus: Reported the flying Ford Anglia to the police.

The Great Humberto: Dudley likes this television programme, which, ironically, sounds like a magician's name!

Mason, Mr.: Rich builder whom Uncle Vernon tries to impress in order to do business with him.

Mason, Mrs.: Mr. Mason's wife is terrified of birds, and gets a nasty shock at the Dursleys'.

McGuffin, Jim: Weatherman who gave a report about downpours of shooting stars the night Voldemort disappeared.

Payne, Mr.: One of the campsite managers at the Quidditch World Cup.

Polkiss, Piers: Dudley's best friend, a scrawny boy with a face like a rat. They attend Smeltings together.

Prentice, Mr.: Mrs. Figg's neighbour (see page 299).

Prime Minister: Unlike most other Muggles, Britain's Prime Minister is aware of the wizarding world. The Minister for Magic communicates with him whenever there is a wizarding crisis that could affect the Muggle world. (Fudge isn't worried about the Prime Minister telling Muggles about wizards, because he doesn't think anyone would believe him if he did.)

Riddle, Mr. and Mrs.: Tom Riddle Sr.'s elderly, snobbish parents.

Riddle Sr., Tom: The Riddles' son (Tom Riddle's father) fell in love with a local woman, but left her when she was pregnant after she told him she was a witch.

Roberts, Mr.: One of the campsite managers at the Quidditch World Cup.

He cannot understand why so many "foreigners" and "weirdos" have suddenly booked campsites, nor why they are having such difficulties sorting out payment (his curiosity leads him to receive multiple Memory Charms). Mr. Roberts is married, with two small children.

Ted: Newsreader who gave a report about hundreds of owls flying by daylight the day after Voldemort disappeared.

Yvonne: A friend of Aunt Petunia's, she vacations in Majorca.

PART TWO:

Hogwarts

HOGWARTS: A HISTORY (AND MUCH MORE!)

Hogwarts was founded over a thousand years ago by the four greatest witches and wizards of the era — Godric Gryffindor, Helga Hufflepuff, Rowena Ravenclaw, and Salazar Slytherin. The castle was built far away from Muggles, as it was a time when those believed to be magical were persecuted. For several years, the four founders peacefully co-existed and educated youngsters who demonstrated magical ability. Then Slytherin, who didn't trust Muggles, decided pure-blood children should be the only ones admitted. Tension broke out amongst the founders, and following a major argument with Gryffindor, Slytherin left Hogwarts for good. After his departure, the fighting stopped but the houses have never since been united the way they were meant to be (see pages 143–145).

Because Voldemort is afraid of Dumbledore, Hogwarts is considered a safe haven against the Dark Arts.

Hogwarts motto: "*Draco dormiens nunquam titillandus*" (Never tickle a sleeping dragon).

Hogwarts coat-of-arms: The Gryffindor lion, Ravenclaw eagle, Hufflepuff badger, and Slytherin snake surrounding a large letter H.

Hogwarts song: Everyone sings the same words, but to their own favourite tune (Fred and George choose a funeral march).

Hogwarts letters: Hagrid says Harry's name has been down for Hogwarts ever since he was born.

Note to Muggles: *In an interview with Scholastic Books in February 2000, J. K. Rowling said there is a quill at Hogwarts that detects births of magical children and writes their names down in a large parchment book. Professor McGonagall checks the book every year, and sends owls to people on their eleventh birthday.*

Annual Hogwarts letters are written in emerald ink on yellowish parchment with a purple wax seal bearing the Hogwarts coat of arms. They are sent to students by owl post during the summer. In addition to admission, letters can provide information about textbook lists, OWL results, and prefectships.

Did you know . . . in an online chat for World Book Day in March 2004, J. K. Rowling explained what happens to magical children before they come to Hogwarts? In the case of witches and wizards raised in the magical world, they either go to a Muggle primary school, or are home-schooled by their parents (as was the case with all the Weasley children). In the case of Muggle-born witches and wizards, a special messenger is sent to their homes to explain everything to their parents — presumably, their parents will have noticed their children have had special abilities over the past ten years and so the news won't come as too much of a shock.

Hogwarts governors: A board of twelve governors oversee various matters in the school, including the appointment and suspension of the Headmaster.

    ✳   In second year, Lucius Malfoy forces the other governors to take drastic action, but the tables are later turned on him.

    ✳   In third year, the governors investigate a complaint about Buckbeak.

Did you know . . . a hogwart is a kind of lily? The name just popped into J. K. Rowling's head when she began writing the series. She couldn't remember where it came from, until a friend reminded her they had seen the flowers at London's Kew Gardens several years earlier. (Hogwarts is also an anagram for "warthogs"!)

GETTING TO HOGWARTS

King's Cross: British Rail station in London from which the Hogwarts Express departs. The Dursleys grudgingly collect Harry from King's Cross at the end of every school year.

JOURNEYS TO KING'S CROSS

First year

The Dursleys drop Harry off.

Second year

Mr. Weasley drives his family and Harry in the magically enhanced Ford Anglia (though Mrs. Weasley ensures the wheels stay on the ground).

Third year

Two cars from the Ministry drive the Weasleys, Harry, and Hermione from the Leaky Cauldron.

Fourth year

Mrs. Weasley arranges for three Muggle taxis to drive her family, Harry, and Hermione from The Burrow.

Fifth year

Harry is escorted to King's Cross on foot by a guard comprised of Mrs. Weasley, Tonks (as an old woman), and his faithful black dog. Mr. Weasley escorts Hermione and Ron, while Lupin escorts Ginny and the twins.

Did you know ... Harry Taylor, who plays the King's Cross station guard, was originally director Chris Columbus's driver during the first two Harry Potter films?

Platform nine and three quarters: Invisible to Muggles, this magical platform is accessed by walking briskly towards the barrier between platforms nine and ten without stopping. Witches and wizards will go straight through the seemingly solid barrier to platform nine and three quarters on the other side. At the end of the school year, students are sent back through the magical barrier spanning the platform in small groups, so as not to attract attention from Muggles.

Did you know ... so many fans visited King's Cross station to take a photo of platforms nine and ten, the station management erected a sign on a bricked-in archway adjacent to the platforms that reads "Platform 9 3/4"? The actual sign and archway can be seen on the cover of this book.

Hogwarts Express: Scarlet-coloured steam train that departs from platform nine and three quarters every first of September at eleven o'clock in the morning. During the journey, students change from their Muggle clothing into their wizarding robes. Hagrid traditionally supervises the students as they get off at Hogsmeade station. He leads first years across the lake in boats, while upper-year students take carriages to the castle. Luggage is left on the train and is taken to Hogwarts separately. The Hogwarts Express takes students back to King's Cross at the end of each year, as well as during Christmas and Easter holidays.

 **Did you know** . . . the train featured as the Hogwarts Express in the films was vandalised in September 2003? Two carriages were completely covered in graffiti, with restoration costs estimated at £3,000 (about $5,400 USD). Commonly known as Loco No. 5972 Olton Hall, the train is operated by the West Coast Railway Company and runs between Scarborough and York in England.

✶ **prefects' carriage:** On the way to Hogwarts, prefects gather in the front two compartments, located at the engine end of the train, to receive instructions from the Head Boy and Girl. Prefects patrol the corridors, discipline any misbehaviour, and supervise students collecting their belongings at the end of the journey.

✶ **trolley witch:** Smiling, dimpled, plump witch who sells wizarding sweets, food, and drink.

carriages: About one hundred musty-smelling stagecoaches, each seating four or five students, go between Hogsmeade station and Hogwarts at the beginning and end of the school year. The coaches smell of mould and straw and seem to be drawn by invisible horses, which are actually Thestrals.

GROUNDS

Though the exact location of Hogwarts is never revealed, it is very likely somewhere in northern Scotland, as Harry and Ron follow the Hogwarts Express several hours due north out of London in second year (not to mention, a Muggle in the Scottish town of Peebles reported seeing them). Hogwarts is also located amongst mountains, and there are certainly lots of mountains in the northern Scottish Highlands.

The Hogwarts grounds are protected by many spells to ward against intruders of both the Muggle and magical kind. For example, Muggles only see an abandoned ruin with signs ordering them to keep out, while magical folk are not allowed to Apparate or Disapparate inside the Hogwarts grounds. During third year, Hogwarts is given extra protection in the form of Dementors, which stand guard around the grounds (although Dumbledore will not let them into the castle).

When first-year students get off the Hogwarts Express, they take a steep, narrow path down to the edge of a great black lake. Hogwarts is north of the lake, situated at the top of a cliff. The first-year boats glide across the lake and through an ivy-covered opening in the cliff. They follow a tunnel to an underground harbour, where a passageway in the rocks leads to the castle grounds. Upper-year students ride to Hogwarts in carriages. The entrance to Hogwarts features a pair of tall stone columns with winged boars on either side of wrought-iron gates, and a long, sloping drive up to the castle.

courtyard: Students take their breaks during the school day in this small, outdoor enclosure.

Forbidden Forest: This dense, dark grove of trees adjacent to the castle has a narrow earthen path winding through it, scattered with brambles, roots, and tree stumps. The forest is black and still, the silence occasionally disrupted by rustling leaves or snapping twigs. There is a feeling of being watched by unseen eyes. The forest is off-limits to all students because of the dangerous creatures that live there.

Inhabitants of the Forbidden Forest include Aragog and his mate, Mosag; centaurs; Grawp; Thestrals; unicorns; and (possibly) werewolves (see Magical Beings and Creatures chapter).

FORAYS INTO THE FORBIDDEN FOREST

First year

* After a Quidditch match, Harry flies into the forest to eavesdrop on a conversation between Snape and Quirrell.
* Malfoy, Harry, Hermione, and Neville accompany Hagrid and Fang into the forest to search for a unicorn by following a trail of its silvery blood.

Second year

* After following some creepy advice, Harry and Ron are completely captivated by what they discover in the forest.

Third year

* A black dog temporarily hides out in the forest.
* The trio see a werewolf race into the forest on their way back to the castle.
* During a rescue mission, Harry and Hermione hide in the forest until the time is right to strike.

Fourth year

* Krum and Harry receive a startling interruption when they walk to the edge of the forest to have a private conversation.
* Moody hunts for Crouch in the forest.

Fifth year

* Hagrid takes the Care of Magical Creatures class into the forest to study Thestrals in their natural habitat.
* Hagrid asks Harry and Hermione to accompany him into the heart of the forest. After introducing them to what he considers a small creature, he asks them for what they consider a giant favour.
* Hermione leads Umbridge (and a confused Harry) to a secret weapon in the depths of the forest. When Harry and Hermione are later reunited with their friends, the forest provides them all with an unseen opportunity to escape.

greenhouses: Located near the vegetable patch. Herbology classes are held in the greenhouses, which contain trestle benches and smell of fertiliser, earth, and perfumed flowers. The more dangerous plants are kept in Greenhouse Three.

Hagrid's cabin: Hagrid lives in a cosy one-roomed wooden hut near the Forbidden Forest. Outside the front door, there is a crossbow and a pair of galoshes. Inside, cured hams and pheasants hang from the ceiling. There is a large fireplace in one corner and a massive bed with a patchwork quilt in the other. The trio often drops in for tea, which is served on an enormous scrubbed wooden table and chairs. Behind the cabin is Hagrid's pumpkin patch, where pumpkins grow large enough to seat three men inside.

Lake: The path to the lake is lined with pine trees, and there is a large beech tree on its shore. In warmer weather, the lake is suitable for swimming (although Krum takes a dip in the grey-coloured water in the middle of January!). Beneath the surface, the lake is home to lots of weeds, small silver fish, and a variety of other creatures.

LAKE DWELLERS

giant squid: Probably the most famous denizen of the lake, the squid can often be seen swimming back and forth across the water and occasionally interacting with students.

Grindylows: Attack a couple of the champions during the second task of the Triwizard Tournament.

Merpeople: Merpeople have greyish skin that ends in a silver tail, and long, wild, dark green hair with yellow eyes and broken yellow teeth. They wear thick ropes of pebbles or chokers of shark-fangs around their necks. Many carry spears and some even keep Grindylows as pets!

Merpeople live in an underwater village of algae-covered stone dwellings. There are rock paintings of them with spears chasing the giant squid. They speak in Mermish, which is comprehensible below water, but sounds like screechy noise above ground. It seems they have no magical abilities. Murcus is the ferocious-looking Merchieftainess, who converses with Dumbledore in Mermish after the second task of the Triwizard Tournament.

Moaning Myrtle: Although her home is in the castle, she sometimes gets flushed out into the lake along with the contents of toilets (yuk!).

Quidditch Pitch: Located on the other side of the grounds from the Forbidden Forest, the enormous pitch is ringed by raised stands that seat hundreds. There is also a broomshed and two changing rooms, each with an equipment cupboard and a captain's office.

Whomping Willow: Definitely not to be confused with the gentler weeping willow, the Whomping Willow violently attacks anything that has the misfortune to come into contact with it. It is a very valuable tree, and several of its boughs need to be put in slings after a particularly nasty encounter in second year.

Like many things at Hogwarts, there is a secret at the root of the Whomping Willow. Lupin tells Harry it was planted the year he came to Hogwarts — students used to try and touch its trunk as a game, but were forbidden to go near it after a boy nearly lost his eye. The tree's motion can be stopped by touching a knot in the trunk.

CASTLE

Hogwarts is a vast castle with lots of towers and turrets. There are one hundred and forty-two staircases, including ones that lead to different places on different days of the week, ones that swivel and ones with vanishing steps that must be jumped over. Often doorways are hidden behind sliding panels or hanging tapestries. Sometimes doors won't open unless they are asked politely or tickled, and sometimes the doors aren't really doors at all.

The castle has lots of mullioned windows and is quite draughty in the colder months — students have been known to wear dragonskin gloves in the corridors between classes! Of course, an old castle like Hogwarts also has numerous secret passageways (and of course, Fred and George know them all!). Fifth years are allowed to be in the corridors until nine o'clock in the evening. After that, watch out for Mrs. Norris!

Armour, Busts, Statues, and Tapestries:

✴ **Barnabas the Barmy:** A tapestry on the seventh floor depicts Barnabas being clubbed by trolls he tried to teach how to do ballet.

✴ **Boris the Bewildered:** His statue on the fifth floor depicts poor old Boris looking confused, with his gloves on the wrong hands.

✴ **bust of a medieval wizard:** Located near the corridor to Umbridge's office, he mutters to himself in Latin.

✴ **Gregory the Smarmy:** Fred and George discovered a secret passageway behind his statue in the east wing during their first week at Hogwarts.

✴ **Humpbacked one-eyed witch:** The hump in her statue opens up, revealing a secret passageway.

✴ **Lachlan the Lanky:** His statue is near the entrance to Gryffindor Tower on the seventh floor.

✴ **Paracelsus:** His bust is near the entrance to Gryffindor Tower on the seventh floor.

* **statue of a knight:** He guards the entrance to the Ravenclaw common room, on the third floor.
* **Stone gargoyle:** Guards the entrance to Dumbledore's office.
* **suits of armour:** Hogwarts suits of armour can walk and talk, and, during the Yule Ball, are bewitched to sing carols. There is a gallery of them located on the third floor near the trophy room.
* **Talking gargoyles:** There is one on either side of the staff room door.
* **Wilfred the Wistful:** His statue is on the way to the Owlery.

Secret passageways: According to the Marauder's Map, there are seven.
* Filch knows about four.
* One is a fairly spacious tunnel behind a large mirror on the fourth floor, but it is caved in.
* One is inaccessible because the Whomping Willow is planted over the entrance.
* One is a little-known passage, entered through the humpbacked witch's statue on the third floor corridor. It is twisting, narrow, and low, with an earth floor. At the end, hundreds of steps lead up to the cellar of Honeydukes sweetshop.

Astronomy Tower: The tallest tower at Hogwarts, with a steep spiral staircase leading up to the top. Students are not allowed up there except for classes.

Chamber of Secrets: Hogwarts co-founder Salazar Slytherin was said to have built an enormous secret chamber within the castle just before he left for good. The Chamber hides a monster that would rid the school of Muggle-born students, whom Slytherin thought were not fit to study magic. Although Hogwarts has been searched many times, no such place was ever found and the Chamber of Secrets eventually became part of the castle's legends.

In reality, Slytherin sealed the hidden Chamber in such a way that only his true heir would be able to command it to open. The entrance is very well-concealed and even after it is opened, the Chamber of Secrets itself is still quite difficult to access. The entrance reveals a long, dark, slimy, and twisting passage, which eventually opens up to a long stone tunnel. The floor of the tunnel is littered with giant coils of skin and the bones of small animals. It leads to a wall with two intertwined, emerald-eyed snakes. When spoken to in a certain way, the snakes unlock and the wall splits open to finally reveal the Chamber. The Chamber of Secrets is a long, large room with a vaulted ceiling. It is bathed in a dull greenish light and is full of shadowy corners. Stone pillars carved with snakes lead to an enormous stone statue of an ancient-looking wizard against the Chamber's back wall. When it is called, Slytherin's monster enters the Chamber through a hole in the statue's mouth.

The Chamber of Secrets was opened once, by the last person anyone would have suspected. Fifty years later, during second year, it seems history is about to repeat itself.

 Did you know . . . the title of the upcoming sixth book, *Harry Potter and the Half Blood Prince*, was once the working title for *Harry Potter and the Chamber of Secrets*? On her official Web site, J.K. Rowling hinted that the "prince" in the title is neither Harry nor Voldemort. . .

Charms classroom: Located on the third floor, not far from a secret passageway. At Christmastime, Flitwick decorates the classroom with live faeries that shimmer and glow.

classroom eleven: Located off the Entrance Hall, in the opposite direction from the Great Hall. Dumbledore transforms the classroom into a forest for Firenze's Divination lessons, with a mossy floor and lots of big, leafy trees. The room is bathed in a soft green light that can be dimmed to reveal planets and stars on the ceiling.

classroom off the Entrance Hall: A small room where the Wand Weighing ceremony and photograph session for the Triwizard Tournament takes place.

Defence Against the Dark Arts classroom: Located on the first floor. In first year, it smelled of garlic to ward off vampires. Cornish pixies vandalised the classroom in second year.

Defence Against the Dark Arts professor's office: Located on the second floor. In second year, Lockhart decorated the office with candles and numerous autographed photos of himself (the inhabitants of which wore hairnets and rollers at night). In third year, Lupin made the office home to a number of Dark creatures that students were studying in class. In fourth year, the room is stocked with Dark detectors and artefacts. In fifth year, Umbridge drapes the room in florals and lace, with bouquets of dried flowers and a wall of ugly ornamental plates featuring moving multicoloured kittens. Her desk is stocked with pink-coloured parchment.

disused classroom: Located near a suit of armour, Harry discovers this fourth floor room by accident when he is escaping from Filch and Snape in first year. All the desks and chairs in the room are pushed against the walls. Harry stumbles across the Mirror of Erised for the first time in this room (until Dumbledore moves it).

Divination classroom: Located on the seventh floor of the North Tower. When the trio get lost on the way to their first Divination lesson, they encounter Sir Cadogan, who leads them on a "quest" through a maze of portraits and corridors to find the classroom. He brings them to the top of a narrow spiral staircase, which has a circular trapdoor on the ceiling with Trelawney's name on a brass plaque. Students climb a silver ladder to get to the classroom.

The classroom looks like a cross between an attic and a teashop, with small round tables and chintz-covered winged armchairs and pouffes. The circular walls hold shelves containing candles, crystal balls, feathers, playing cards, teapots, and teacups. It is a gloomy room, with dim lights covered in crimson scarves and curtains that are always closed. It is also dusty and very stuffy, with a large fireplace that burns with a smoky, overpowering perfume. Trelawney always makes a dramatic entrance out of the shadows.

Dumbledore's office: While Dumbledore's actual living quarters are still a mystery, his second-floor office is certainly well-known! A large stone gargoyle protects the wall that conceals the office's entrance. After the password is spoken, the gargoyle moves aside and the wall opens up, revealing an escalator-like spiral stone staircase. The staircase stops in front of an oak door with a brass griffin knocker.

The office is large and circular, with portraits of former Hogwarts heads covering the walls. Fawkes's perch is behind the door. In addition to Dumbledore's large, claw-footed desk and high-backed chair, there are several spindle-legged tables on which strange silver instruments sit whirring and emitting puffs of smoke. The Sorting Hat stands on a shelf behind Dumbledore's desk, next to which is a glass case containing Godric Gryffindor's sword. A black cabinet holds Dumbledore's Pensieve.

    ✶ **passwords:** cockroach cluster, Fizzing Whizzbee, lemon drop, sherbet lemon

VISITS TO THE HEADMASTER'S OFFICE

Second year

✶ Harry is sent to Dumbledore's office just before Christmas, after two more Petrification victims are found.

Fourth year

✶ Harry has a pensive moment while waiting for Dumbledore in his office. He returns to the office later in the year to relate his encounter in the graveyard after the third task of the Triwizard Tournament.

Fifth year

✶ Harry and Ron are brought to the office after Harry's disturbing vision.
✶ Harry is escorted to Dumbledore's office after the DA is discovered. Dumbledore's office later seals itself off to Umbridge and will not permit her to enter.
✶ Dumbledore Portkeys Harry from the Ministry to his office, where they have a long overdue chat.

dungeons: Potions classes are held in a large, cold dungeon. The stone walls are lined with preserved animals floating in jars. Brass scales and jars of ingredients sit on top of twenty wooden desks, each of which has a cauldron adjacent to it. There are stone basins in the corner with jets of water coming from a gargoyle's head to do the washing up after class.

Nearly Headless Nick also holds his Deathday Party in one of the biggest and coldest dungeons, which he decorates in black velvet with hundreds of blue-flamed black candles.

Entrance Hall: This massive hallway on the ground floor has a high, cavernous ceiling with stone floors and walls that are lit by flaming torches. Double oak doors lead out to the Hogwarts grounds, while a grand marble staircase leads to the upper floors. Various doors beside the staircase lead down to the kitchens, dungeons, and the Hufflepuff and Slytherin residences. First years wait to be sorted in a small chamber off the Entrance Hall.

Filch's office: Drab, dimly lit, and windowless, Filch's fishy-smelling office contains stacks of wooden cabinets with files on troublemaking students (Fred and George have a whole drawer to themselves). Filch keeps a list of forbidden objects in his office, many of which he has confiscated from students, including the Marauder's Map (before the twins, well, filched it!). He also has a set of well-oiled, polished chains — just in case certain kinds of punishment are ever reinstated.

Flitwick's office: Located on the seventh floor, thirteen windows from the right of the West Tower.

Great Hall: Double doors off the Entrance Hall lead to an enormous grand dining room. There are four long house tables and a raised High Table for the teachers at the far end, where Dumbledore sits in a high-backed golden chair. The Great Hall has high windows, and is lit by thousands of candles that float in midair. The ceiling is bewitched to reflect the current condition of the sky.

✷ Feasts:

start-of-term feast: The Sorting Hat ceremony takes place, followed by Dumbledore's speech and announcements and the singing of the school song.

Welcoming Feast: A special feast held in fourth year on Friday the thirtieth of October, to welcome the Beauxbatons and Durmstrang students. The entire castle is cleaned in honour of their arrival, and the Great Hall is decorated with silk house and school banners.

Hallowe'en Feast: Thousands of live bats cover the walls and ceiling, while the tables are covered in carved, candlelit pumpkins. In second year there are dancing skeletons for entertainment, while in third year, the castle ghosts perform formation gliding amid a backdrop of animated orange streamers. The Triwizard Tournament champions' names are drawn from the Goblet of Fire during the feast in fourth year.

Yule Ball Feast: Held during the Yule Ball, on Christmas Day in fourth year, the traditional house tables are replaced by about a hundred smaller ones, each seating about a dozen and lit by lanterns. Small menus rest on top of golden plates — after the name of the desired food is spoken out loud, it magically appears on the plate.

Valentine's Day: As a "morale-booster" in second year, Lockhart decorates the Great Hall with large pink flowers and makes heart-shaped confetti fall from the ceiling (to the mutual disgust of most students and staff). He also brings in twelve golden wing–wearing, harp–carrying dwarves (who look about as pleased to be there as the students and staff do) to distribute Valentines throughout the day. To Harry's complete embarrassment, one of them gruffly tackles him on his way to class to deliver an anonymous singing Valentine.

Leaving (end-of-term) Feast: The House Cup is awarded, and the Great Hall is decorated in the colours of the winning house. In second year, the feast was held late at night after Harry's experience in the Chamber of Secrets, and students attended in their pyjamas. Out of respect for the person who dies in fourth year, there are black drapes behind the High Table instead of decorations, and Dumbledore asks everyone to stand in a toast to honour the deceased.

Christmas: Each year, there are twelve enormous, frost-covered Christmas trees, variously adorned with tiny icicles, luminous holly berries, golden owls and bubbles, glittering stars, and hundreds of candles. Mistletoe and holly cover the walls and ceiling, from which warm, dry, enchanted snow falls.

CHRISTMAS PRESENTS

First year

Harry: large box of Chocolate Frogs (Hermione), fifty pence (the Dursleys), hand-whittled wooden flute (Hagrid), home-made fudge and hand-knitted green jumper (Mrs. Weasley), Invisibility Cloak (Dumbledore)
Ron: box of Bertie Bott's Every Flavour Beans (Hermione), hand-knitted maroon jumper with a yellow R (Mrs. Weasley)
Percy, "Gred," and "Forge": hand-knitted jumpers with their initials in yellow, which the twins jokingly say their mother knitted because she can't tell them apart (Mrs. Weasley)

Second year

Harry: *Flying with the Cannons* (Ron), luxury eagle-feather quill (Hermione), plum cake and hand-knitted jumper (Mrs. Weasley), toothpick (the Dursleys), treacle fudge (Hagrid)

Third year

Harry: nut brittle, mince pies, Christmas cake, and hand-knitted scarlet jumper with a Gryffindor lion (Mrs. Weasley), Marauder's Map (early gift from Fred and George), Firebolt (Sirius)
Ron: hand-knitted maroon jumper and socks (Mrs. Weasley)

Fourth year

Dobby: mustard-coloured socks (Harry), violet-coloured socks and hand-knitted jumper (Ron, courtesy of Mrs. Weasley)

Harry: Dungbombs (Ron), mince pies and hand-knitted green jumper with a dragon (Mrs. Weasley), mismatched hand-knitted socks (Dobby), penknife (Sirius), *Quidditch Teams of Britain and Ireland* (Hermione), sheet of tissue (the Dursleys), sweets (Hagrid)

Hermione: Omnioculars (Harry — bought during the summer at the Quidditch World Cup)

Ron: Chudley Cannons hat (Harry), Omnioculars (early gift from Harry at the Quidditch World Cup, although Ron thinks he repaid Harry with the Leprechaun gold he caught)

Fifth year

Harry: homework planner (Hermione), *Practical Defensive Magic and its Use Against the Dark Arts* books (Sirius and Lupin), fanged brown furry wallet (Hagrid), model Firebolt (Tonks), large box of Bertie Bott's Every Flavour Beans (Ron), mince pies and hand-knitted jumper (Mr. and Mrs. Weasley), bad painting of Harry (Dobby)

Hermione: *New Theory of Numerology* (Harry), "unusual" perfume (Ron)

Kreacher: patchwork quilt (Hermione)

Mr. Weasley: screwdrivers and wire (Harry)

Ron: broom compass (Harry), homework planner (Hermione)

Great Hall antechamber: A little room behind the Great Hall where Triwizard Tournament champions receive their instructions for the first task. It is accessed through a door behind the staff table, and has a fireplace and a candle-filled chandelier. The walls are covered with paintings of witches and wizards, including the Fat Lady's friend Violet. The champions' families are received here prior to the third task.

hospital wing: The hospital wing has multiple beds, like a dormitory, each with a bedside cabinet and portable screen for privacy. Madam Pomfrey's office is at the end of the ward.

★ Medicinal Magic:

Blood-replenishing Potion: Mr. Weasley takes this after being bitten by a snake.

bright blue liquid: Spoon-fed to Montague for his confusion and disorientation.

Bubotuber pus: Excellent treatment for acne.

Calming Draught: Combats anxiety and stress.

chocolate: Dumbledore, Lupin, and Madam Pomfrey all favour chocolate as a remedy for shock (especially after encountering Dementors). Eating it spreads warmth throughout the body.

Dr. Ubbly's Oblivious Unction: Applied to the welts on Ron's arms after he is attacked by brains.

dragon meat steak: Raw and green-blooded, Hagrid uses one to soothe the stinging in his black eye.

dreamless sleep potion: Purple liquid that instantly puts the drinker in a deep sleep.

Mandrake Restorative Draught: When they reach maturity, Mandrakes are chopped up and stewed to make this draught, which revives people who have been Petrified.

Murtlap essence: Hermione prepares a bowl of yellow liquid containing pickled and strained Murtlap Tentacles to soothe the pain in Harry's hand after detention. Murtlap essence also cures boils.

Pepperup Potion: Perks up those who have the flu, but leaves the person smoking from the ears for several hours. It tastes peppery and burns the throat.

Phoenix tears: Have the ability to heal wounds, although they are not used in the hospital wing.

Skele-Gro: Regrows bones, which is a painful procedure — the area to be regrown feels like stabbing pain, then like it is full of splinters. Skele-Gro is a steaming liquid with a burning taste that induces coughing.

smoking purple liquid: cleans cuts.

thick orange paste: heals burns.

TRIPS TO THE HOSPITAL WING

First year

Neville: Covered in boils after a mishap in Potions; breaks his wrist during his first flying lesson; knocked out after fighting during a Quidditch match.

Ron: Bitten by a dragon (though he told Madam Pomfrey it was a dog), the cut turned green and his hand swelled up to twice its usual size.

Harry: Unconscious for three days following his experience in the chamber with the Philosopher's Stone (Fred and George send a lavatory seat as a get-well-soon present, which Madam Pomfrey confiscates).

Second year

Ginny: Coerced into taking Pepperup Potion because Percy thought she looked ill; recovers from her experience in the Chamber of Secrets.

Harry: Spends a night regrowing thirty-three bones in his right arm, after they are broken during a Quidditch match and accidentally removed by an inept spell.

Hermione: Recovers for about five weeks after accidentally transforming into a cat. She sleeps with a get-well-soon card from Lockhart under her pillow, much to Harry and Ron's disgust!

Colin Creevey, Justin Finch-Fletchley, Nearly Headless Nick, Hermione, Penelope Clearwater: Revived with Mandrake Restorative Draught after each of them has a petrifying experience during the year.

Lockhart: Doesn't remember why he is sent there.

Third year

Harry: After he collapses following an encounter with Dementors, Madam Pomfrey visits Harry in McGonagall's office to monitor his recovery; recovers for a weekend after falling fifty feet from his broom during a Quidditch match; collapses again after coming into contact with Dementors at the end of the year.

Malfoy: Right arm bandaged and put in a sling after being attacked in Care of Magical Creatures class. Malfoy claims he can't use his arm for three months afterwards.

Unnamed Gryffindor fourth year and Slytherin sixth year: Leeks grow out of their ears following a tussle in a corridor before a Quidditch match.

Ron: Breaks his leg after catching it in one of the Whomping Willow's roots, and is later knocked out.

Hermione: Collapses after coming into contact with Dementors. Snape also (wrongly) suggests Harry, Hermione, and Ron have been placed under a Confundus Charm, and they are held for observation overnight.

Fourth year

Fred, George, Fawcett, and Summers: Spout long white beards after crossing an Age Line.

Hermione: Her front teeth grow past her collar when she is hit by a wayward Densaugeo spell, but it turns out to be a blessing in disguise; fingers erupt in painful yellow boils after coming into contact with undiluted Bubotuber Pus.

Goyle: Boils erupt all over his face when he is hit by a wayward Furnunculus Curse.

Cedric and Harry: Receive burns (Cedric) and gashes (Harry) from dragons.

Cedric, Cho, Gabrielle, Hermione, Harry, Krum, Ron: Wrapped in blankets and given Pepperup Potion following the second task. Fleur has numerous cuts but refuses to let Madam Pomfrey tend to them.

Moody: Recovers from his experience in the trunk.

Harry: Given a dreamless sleep potion following his encounter in the graveyard.

Fifth year

Katie Bell: Bleeds uncontrollably after Fred accidentally gives her a Blood Blisterpod to stop her bloody nose during Quidditch practice.

Alicia Spinnet: Her eyebrows grow down to her mouth when she is jinxed before the Gryffindor-Slytherin Quidditch match.

Hannah Abbott: Suffers from anxiety and stress whilst studying for OWLS.

Marietta Edgecombe: Suffers from a rather telling and very stubborn case of acne.

Montague: Turns up inside a toilet after being missing for several days. He remains confused and disoriented for quite some time.

Jack Sloper: Knocks himself out during Quidditch practice.

Warrington: Skin develops a condition where it looks like it has been coated in cornflakes.

McGonagall: Hit with four Stunning Spells in the chest.

Hermione, Neville, Ginny, and Ron: Assorted injuries following their experience at the Department of Mysteries.

Umbridge: Suffers from shock after her experience in the Forbidden Forest.

kitchens: A door to the right of the marble staircase in the Entrance Hall leads down to a brightly lit, broad stone corridor, decorated with paintings of food. One painting features a large silver bowl of fruit — tickling the large green pear will transform it into the door handle of the Hogwarts kitchen. It is an enormous room with a high ceiling and large fireplace. Lots of brass pots and pans hang from the walls. Four long wooden tables correspond to the house tables directly above them in the Great Hall. Meals are set out on the tables, then magically sent up through the ceiling.

Wizard Cuisine

* **Cauldron Cakes**
* **Ginger Newts**
* **Pumpkin Pasties**
* **treacle tarts**
* **Hagrid's cuisine:** doughy biscuits, stoat sandwiches (his favourite), beef casserole (watch out — contains talons!), and dandelion juice

British and European Cuisine

* **bangers:** sausages
* **Bath buns:** dense, sweet, and rich, these sugar-topped, currant and fruit peel–filled buns were first made in the city of Bath over three hundred years ago.
* **biscuit:** cookie
* **black/blood pudding:** pork sausage containing blood and suet
* **blancmange:** thick, sweet, almond-flavoured milk pudding (French)
* **bouillabaisse:** shellfish-based stew (French)
* **chipolata:** small pork sausage
* **chips:** French fries
* **(flaming) Christmas pudding:** Traditional holiday dessert. Dense, dark cake that is steamed, containing dried fruit and (usually) alcohol. A coin is often hidden inside, bringing good luck to whomever finds it.
* **clotted cream:** unsweetened cream containing fifty-five per cent fat (!), usually from Cornwall or Devon.
* **crisps:** potato chips
* **crumpet:** cratered, round, eggless bread made with yeast, served toasted and buttered. (It is also slang for a good-looking female.)
* **gateau:** cake (French)
* **ice lolly:** popsicle
* **jelly:** Jell-O
* **joint:** a piece of roasted meat traditionally served for Sunday dinner
* **kippers:** smoked herrings, traditionally eaten for breakfast
* **knickerbocker glory:** sundae made with layers of fruit and ice cream, served in a tall glass and eaten with a long spoon

* **mince:** ground beef
* **mint humbugs:** mint-flavoured hard boiled sweets
* **Cornish pasty:** half-moon shaped pastry with thick scalloped crust, traditionally filled with a mixture of beef, turnip, onion, and potato
* **porridge:** breakfast food, usually served hot, consisting of oatmeal boiled with milk or water until thick
* **pudding:** dessert
* **rock cakes:** small cakes containing dried fruit, with a hard, dense texture
* **runner-beans:** string beans
* **sherbert lemons:** fizzy, lemon-flavoured sweets (one of Dumbledore's favourites)
* **spotted dick:** steamed sponge pudding made from suet, containing currants
* **sweets:** candy
* **treacle:** thick, sweet syrup, similar to molasses and generally dark in colour
* **trifle:** traditional dessert made with layers of custard, sponge cake (sometimes soaked in alcohol), jelly, fruit, and whipped cream.
* **tripe:** lining of a cow's stomach (not to be confused with haggis). It also means foolish talk or nonsense.
* **whelk:** small, edible sea snail
* **Yorkshire pudding:** light, puffy bread made from batter, traditionally baked and served with roast beef

Library: Hogwarts's enormous library features tens of thousands of books on thousands of shelves in hundreds of narrow rows. It closes at eight o'clock at night. The Restricted Section, located at the back of the library, houses books about Dark Magic that are off-limits to everyone except older-year students studying advanced Defence Against the Dark Arts. Students need a signed note from a teacher to access the restricted section, which is cordoned off from the rest of the library by rope. The books here are written in different wizarding languages. Some have no titles, some are bloodstained, one makes a faint whispering noise, and another lets out a blood-curdling scream if touched.

✶ Hogwarts Library Books:
An Anthology of Eighteenth-Century Charms: Harry searches this for help with the second task of the Triwizard Tournament.

Ancient Runes Made Easy: Hermione reads this in second year to learn more about the subject, which she plans to sign up for in third year.

Asiatic Anti-Venoms: Harry suddenly becomes very interested in this when Hermione asks if he's given any further thought to her teaching proposal.

Basic Hexes for the Busy and Vexed: Harry looks through this book during research for the first task of the Triwizard Tournament.

Dragon Breeding for Pleasure and Profit: Hagrid borrows this for "research purposes." It says dragon eggs must be kept in a fire to mimic their mothers' breath, then the baby must be fed a bucket of brandy and chicken blood every half-hour after hatching.

Dragon Species of Great Britain and Ireland: Hagrid looks through this for information about Norbert.

Dreadful Denizens of the Deep: Harry searches this for help with the second task of the Triwizard Tournament.

Fowl or Foul? A Study of Hippogriff Brutality: Ron studies this when researching how to help Buckbeak.

From Egg to Inferno, A Dragon Keeper's Guide: Hagrid looks through this for information about Norbert.

Great Wizards of the Twentieth Century: The trio search through this to find out about Nicolas Flamel.

A Guide to Medieval Sorcery: Harry searches this for help with the second task of the Triwizard Tournament.

The Handbook of Hippogriff Psychology: Ron studies this when researching how to help Buckbeak.

Hogwarts: A History: Hermione frequently references this to quote facts about the castle (despite being outraged that the "oppression" Hogwarts shows towards house-elves is not mentioned in its pages).

Important Modern Magical Discoveries: The trio search this to find out about Nicolas Flamel.

Madcap Magic for Wacky Warlocks: Harry searches this for help with the second task of the Triwizard Tournament.

Men Who Love Dragons Too Much: Harry and Hermione look through this during their research for the first task of the Triwizard Tournament.

Moste Potente Potions (Restricted Section): Hermione convinces Lockhart to sign a note (which she wants to keep, as it has his autograph!) permitting her to go into the Restricted Section, where she checks out this large, mouldy-looking book. It contains many disturbing drawings and recipes for potions with frightening side effects.

Notable Magical Names of Our Time: The trio search this to find out about Nicolas Flamel.

Olde and Forgotten Bewitchments and Charmes: Hermione pores over this tiny-printed book to try and find something that will help Harry with the second task of the Triwizard Tournament.

Powers You Never Knew You Had and What to Do With Them Now You've Wised Up: Harry searches this for help with the second task of the Triwizard Tournament.

Quidditch through the Ages: Hermione scours this for useful tips prior to her first flying lesson. Harry finds it a very interesting read, until Snape confiscates it.

Saucy Tricks for Tricky Sorts: The trio search this to try to find something that will help Harry with the second task of the Triwizard Tournament.

A Study of Recent Developments in Wizardry: The trio search this to find out about Nicolas Flamel.

Weird Wizarding Dilemmas and Their Solutions: The trio search this to try and find something that will help Harry with the second task of the Triwizard Tournament. (It includes a section on growing nose hair into ringlets, which Fred thinks would be quite a conversation piece!)

Where There's a Wand, There's a Way: Harry searches this for help with the second task of the Triwizard Tournament.

Did you know . . . the five books in the Harry Potter series published to date (hardcover editions) comprise between 2,212 (British edition) and 2,689 (American edition) pages in English? (Some foreign translations of the series are over 3,200 pages long!)

McGonagall's office: Located on the first floor, it is a tiny office with a large, cheery fireplace. A certain Cup has taken up residence there over the past couple of years.

Moaning Myrtle's bathroom: Haunted for over fifty years by Moaning Myrtle, who often floods the toilets and sinks as a result of her incessant tantrums (hence the perpetual "out of order" sign on the door). It is a gloomy, secretive, candlelit chamber that is in a general state of disrepair, with a large cracked dirty mirror, a damp floor, doors that fall off their hinges, and chipped sinks.

Owlery: School and students' owls sleep and eat in this circular room, located at the top of the West Tower. It is made of stone, with rafters that go all the way up to the ceiling, and has a floor covered in straw, droppings, and rodent skeletons. The Owlery's windows have no glass because of the constant takeoffs and landings of its residents, so it is always cold.

Prefects' bathroom: Located on the fifth floor, four doors to the left of Boris the Bewildered's statue. Prefects bathe in the lap of luxury — the room features a sunken white marble bathtub the size of a swimming pool, complete with diving board. Around the edges of the tub there are a hundred golden taps with jewelled handles, each containing a different kind of bubble bath. The bathroom is lit by a candle chandelier and has long white linen curtains. There is a pile of fluffy white towels in the corner, and a gold-framed painting of a blonde mermaid on the wall. The password to enter is "Pine-fresh."

Room of Requirement: The Come and Go Room, as the house-elves call it, is very difficult to find. It will only reveal itself when a person has a dire need for something; the room will magically appear and be equipped with whatever the person needs. Very few people know about the room — they find it by accident, but often cannot find it again.

The room is located on the seventh floor, not far from a boys' bathroom. To find it, a person must walk past the wall opposite the tapestry of Barnabas the Barmy and concentrate on what is needed. After doing this three times, a polished door with a brass handle will appear in the wall.

REQUIREMENTS OF THE ROOM

✷ Once, Dumbledore took a wrong turn on the way to the bathroom and found himself in a room with a collection of chamber pots. When he went back later, the room had vanished (because he only needed it when his bladder was full!).

✷ Dobby uses the room to hide Winky when she is drunk — he finds antidotes to Butterbeer and an elf-sized bed for her to sleep in.

✷ When Fred and George hid from Filch, the room was just a broom cupboard.

✷ Filch finds additional cleaning supplies in the room when he runs out.

✷ Harry uses the room to hold DA lessons. It becomes a large room containing dark detectors, big silk cushions, and bookcases filled with defence books.

second floor corridor: In second year, this corridor near Moaning Myrtle's bathroom was the scene of a number of ominous events. It is where the first Petrified victim was found, along with a warning message on the wall written in foot-tall letters. A second, even more sinister message was found on the corridor wall later in the year.

staff room: Located on the ground floor, it is a large, panelled room containing mismatched dark wooden chairs and an ugly wardrobe full of the teachers' cloaks (and, on one occasion, a Boggart). A pair of talking stone gargoyles flank the entrance.

Snape's office: Snape's office is cold, inaccessible, and full of strange, hidden things, much like Snape himself. Located in the dungeons, it has a fireplace that never seems to be lit and lots of glass jars full of coloured potions with creepy things floating inside. A large corner cabinet holds his private store of Potions ingredients. Snape uses a spell to seal the office, as he knows it has been broken into before.

third floor corridor: Located behind a locked door, this corridor is off-limits to all students during first year, and with good reason. Those who find themselves trapped behind the door are in for a triple shock.

trophy room: Located on the third floor. It has doors at either end that are never locked, and is full of at least a hundred silver and gold awards, cups, medals, plates, shields, statues, and a list of old Head Boys.

AWARDS

House Cup: Awarded annually to the House with the most points.

Medal for Magical Merit: Tom Riddle won this as a student.

Quidditch Cup: Won by Slytherin for seven consecutive years before Harry started Hogwarts, but a different name appears on it more frequently these days.

Special Award for Services to the School: A burnished gold shield Tom Riddle received during his fifth year (Ron particularly remembers this award because he belched slugs all over it). Harry and Ron receive the same award in second year, following their experience in the Chamber of Secrets.

STUDENT ACTIVITIES AND APPOINTMENTS

There's more to life at Hogwarts than spellbooks and Potions experiments! Depending on their interests, students can participate in a number of extracurricular activities, covering everything from Gobstones to Quidditch.

As per the school rules, students are also allowed to form groups of their own pertaining to study and homework. However, this changes in fifth year with the establishment of Educational Decree Number Twenty-four, which immediately disbands all clubs, groups, organisations, societies, and teams of three or more students. Permission must be granted before the activities can be reformed, and any student forming or belonging to a non-approved activity will be expelled.

The staff also appoint selected students to various positions each year, including prefects, Head Girl and Boy, and the four Quidditch Captains.

Charms Club: Vicky Frobisher belongs to this society, and said she would choose it over Quidditch training if she were chosen to play on the team.

Duelling Club: In second year, Lockhart (with Snape as a very reluctant "assistant") starts a Duelling Club so students can learn to defend themselves. Students are paired off and taught the proper procedure for duelling — they must bow, hold their wands up like swords ("the accepted combative position," according to Lockhart), count to three, and then cast spells in an attempt to disarm each other. Harry and Malfoy are volunteered to demonstrate how to block unfriendly spells — however, in this case, words speak louder than actions.

Dumbledore's Army (DA): After suffering through several years of hit-and-miss Defence Against the Dark Arts classes, a group of students literally decide to take matters into their own hands by attending secret defensive training lessons in fifth year.

Known as the DA, the group is under Harry's leadership but it is largely Hermione's brainchild. She proposed the idea to Harry, organised the first meeting, roused dubious attendees with an impassioned speech, coordinated security measures, communicated meeting times to members, suggested Harry be officially elected as leader, and asked the members to come up with a name (which Cho and Ginny chose).

Interestingly, a number of parallels exist between the DA and the Order of the Phoenix: both are shrouded in secrecy, both hold meetings in inconspicuous locations that cannot be detected by passers-by, both are designed to educate members in the fight against the Dark Arts, and both are led by powerful wizards who have first-hand experience with Voldemort. (Although hopefully, the DA's fate won't be a sneak preview for what will happen to the Order!)

Although hesitant at first, Harry eventually warms to the idea of teaching. He takes great pride in seeing his fellow students improve their skills in several key spells, including the Disarming Charm, Impediment Jinx, Patronus Charm, Reductor Curse, Shield Charm, and Stunning Spell. The breakout star is undoubtedly Neville, who develops a newfound confidence and masters things quickly. His concentration, determination, and perseverance take Harry by surprise.

The defensive magic taught in the DA is put to good use by its members in various situations throughout the remainder of the school year.

DA MEMBERS

Hannah Abbott, Katie Bell, Susan Bones, Terry Boot, Lavender Brown, Cho Chang, Michael Corner, Colin Creevey, Dennis Creevey, Marietta Edgecombe, Justin Finch-Fletchley, Seamus Finnigan, Anthony Goldstein, Hermione Granger, Angelina Johnson, Lee Jordan, Neville Longbottom, Luna Lovegood, Ernie Macmillan, Padma Patil, Parvati Patil, Harry Potter, Zacharias Smith, Alicia Spinnet, Dean Thomas, Fred Weasley, George Weasley, Ginny Weasley, Ron Weasley.

Gobstones Club: Presumably, members play Gobstones, a wizarding game similar to marbles.

Head Girl and Head Boy: Pair of seventh-years who are considered the overall top students and role models for the rest of the school. The Head Girl and Boy are chosen by the staff, normally from the existing group of prefects. Their duties generally include overseeing the prefects and students and representing the school at various events. They wear badges with their titles on them (the twins enjoy bewitching Percy's badge to read "Bighead Boy" and "Humongous Bighead").

Inquisitorial Squad: In fifth year, a group of students are appointed to enforce rules and carry out the orders of the Hogwarts High Inquisitor, acting as her eyes and ears throughout the castle (sort of like a junior version of the Death Eaters). Members wear a tiny silver "I" on their robes and have the authority to deduct house points and inspect all mail entering and exiting Hogwarts. They can use physical force as a weapon, if necessary. Unsurprisingly, members of the Inquisitorial Squad are comprised entirely of Slytherins, including Millicent Bulstrode, Crabbe, Malfoy, Montague, Pansy Parkinson, and Warrington.

Prefects: Students who are given a small amount of authority by the staff to assist with the supervision of younger students and carry out other miscellaneous duties (at Hogwarts, these include patrolling the corridors and overseeing the decorations at Christmas). Prefects are appointed by the staff and are usually model students who set good examples and show signs of leadership. One male and female prefect are chosen from fifth, sixth, and seventh years for each house. Prefects wear badges with a "P" over their house crests. Past prefects include Tom Riddle, Lily Evans, Remus Lupin, Bill Weasley, Percy Weasley, Penelope Clearwater, and Cedric Diggory.

FIFTH YEAR PREFECTS

Gryffindor: Hermione Granger, Ron Weasley
Hufflepuff: Hannah Abbott, Ernie Macmillan
Ravenclaw: Anthony Goldstein, Padma Patil
Slytherin: Draco Malfoy, Pansy Parkinson

S.P.E.W. (**Society for the Promotion of Elfish Welfare**): Although elf enslavement is a centuries-old practice in the wizarding world, Hermione is horrified to learn how some house-elves are treated by their masters. She is further horrified to discover Hogwarts has over one hundred house-elves, who do not receive wages, benefits, or holidays, and decides to form S.P.E.W. as a means of empowering the creatures. (The group was originally going to be called "Stop the Outrageous Abuse of Our Fellow Magical Creatures and Campaign for a Change in Their Legal Status," but as this wouldn't fit on the badges, it is the heading of the manifesto instead.)

S.P.E.W.'s goals are to ensure house-elves are paid and have decent working conditions, although Hermione eventually hopes to get a house-elf into the Department for the Regulation and Control of Magical Creatures. She charges two Sickles for membership and a badge, and plans to use the funds raised to start a leaflet campaign. Much to Harry and Ron's dismay, they are conscripted as secretary and treasurer. Although Harry seems to quietly indulge her, Ron loudly disagrees with "spew"'s policies, suggesting house-elves are happy as they are and don't mind being treated like servants.

Fred and George tease Hermione about leading the house-elves into rebellion or on strike (prompting Ron to nickname the group the "House-Elf Liberation Front"), while Hagrid insists most house-elves wouldn't want freedom even if it was offered as it is in their nature to look after others. The criticism does nothing to discourage Hermione's enthusiasm. In fact, after discovering a lone house-elf who embraces S.P.E.W.'s vision, she is more motivated than ever before. In fifth year, she steps up her efforts and tries to trick the house-elves into freeing themselves.

Although most people scoff at S.P.E.W., Hermione may be on to something. As Dumbledore says, house-elves are what they have been made by wizards. He believes in treating them with kindness and courtesy instead of taking them for granted, as many wizards have done for centuries. If shown proper respect, house-elves could prove to be extremely valuable in the fight against the Dark Arts, as they have a powerful magic of their own.

 **Did you know** . . . J. K. Rowling used to work for Amnesty International as a research assistant for human rights abuses in Africa? In an interview with the CBC in July 2000, Rowling indicated Hermione's political conscience and interest in civil rights developed from this experience.

S.P.U.G. (**Society for the Protection of Ugly Goblins**): Ron jokes about Hermione next starting up this organisation for the well-being of "poor ickle goblins."

GHOSTS

"I know nothing of the secrets of death, Harry, for I chose my feeble imitation of life instead."
— Nearly Headless Nick, *Harry Potter and the Order of the Phoenix*

Approximately twenty ghosts haunt Hogwarts. They are pearly-white, translucent, and feel ice-cold to people who touch them. Only wizards can come back as ghosts, although very few choose to do this (it is not known why).

Bloody Baron: Slytherin house ghost. He is silent and intimidating, with blank staring eyes, a gaunt face, and robes stained with silvery blood. The Bloody Baron is also the only ghost Peeves will obey.

Chameleon Ghouls: Although none have been found in Hogwarts so far, these ghosts can disguise themselves as other objects.

Fat Friar: The Hufflepuff house ghost, a plump and jovial little monk.

The Grey Lady: Ravenclaw house ghost. Not much is known about her, other than she is tall.

Moaning Myrtle: Myrtle has haunted the girls' bathroom on the first floor for many years. A former Muggle-born student, she was crying in the bathroom after being teased when she heard something strange outside her cubicle. When Myrtle opened the door to investigate, she received the shock of her life.

Perpetually miserable and mopey-looking, Myrtle is squat and unattractive, with lank hair and spots. She always seems to be crying and wears thick pearly glasses on her small eyes. Melodramatic, highly sensitive, and almost paranoid, Myrtle always thinks the worst of situations and people — she frequently dives head-first into the toilet when she feels wronged, crying in the U-bend. Hypocritically, Myrtle takes great glee in other peoples' misfortunes. After Harry returns from his experience in the Chamber of Secrets, Myrtle is most disappointed he hasn't died — it seems she has developed a bit of a crush on him, and was hoping he would share her toilet!

In fourth year, Myrtle turns up in another bathroom, the Prefects', during Harry's attempt to decipher a clue for the Triwizard Tournament. Although Harry is furious she has been spying on him in the bath, he softens when she helps him. (She also expresses her disappointment that Harry doesn't visit anymore.) Myrtle sees Harry during the second task and points him in the right direction, but won't go any closer because she doesn't like the Merpeople.

Peeves: Peeves is a nasty little poltergeist who annoys the ghosts, staff, and students with his rudeness and pranks. He has a malicious face, with wicked, dark eyes, a wide mouth, a greasy voice, and an evil cackle. Peeves wears a bell-covered hat and an orange bowtie. He is only afraid of the Bloody Baron, but also knows better than to taunt Dumbledore.

Peeves thrives on chaos. He gleefully shouts out bad news, often jumping to the wrong conclusions about things. He is also fond of making up impromptu songs-and-dances about various people, including Harry ("potty wee Potter") and Lupin ("Loony, loony Lupin").

Filch has been itching to get rid of Peeves for ages. After a missed chance in fourth year, he is thrilled when another opportunity presents itself the following year. Peeves doffs his hat and salutes Fred and George, stepping up his own mischief-making after they leave Hogwarts.

PEEVES'S PRANKS

* "accidentally" hurled chairs at Harry when he was practising the Summoning Charm
* blew ink pellets at students through a peashooter
* burst out from blackboards
* chased and hit Umbridge with a sock full of chalk and a walking stick
* dropped wastepaper baskets on peoples' heads and a sack of tarantulas into the Great Hall during breakfast
* flooded the second floor after pulling the taps off in the bathrooms
* glided along after Umbridge and blew raspberries at her
* hid inside suits of armour when the armour sang Christmas carols, filling in the lyrics with rude ones of his own
* invisibly grabbed peoples' noses
* "juggled" flaming torches over the heads of students and ink wells that smashed on the floor
* loosened the carpet so people would trip and pulled rugs out from under their feet, and loosened a chandelier (with McGonagall's help!)
* pelted people with chalk
* played tennis in the Entrance Hall
* relayed gossip and tattled on students who were out of bed after curfew
* shut Mrs. Norris inside a suit of armour
* smashed cabinets and lanterns
* smeared ink on the telescope eyepieces
* snuffed out candles
* stuffed chewing gum into keyholes
* threw water balloons and walking sticks
* toppled stacks of parchment out windows or into the fire

* tried to overturn a vase on Harry
* tried to strangle Ron with tinsel
* upended tables, suits of armour, and vases
* woke Harry up in the wee hours of the morning
* wreaked havoc in the kitchen and terrified the house-elves after being barred from the fourth year start-of-term feast
* wrote rude words on blackboards

Did you know . . . the part of Peeves in the *Harry Potter and the Philosopher's Stone* film was played by British comedian Rik Mayall, but was edited out due to time constraints?

Professor Binns: The only ghost on staff, he teaches History of Magic.

Sir Nicholas de Mimsy-Porpington (Nearly Headless Nick): The Gryffindor house ghost, Nearly Headless Nick has long curly hair and wears a feathered hat, tunic, ruff, and tights. He was the victim of a botched beheading (forty-five swings with a blunt axe), and can make his entire head swing off his neck like a hinge. Sir Nicholas decided to come back as a ghost instead of "going on," because he was afraid of death.

Did you know . . . J. K. Rowling initially wrote a ballad for Nearly Headless Nick to sing, about how he came to be almost decapitated? Though she removed the song from *Harry Potter and the Chamber of Secrets*, it can still be found in its entirety on her official Web site.

Sir Patrick Delaney-Podmore (Sir Properly Decapitated-Podmore): Although not a Hogwarts ghost, Sir Patrick organises the Headless Hunt, which Nearly Headless Nick desperately wants to attend. A bit of a cut-up and very popular with his fellow ghosts, Sir Patrick makes a grand entrance at the Deathday Party. Nearly Headless Nick asks Harry to make him sound scary and formidable in front of Sir Patrick, which Harry tries but fails to do.

Wailing Widow: A guest at the Deathday Party, from Kent.

Ghostly Goings~On

Deathday Party: In honour of his five hundredth Deathday, Nearly Headless Nick throws himself a party on Hallowe'en of second year. The celebration features a thirty-piece orchestra playing musical saws that sound like nails scratching down a blackboard. Food includes putrid fish, burnt cake, maggoty haggis, mouldy cheese, fungus-covered nuts, and a tombstone-shaped cake, all of which are left to rot to increase their flavour (although the ghosts can't taste anything, anyway). Hundreds of ghosts are in attendance including nuns, knights, prisoners in chains, and assorted otherworldly Hogwarts residents.

Did you know ... In first year, Nearly Headless Nick says he hasn't eaten for "nearly four hundred years," yet in second year, he celebrates his five hundredth Deathday? Despite this discrepancy, most of the dates in the Harry Potter series can be devised from the date of death on Nearly Headless Nick's cake — 1492 — as it is the only concrete date mentioned anywhere in the books. Five hundred years after this date would mean the Deathday Party and Harry's second year at Hogwarts was in 1992, which means Harry was born in 1980 (he turned twelve before second year), which means Lily and James were killed on Hallowe'en in 1981, and so on.

formation gliding: The Hogwarts ghosts provide the entertainment at the third year Hallowe'en Feast by gliding in formation around the Great Hall. Nearly Headless Nick also re-enacts his failed beheading.

ghosts' council: Hogwarts ghosts form a group to discuss various issues related to them. A council was held when Peeves wanted to go to the fourth year start-of-term feast, but the Bloody Baron said no.

Headless Hunt: An event for decapitated ghosts and ghost horses that includes activities such as Head Polo and Horseback Head-Juggling. Nearly Headless Nick was refused admission because he is not properly beheaded. To his chagrin, members of the Headless Hunt start a game of Head Hockey at Nearly Headless Nick's Deathday Party, completely detracting from his speech.

HOUSES

"The four houses are called Gryffindor, Hufflepuff, Ravenclaw, and Slytherin. Each house has its own noble history and each has produced outstanding witches and wizards."
— Professor McGonagall, *Harry Potter and the Philosopher's Stone*

During their first year, students are put into one of four houses. For the duration of their time at Hogwarts, students eat, sleep, attend classes, and spend free time with the other members of their house, much like a family. The houses are named after the founders of the school.

Gryffindor, Godric: From the moors (broad open fields full of hills). Godric's Hollow, where the Potters lived, may bear some relation to Gryffindor, as may the Potters themselves. Gryffindor believed anyone who had magical ability should be welcomed at Hogwarts, including Muggle-borns. He is also the original owner of the Sorting Hat.

"Gryffin" is a variation of "Griffin" (or Gryphon), a creature with the body of a lion and the head and wings of an eagle (and sometimes, the tail of a serpent) — a union symbolising strength and intelligence. Griffins are a combination of the king of the beasts (earth) and the king of the birds (air), and as such, have come to represent the dual nature of Christ (human and divine). They were also considered enemies of serpents and basilisks, which were seen as Satanic demons. *D'or* is French, meaning "golden." Gryffindor's mascot is, naturally, a lion.

Gryffindors are associated with boldness, bravery, chivalry, daring, and nerve. However, they can also suffer from a lion's pride and a stubborn or temperamental nature. Their bravery and daring can make them impulsive and prone to taking rash actions without thinking things through first.

✳ **Godric Gryffindor's sword:** A silver sword with a hilt covered in large rubies. When Harry magically obtains the sword in a battle to the death, Dumbledore tells him only a "true Gryffindor" could have done this. Could Dumbledore possibly mean Harry is an ancestor of Godric Gryffindor?

Hufflepuff, Helga: From the valley. Hufflepuff seemed to have an open mind and a tolerant nature — she believed in diversity and wanted Hogwarts to include students from all backgrounds. Hufflepuff believed in treating everyone equally and fairly.

The origins of the word "Hufflepuff" are unknown, although it does sound a bit like "huff and puff," something the wolf did to blow down the houses in the *Three Little Pigs*. Hufflepuff's mascot is a badger, which is associated with perseverance (to "badger" someone means to continually persist in asking them something). In Native American totems, the badger represents industriousness, and the ability to reach a desired goal.

Hufflepuffs are associated with fairness, hard work, justice, loyalty, and patience. However, they don't generally get a lot of recognition or attention, and according to Hagrid, are commonly thought of as "a lot o' duffers" (plodding, slow types). Hufflepuffs may be the embodiment of the expression "nice guys finish last."

Ravenclaw, Rowena: From the glen (deep narrow valley, usually between mountains). Ravenclaw preferred to teach those who had the sharpest minds. Whether the students were pure-blood or Muggle-born didn't matter; all that was important to her was their intelligence. The name Rowena is the feminine form of Rowen, which could be derived from the Norse *runa* (meaning mystery or secret), or simply named after the rowen tree, which has been considered magical by different cultures all over the world for many centuries. The rowen tree is said to guard against dark magic and evil spirits, and is especially attractive to faeries.

Surprisingly, the mascot of Ravenclaw is not a raven, but an eagle (the "raven" in the name refers to the eagle's black claws). While ravens are depicted as highly intelligent birds in folklore, they are also considered symbolic of death and destruction. As king of the birds, eagles are thought of as intelligent, powerful, and highly skilled. Eagles are characterised by their extraordinarily high flight, symbolising the setting (and achievement) of lofty goals. They represent success, strength, and protection from evil.

Ravenclaws are associated with cleverness, knowledge, learning, wisdom, and wit. The downside to this is that others can perceive them as overly-analytical, haughty, and even arrogant. Their intellectual approach to problems can hinder their decision-making abilities because they must examine things from all angles.

Slytherin, Salazar: From fen (low flat wetlands). Slytherin only wanted to teach those whose ancestry was purest. His almost maniacal preference for pure-blood students caused a deep rift with the other founders, the echoes of which can still be seen between Slytherin and the other houses over a thousand years later.

"Slytherin" sounds like "slithering," a movement associated with snakes. Indeed, Slytherin was a Parselmouth and went by the nickname "serpent tongue," which is why he chose a snake to represent his house. Snakes and serpents have an almost universal historical affiliation with evil and deceit. However, the manner in which a snake occasionally shed its skin was believed to symbolise reincarnation and immortality (is it any wonder Voldemort was a Slytherin?).

Slytherins are associated with cunning, determination, a disregard for the rules, and shrewdness. According to Hagrid, every witch or wizard who "went bad" during Voldemort's time was from Slytherin. Despite this reputation, Slytherins do possess several traits that can be seen as positive, including ambition, resourcefulness, and a sense of duty and pride.

Sorting Hat: This old, dirty, patched and worn hat once belonged to Gryffindor and is now responsible for putting students into their houses. It has a tear near the brim that opens up like a mouth and sings during the Sorting Ceremony. Each year, the hat sings a different song explaining the history of Hogwarts and the general characteristics associated with the houses. However, in fifth year the Sorting Hat's song warns against repeating past mistakes, and urges students to overcome house differences and unite to defeat external enemies. According to Nearly Headless Nick, the Hat has given out similar warnings before, when it felt Hogwarts was in danger.

Sorting Ceremony: During the start-of-term feast on the first of September, the Sorting Hat is tried on by all first years in alphabetical order. Based on what the Hat finds in a student's head, it shouts out which house is the best match. Sometimes students' heads reveal characteristics found in more than one house. In these cases, the Sorting Hat likely determines which characteristics are the most dominant. For example, this could help explain how Harry and Hermione were sorted into Gryffindor instead of Slytherin and Ravenclaw, respectively.

Sometimes the Hat only takes a moment to decide where a student belongs (as was the case with Malfoy), but in some cases it takes longer (as it did with Neville, Seamus, and Harry). The Hat has also been known to consult with students on occasion before placing them in their houses.

Did you know . . . according to J. K. Rowling's official Web site, some of the ways she originally considered for students to be sorted included a panel of ghosts or prefects making the decision, passing through a magical gateway, and drawing names out of a hat? The Sorting Hat evolved from this last option.

House points: Students earn points for their house through their accomplishments and lose them through misbehaviour. Teachers and prefects can award or deduct points, although members of the Inquisitorial Squad were given this privilege by Umbridge in fifth year.

hour-glasses: Four giant hour-glasses in the Entrance Hall are filled with coloured stones that record the points for each house. Ravenclaw's hour-glass contains sapphires, Gryffindor's has rubies, and Slytherin's has emeralds (Hufflepuff's stones are unknown). Whenever points are deducted from a house, stones automatically fly upwards from the bottom to the top bulb.

HOUSE POINT ADDITIONS AND DEDUCTIONS

First year

✳ Snape deducts a point from Harry for being cheeky, and another for failing to help Neville.

✳ McGonagall deducts five points from Hermione for attempting to take on the troll, then awards five points each to Harry and Ron for rescuing her.

✳ Snape deducts five points from Harry for taking a library book outside the castle.

✳ Snape deducts five points from Ron for fighting with Malfoy.

✳ McGonagall deducts twenty points from Malfoy for skulking around late at night and lying about Harry having a dragon (which was actually true). She deducts fifty points each from Harry and Hermione for concocting the story about the dragon to lure Malfoy into trouble, and for being in the out-of-bounds Astronomy Tower at one o'clock in the morning. She also deducts fifty points from Neville for being out of bed.

✳ At the end-of-term feast, Dumbledore awards fifty points to Ron for his chess game victory, fifty points to Hermione for her logic, sixty points to Harry for his courage, and ten points to Neville for standing up to his friends.

Second year

✳ Sprout awards ten points to Hermione for naming the properties of a Mandrake and another ten for explaining why it is dangerous.

✳ Lockhart awards ten points to Hermione for getting full marks on her "quiz."

* Percy deducts five points from Ron for playing "detective" (but it is more likely he deducted the points because Ron made a nasty comment about him).
* Harry is awarded fifty points for his spectacular performance during the Quidditch match where he was chased by a rogue Bludger.
* Harry believes Percy is going to deduct five points after he witnesses Harry casting the Disarming Charm on Malfoy in a corridor.
* Dumbledore awards two hundred points each to Harry and Ron (as well as a Special Award for Services to the School) for their experience in the Chamber of Secrets.

Third year

* Snape deducts five points from Hermione for helping Neville correct his Shrinking Solution.
* Lupin awards five points to every student who took on the Boggart in his class (ten points to Neville for doing it twice), and five points to Harry and Hermione for correctly answering questions.
* Snape deducts ten points from Harry for being ten minutes late for Defence Against the Dark Arts, and another five for asking about Lupin. In the same class, he deducts five points from Hermione for being an "insufferable know-it-all."
* Snape deducts fifty points from Ron for throwing a crocodile heart in Malfoy's face.
* McGonagall deducts fifty points from Slytherin when a group of students, led by Malfoy, pulls a prank during a Quidditch match designed to terrify Harry.

Fourth year

* Snape deducts fifty points from Gryffindor when Harry and Ron shout at him after he insults Hermione.

✳ Snape deducts ten points respectively from Hufflepuff and Ravenclaw when he catches Stebbins and Fawcett in a rose bush during the Yule Ball.

✳ Snape deducts ten points from Hermione for talking in class and a further ten points after he spots her copy of *Witch Weekly*.

Fifth year

✳ Umbridge deducts ten points from Harry for mentioning Voldemort in class.

✳ McGonagall awards ten points to Hermione for successfully Vanishing a snail.

✳ Grubbly-Plank awards fifteen points to Hermione for answering questions about Bowtruckles.

✳ Umbridge deducts five points from Hermione when she "disrupts" class with a "pointless" question.

✳ McGonagall deducts five points from Angelina after she causes a disturbance by yelling at Harry for missing Quidditch practice.

✳ McGonagall deducts five points from Harry for failing to learn his lesson about Umbridge.

✳ Snape deducts ten points from Gryffindor after wrongly assuming Neville, Harry, and Ron have been fighting with Malfoy.

✳ Hagrid awards ten points to Hermione for answering a question about Thestrals.

✳ Umbridge deducts fifty points from Harry after learning of his interview in *The Quibbler*.

✳ Professor Sprout awards twenty points to Harry for handing her a watering can.

✳ Umbridge awards fifty points to Malfoy for catching Harry as he fled from the Room of Requirement.

✳ Malfoy deducts five points from Ernie Macmillan for contradicting him. He deducts five points from Harry because he doesn't like him, five from Ron because his shirt is untucked, five from Hermione when she speaks badly of Umbridge, and another ten because Hermione is a "Mudblood."

* When Montague tries to deduct points from Fred and George, they shove him into a Vanishing Cabinet.

* Snape deducts ten points from Harry after catching him with his wand drawn on Malfoy.

* McGonagall awards fifty points each to Harry, Hermione, Neville, Ron, Ginny, and Luna for alerting the world to Voldemort's return.

House Cup: Awarded at the end of the year to the house with the most points. Slytherin had won the cup for six consecutive years prior to Harry's arrival at Hogwarts.

Detentions

First year

* McGonagall gives Malfoy, Harry, Hermione, and Neville detention after catching them out of bed in the middle of the night. Their punishment is to accompany Hagrid into the Forbidden Forest and search for an injured unicorn.

Second year

* McGonagall gives Harry and Ron detention for flying the Ford Anglia. Ron must polish the silver in the trophy room by hand under Filch's supervision, while Harry must address envelopes for Lockhart's fan mail.

Third year

* Snape gives Ron detention for criticising him when he substitutes for Lupin in Defence Against the Dark Arts. Ron has to scrub the bedpans in the hospital wing by hand.

* McGonagall gives Malfoy, Crabbe, Goyle, and Marcus Flint detention for their prank during the Quidditch match.
* McGonagall gives Neville detention for losing the list of passwords to Gryffindor Tower, which resulted in a serious breach of security. Neville was also forbidden to go to Hogsmeade for the remainder of the year.

Fourth year

* Not a detention, but memorable enough to be worth noting: Moody punishes Malfoy for attacking Harry when his back is turned by transfiguring Malfoy into a ferret and bouncing him ten feet off the floor repeatedly.
* Snape gives Neville a detention disembowelling a barrel full of toads after he melts his sixth cauldron.
* Snape gives Harry and Ron detention pickling rats' brains for two hours after Harry and Ron shout at him for insulting Hermione.

Fifth year

* Umbridge gives Harry detention for the remainder of the week (which McGonagall will not dismiss) after he stands up to her in class regarding Voldemort. Harry has to write lines — "I must not tell lies" — with Umbridge's quill, which repeatedly cuts the words into the back of his hand as they appear on his parchment in blood.
* Harry gets another week of similar detentions from Umbridge for making another comment about Voldemort, and one more for insulting Malfoy.
* McGonagall gives Harry and George a week's detention after they fight with Malfoy following their Quidditch match, but Umbridge overrides this and imposes a more severe punishment, which extends to Fred as well.
* Crabbe is given detention writing lines after he attacks Harry with a Bludger during their Quidditch match. It is unknown if he had to write regular lines, or the Umbridge variety.
* Umbridge gives Lee Jordan a detention similar to Harry's after he makes a joke about Educational Decree Number Twenty-six.
* Umbridge gives Harry a week's detention after learning of his interview in *The Quibbler*.

✱ Umbridge puts four classes in detention after failing to discover why students are repeatedly fainting, bleeding, and vomiting.

Gryffindor

"Said Gryffindor, 'We'll teach all those with brave deeds to their name . . .'"
— The Sorting Hat's song, *Harry Potter and the Order of the Phoenix*

> **Colours:** gold and scarlet
> **Mascot:** lion
> **Banner:** red with a gold lion
> **Head:** Professor McGonagall
> **Ghost:** Nearly Headless Nick
> **Location:** Gryffindor Tower is located on the seventh floor

common room: A cosy, round room full of squashy armchairs and lop-sided tables. It has a fireplace with a hearthrug and a grandfather clock near the door. Two other doors lead to stone spiral staircases to the girls' and boys' dormitories. A noticeboard lists the Quidditch practice timetable, school rules and announcements, advertisements for various clubs and outings, lost and found items, things for sale, and Chocolate Frog Card trades (and in fifth year, it includes a notice calling for volunteers to test Fred and George's Skiving Snackboxes!).

The Fat Lady: A Gryffindor institution since Mr. and Mrs. Weasley were students, the Fat Lady wears a pink silk dress and guards the entrance to Gryffindor Tower from her painting. After the password is spoken, her painting swings open to reveal the round entrance to the common room.

The Fat Lady has been known to be irresponsible and moody. She sometimes goes off visiting other paintings and inadvertently locks people out. She can also get rather shirty with students who wake her up to let them in or change their mind about entering. When the Fat Lady is attacked in third year, she flees in fear and a temporary replacement is found.

Sir Cadogan: Full of bravado but lacking in logic, this short and squat knight-in-armour usually resides in a large painting with his fat little pony. He is over-enthusiastic and hapless, and leaps from painting to painting on one of his much-loved "quests" to show the trio the way to their first Divination lesson.

Sir Cadogan takes over the Fat Lady's post for a period in third year after she is attacked. He frustrates the Gryffindors by challenging them to duels and creating difficult, frequently changing passwords. He keeps the right people out for the wrong reasons and lets the wrong people in for the right reasons, which eventually gets him sacked.

passwords: balderdash, banana fritters, Caput Draconis, fairy lights, flibbertigibbet, Fortuna Major, Mimbulus mimbletonia, oddsbodikins, pig snout, scurvy cur, wattlebird.

 Did you know . . . the wattlebird is a real bird, found in Australia, with fleshy, wrinkled skin (wattles) that droops down over its ears?

dormitories: Harry's dormitory — which he shares with Dean, Neville, Ron, and Seamus — is a round room at the top of Gryffindor Tower with high, narrow windows. It contains a long mirror, five four-poster beds with crimson velvet curtains, and a trunk at the foot of each bed.

Interestingly, girls can enter the boys' dormitory (as Hermione and Ginny have done), but the reverse does not hold true. According to *Hogwarts: A History*, the founders thought boys were less trustworthy than girls, resulting in a rule that barred boys from the girls' dormitories. When Ron tries to climb the stairs to Hermione's dormitory, a loud alarm sounds and the staircase turns into a slide, denying him access.

known alumni: Sirius Black, Albus Dumbledore, Lily Evans, Rubeus Hagrid, Remus Lupin, Peter Pettigrew (assumed), James Potter, Molly Prewett, Arthur Weasley, Bill Weasley, Charlie Weasley

the Marauders: Name associated with James Potter (Prongs), Sirius Black (Padfoot), Remus Lupin (Moony), and Peter Pettigrew (Wormtail) during their time at Hogwarts.

Extremely intelligent, James and Sirius were the leaders of the group and carried themselves in a haughty, arrogant way. They were show-offs who had a reputation as a pair of troublemakers and were constantly in detention. Lupin seemed to be a little more serious, and was even made prefect in the hopes he might "exercise some control" over his friends; however, he seemed to look the other way whenever they misbehaved. Smaller and less confident, Pettigrew showered James and Sirius with adoration and took great delight in watching them torment and humiliate people, especially Snape.

Lupin was afraid his friends would abandon him once they discovered his darkest secret, but instead they found a way to share the experience with him. As Animagi, their presences helped to soften the impact of his own transformation. Each month, the four roamed the Hogwarts grounds and beyond, and the knowledge they gathered of these areas led to the creation of the Marauder's Map. (A marauder is someone who roams around, like a vagabond, in search of things to plunder.)

As a student, Snape never liked the group, and was always trying to find out what they were up to. He discovered Lupin's secret one night in a prank set up by Sirius that would have cost Snape his life, if James hadn't saved him at the last minute. The incident fuelled Snape's deep-seated (and mutual) hatred for them that lasted his entire life (and was passed down a generation to Harry, it seems).

Sorted Gryffindors

Unknown year: Vicky Frobisher, Geoffrey Hooper, Andrew Kirke, Jack Sloper, Patricia Stimpson, Kenneth Towler
Four years ahead: Percy Weasley, Oliver Wood
Two years ahead: Angelina Johnson, Lee Jordan, Alicia Spinnet, Fred Weasley, George Weasley
One year ahead: Katie Bell

Note to Muggles: *Although Katie is always grouped in with Angelina and Alicia because all three are Chasers, Ginny says in fifth year that she plans on trying out for Chaser "as Angelina and Alicia are both leaving next year." This implies Katie will still be on the team the following year (otherwise Ginny would have said all three were leaving); therefore, we can assume Katie must be a year behind her friends.*

Same year as Harry: Lavender Brown, Seamus Finnigan, Hermione Granger, Neville Longbottom, Parvati Patil, Harry Potter, Dean Thomas, Ron Weasley
One year behind: Colin Creevey, Ginny Weasley
Three years behind: Dennis Creevey, Natalie McDonald
Four years behind: Euan Abercrombie

Note to Muggles: *J.K. Rowling admitted in an online chat for World Book Day in March 2004 that there were two other Gryffindor girls in Harry's year (to even out the number of boys and girls), but didn't remember their details! Guess they can't be very important to the series in that case . . .*

Hufflepuff

"Said Hufflepuff, 'I'll teach the lot, and treat them just the same.'"
— The Sorting Hat's song, *Harry Potter and the Order of the Phoenix*

> **Colours:** black and yellow
> **Mascot:** badger
> **Banner:** yellow with a black badger
> **Head:** Professor Sprout
> **Ghost:** Fat Friar
> **Location:** A door to the right of the marble staircase in the Entrance Hall leads downstairs to a broad stone corridor. Hufflepuff residence is located somewhere off this corridor.

known alumni: Fat Friar

Sorted Hufflepuffs

Unknown year: Zacharias Smith, Stebbins, Summerby, Summers
Two years ahead: Cedric Diggory
Same year as Harry: Hannah Abbott, Susan Bones, Justin Finch-Fletchley, Ernie Macmillan
Three years behind: Eleanor Branstone, Owen Cauldwell, Laura Madley, Kevin Whitby
Four years behind: Rose Zeller

 Did you know . . . J. K. Rowling said that when she took an online Sorting Hat quiz, it sorted her into Hufflepuff?

Ravenclaw

"Said Ravenclaw, 'We'll teach those whose intelligence is surest.'"
— The Sorting Hat's song, *Harry Potter and the Order of the Phoenix*

> **Colours:** bronze and blue
> **Mascot:** eagle
> **Banner:** blue with a bronze eagle
> **Head:** Professor Flitwick
> **Ghost:** Grey Lady
> **Location:** In a tower on the west side of the castle. Accessed through a statue of a knight.

 **Note to Muggles:** *Although it is not stated in the Harry Potter series that Professor Flitwick is the head of Ravenclaw, J. K. Rowling confirmed this during an online chat with Barnes & Noble in October 2000.*

Similarly, there is nothing in the series stating the Grey Lady is the Ravenclaw ghost, but J. K. Rowling verified this in a separate interview. Readers were introduced to the Grey Lady when Harry and Ron passed the ghost of a "tall witch" in the corridor on their way to the Mirror of Erised.

(She also shows up in the Harry Potter and the Philosopher's Stone *film — in the Sorting Hat scene, Nearly Headless Nick, the Bloody Baron, the Fat Friar, and an unidentified tall witch are the first four ghosts shown. As the other three ghosts belong to Gryffindor, Slytherin, and Hufflepuff respectively, it seems logical the tall witch must belong to Ravenclaw.) J. K. Rowling has said the Grey Lady will return in future books.*

known alumni: Lasuris Bonao

Sorted Ravenclaws

Unknown year: Bradley, Chambers, Michael Corner, Roger Davies, Fawcett
Four years ahead: Penelope Clearwater
One year ahead: Eddie Carmichael, Cho Chang, Marietta Edgecombe
Same year as Harry: Terry Boot, Mandy Brocklehurst, Anthony Goldstein, Padma Patil, Lisa Turpin
One year behind: Luna Lovegood
Three years behind: Stewart Ackerley, Orla Quirke

Slytherin

"Said Slytherin, 'We'll teach just those whose ancestry is purest.'"
   — The Sorting Hat's song, *Harry Potter and the Order of the Phoenix*

> **Colours:** silver and green
> **Mascot:** serpent
> **Banner:** green with a silver serpent
> **Head:** Professor Snape
> **Ghost:** Bloody Baron
> **Location:** A door to the right of the marble staircase in the Entrance Hall leads downstairs to a broad stone corridor. Slytherin residence is located on the same level as the dungeons, through a series of labyrinthine corridors.

common room: A hidden door appears in a stone wall after the password is spoken. It slides opens to reveal a long room with a low ceiling and rough stone walls with round green lamps hanging on chains. There is a fireplace with a carved mantelpiece and an assortment of carved chairs.

password: pure-blood

known alumni: Avery, Bellatrix Black, Narcissa Black, Rabastan Lestrange, Rodolphus Lestrange, Lucius Malfoy, Phineas Nigellus, Tom Riddle, Rosier, Severus Snape, Wilkes

Note to Muggles: *While it is a natural assumption most of the Death Eaters are Slytherin alumni, only those listed above have been officially confirmed as such in the series.*

Sorted Slytherins

Unknown year: Miles Bletchley, Terence Higgs, Montague, Adrian Pucey, Warrington
Five years ahead: Marcus Flint

Did you know . . . although it is mentioned Marcus Flint is in sixth year during Harry's first year, he is still mentioned as a seventh year student in Harry's third year? (When asked about this, J. K. Rowling explained it by saying Flint failed a year!) Because of this, fans termed any errors they found in the series "Flints."

Three years ahead: Bole, Derrick
Same year as Harry: Millicent Bulstrode, Vincent Crabbe, Gregory Goyle, Draco Malfoy, Theodore Nott, Pansy Parkinson, Blaise Zabini
Three years behind: Malcolm Baddock, Graham Pritchard

ACADEMICS

"And then, once you had managed to find them, there were the lessons them-selves. There was a lot more to magic, as Harry quickly found out, than waving your wand and saying a few funny words."
— *Harry Potter and the Philosopher's Stone*

A Hogwarts education is seven years long, and corresponds to the middle and high school years in the Muggle world. The school year begins on September the first and finishes at the end of June. It is divided into three terms, with a three-week Christmas break and a shorter holiday over Easter.

Classes are about forty-five minutes in length (we know this because double Potions is an hour and a half long), and the school day ends around five o'clock (one of Fred and George's pranks takes place "just after lessons end" when everyone is still in the corridors, and they tell Ron to show up "round about five o'clock" to see it).

Final exams are held in June each year, and there is a free week after exams are over until the results come out (except for OWL and NEWT students, whose results are owled to them during the summer).

Notes are distributed to all students before summer holidays, reminding them they are not allowed to use magic over summer holidays if they are under-age (seventeen is the legal age in the wizarding world). Magic is also not allowed in corridors between classes.

First year (age eleven)

Curriculum: Astronomy, Charms, Defence Against the Dark Arts, Herbology, History of Magic, Potions, Transfiguration, flying lessons

All students must take all classes.

First year requirements

- ✳ one wand
- ✳ one standard size-2 pewter cauldron
- ✳ one set glass or crystal phials
- ✳ one telescope
- ✳ one set brass scales
- ✳ owl, cat, or toad (optional)
- ✳ first years are not permitted to have their own broomsticks

Second year (age twelve)

Curriculum: same as first year (minus flying lessons)

Over Easter holidays, students must choose their new classes for third year. Percy offers advice to Harry about what to take ("play to your strengths," which, to Harry, means Quidditch), Neville receives a battery of letters from his family, each with different suggestions, Dean Thomas closes his eyes and stabs his wand randomly at the list, and Hermione listens to no one and signs up for everything.

Exams: As a special treat, McGonagall cancels all exams following the events in the Chamber of Secrets.

Third year (age thirteen)

Curriculum: Ancient Runes, Arithmancy, Astronomy, Care of Magical Creatures, Charms, Defence Against the Dark Arts, Divination, Herbology, History of Magic, Muggle Studies, Potions, Transfiguration

Harry, Ron, and Hermione take Astronomy, Care of Magical Creatures, Charms, Defence Against the Dark Arts, Herbology, History of Magic,

Potions, and Transfiguration together. Harry and Ron (and Hermione, to begin with) also take Divination, while Hermione chooses Ancient Runes, Arithmancy, and Muggle Studies for her additional classes.

Harry and Ron are perplexed by Hermione's frequent disappearances and reappearances during the day and her seemingly impossible schedule, which indicates multiple classes at the same time. Her heavy courseload begins to take its toll as the year goes on. The boys suggest she is overloaded, but Hermione insists she can manage, although she is the first to the library in the morning and the last to leave the common room at night. At the end of the year, Hermione gives up her secret study aide in favour of a more manageable courseload the next time around.

Exam Schedule

(Hermione refuses to explain how she plans to sit two exams simultaneously)

* **Monday:** Transfiguration (morning), Arithmancy (morning — Hermione only), Charms (afternoon), Ancient Runes (afternoon — Hermione only)
* **Tuesday:** Care of Magical Creatures (morning), Potions (afternoon), Astronomy (midnight)
* **Wednesday:** History of Magic (morning), Herbology (afternoon)
* **Thursday:** Defence Against the Dark Arts (morning), Divination (afternoon — Harry and Ron), Muggle Studies (afternoon — Hermione)

Fourth year (age fourteen)

Curriculum: same as third year

Harry, Ron, and Hermione take Astronomy, Care of Magical Creatures, Charms, Defence Against the Dark Arts, Herbology, History of Magic, Potions, and Transfiguration together. Harry and Ron continue with Divination, while Hermione continues with Ancient Runes and Arithmancy.

The amount of homework is stepped up in preparation for OWLs the following year.

Exams: Exams finish on the twenty-fourth of June, the same day as the third task of the Triwizard Tournament. Champions are exempt from sitting exams.

Fifth year (age fifteen)

Curriculum: Same as fourth year

Considered a very difficult year (Fred and George recall their classmates having numerous tears and tantrums), due to OWLs. Hermione constantly reminds Harry and Ron how hard they must work, and threatens to stop allowing them to copy their homework from her any more. Although she takes more subjects than they do, she does exceedingly well and has no trouble keeping up, while they fall behind in their homework due to Quidditch practices, detentions, or prefect duties.

Careers Advice: Students are given careers advice from their head of house in order to help determine their course selection for NEWT studies. Harry wants to be an Auror, a profession Ron seems interested in as well. Hermione keeps her options open — she wants to do something "worthwhile" and wonders about the possibility of taking S.P.E.W. further.

CAREER OPTIONS MENTIONED

Auror: Requires five "E"-level NEWTs, including Charms, Defence Against the Dark Arts, Potions, and Transfiguration, plus aptitude and character tests at the Ministry. Auror training takes three years, and is extremely difficult — no new Aurors have been taken on in the past three years. McGonagall vows to do everything she can to help Harry become an Auror after Umbridge dismisses the idea.

Cultivated Fungus Trade
Curse Breaking (wizard banking): Requires training in Arithmancy.
Healing: Requires "E"-level NEWTs in Charms, Defence Against the Dark Arts, Herbology, Potions, and Transfiguration.
Ministry of Magic: Various departments and positions.
Muggle Relations: Requires an OWL in Muggle Studies, as well as "enthusiasm, patience, and a good sense of fun."
Training Security Trolls

OWLS: Ordinary Wizarding Levels, a play on "O Levels" (Ordinary Levels), similar exams that were once a standard in the British education system. OWLS are very important and can affect the jobs wizards can apply for. The exams take place in the Great Hall over two weeks, with theoretical exams in the mornings and practical exams in the afternoon (except for Astronomy, which obviously must be taken at night). Results are sent by owl post in July.

Timetable:

* **Monday:** Charms
* **Tuesday:** Transfiguration
* **Wednesday:** Herbology
* **Thursday:** Defence Against the Dark Arts
* **Friday:** Ancient Runes (Hermione)
* **Monday:** Potions
* **Tuesday:** Care of Magical Creatures
* **Wednesday:** Astronomy theoretical (morning), Divination (afternoon — Harry and Ron), Arithmancy (afternoon — Hermione), Astronomy practical (eleven o'clock at night)
* **Thursday:** History of Magic

OWL Grade Levels:

* ✶ O: Outstanding
* ✶ E: Exceeds Expectations
* ✶ A: Acceptable (last passing grade to go on to NEWT level in a subject)
* ✶ P: Poor
* ✶ D: Dreadful
* ✶ T: Troll (Fred and George may have made this one up!)

Did you know . . . in an online chat for World Book Day in March 2004, J. K. Rowling confirmed the maximum number of OWLs a student can earn is twelve? Presumably, this would be one each for Ancient Runes, Arithmancy, Astronomy, Care of Magical Creatures, Charms, Defence Against the Dark Arts, Divination, Herbology, History of Magic, Muggle Studies, Potions, and Transfiguration. (So, how did Barty Crouch Jr., Bill, and Percy find time to take all twelve classes?)

Wizarding Examinations Authority: Body of witches and wizards that oversee OWLS.

OWL Examiners

* ✶ **Griselda Marchbanks:** Head of the Wizarding Examinations Authority for quite some time — she examined Dumbledore during his NEWTs! She is small, stooped, and slightly deaf, with a heavily lined face. Malfoy claims his family is friendly with her, but she is actually a friend of Neville's Gran (and a bit like her in temperament, according to Neville!).
* ✶ **plump little witch**
* ✶ **Professor Tofty:** Oldest of all the examiners, he is bald, wears a pince-nez, and has knarled, veiny hands. His voice quivers when he speaks. Professor Tofty knows who Harry is and seems to like him. He is good friends with Tiberius Ogden of the Wizengamot.
* ✶ **wizard with a wart on his nose**

Sixth year (age sixteen)

Many of the subjects Harry needs to continue with in order to become an Auror require very high OWL grades. McGonagall will not accept Harry in Transfiguration unless he receives an "E," and Snape will not let Harry continue with Potions unless he receives an "O."

Seventh year (age seventeen)

NEWTS: Nastily Exhausting Wizarding Tests, a play on "A Levels" (Advanced Levels), similar exams that were once standard in the British education system. Percy receives outstanding marks in his NEWTS.

Ancient Runes

English runes were ancient Teutonic and Norse alphabets and symbols that were assigned magical and mystical properties. Runic characters represented various deities, events, letters, and qualities, and their magic was sought for divination, healing, psychic power, love, fertility, protection from evil, and victory in battle. The word "rune" comes from either the Indo-European *ru* or the Norse *runa*, both meaning mystery or secret.

Teacher: Unknown
Location: Unknown
Time: Unknown
Textbooks: *Ancient Runes Made Easy* (third year), *Magical Hieroglyphs and Logograms* (fifth year), *Spellman's Syllabary* (fifth year), *Rune Dictionary*
Material Covered/Homework: Rune translations
OWL: Hermione is angry with herself for mis-translating the rune *ehwaz* (partnership) as *eihwaz* (defence)

Did you know . . . in the film *Harry Potter and the Prisoner of Azkaban*, Sirius Black's "Have You Seen This Wizard" poster contains two runes? They are *perth* (looks like a sideways top hat) and *algiz* (looks like a "Y" with an extra line up the middle). Perth means secret or hidden things, as well as new beginnings and rebirth after death. Algiz means protection, or a mentor or advisor.

Arithmancy

A form of numerology based on Ancient Greek and Chaldean methods, Arithmancy involves predicting the future using numbers, especially those related to the letters in a person's name. The word Arithmancy comes from the Greek *arithmos* (number) and *manteia* (divination).

Hermione somehow finds the time to take Arithmancy starting in third year. It is her favourite class, even though she considers it the most difficult of all the subjects she is taking.

Teacher: Professor Vector
Location: Unknown
Time: nine o'clock in the morning (third year); Monday afternoons (fourth and fifth years)
Textbook: *Numerology and Grammatica*
Material Covered/Homework: Very complicated-looking number charts
OWL: No information given, but Hermione thinks she did "all right."

Did you know . . . in ancient Greece, the number and value of the letters in the names of two combatants was studied to predict whom the victor would be? The victor was said to be the combatant with the greater value. As both Harry James Potter and Tom Marvolo Riddle calculate down to the number one, there is no predicting who would emerge victorious in a battle between them. The number one in numerology indicates an individual who makes a great leader, provided he does not let his natural tendency to dominate lead him down the path of tyranny.

Astronomy

One of the oldest sciences, Astronomy is the study of the celestial bodies in outer space, including stars, constellations, and planets. The study of astronomy includes everything from the creation of the universe to the passage of time and seasons to gravity. Little is known of Hogwarts' Astronomy classes; however, they seem to focus more on a formal study of planets and stars.

Teacher: Professor Sinistra
Location: Astronomy Tower
Time: Wednesdays at midnight (first year); Wednesdays, Gryffindor/Hufflepuff class (fifth year)
Textbook: Unknown
Material Covered/Homework: learn names of moons of Jupiter (first year); fill out star charts (third year); essay on Jupiter's moons, more star charts (fifth year)
OWL: THEORETICAL — includes Jupiter's moons; PRACTICAL — fill in blank star charts using telescopes. Harry mislabels Venus and Mars.

Did you know . . . several of the characters in the Harry Potter series are named after constellations and stars, including Alphard, Andromeda, Bellatrix, Draco, Regulus, and Sirius?

Care of Magical Creatures

The study of magical beasts, or Magizoology, covers everything from ferocious crossbreeds to dull, slimy worms. Naturally, Hagrid leans towards the former rather than the latter, which causes him a great deal of trouble on more than one occasion.

Teachers: Hagrid; Professor Grubbly-Plank (temporary during fourth and fifth year)

Locations: Depending on the creature being studied, class is taught in the area and paddocks near Hagrid's Hut or the Forbidden Forest

Time: After lunch (third year); Monday mornings (fourth year); Tuesday afternoons and Wednesdays (fifth year). Gryffindors always have class with Slytherins

Textbooks: *The Monster Book of Monsters* (third year); *Fantastic Beasts and Where To Find Them*

Material Covered/Homework: How to approach and ride Hippogriffs, care and feeding of Flobberworms, observing salamanders (third year); raising Blast-Ended Skrewts, observing unicorns and their foals, watching Nifflers seek buried treasure (fourth year); drawing Bowtruckles, trying to observe Thestrals, observing Crups (fifth year)

Third year exam: Ensure a tub of Flobberworms are still alive after looking after them for an hour

OWL: PRACTICAL — covers Bowtruckles, Fire Crabs, Knarls, and unicorns

Charms

Students learn a variety of charms, curses, hexes, jinxes, and spells. Some are defensive, some are practical, while others seem rather frivolous. Certain charms are also taught in advanced Defence Against the Dark Arts and Transfiguration classes.

Teacher: Professor Flitwick

Location: Charms classroom, first floor

Time: Wednesdays (fourth year); double class Tuesday mornings (fifth year)

Textbooks: *The Standard Book of Spells, Grades 1 through 5; Magical Theory* (first year); *Achievements in Charming* (fifth year)

Material Covered/Homework: Levitation spells (first year); Cheering Charms (third year); Summoning Charms, Banishing Charms (fourth year); revision of Summoning Charms and Silencing Charms, and teacups are charmed to sprout legs and run across desks (fifth year)

First year exam: Make a pineapple tap dance across a desk. (Brainy Hermione receives one hundred and twelve per cent!)

Third year exam: Harry is a bit too enthusiastic when casting a Cheering Charm on Ron, who laughs uncontrollably for an hour

OWL: THEORETICAL — Two hours long, includes Cheering Charms and Wingardium Leviosa; PRACTICAL — About ten minutes long, includes Colour Charms, Levitation Charms, and making an egg cup do cartwheels. Harry accidentally enlarges his rat to badger size when he is meant to be turning it orange, Malfoy's Levitation Charm goes awry, and Ron mistakenly changes a plate into a mushroom.

Did you know . . . J. K. Rowling said if she were to be a teacher at Hogwarts, she would probably teach Charms?

List of Spells

Note to Muggles: *Wherever possible, incantations have been given in parentheses beside the spell's name. If the spell's name is not known, it is listed by incantation instead.*

- ✳ **Age Line:** Thin golden line drawn in a ten-foot circle on the floor that detects, repels, and alters anyone under a certain age who crosses it.

* **"Alohomora":** Unlocks doors.
* **Animagi transfiguration spell:** Transforms an Animagus into its human form. Casting the spell emits blue-white light from a wand.
* **Anti-Cheating spell:** Used on quills during exams.
* **Anti-Disapparation Jinx:** Prevents a wizard from Disapparating, forcing him to stay where he is.
* **"Aparecium":** Reveals invisible ink.
* **Apparation/Disapparation:** The ability to disappear from one location and re-appear in another instantly. It is not easy to Apparate and there can be consequences if it is not done properly, such as splinching (literally being in two places at the same time!) As with driving in the Muggle world, Apparation carries certain restrictions. Underage wizards are not allowed to Apparate, and those who do so must pass a test and carry a licence.
* **arrow spell:** Shoots silver jets of light that look like arrows from the tip of a wand.
* **"Avis":** Conjures a flock of birds from the tip of a wand.
* **Babbling Curse:** Presumably causes someone to chatter foolishly without stopping. Lockhart allegedly cured a Transylvanian suffering from this.
* **Banishing Charm:** Repels objects.
* **Bat Bogey Hex:** One of Ginny's specialities, it covers the victim's face in large, winged bogeys!
* **Body-Bind curse ("Petrificus Totalus"):** Similar to Petrification, it makes the victim's entire body go rigid; however, unlike Petrification, the victim is still conscious.
* **bubble spell:** Conjures golden bubbles.
* **Bubble-Head Charm:** Conjures a large bubble around the caster's head.
* **Charm to Cure Reluctant Reversers:** Mentioned in the *Handbook of Do-it-Yourself Broomcare*.
* **Cheering Charm:** Creates a feeling of great contentment.
* **"Colloportus":** Seals doors with a squelching noise.
* **Colour Change Charm:** Turns objects different colours.
* **Confundus Charm:** Causes the victim to become befuddled and confused.

* **Conjunctivitus Curse:** Impairs a victim's eyesight.
* **Conjuring Spells:** Temporarily creates an object out of thin air or from the tip of a wand.
* **Cruciatus Curse ("Crucio"):** See page 180.
* **Curse of the Bogeys:** Possibly related to the Bat Bogey Hex.
* **Dark Mark ("Morsmordre"):** Conjures an enormous serpent-tongued skull composed of glittering emerald stars that floats high into the sky and burns in a haze of green smoke. Known as the Dark Mark, the skull is Voldemort's calling card and is conjured whenever he or his Death Eaters have killed.
* **"Deletrius":** Deletes the smoky remnants of spells created by Prior Incantato.
* **"Densaugeo":** Enlarges teeth.
* **"Diffindo":** Tears object in half.
* **Disarming Charm ("Expelliarmus"):** Blasts a wand (or weapon) out of an opponent's hand. The force is often strong enough that the opponent is knocked off his feet. Casting the spell emits a flash of scarlet light.
* **Disillusionment Charm:** Disguises a person or object by turning it into the colour and texture of its surroundings, like a chameleon. When a Disillusionment Charm has been placed on a person it feels like an egg has been cracked over their head, as a cold trickling sensation flows down the body. Conversely, a warm trickling sensation is felt when the charm is removed.
* **"Dissendium":** Reveals the secret passageway in the hump of the humpbacked witch's statue.
* **Drought Charm:** Dries up small bodies of water.
* **"Enervate":** Revives someone who has been Stunned.
* **Engorgement Charm ("Engorgio"):** Expands an object in size.
* **Enlargement Charm:** Similar to an Engorgement Charm, it also makes objects bigger.
* **Entrail-expelling Curse:** Turns a person's internal organs out (yuk!).
* **Entrancing Enchantments:** Romantically bewitches a person, making him or her attracted to the caster. On Valentine's Day, Lockhart suggests Flitwick ("the sly old dog!") knows more about

these than any other wizard he's met — much to the tiny professor's complete embarrassment.

* **"Ferula":** Conjures a wooden splint and bandages in midair.
* **Fidelius Charm:** Very complicated charm that involves magically hiding information inside a person, known as a Secret-Keeper. As long as the Secret-Keeper does not reveal the secret, the information is completely protected and impossible for anyone else to discover, no matter how hard they search. The Fidelius Charm is particularly useful for concealing the location of places and people.
* **"Finite Incantatem":** Immediately ends the effects of a spell.
* **fire spell:** Conjures flames that can be held, thrown, moved to a specific location, or carried around in a container. Hermione specialises in conjuring portable waterproof flames that are bright blue in colour.
* **"Flagrate":** Conjures a thin line of fire in midair.
* **Flame-Freezing Charm:** Causes flames to tickle instead of burn. Medieval witches and wizards would cast this on the fire when being burnt at the stake by Muggles, and pretend to scream in pain.
* **Four-Point Spell ("Point me!"):** Points a wand due North, so the caster can check direction, like a compass.
* **Freezing Charm:** Immobilises objects and stops them from moving.
* **Furnunculus Curse:** Causes boils to erupt on the victim's skin.
* **Growth Charm:** Presumably similar to an Enlargement Charm, it also makes objects bigger.
* **Hair-thickening Charm:** Makes hair grow longer and stronger.
* **Homorphus Charm:** Lockhart allegedly performed this "immensely complex" charm on a werewolf to transfigure it back into a man.
* **Horn tongue:** Causes a horn to grow on the victim's tongue.
* **hot air charm:** Casts a jet of hot air from the tip of a wand.
* **Hover Charm:** Makes objects float.
* **Hurling Hex:** Presumably throws (hurls) a person from a broom.
* **Impediment Jinx:** Slows down and obstructs attackers.
* **Imperius Curse ("Imperio"):** See page 179.

* **Imperturbable Charm:** Creates a protective barrier around an object that repels contact from other objects.
* **"Impervius":** Repels water from the surface of an object.
* **Inanimatus Conjurus Spell:** Taught in Transfiguration, it presumably conjures inanimate objects.
* **"Incarcerous":** Conjures ropes in midair. Possibly, a variation of this is used to conjure cords, ropes, and long thin flames from the tip of a wand, but the incantation is not given.
* **"Incendio":** Creates fire.
* **Instant scalping:** Immediately removes hair from the head.
* **Jelly-Legs Jinx:** Makes a victim's legs unstable and wobble out of control.
* **Killing Curse ("Avada Kedavra"):** See page 180.
* **Leg-Locker Curse ("Locomotor Mortis"):** Impedes movement by making a victim's legs stiff and rigid.
* **Levitation Charm:** Makes objects rise in the air.
* **liquid silver:** Conjures a streak of liquid silver that can form itself into an object.
* **Locomotion Charm ("Locomotor"):** Moves objects.
* **"Lumos":** Casts a beam of light from the tip of a wand.
* **Memory Charm ("Obliviate"):** Modifies or erases a victim's memories. It is usually performed on Muggles by the Ministry to make them forget about any magic they have encountered. A Memory Charm can be broken by a very powerful wizard but can cause irreversible brain damage.
* **message dart:** Conjures a silvery dart from the tip of a wand that flies through the air like a small, ghostly bird until it finds its target. The dart notifies the person it locates that he or she is needed by the sender.
* **"Mobiliarus":** Makes a tree move.
* **"Mobilicorpus":** Makes a body move.
* **Muggle-Repelling Charms:** Spells that ward off Muggles from a magical place if they approach it by convincing them they have urgent business elsewhere.
* **"Nox":** Extinguishes light.

★ **Obliteration Charm:** Erases evidence of an object's existence (such as the removal of footprints in the snow).

★ **"Orchideous":** Conjures a bouquet of flowers from the tip of a wand.

★ **packing spell:** Summons objects into a trunk.

★ **Patronus Charm ("Expecto Patronum"):** Repels Dementors.

★ **pepper breath:** Makes a victim's breath hot and fiery.

★ **Permanent Sticking Charm:** Binds one object to another permanently.

★ **"Portus":** Transforms an object into a Portkey. Casting the spell engulfs the object in a blue light for a few seconds and causes it to tremble.

★ **"Prior Incantato":** Reveals the last spell a wand cast. When the caster's wand tip touches another wand tip, the last spell the other wand cast is shown in the form of a dense, grey, smoky shadow, like a ghost spell.

★ **"Priori Incantatem":** Similar to Priori Incantato in nature, although it is an effect and not a spell. Normally, if brother wands (wands that share their core substance from the exact same source) are forced to do battle, they will not work properly against each other. Depending on the power of the wizards involved, one of the wands will force the other to reveal the spells it has cast in reverse-order (the last spell cast will emerge first, then the second-last spell, and so on), like echoes.

★ **Protean Charm:** NEWT-level charm (which Hermione masters in fifth year!) that enables an object to change its form. Objects that are linked to the main object will also take on the new form. (In Greek mythology, the sea god Proteus would tell the future to those who could catch him, but assumed various forms in order to avoid getting caught.)

★ **"Quietus":** Returns the caster's amplified voice to normal volume.

★ **"Reducio":** Returns an enlarged object to normal size.

★ **Reductor Curse ("Reducto"):** Blasts objects out of the way.

★ **"Relashio":** Casts a jet of sparks from the tip of a wand. Underwater, it casts a jet of boiling water instead.

* **"Reparo"**: Repairs broken objects, such as glass.
* **"Riddikulus"**: Charm to repel a Boggart. It must be cast while consciously forcing the Boggart to turn into something the caster finds funny, as Boggarts are destroyed by laughter.
* **Scouring Charm ("Scourgify")**: Scrubs objects clean.
* **"Serpensortia"**: Conjures a snake from the tip of a wand.
* **Severing Charm**: Cuts objects.
* **Shield Charm ("Protego")**: Creates a temporary invisible wall around the caster that deflects minor spells during an attack.
* **Shock Spells**: Offered as a treatment at St. Mungo's. (Possibly the wizarding world's answer to electroshock therapy?)
* **Silencing Charm ("Silencio")**: Makes a person or creature mute.
* **Slug-vomiting Charm**: Makes a victim vomit slugs. There appears to be no spell to stop the effects, other than waiting it out.
* **"Sonorus"**: Amplifies the caster's voice.
* **space enlargement spell**: Creates additional room inside an object, such as a car or tent, without altering its normal exterior appearance.
* **Stealth Sensoring Spells**: Covertly monitor an area to detect intruders and alert the owner if the area's security has been breached (like the magical equivalent of a burglar alarm).
* **Stinging Hex**: Leaves a painful welt on the victim's skin.
* **Stunning Spell ("Stupefy")**: Immobilises people or creatures. Casting the spell emits red light from a wand.
* **Substantive Charm**: Seamus and Dean study the definition of this in preparation for their OWL. (The word "substantive" means the essence or essential element of an object.)
* **Summoning Charm ("Accio")**: Commands an object to fly to the caster.
* **Switching Spell**: Substitutes one object for another (such as wine gums for fangs).
* **Talon-clipping charm**: Cuts dragons' claws.
* **"Tarantallegra"**: Makes a victim's legs dance uncontrollably.
* **Tickling Charm ("Rictusempra")**: Makes a victim laugh uncontrollably. Casting the spell emits silver light from a wand.
* **Transmogrification Torture**: Lockhart believes this is what

"killed" the first Petrification victim. (To "transmogrify" something means to change it into a different form, especially one that is bizarre-looking.)

* **Trip Jinx:** Makes a victim stumble and fall.
* **Twitchy Ears Hex:** Makes a victim's ears twinge and spasm.
* **Unbreakable Charm:** Prevents objects, such as glass, from breaking.
* **Vanishing Spell ("Evanesco"):** Makes an object disappear. Vanishing Spells are taught in Transfiguration. The more complex the object to Vanish, the more difficult the spell is to perform.
* **"Waddiwasi":** Lupin uses this spell to expel a wad of chewing gum from one place (a keyhole) and direct it to another (up Peeves's nostril!).
* **wand sparks spell:** Casts sparks of various colours from the tip of a wand that can be used as a warning or signal.
* **wand writing spell:** Conjures a golden ribbon from the tip of a wand that forms itself into words or numbers.
* **"Win-*gar*-dium Levi-*o*-sa" (not Levi-osa!):** Makes objects fly. Used with a "swish and flick" wrist movement.

Defence Against the Dark Arts

CONSTANT VIGILANCE! Defence Against the Dark Arts class is somewhat erratic, depending on the teacher. In some years, students are given hands-on training in the ways to combat Dark creatures and curses, whilst in others, a highly-structured theory-only curriculum is imposed ("wands away, quills out!"). At other times, it seems like nothing useful is taught at all. Strangely, no teacher in this post seems to be able to last longer than a year. Perhaps Dumbledore will finally give Snape a crack at teaching the class one year . . .

Teachers: Professor Quirrell (first year); Professor Lockhart (second year); Professor Lupin (third year); Professor Moody (fourth year); Professor Umbridge (fifth year)

Location: Defence Against the Dark Arts classroom

Time: Mondays after lunch (third year); Thursdays after lunch (fourth year); Monday afternoon double class (fifth year)

Textbooks: *The Dark Forces: A Guide to Self-Protection, Break with a Banshee, Gadding with Ghouls, Holidays with Hags, Travels with Trolls, Voyages with Vampires, Wanderings with Werewolves, Year with the Yeti, Defensive Magical Theory*

Material Covered/Homework: Ways of treating werewolf bites (first year); Cornish Pixies, fifty-four question quiz about Lockhart, dramatic re-enactments from his books, and composition of poems about his defeat of the Wagga Wagga werewolf (second year); Boggarts, Grindylows, Hinkypunks, Kappas, Red Caps, ways to recognise and kill werewolves, essay on vampires (third year); Unforgivable Curses, hex deflection (fourth year); defensive theory, including non-offensive responses, counter-jinxes, and negotiation (fifth year)

Third year exam: Outdoor obstacle course — wade across a pool containing a Grindylow, cross a series of Red Caps, navigate through a marsh containing a Hinkypunk, and do battle with a Boggart in a trunk

OWL: THEORETICAL — Harry feels he did very well. PRACTICAL — includes counter-jinxes, defensive spells, and Riddikulus. For a bonus point, Professor Tofty asks Harry to produce a Patronus.

BOGGARTS

Dean: severed hand
Harry: Dementor
Hermione: Ron sniggers it must be homework that is less than perfect!
Neville: Professor Snape
Parvati: mummy
Professor Lupin: full moon
Ron: giant spider
Seamus: banshee
unnamed students: rat, rattlesnake, and a bloody eyeball
Mrs. Weasley: Although obviously not part of the class, Mrs. Weasley's Boggart turns into the dead bodies of Mr. Weasley, Bill, Percy, Fred, George, Ron, and Harry.

Patronus Charm ("**Expecto Patronus**"): Dementors are repelled by the highly advanced Patronus Charm, which Lupin teaches Harry to help him conquer his fear of the creatures.

A Patronus works on the premise that thinking good thoughts can overcome depression. It is a positive force that guards and shields the caster of the spell from Dementors by projecting the things Dementors feed upon (for example, love and happiness) — but as a Patronus cannot feel despair, Dementors cannot hurt it.

Saying the incantation whilst concentrating on a very happy memory will conjure a Patronus from the tip of a wand in a silvery, animal-shaped form. Conjuring a Patronus can be quite difficult. Usually, the first few attempts only produce an opaque smoky shadow. A fully-defined Patronus is called a corporeal Patronus (the Latin for "body" is *corpus*).

Patronuses (Patroni?)

Each Patronus is unique to the wizard who conjures it.

Note to Muggles: *Hermione and Cho's Patronuses are not conjured as part of Lupin's class.)*

★ **Cho:** Swan — symbolises grace, faithfulness, solitude, sensitivity, self-image, and intuition. Swans also mate for life and grieve the deaths of their mates deeply.
★ **Harry:** Stag — represents nobility, pride, independence, boldness, strength, and bravery.
★ **Hermione:** Otter — symbolises female magic, empathy, helpfulness, curiosity, and power. (Otters are also J. K. Rowling's favourite animal!)

Unforgivable Curses

These three curses are illegal because of the results they produce — mind control, torture, and death. They are associated with the Dark Arts, and were commonly used by Voldemort's supporters during his reign. Casting any of the Unforgivable Curses on another person is punishable by the heaviest sanctions in wizarding law — a life sentence in Azkaban.

It takes powerful magic to perform an Unforgivable Curse. In order to cast one, there must be conscious intent by the caster to do harm. The caster must not only want to cause pain, but to enjoy it — righteous anger is not a strong enough motivating force for the curses to work.

According to the Ministry, Dark curses are not meant to be taught until sixth year (in fourth year students are supposed to just learn counter-curses). However, Dumbledore believes the fourth years can manage them.

★ **Imperius Curse ("Imperio"):** Forcibly controls another person's actions. It can be fought, but extreme strength of character is needed to do so. Being under the Imperius Curse feels almost relaxing — all thoughts are wiped from the victim's head and are replaced by a vague sort of happiness. *Impero* means to command, rule or give orders in Latin.

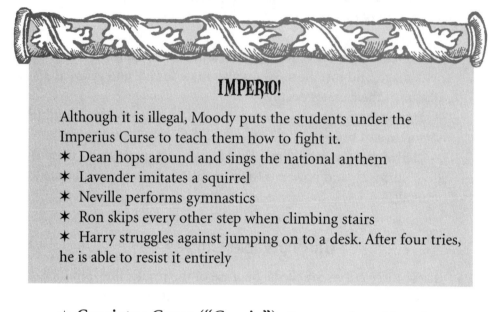

IMPERIO!

Although it is illegal, Moody puts the students under the Imperius Curse to teach them how to fight it.
✱ Dean hops around and sings the national anthem
✱ Lavender imitates a squirrel
✱ Neville performs gymnastics
✱ Ron skips every other step when climbing stairs
✱ Harry struggles against jumping on to a desk. After four tries, he is able to resist it entirely

✱ **Cruciatus Curse ("Crucio"):** Causes unbearable pain. *Cruciatus* means "to torture" in Latin. Neville has an odd reaction to seeing this curse demonstrated on a spider in class, and readers later discover why.

✱ **Killing Curse ("Avada Kedavra"):** Causes instantaneous death, with no visible marks on the victim. A jet of bright green light and a rushing noise are always seen and heard when the spell is cast. A wizard must be very powerful to cast the killing curse. Harry is the only person who has ever survived it, even though there is no counter-curse or method of blocking it. In Aramaic (an ancient language closely related to Hebrew), *avada kedavra* means "may the thing be destroyed." Ironically, it also sounds similar to "abra-cadabra," which is a charm to cure illness from the Kabbalah, the mystical interpretation of the Jewish Scriptures.

Divination

Divination is the study of the unknown using a variety of methods, including Astrology (stars), Cheiromancy (palm reading), Oneiromancy (dream interpretation), Scrying (looking into reflective surfaces, such as water, mirrors, and crystal balls), and Tasseomancy (tea leaf reading). The word Divination comes from the Latin *divinare*, meaning "predict, prophecy, or divine the future."

Trelawney considers Divination a noble and sacred art. Books and exams aren't of much use in Divination; if students do not have the Gift of Sight, there isn't much they can be taught (much to Hermione's horror). Firenze dismisses Trelawney's beliefs as "fortune-telling." Instead, he teaches the centaurs' way of interpreting the stars, which is much more impartial and objective, but very slow.

Teachers: Professor Trelawney; Firenze (fifth year)

Locations: Top of the North Tower (Trelawney); classroom eleven (Firenze)

Time: Nine o'clock in the morning (third year); Monday afternoon double class (fourth year); Monday afternoons and Wednesday mornings (fifth year)

Textbooks: *Unfogging the Future*, *The Dream Oracle* (fifth year)

Material Covered/Homework: Tea leaf reading, palm reading, fire omens, and crystal ball gazing (third year); star charts (fourth year); dream interpretation and dream diaries, lectures about predicting the future in smoke and flame patterns from burnt herbs (fifth year)

Third year exam: Crystal ball gazing. Ron and Harry make things up (Trelawney seems disappointed there is no death in Harry's vision!)

OWL: PRACTICAL: includes crystal balls, tea leaf reading, and palmistry. Both Harry and Ron think they did very poorly.

Did you know . . . there are over one hundred and sixty different kinds of Divination practised around the world, including Batraquomancy (divination by frogs), Tiromacy (divination by cheese), and Gastromancy (divination by sounds from the belly)?

Crystal Balls ("the Orb")

The Orbs in Trelawney's classroom are full of pearly white mist that gives off a milky glow. She introduces crystal balls earlier than expected — the Fates told her the students' exam would include an area about the Orb, so she wanted to give them as much practice as possible. Trelawney doesn't expect any of her students to See on their first attempt, as it is a refined art. Predictably, she sees a Grim in Harry's crystal ball.

A crystal's size is not as important as its clarity, as flaws can distract from Seeing. The best results are obtained in near or total darkness, preferably by candlelight. By focusing on the centre of the crystal, a Seer will notice clouds and mist that spreads outwards and reveals images. According to legend, Merlin used a crystal ball.

Tea Leaf Reading

Students drink a cup of tea until only the dregs remain, then swirl them around three times using the left hand and turn the cup upside-down on the saucer. Patterns formed by the tea leaves are interpreted according to what they symbolise. According to common practice, the closer the leaves are to the rim, the more immediate the timing of the prediction.

Tea leaf reading dates back hundreds of years, and is commonly associated with gypsies and the English.

TEA LEAF SYMBOLS

acorn: windfall, unexpected gold
bowler hat–shaped blob: Ron reckons this means Harry will work for the Ministry one day. (Hmm . . . is this just a throw-away line, or is J. K. Rowling making a prediction of her own?)
club: an attack
cross: trials and suffering
falcon: deadly enemy
Grim: death omen
skull: danger
sun: great happiness

Star Charts

Students learn the movements of the planets and the "steps of the celestial dance." Using a circular chart, students detail the positions of the planets at the time of their birth and in the present day (like a horoscope). Harry and Ron make their answers up — being sure to include lots of tragedy and misfortune — and (not so) surprisingly, receive top marks!

Natal charts (indicating the positions of the planets at the time of a person's birth) include the twelve signs of the zodiac, twelve houses, and ten planets (including the sun and moon). The sun sign, moon sign, ascendant, and planet ruling the ascendant are the four most important aspects of a natal chart, and the exact hour and minute of a person's birth must be known in order to accurately determine them.

HARRY AND RON'S PLANETARY "PREDICTIONS"

★ Ron will develop a cough, lose a treasured possession, lose a fight, drown (twice), and be trampled by a Hippogriff.
★ Harry will suffer burns, get stabbed in the back by someone he thought was a friend, lose a bet, and be decapitated.

Dream Interpretation

Interpreting dreams dates as far back as ancient Greek and Roman times. Dreams were seen as messages from the gods, and dream interpreters were thought to possess a divine gift.

Thousands of years later, psychoanalyst Sigmund Freud revolutionised the study of dreams by connecting dreams with the unconscious mind. Because a person's guard is down during sleep, the unconscious can express its hidden desires, impulses, and thoughts without fear of repression. Like Trelawney, Freud analysed the symbolism in dreams — but instead of using his findings to predict the future, he used them to gain a deeper understanding of a person's psyche and personality.

DREAMS

Harry: refuses to share his dreams (nightmares) as he already knows what they mean, although when Umbridge inspects the class he makes up a dream about Snape drowning in a cauldron. Dreaming of someone drowning suggests being too deeply involved in something that is beyond your control. Trelawney interprets everything Harry has written in his dream diary as signs of a premature, grizzly death.

Neville: giant pair of scissors wearing his Gran's hat. Scissors in dreams indicate decisiveness and control, or the need to cut things or people out of your life, whilst dreaming of a hat indicates your role and responsibilities in your life. It can also mean you are hiding something.

Ron: playing Quidditch (Harry reckons this means Ron is going to be devoured by a giant marshmallow). A dream about playing a sport represents the learning of talents and achievements of your goals, as well as the importance of teamwork and harmony. Ron also makes up a dream about buying shoes. Shoes in dreams signify a person's approach to life, and generally suggest you are down to earth or grounded.

Other Kinds of Divination Mentioned

✷ **Heptomology:** A possible definition is predicting the future through the study of the number seven, or things grouped in sevens (*hepta* means "seven" in Greek). Another possibility is that "hepto" is a medical abbreviation for hepatology, or the study of the liver. An ancient form of divination was hepatoscopy — examining the liver of sacrificial animals.

✷ **Ornithomancy:** Popular during ancient Roman times, it involves predicting the future by interpreting bird song, or the flight patterns of birds.

Herbology

Students learn about the care and uses of magical plants and flowers. There is some overlap between Herbology and Potions, as many herbs, plants, and botanical extracts are used in preparing potions.

Teacher: Professor Sprout
Locations: Greenhouses One (first year) and Three (second year onwards), behind the castle
Time: three times a week (first year); double class (second year); Monday mornings (fourth year); Tuesday afternoons and Wednesday morning double class (fifth year). Gryffindors always have class with Hufflepuffs.
Textbook: *One Thousand Magical Herbs and Fungi*
Material Covered/Homework: Devil's Snare (first year); repotting Mandrakes, pruning Abyssinian Shrivelfigs, leaping toadstools (second year); shelling Puffapod beans (third year); squeezing and bottling Bubotuber pus, repotting Bouncing Bulbs, pruning Flutterby Bushes (fourth year); essay on self-fertilising shrubs (fifth year)
OWL: PRACTICAL — Harry is bitten by a Fanged Geranium

Did you know . . . the names of many females in the Harry Potter series are flower-based, including Lily, Fleur, Lavender, Narcissa, Pansy, Petunia, Poppy (Pomfrey), and Rose (Zeller)?

Magical Plants and Flowers

Note to Muggles: *For plants and flowers used in Potion-making, see the Potions section.*

✳ **Abyssinian Shrivelfigs:** Used in Shrinking Solutions. Figs (which have a shrivelled appearance) are a staple of Ethiopia, the modern name for Abyssinia.
✳ **Bouncing Bulbs**
✳ **Bubotubers:** Look like giant black slugs dotted with shiny liquid-filled swollen spots that contain a thick, yellow-green pus that smells like petrol. Although the pus is an excellent treatment for acne, dragon-hide gloves must be worn when squeezing Bubotubers as the undiluted pus can damage skin.

* **Chinese Chomping Cabbage:** Hermione copies a diagram of this in fifth year.
* **Devil's Snare:** Ugly-looking plant with long snakelike vines. If a person encounters Devil's Snare, the vines will reach out like tentacles and wrap around their body, eventually strangling them. If trapped in Devil's Snare, the key to survival is to relax — the plant will twist itself more tightly around victims if they struggle. Devil's Snare will also loosen its grip if in the presence of fire, as it only thrives in damp and darkness.
* **dragon dung compost:** Sprout's favourite fertiliser.
* **Fanged Geraniums**
* **Flitterbloom:** Often mistaken for Devil's Snare because of their similar appearance, except Flitterbloom isn't deadly.
* **flowers** as big as cabbages hang from the greenhouse ceiling, others are the size of umbrellas
* **Flutterby Bush**
* **Gillyweed:** Looks like a ball of slimy green-grey rat tails. It tastes rubbery but will give the eater temporary gills and webbed hands and feet, enabling underwater survival. Gillyweed was stolen from Snape's private stores in fourth year.
* **honking daffodils**
* **leaping toadstools**
* **Mandrakes (Mandragora):** Used in many antidotes, Mandrakes are a potent restorative that, when fully mature, can revive people who have been cursed, transfigured, or Petrified. Mandrake seedlings look like small, ugly babies with green mottled skin and purplish leaves that grow out of their heads. When immature, their cry will cause anyone who hears it to faint; when mature, their cry is deadly (students must wear ear-muffs when working with Mandrakes).

Native to the Mediterranean and Himalayan regions, mandrakes in the Muggle world are part of the nightshade family, and were used as a narcotic during the Middle Ages. Muggle mandrakes are surrounded by much of the same mythology as their magical counterparts — they have mystical properties (increasing passion, wealth, and fertility), their roots roughly resemble the human form, and it was once believed that if you plucked them, they would scream so loudly that anyone who heard their cry would die.

✴ **Mimbulus mimbletonia:** Very rare plant that is grey in colour and pulsates slightly, like a diseased internal organ. It looks like a cactus, only with boils instead of spines. The boils squirt Stinksap as a defence mechanism if the plant is poked. As it ages, the Mimbulus mimbletonia makes crooning noises when touched.

✴ **Puffapods:** Plants with fat pink pods containing beans that bloom instantly if dropped.

✴ **Screechsnap seedlings:** Wriggle and make squeaking noises when not looked after properly.

✴ **Self-fertilising shrubs**

✴ **Stinksap:** Thick, non-poisonous dark green liquid that smells like rancid dung.

✴ **Venomous Tentacula:** Spiky plant that "teethes." It is dark red in colour with creeping feelers.

✴ **Venomous Tentacula seeds:** Considered a Class C Non-Tradeable Substance, these black wrinkled pods make faint rattling noises.

History of Magic

Although the history of magic is actually quite interesting, Professor Binns manages to make it sound boring and dreary. Lessons are always the same, and consist of lots of note-taking during his monotonous lectures. Harry and Ron have scraped by through the years by copying Hermione's notes.

Teacher: Professor Binns
Location: First floor classroom
Time: Wednesday afternoons (second year); Tuesday mornings and Fridays (fourth year); Monday mornings (fifth year)
Textbook: *A History of Magic*
Material Covered/Homework: essay on The Medieval Assembly of European Wizards, International Warlock Convention of 1289, impromptu lesson on Hogwarts's history and the Chamber of Secrets (second year); summer homework essay on

fourteenth century witch-burning (third year); weekly essays about the goblin rebellions (fourth year); giant wars (fifth year)

First year exam: Wizards who invented self-stirring cauldrons

Third year exam: Medieval witch hunts

Fourth year exam: Goblin rebellions. Ron can't remember the names so he makes ones up, such as Bodrod the Bearded and Urg the Unclean.

OWL: THEORETICAL — includes wand legislation, goblin riots, the Statute of Secrecy, and the International Confederation of Wizards.

Historical Wizards and Witches

Bonaccord, Pierre: First Supreme Mugwump of the International Confederation of Wizards. Wizards from Liechtenstein disapproved of his appointment because he wanted to give trolls rights — they were having difficulties with a tribe of mountain trolls.

Elfric the Eager: Wizard who staged an uprising.

Emeric the Evil: Wizard mentioned in passing in class.

Flamel, Nicolas: Famous for his work in alchemy with his partner Dumbledore, Flamel is the only known maker and owner of the Philosopher's Stone. Although the Stone can provide great wealth and immortality, it also has tremendous power for misuse if it falls into the wrong hands. This causes Flamel to come to a decision about the Stone's future, which has far-reaching implications for his own future, as well. According to a library book Hermione finds in first year, Flamel turned six hundred and sixty-five years old "last year." It says he is an opera lover and lives in Devon with his wife.

Did you know . . . there really was a Nicolas Flamel? Born in France in 1330, Flamel and his wife, Perenelle, had a successful business selling and collecting books. He came across a mystical book containing ancient Greek and Hebrew writings, and spent many years travelling around the world consulting with scholars to translate and interpret the text. Flamel used his new knowledge to become one of the most accomplished alchemists of his time — it is said he successfully produced the Philosopher's Stone, which he used to turn lead into gold and achieve immortality. Despite this, his date of death is listed as 1410 . . . although legend has it his grave is empty!

Flamel, Perenelle: Flamel's wife. In first year, Hermione's library book lists her as six hundred and fifty-eight years old. Like her husband, Perenelle was a real person, although her name has been written as "Petronella" and "Perelle." Interestingly, "Perenelle" sounds like "perennial," meaning long-lasting or enduring through many years.

Uric the Oddball: Wizard mentioned in passing in class.

Wendelin the Weird: Medieval witch who so enjoyed the tickling sensation of being burnt at the stake, she allowed herself to be caught by Muggles forty-seven times.

Historical Events and Laws

1637 Werewolf Code of Conduct: Studied in first year. Presumably, it addresses the behaviour of those who are werewolves.

goblin rebellions: Took place in the seventeenth and eighteenth centuries. The Hog's Head, in Hogsmeade, was headquarters for the goblin rebellion of 1612.

International Warlock Convention of 1289: Included a sub-committee of Sardinian sorcerers.

International Confederation of Wizards: The Confederation met for the first time in France. Goblins were not permitted to attend, and warlocks from Liechtenstein refused to join because they did not approve of Pierre Bonaccord's appointment as Supreme Mugwump.

Statute of Secrecy: Breached in 1749, possibly by vampires.

Warlocks' Convention of 1709: Officially outlawed dragon breeding due to physical dangers and fear of discovery by Muggles.

Muggle Studies

Hermione takes this in third year, much to Ron's disbelief ("You're Muggle-born!"), because she thinks it will be interesting to study Muggles from a wizarding perspective. Though some consider Muggle Studies an easy class, Percy thinks it is important for wizards to understand the non-magical world, especially if they plan on working in close contact with Muggles (for example, Mr. Weasley's position at the Ministry).

Teacher: Unknown
Location: First floor
Time: nine o'clock in the morning
Textbook: *Home Life and Social Habits of British Muggles*
Material Covered/Homework: essay — "Explain why Muggles Need Electricity." Hermione has four hundred and twenty-two pages of reading to get through in one weekend.
Exam: Hermione earns three hundred and twenty per cent!
OWL: Details unknown

Did you know . . . the word "Muggle" made its debut in the *Oxford English Dictionary* in 2003? The entry reads: "Muggle (noun): In the fiction of J.K. Rowling, a person who possesses no magical powers. Hence in allusive and extended uses, a person who lacks a particular skill or skills, or who is regarded as inferior in some way."

Potions

Through a combination of theoretical and practical work, students learn about the preparation and effects of magical potions and substances. They also study poisons and antidotes, and learn about the attributes of different potion ingredients, from the everyday to the exotic. Snape considers potion-making a subtle science and exact art, and has a very low tolerance for students' mistakes (particularly if they are made by Gryffindors).

Teacher: Professor Snape
Location: Dungeons
Time: Friday mornings (first year); Thursday afternoons (second year); Monday and Thursday mornings (third year); Friday afternoons (fourth year); Monday mornings and Thursdays (fifth year). Gryffindors always have double classes with Slytherins.
Textbooks: *One Thousand Magical Herbs and Fungi, Magical Drafts and Potions*
Material Covered/Homework: Boil-curing potion (first year); Hair Raising Potion, Swelling Solution (second year); summer homework essay on Shrinking Potions, essay on Undetectable Potions (third year); Wit-Sharpening Potion, Shrinking Solution, research on antidotes (fourth year); Draught of Peace, Strengthening Solution, Invigoration Draught, essays on moonstone and venom antidotes (fifth year)
First year exam: Make a Forgetfulness Potion
Third year exam: Make Confusing Concoction
OWL: THEORETICAL — includes Polyjuice Potion. PRACTICAL — Not as horrible as Harry had expected, as Snape wasn't present.

Did you know . . . J. K. Rowling said if she could take Polyjuice Potion for an hour, she would like to become Tony Blair? The author said her first order of business as the British Prime Minister would be to call a press conference and announce all the new policies she'd like to implement!

Potions

✻ **Ageing Potion:** Makes the drinker a little or a lot older, depending on how much is drunk.

✻ **Babbling Beverage:** Presumably makes the drinker speak nonsense.

✻ **Baruffio's Brain Elixir:** Presumably boosts brain power. It is sold as a black-market concentration and study aid for OWL and NEWT students.

✻ **bezoar (pronounced "bez-war"):** Stone found in a goat's stomach that will save a person from most poisons.

✻ **Boil-curing potion:** Contains crushed snake fangs, dried nettles, stewed horned slugs, and porcupine quills.

✻ **Confusing Concoction:** Presumably befuddles the drinker.

✻ **Deflating Draught:** Antidote to Swelling Solution. It reduces objects that have been inflated back to their original size.

✻ **Draught of Living Death:** Very powerful sleeping potion containing powdered root of asphodel and infusion of wormwood.

✻ **Draught of Peace:** Soothes anxiety and agitation. It must be prepared very precisely — if mixed incorrectly, it can put the drinker into a heavy, sometimes irreversible, sleep.

✻ **Elixir of Life:** Product of the Philosopher's Stone that makes the drinker immortal.

✻ **Forgetfulness Potion:** Presumably makes the drinker forget things (it could be the potion equivalent of a Memory Charm).

✻ **Hair Raising Potion:** Presumably makes hair stand on end.

✻ **Invigoration Draught:** Presumably stimulates or revitalises the drinker.

✻ **Love Potion:** Makes the drinker fall in love. Love Potions are not allowed at Hogwarts, but that doesn't stop Lockhart from suggesting students ask Snape to show them how to brew one on Valentine's Day (though the mutinous expression on Snape's face suggests any student actually considering this should think otherwise).

✻ **Mandrake Restorative Draught:** See page 120.

✻ **Pepperup Potion:** See page 120.

✻ **photo developing potion:** Animates objects in pictures when used to develop film.

✳ **Polyjuice Potion:** Temporarily turns the drinker into another person (though it is not to be used for animal transformations!). It takes about a month to brew, and is made from an extremely complicated recipe. Ingredients include Bicorn horn (powdered), Boomslang skin (shredded), fluxweed (picked during a full moon), knotgrass, lace-wing flies (stewed for twenty-one days), leeches, and a bit of whomever the person wants to become. Polyjuice Potion looks like thick, dark mud and tastes like overcooked cabbage. It causes a writhing and burning sensation inside the drinker's body, making the skin bubble and melt like hot wax as it reconfigures itself into the features of the other person.

✳ **Scintillation Solution:** "Scintillating" means enthusiastic and energetic, so presumably the drinker develops these qualities. Taught in Kwikspell correspondence courses.

✳ **Shrinking Solution:** Makes things smaller. It should be bright green in colour if prepared correctly. Shrinking Solution contains caterpillar, daisy roots, leech juice, rat spleen, and skinned Abyssinian Shrivelfig.

✳ **Sleekeazy's Hair Potion:** Hermione uses this to make her hair smooth and shiny for the Yule Ball.

✳ **Sleeping Draught:** Makes the drinker fall asleep, although it is possibly not as strong or long-lasting as the Draught of Living Death.

✳ **Strengthening Solution:** Presumably fortifies objects or makes them stronger. Strengthening Solution should be turquoise in colour if prepared correctly. After the initial mixture is prepared, it must mature for a few days before the remainder of the ingredients are added.

✳ **Swelling Solution:** Makes objects grow larger.

✳ **Undetectable Poisons:** Presumably, poisons that have no odour, taste, or colour and could be added to other substances without being noticed.

✳ **Veritaserum (Truth Potion):** Makes the drinker tell the truth (usually, three drops is enough to elicit a confession). It is a concentrated, clear liquid that takes a full month to mature. Veritaserum is extremely powerful, and its use is strictly controlled by the Ministry.

* **Wit-sharpening Potion:** Presumably sharpens the drinker's intellect. It contains armadillo bile, chopped ginger roots, and ground scarab beetles.
* **Wolfsbane Potion:** When drunk the week before a full moon, it prevents a person from losing their mind and turning into a werewolf — instead, the drinker will transform into a regular wolf and can wait safely for the full moon to pass. Wolfsbane Potion is a complicated potion that must be brewed every month. It tastes awful and is served in a goblet that continues to smoke even after the potion has been drunk.

Transfiguration

Transfiguration involves transforming an object or person into something else. It is some of the most complex and dangerous magic taught, and involves lots of complicated note-taking. Transfiguration covers several areas, including partial transformations (Switching), making objects disappear entirely (Vanishing), creating objects out of nothing (Conjuring) and human-to-animal transformations (Animagi). Human transfiguration is taught in sixth year.

Teacher: Professor McGonagall

Location: Unknown

Time: Following Divination (third year); Thursdays (fourth year); Tuesday mornings double class, Wednesday afternoons (fifth year)

Textbooks: *A Beginner's Guide to Transfiguration, Intermediate Transfiguration*

Material Covered/Homework: Transform matches into needles, McGonagall transforms her desk into a pig (first year); transform beetles into buttons and rabbits into slippers (second year); McGonagall demonstrates Animagi transformations (third year); transform hedgehogs into pincushions, guinea-fowls into guinea-pigs, Switching Spells, describe how Transforming Spells must be adapted when performing Cross-Species Switches (fourth year); Vanishing Spells, essay on Inanimatus Conjuring Spell,

Hermione studies diagrams of how to turn an owl into a pair of opera glasses (fifth year).

First year exam: Transform a mouse into a snuff-box (points given for prettiness, but deducted if the box still has whiskers)

Third year exam: Transform a teapot into a tortoise (very difficult — several tortoises wind up with patterned shells or spouts instead of tails)

OWL: THEORETICAL — includes Switching Spells. PRACTICAL — includes Vanishing Spells. Harry successfully Vanishes iguanas, but poor Hannah Abbott turns her ferrets into a flock of flamingos.

Flying

The basics of flying are taught in first year. Flying is a skill that cannot be taught from a textbook; it seems to be naturally present (or not) to varying degrees — Harry is a born flyer, whilst Neville has great difficulty. It is possible brooms can detect fear or confidence in a person's voice, and react accordingly. Although first years are not allowed their own brooms, many (including Malfoy, Ron, and Seamus) have already practised flying before starting at Hogwarts.

Teacher: Madam Hooch

Location: Lawn on the opposite side of the Forbidden Forest

Time: Thursday afternoons. Gryffindors have class with Slytherins.

Textbooks: Unknown (likely none)

Material Covered/Homework: how to command a broom to fly up into the hands, correct mounting and gripping, kick-off techniques

First year exam: Unknown, but presumably there is some sort of grading system

Legilimency and Occlumency

Legilimency: On a basic level, Legilimency (pronounced "La-jill-a-men-see") is the ability to read minds (in Latin, *legens* is a reader and *mens* means mind). However, given the complexities of the human brain, a better definition is the extraction and interpretation of memories, feelings, and emotions from someone else's mind.

Normally, it is important to maintain eye contact when performing Legilimency (which gives new meaning to the phrase "the eyes are the windows to the soul"). Best results are achieved when the person whose mind is being broken into is relaxed or unaware. Legilimency is not a common skill and takes great power to master.

★ **Legilimens:** Both the name given to a practitioner of Legilimency, and the incantation used to perform it.

Occlumency: A useful but obscure branch of magic, Occlumency (pronounced "Aw-clue-men-see") deals with defending and sealing the mind against external intrusion and influence (in Latin, *occulto* means to hide or conceal, and *mens* means mind). It is not unlike fighting the Imperius Curse.

Occlumency is the method used to block Legilimency. Although wands can be used defensively to disarm a Legilimens, the best way to block mental intrusions is to calm and focus the mind, clearing it of all thoughts and feelings.

Note to Muggles: *Here is an example of how Legilimency and Occlumency work: Voldemort can almost always tell when he is being lied to by examining the other person's mind (Legilimency). But if a person were able to turn off or block the part of the mind that would give away the lie (Occlumency), he or she could lie to Voldemort successfully without being detected.*

Harry's Occlumency Lessons

In fifth year, Dumbledore wants Harry to learn Occlumency because Harry is connected to Voldemort through his scar, which makes him vulnerable to all manner of things. Although

Dumbledore could teach Harry himself, he instructs Snape to privately tutor him instead (an arrangement neither Snape nor Harry is pleased with).

The lessons are disguised as remedial Potions, and are held in Snape's office. To Harry's frustration (and Ron's suspicion), things do not go as planned, and after Harry uses a Pensieve to perform a little Legilimency of his own, Snape puts an end to the lessons entirely. Harry's refusal to resume learning Occlumency after this has serious consequences.

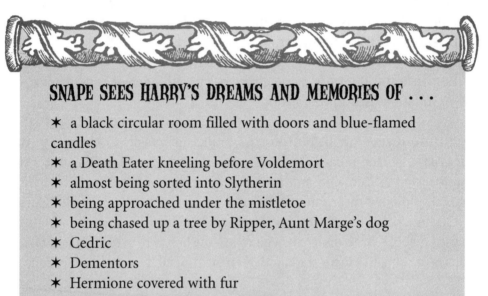

SNAPE SEES HARRY'S DREAMS AND MEMORIES OF . . .

* a black circular room filled with doors and blue-flamed candles
* a Death Eater kneeling before Voldemort
* almost being sorted into Slytherin
* being approached under the mistletoe
* being chased up a tree by Ripper, Aunt Marge's dog
* Cedric
* Dementors
* Hermione covered with fur
* his parents in the Mirror of Erised
* running along a corridor towards a door, but turning down a flight of stairs instead
* the Hungarian Horntail
* Uncle Vernon nailing the letterbox shut
* various traumatic childhood incidents caused by Dudley and his gang
* watching Dudley ride a new bicycle

HARRY SEES SNAPE'S MEMORIES OF . . .

✴ a girl laughing as he tries to mount a broomstick
✴ being a teenager in his bedroom
✴ his parents arguing as he cries

OTHER WIZARDING SCHOOLS

"Harry laughed, but didn't voice the amazement he felt at hearing about other wizarding schools. He supposed, now he saw representatives of so many nationalities in the campsite, that he had been stupid never to realise that Hogwarts couldn't be the only one."
— *Harry Potter and the Goblet of Fire*

Traditionally there is a lot of rivalry between magical schools, so in order to prevent their secrets being stolen, their locations are made Unplottable and concealed by bewitchments and Muggle-Repelling Charms. The three largest schools in Europe are Beauxbatons, Hogwarts, and Durmstrang.

Beauxbatons Academy of Magic: Co-educational French school of witchcraft and wizardry that participates in the Triwizard Tournament in fourth year. Beauxbatons is French for "handsome sticks." Its coat of arms is two gold wands, crossed over each other, emitting three stars each. The Beauxbatons delegation travels to Hogwarts in a giant flying powder-blue carriage pulled by a dozen giant winged palominos.

Beauxbatons students wear robes of pale blue silk and seem accustomed to having the best of everything. The Palace of Beauxbatons is opulent and luxurious. It features choirs of wood-nymphs and unmeltable ice sculptures around the dining chamber at Christmas. At Hogwarts the Beauxbatons students give off an air of snobbery and unhappiness as they survey their new surroundings, criticising everything from the food to the décor to the weather. They sit with the Ravenclaws for meals, and those who are not chosen as champion in the Triwizard Tournament sulk and sob.

✴ **Maxime, Madame Olympe:** Headmistress. Madame Maxime has a handsome, olive complexion with large black eyes, a beaky nose and hair that is pulled back into a neat bun. She is the picture of elegance in her black satin outfit, high heels, and opal jewellery.

Madame Maxime carries herself regally and imperiously, which is no small feat given her size — roughly the same as Hagrid. He is rather smitten with her, but when he suggests they share the same heritage, Madame Maxime is highly insulted (*"I 'ave big bones!"*). Her first name, Olympe, is likely taken from Mount Olympus, the largest mountain in Greece, and home to all the gods. In Latin, *Maxima* means "greatest."

"Dumbly-Dorr" thinks Madame Maxime is an excellent headmistress and dancer.

✴ **curly-haired witch:** During the commotion after the Quidditch World Cup final, she asks Harry, Hermione, and Ron in French where Madame Maxime is, as the students have lost her.

✴ **Delacour, Fleur:** Beauxbatons' champion in the Triwizard Tournament. Fleur is a head-turner, with long silvery blonde hair and large blue eyes. Ron has a crush on her, although he insists she is not "normal," and he is right — her *"grandmuzzer"* was a Veela. Her full name means "Flower of the court," indicating both beauty and a regal bearing. Haughty, disdainful, and petulant, Fleur stamps her feet when she is displeased and tosses her hair when she flirts. She is a bit of a snob and continually complains about how inferior Hogwarts is to Beauxbatons, but warms towards some of the students after receiving assistance following an unexpected attack. During fifth year, Fleur comes to London to *"eemprove 'er Eeenglish"* and finds a job at Gringotts, where Bill Weasley seems to be giving her private lessons.

✴ **Delacour, Gabrielle:** Fleur's younger sister, to whom she is very close. Gabrielle is about eight, with the same long silvery hair as Fleur.

✳ **Delacour, Madame:** Fleur's mother, who comes to watch Fleur compete in the third task.

Brazil: Bill Weasley used to have a pen-friend at a wizarding school in Brazil when he went to Hogwarts. He wanted to go on exchange, but the Weasleys couldn't afford it. His pen-friend was so upset, he sent Bill a cursed hat that made his ears shrivel up.

Durmstrang Institute: School of wizardry that participates in the Triwizard Tournament in fourth year. Durmstrang's exact location is not known, but it is likely somewhere in northeastern Europe or northern Asia. "Durmstrang" is a play on the German phrase *sturm und drang*, which means "storm and stress," or turmoil. The Durmstrang delegation arrives on a ghostly, skeletal-looking ship, which rises out of the centre of the Hogwarts lake.

Durmstrang students wear fur capes and blood-red robes. They seem to be impressed with Hogwarts, as their own school is rather bare and spartan — while the grounds are quite large, the castle only has four floors and the fires are lit for magical purposes only.

According to Malfoy, Durmstrang teaches the Dark Arts instead of just defence against them, and does not admit Muggle-borns. Lucius Malfoy considered sending Malfoy there, but Malfoy's mother didn't want him so far away. Not surprisingly, the Durmstrang students sit with the Slytherins for meals.

✳ **Karkaroff, Igor:** Headmaster. Karkaroff is tall, thin, and severe-looking. He has short white hair and a goatee that curls around at the end (all the better to hide his weak chin). His steely smile does not reach his eyes, which are shrewd and cold, like two chips of ice. Karkaroff wears sleek silver furs and speaks in an oily, insincere tone. His surname may be a play on Boris Karloff, an actor known for playing creepy characters, including Dr. Jekyll and Mr. Hyde and Frankenstein (he also narrated the TV movie *How the Grinch Stole Christmas*).

Karkaroff acts strangely around both Moody and Snape, although for entirely different reasons. He has a shady past, a mysterious present, and a questionable future. He is untrustworthy, but also trusts no one — his only allegiance is to himself. Though this reticence helped him in the past, it may come back to haunt him in the future.

⋆ Krum, Viktor (Vicky): Durmstrang champion in the Triwizard Tournament. Eighteen-year-old Krum looks like a large bird of prey — he has a large curved nose, thick black eyebrows, and a sallow complexion. He is thin and duck-footed, with stooping posture. Krum is broody and scowls a lot, but his mannerisms are somewhat understandable — not only is he in his final year of school and competing in the Triwizard Tournament, he is also the Seeker for the Bulgarian National Quidditch Team.

Krum prefers Hogwarts to Durmstrang. He spends a lot of his time at Hogwarts in the library, partly as an escape from starstruck autograph hounds. Despite his fame, he was initially too shy to approach Hermione, whom he met in the library. At first, Hermione dismisses Krum as grumpy-looking, but this changes as she gets to know him better. He becomes quite taken with her, but is concerned her affections may lie elsewhere.

Viktor is impressed with Harry's wizarding abilities and considers him an equal, to Harry's great surprise. This is quite true, as there are many similarities between the two boys — both live their lives in the spotlight yet are quiet and reserved by nature; both are excellent Quidditch Seekers; both are brave, powerful, and highly skilled wizards; both are mature for their ages; and both have similar physical builds (dark hair, slight frame).

Did you know . . . the face of Viktor Krum may be the new face of Bulgarian tourism? The country's National Tourism Advertising and Information Agency is considering using the actor cast as Krum in the upcoming *Harry Potter and the Goblet of Fire* film as a spokesperson to promote Bulgaria, hoping kids will encourage their parents to visit the country.

⋆ Krum, Mr. and Mrs.: Krum's parents, who come to watch him compete in the third task. They are dark-haired, and his father has a hooked nose.

✴ **Poliakoff:** Durmstrang champion hopeful who is told off by Karkaroff for messy eating.

The Salem Witches' Institute: Witches from this organisation in Massachusetts, America, attended the Quidditch World Cup.

THE TRIWIZARD TOURNAMENT

Considered an excellent way to create bonds between young wizards and witches from around the world, the 422nd Triwizard Tournament is held at Hogwarts during fourth year. The Tournament was established about seven hundred years ago as a friendly competition between Beauxbatons, Durmstrang, and Hogwarts, who took turns hosting every five years.

One designated champion from each school competed in three magical tasks — until the number of fatalities put an end to the Tournament. There were several failed attempts to revive the Triwizard Tournament over the centuries, but the Ministry finally agreed to bring it back after imposing an age restriction on participants. Champions must be of legal age (seventeen), due to the dangerous and difficult nature of the tasks.

A small handful of students from Beauxbatons and Durmstrang students arrive at six o'clock in the evening on Friday the thirtieth of October. The guests stay at Hogwarts for the duration of the year, as the Tournament is spread out over several months.

Note to Muggles: *If the Triwizard Tournament was really created about seven hundred years ago and held every five years, then the Hogwarts Tournament should only be the 140th — and that doesn't count the period of time the Tournament was cancelled, which would lower the number even further!*

Goblet of Fire: Stored in an ancient, jewel-encrusted wooden chest, the goblet is a large, rough-looking wooden cup full of blue-white flames.

Prospective champions submit their names and schools on pieces of parchment and drop them into the flames, which turn red and emit sparks. (An Age Line is drawn around the Goblet to prevent underage students from entering.) Placing a name in the Goblet is considered a binding magical contract, and those chosen to be champions must go through with the Tournament until the end. During the Hallowe'en Feast, the Goblet impartially selects one champion from each school, and then its flames are extinguished until the next Tournament.

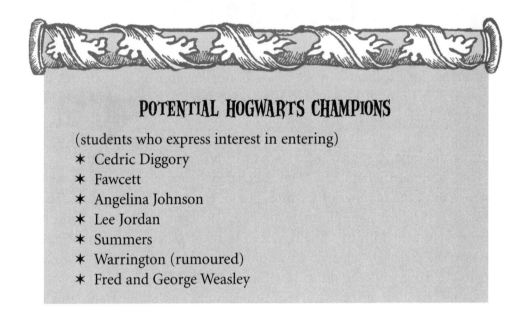

POTENTIAL HOGWARTS CHAMPIONS

(students who express interest in entering)
* Cedric Diggory
* Fawcett
* Angelina Johnson
* Lee Jordan
* Summers
* Warrington (rumoured)
* Fred and George Weasley

Did you know . . . two walk-on roles in the upcoming *Harry Potter and the Goblet of Fire* film fetched £9,000 ($16,000 USD) and £10,000 ($18,000 USD) in an auction at a Multiple Sclerosis Scotland benefit in November 2003, where J. K. Rowling was the guest of honour?

Wand Weighing ceremony: Before the Tournament begins, Mr. Ollivander (see page 247) examines each champion's wand and performs a test spell to ensure it works properly.

judges panel: Consists of Bagman (commentator), Crouch, Dumbledore, Karkaroff, and Madame Maxime. Percy and Fudge substitute as judges in the last two tasks.

scoring: For each task, the judges individually give each champion a mark out of ten, which shoots out of their wands in a silver ribbon. All five judges' marks are added together to give the champion a total score out of fifty for the task. The champion with the highest total score at the end of the three tasks is declared the winner, and receives one thousand Galleons and the Triwizard Cup.

Triwizard tasks: The tasks test the champions' powers of deduction, daring, magical skill, and ability to cope with danger. Champions are armed only with their wands, and are forbidden to ask for or receive help in preparation. (The good news is the champions are exempt from year-end exams.) Despite the strict rules, cheating is a traditional part of the Tournament and the champions are offered assistance from various teachers, judges, house-elves, ghosts, and each other!

First task

November 24
* Champions must get past a fifty-foot tall, fire-breathing dragon and collect its golden egg.

Second task

February 24, at half-past nine in the morning
* Champions must decipher a hidden message, then overcome a suffocating obstacle to retrieve something valuable that was taken from them.

Third task

June 24, at dusk, a week before the end of term
✷ Champions must battle spells and creatures to reach the centre of a maze and touch the Triwizard Cup.

Yule Ball: A traditional part of the Triwizard Tournament, the Yule Ball is held on Christmas Day, from eight o'clock in the evening until midnight in the Great Hall. It is open to fourth year students and above, although younger students can be invited as their partners. Dress robes must be worn, and the champions and their partners traditionally open the ball with a dance.

Hogwarts is transformed into a magical winter wonderland for the Yule Ball. The front lawn has been decorated like a grotto, with fountains, carved benches, ornamental paths, stone statues of Father Christmas and his reindeer, and live, multi-coloured faeries perched in conjured rose bushes. (Snape takes great satisfaction in blasting the rose bushes apart and deducting house points from the young couples he discovers inside.) Inside, the Great Hall has been dusted in silver frost and draped with garlands of ivy and mistletoe, and the house tables have been replaced by smaller round tables, lit by lanterns. The evening features a performance by the Weird Sisters.

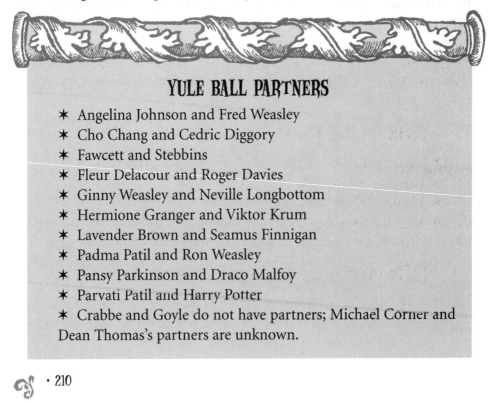

YULE BALL PARTNERS

* Angelina Johnson and Fred Weasley
* Cho Chang and Cedric Diggory
* Fawcett and Stebbins
* Fleur Delacour and Roger Davies
* Ginny Weasley and Neville Longbottom
* Hermione Granger and Viktor Krum
* Lavender Brown and Seamus Finnigan
* Padma Patil and Ron Weasley
* Pansy Parkinson and Draco Malfoy
* Parvati Patil and Harry Potter
* Crabbe and Goyle do not have partners; Michael Corner and Dean Thomas's partners are unknown.

HOGWARTS QUIDDITCH TEAMS AND MATCHES

Madam Hooch oversees trials, held in the second week of September. In fifth year, all Quidditch teams are disbanded as part of an Educational Decree, and permission must be sought to reform them.

Gryffindor (scarlet robes)

When Harry starts Hogwarts, Gryffindor hasn't won the Quidditch Cup since Charlie Weasley graduated. James Potter was on a Quidditch Cup–winning team during his days at Hogwarts, too. Harry's natural flying abilities earn him a spot on the team in his first year, against the normal school rules. He is the youngest player at Hogwarts in a century.

First to third years (captain: Oliver Wood)

* **Chasers:** Katie Bell, Angelina Johnson, Alicia Spinnet
* **Beaters:** Fred Weasley, George Weasley
* **Keeper:** Oliver Wood
* **Seeker:** Harry Potter

Fifth year (captain: Angelina Johnson)

Ron is chosen as Keeper despite not being the best flier or most talented at tryouts. Angelina schedules practices twice weekly and is counting on Ron inheriting his brothers' talents, but he has trouble with nerves. As a result of another Educational Decree, replacement players for some positions must be found later in the year.

* **Chasers:** Katie Bell, Angelina Johnson, Alicia Spinnet
* **Beaters:** Fred Weasley, George Weasley (replacements: Andrew Kirke, Jack Sloper)
* **Keeper:** Ron Weasley
* **Seeker:** Harry Potter (replacement: Ginny Weasley)

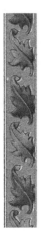

Did you know . . . there has been some debate as to what position James Potter played? In the *Harry Potter and the Philosopher's Stone* film, Hermione tells Harry he will be a great Seeker because it is "in his blood," and points to an engraved trophy reading "J. Potter — Seeker." In *Harry Potter and the Order of the Phoenix*, Harry sees a memory of his father as a student playing with a Snitch, which would also suggest James was a Seeker (although he admits to having stolen the Snitch) . . . but in an interview with Scholastic Books that predates both the film and book, J. K. Rowling said James was a Chaser. Then again, there's no reason why James, like Ginny, couldn't have been interested in more than one position!

Hufflepuff (canary-yellow robes)

Oliver thinks Cedric has put together an excellent team.

Third year (captain: Cedric Diggory)

* **Chaser:** Zacharias Smith
* **Seeker:** Cedric Diggory

Note to Muggles: *Although Zacharias was not mentioned during third year, we know he is on the team because Harry vaguely recognises him from Quidditch when they meet in fifth year. At that point, fifth year Quidditch matches haven't started yet, and there was no Quidditch in fourth year, so Harry must have recognised Zacharias from third year, the last time he played.*

Fifth year (captain: unknown)

* **Chaser:** Zacharias Smith
* **Seeker:** Summerby

Ravenclaw (blue robes)

Ravenclaw has an all-male team, except for Cho, who has had some problems with injuries — but this doesn't stop Oliver from suggesting to Harry that he knock her off her broom! Cho flies poorly in fifth year and worries about being kicked off the team.

Third year (captain: Roger Davies)

* **Chaser:** Roger Davies
* **Seeker:** Cho Chang

Fifth year (captain: Roger Davies)

* **Chasers:** Bradley, Chambers, Roger Davies
* **Seeker:** Cho Chang

Slytherin (green robes)

Slytherin had won the Quidditch Cup seven years in a row prior to Harry's arrival at Hogwarts. They are an all-male team and play dirty, with lots of fouls.

First year (captain: Marcus Flint)

* **Chasers:** Marcus Flint, Adrian Pucey
* **Keeper:** Miles Bletchley
* **Seeker:** Terence Higgs

Second year

Same as first year, except Malfoy becomes the new Seeker after his father buys Nimbus Two Thousand and One brooms for the entire team.

Third year (captain: Marcus Flint)

Lee Jordan comments during a match that Flint has made changes to the team, emphasizing size over skill.

* **Beaters:** Bole, Derrick
* **Chasers:** Marcus Flint, Montague, Warrington
* **Keeper:** Miles Bletchley
* **Seeker:** Draco Malfoy

Fifth year (captain: Montague)

* **Beaters:** Vincent Crabbe, Gregory Goyle
* **Chasers:** Montague, Pucey, Warrington
* **Keeper:** Miles Bletchley
* **Seeker:** Draco Malfoy

Matches

According to Oliver, the longest Quidditch match played at Hogwarts was three months!

First year

Gryffindor v Slytherin (November)
Score: Gryffindor wins by one hundred and seventy points to sixty after Harry catches (nearly swallows) the Snitch.
* Harry seems to have no control over his broom, until Hermione intervenes from the stands.

Gryffindor v Hufflepuff (after Christmas holidays)
Score: Unknown, but Gryffindor wins when Harry catches the Snitch in what appears to be record time — the game lasts barely five minutes.
* Snape referees, showing his extreme bias against Gryffindor.
* With this win, Gryffindor takes over the lead for the House Cup from Slytherin. However, it is a short-lived victory when Harry is held responsible for losing Gryffindor the same number of points they won in the match. His teammates are furious and he offers to resign, but Oliver won't let him.

Gryffindor v Ravenclaw (end of year, after exams)
Score: Unknown, but according to Ron, Gryffindor lost by a wide margin. (In second year, this match is referred to as the worst defeat for Gryffindor in three hundred years.)
* Harry was in the hospital wing and did not play.

Second year

Gryffindor v Slytherin (November)
Score: Although Slytherin leads sixty to zero, Gryffindor wins when Harry catches the Snitch.
* Oliver is desperate to teach Slytherin a lesson for letting Malfoy buy his way onto the team.
* Harry is chased by a rogue Bludger, which hits him in the elbow and breaks his right arm. Lockhart's attempt to administer first aid turns out to be disastrous.

Gryffindor v Hufflepuff (after Easter holidays)

Score: McGonagall cancels the match after two students are found Petrified. She later announces all remaining matches and practices are postponed indefinitely.

Third year

Gryffindor v Hufflepuff (November)

Score: Although Gryffindor is up by fifty points, Cedric catches the Snitch after Harry falls off his broom. Demonstrating true Hufflepuff fairness, Cedric suggests a re-match, but even Oliver agrees (though he tries to drown himself in the shower after the match) they earned their victory.

✷ Gryffindor was supposed to face Slytherin, but Malfoy's "injury" was used as an excuse for Slytherin to get out of the match (the real reason is the stormy weather). Oliver is furious because the Gryffindor players have based their practices on Slytherin's style of play and are unprepared for Hufflepuff.

✷ Harry faces a number of obstacles during the match, including gale-force winds and rain, an enormous black dog in the stands he assumes is a Grim, and a pitch invasion by about a hundred Dementors.

Ravenclaw v Hufflepuff (end of November)

Score: Unknown, but Ravenclaw wins by a wide margin.

Ravenclaw v Slytherin (January)

Score: Unknown, although Slytherin narrowly wins.

Gryffindor v Ravenclaw (February)

Score: Gryffindor has eighty points to Ravenclaw's thirty when Harry catches the Snitch, putting the final score at two hundred and thirty to thirty.

✷ Percy and Penelope have a ten Galleon bet on the outcome.

✷ This is Harry's first match against Cho.

✷ Harry produces a non-corporeal Patronus when he dispels three "Dementors" during the match.

Gryffindor v Slytherin (first Saturday after Easter holidays)

Score: Despite Malfoy's interference, Harry catches the Snitch and Gryffindor wins with a score of two hundred and thirty to twenty. With this victory, Gryffindor also wins the Quidditch Cup — Oliver is so ecstatic, he cannot stop sobbing (the only person crying harder is McGonagall).

✶ This is the most anticipated match of the year — Hermione is so anxious, she even abandons studying — due to the increasing animosity between Harry and Malfoy. There are approximately eight hundred spectators, with three-quarters (including the Hufflepuffs and Ravenclaws) supporting Gryffindor.

✶ Oliver is so afraid of sabotage leading up to the match, he arranges for Harry to be escorted everywhere.

✶ Both teams play dirty and earn multiple penalties (although Gryffindor's tactics are largely in retaliation against Slytherin's).

Fourth year

✶ No Quidditch due to the Triwizard Tournament.

Fifth year

✶ Quidditch teams are disbanded due to Educational Decree Number Twenty-four and cannot be reformed without consent from the High Inquisitor. Umbridge grants permission to the Slytherins immediately, but needs time to "consider" (and intervention from Dumbledore) before agreeing to reinstate the Gryffindor team.

Gryffindor v Slytherin (November)

Score: Slytherin has forty points to Gryffindor's ten when Harry catches the Snitch. Gryffindor wins with a final score of one hundred and sixty to forty.

✶ The students and Heads of both houses become very competitive in the days leading up to the match, as it is the first held in quite a while.

✴ The Slytherins wear badges and sing "Weasley is our King" to exploit Ron's nervousness when he plays in his first match.

✴ Crabbe and Malfoy prove they are poor losers by attacking Harry physically and making spiteful comments about his mother and the Weasleys, but when Harry and the Weasleys retaliate, they face serious consequences.

Gryffindor v Hufflepuff (February)

Score: Despite Ginny catching the Snitch when the Hufflepuff Seeker sneezes, Hufflepuff still wins by a score of two hundred and forty to two hundred and thirty.

✴ The match only lasts twenty-two minutes, and Gryffindor plays very poorly.

Hufflepuff v Slytherin (Saturday in May)

Score: Unknown, although Hufflepuff narrowly wins.

Gryffindor v Ravenclaw (last weekend in May)

Score: Unknown, however Ginny grabs the Snitch away from Cho (who cries, of course). With this victory, Gryffindor wins the Quidditch Cup.

✴ Ron seems to develop a newfound confidence and does not let in many goals. He is treated like a hero after the match.

PART THREE:
The Wizarding World

QUIDDITCH

Quidditch is extremely popular and followed by wizards and witches from all over the world. Though it seems to incorporate some elements from Muggle football (soccer), basketball, and baseball, Quidditch is a uniquely magical sport. It is played on broomsticks with four balls by two teams with seven players each. Points are scored by putting the Quaffle through the other team's hoops, or by catching the Golden Snitch (which ends the match). Quidditch is fast-paced and often dangerous. Fouls and injuries are common, although deaths during matches are rare (however, referees have been known to vanish and turn up months later in the Sahara desert).

Note to Muggles: *This list of the Quidditch teams, terms, and manoeuvres mentioned in the Harry Potter book series is comprehensive, but not complete. To learn about the complete history of Quidditch, see* Quidditch through the Ages *by Kennilworthy Whisp (Whizz Hard Books, 129b Diagon Alley). J. K. Rowling wrote this book in 2001 as a fundraiser for Comic Relief, a UK-based charity that helps underprivileged children in some of the poorest countries in the world.*

Equipment

✳ **Broomsticks:** Hogwarts brooms tend to be older models, with twigs sticking out here and there, and need to be defrosted in cold weather. Some fly slightly to the left or vibrate if flown too high. They are stored in the broomshed adjacent to the pitch.

✳ **Bat:** Small heavy clubs used to hit Bludgers.

✳ **Bludgers:** Two animated black balls smaller than a Quaffle that try to knock players off their brooms.

* **Quaffle:** Red ball the size of a football.
* **Snitch:** Animated gold ball the size of a large walnut with silver fluttering wings. It is very fast and difficult to see.

Pitch

Raised stands seating hundreds. At each end of the pitch, there are three fifty-foot-tall goalposts with hoops on the end. The pitch must be booked by the captains or heads of houses for practices.

Changing Room

Contains an equipment cupboard and a Captain's office. Players don their robes here before their matches and listen to pep-talks and strategy from their captains.

Players

* **Beaters (two):** Protect team from Bludgers by hitting them towards their opponents.
* **Chasers (three):** Score ten points each time they get the Quaffle through their opponents' hoops.
* **Keeper (one):** Defends the hoops.
* **Seeker (one):** Catches the Snitch. This ends the game and earns an extra one hundred and fifty points for the team. Seekers are generally the smallest and fastest players but suffer the most serious accidents.

Did you know . . . J. K. Rowling thinks she would be dreadful at Quidditch? In an online chat for World Book Day in March 2004, she said, "I'm not sporty, I'm not great with heights, and I'm clumsy as well — Neville['s flying ability] would be about my standard!"

Quidditch Plays and Penalties

✴ There are seven hundred ways of committing a foul — all of which happened during a Quidditch World Cup match in 1473.

✴ **cobbing:** Penalty for excessive elbowing.

✴ **Hawkshead Attacking Formation:** Flying move involving all three Chasers.

✴ **Porskoff Ploy:** Move involving a Chaser flying upwards with the Quaffle but dropping it to a teammate below.

✴ **Sloth Grip Roll:** Angelina makes the Gryffindor team practice this upside-down hanging move.

✴ **Wronski Feint ("Wonky Faint"):** A steep dive one Seeker instigates after pretending to see the Snitch, knowing the other Seeker will follow. The instigating Seeker diverts at the last second, resulting in the other Seeker crashing.

Did you know . . . in the ancient Greek translation of the series, Quidditch is known as Ikarosfairike or "Ikarus ball"? The name refers to the Greek myth of Icarus, who flew too close to the sun with his father, Daedalus, on wings made from wax and feathers. Icarus's wings melted and he fell into the sea and drowned.

QUIDDITCH WORLD CUP

The final match of the 422nd Quidditch World Cup takes place in August, two weeks before fourth year begins. One hundred thousand or so magical folk from around the world have tickets for the final. Tickets are very hard to come by, but Mr. Weasley manages to get some from Ludo Bagman.

Arrivals are staggered depending on ticket price — the more expensive the ticket, the later the arrival time can be (cheap ticket-holders must arrive two weeks in advance). A nearby woods is used as an Apparation site, and there are two hundred Portkey points around Britain with numerous more across five continents. Limited use of Muggle transportation is also permitted. In order to avoid being noticed, wizards travel to the Quidditch World Cup disguised as Muggles, however most have no real concept of Muggle clothing — outfits seen include a kilt and poncho ensemble, a tweed suit with thigh-high galoshes, and a nightgown.

Britain has not hosted a Cup final in thirty years. As there was no magical site in existence that could hold that many spectators, a stadium large enough to fit ten cathedrals was created on a deserted moor. The stadium is accented in gold and purple and bathed in a golden light. It features a Top Box with the best view of the pitch, halfway between the goalposts and opposite a blackboard featuring wizarding advertisements. There is ample room surrounding the stadium for spectators to camp. Five hundred Ministry employees have spent months setting up Muggle-Repelling Charms around the site.

Magic is not permitted on the campsite grounds, but it is still apparent the campers are not Muggles — many tents feature weather-vanes, chimneys, turrets, gardens, doorbells, and in one case, live peacocks! Though the Weasleys' tents appear to be Muggle-sized, inside they are furnished three-room flats. Curiously, Harry notes the decor and smell is exactly the same as Mrs. Figg's home. Ireland supporters' tents are covered in shamrocks, whilst Bulgarian supporters paper their tents with posters of a scowling Viktor Krum.

Organisers and Spectators

* **African wizards:** Three African wizards dressed in long white robes roast a rabbit over purple flames outside their tent.

* **American witches:** Middle-aged witches from the Salem Witches Institute merrily gossip outside their tents.

* **Archie:** Elderly wizard who stubbornly refuses to trade his flowery night-gown for a pair of trousers because he likes a "healthy breeze" around his privates(!).

* **Basil:** Poncho and kilt–clad Ministry wizard in charge of Portkeys.

* **Bulgarian Minister for Magic:** Mr. Oblansk (or, as Fudge says, Obalonsk) recognises Harry because of his scar, although the Minister doesn't seem to understand English.

* **Mrs. Finnigan:** Seamus's sandy-haired mother expectantly asks Harry, Hermione, and Ron if they will be supporting Ireland (naturally!).

* **goblins:** A group of goblins examine their winnings after successfully betting on the final, paying no attention to the commotion around them.

* **Kevin:** Two-year-old wizard who uses his father's wand to inflate a slug.

* **Hogwarts students:** Cho, Cedric, Dean, Ernie, Fred, George, Ginny, Harry, Hermione, Malfoy, Seamus, and Ron all attend the final.

* **The Lovegoods:** Luna and her father arrive a week before the final begins.

* **Lucius and Narcissa Malfoy:** Attend as guests of Fudge after Lucius Malfoy makes a large donation to St. Mungo's.

* **Madame Maxime and Beauxbatons students:** Separated during the commotion after the final.

* **Ministry employees:** Ludo Bagman, Bode, Croaker, Barty Crouch Sr., Amos Diggory, Cornelius Fudge, Cuthbert Mockridge, Arnold Peasegood, Percy, Mr. Weasley, and Gilbert Wimple all attend the final.

* **Stan Shunpike and several young wizards:** Harry, Hermione, and Ron overhear them lying about their occupations to try and impress a group of Veela (Ron slips under their spell momentarily and claims to have invented a broomstick that can fly to Jupiter!).

* **two little witches:** Ride toy broomsticks around the campsite.

* **Bill and Charlie Weasley:** Came back from abroad just to see the final.

* **Mr. and Mrs. Wood and Oliver:** Oliver introduces Harry to his parents.

Merchandise

* Bulgarian scarves with roaring lions
* flags that play the national anthems
* flying model Firebolts
* moving figurines of players
* Omnioculars
* pointed green hats with dancing shamrocks
* rosettes (green for Ireland, red for Bulgaria) that shout the players' names
* velvet-covered tasselled programmes

Betting

Bagman eagerly accepts bets on the outcome of the final from any and all takers.

* **Fred and George:** To their father's dismay, the twins bet thirty-seven Galleons, fifteen Sickles, and three Knuts (and a fake wand) that Ireland will win, but Krum will catch the Snitch.
* **Pontner, Roddy:** Bets Bulgaria will score first.
* **Timms, Agatha:** Bets half-shares in her eel farm that the match will go on for a week.
* **Mr. Weasley:** Bets a Galleon that Ireland will win.

Preliminary Matches

* **England v Transylvania:** A huge embarrassment for England, as Transylvania won three hundred and ninety to ten.
* **Scotland v Luxembourg:** Luxembourg won.
* **Wales v Uganda:** Uganda won.
* **Ireland v Peru (semi-final):** Ireland won.

Did you know ... the Quidditch World Cup standings partly echo the (Muggle) World Cup standings from 1994? Scotland, Wales, and England all failed to qualify for that tournament (a similarly huge embarrassment for England, as it was the first time in sixteen years they hadn't qualified), so many Britons chose to support Ireland instead.

Final: Ireland v Bulgaria

After a very close match, both teams enter the Top Box for the awarding of the golden Quidditch World Cup. They are individually introduced to the crowd and shake hands with the Ministers for Magic from both countries.

✶ Bagman commentates from the Top Box, where Fudge, Harry, Hermione, the Malfoys, Mr. Oblansk, Winky (who saves a seat for no-show Crouch), and the Weasleys watch the match.

✶ **Mostafa, Hassan:** Gold-robed referee. He is a small, skinny, and bald Egyptian wizard with a bushy moustache. During the match, Mostafa seems to have more trouble with the mascots than the players!

✶ **mediwizards:** Use potions, not to mention the odd swift kick in the shins, to revive people during the match.

Ireland (green robes)

The year before the tournament, the Irish side puts in an order for seven Firebolts.

PLAYERS

- ✶ **Connolly:** Male Beater
- ✶ **Lynch, Aidan:** Seeker
- ✶ **Moran:** Female Chaser
- ✶ **Mullet:** Female Chaser
- ✶ **Quigley:** Beater
- ✶ **Ryan, Barry:** Keeper
- ✶ **Troy:** Chaser

 Did you know . . . according to J. K. Rowling's official Web site, Moran, Troy, and Quigley are the surnames of three of her good friends? The real-life Troy is a big supporter of West Ham Football Club, and it is in her honour Dean Thomas is a supporter, too!

Mascot

leprechauns: Tiny bearded men who fly onto the pitch in a swarm of green and gold. The leprechauns form themselves into rainbows and shamrocks whenever Ireland scores, and take great delight in taunting the Veela.

In Irish folklore, leprechauns are crafty, mischievous male faeries who hide their treasure from humans. It is said the end of a rainbow reveals where a leprechaun's pot of gold is hidden. A leprechaun must lead a person to his treasure if he is captured; however, this is almost impossible to do. Even if a leprechaun is caught, he will vanish after tricking his captor into looking away for an instant.

Leprechaun gold: The leprechauns shower the spectators with these gold coins that vanish after a few hours, much to the dismay of the crowd, not to mention Fred, George, and Ron.

Bulgaria (scarlet robes)

 Did you know . . . J. K. Rowling chose Bulgaria to play in the Quidditch World Cup because she was inspired by the country's surprise fourth place finish in the 1994 (Muggle) World Cup?

PLAYERS

* **Dimitriov:** Chaser
* **Ivanova:** Chaser
* **Krum, Viktor:** Seeker
* **Levski:** Chaser
* **Volkov:** Beater
* **Vulchanov:** Beater
* **Zograf:** Keeper

Mascot

Veela: Beautiful, seemingly non-human women with long white-gold hair and skin that shines like the moon. The Veela glide onto the pitch and begin a frenzied dance that bewitches many of the wizards in the crowd, and are so distracting they are threatened with ejection. After the leprechauns taunt them, the Veela turn spiteful. They sprout scaly wings and their faces morph into long, sharp bird heads.

According to eastern European mythology, vila are warrior spirits who can evoke whirlwinds and storms. They appear as beautiful, long-haired women but can also shapeshift into a variety of animal forms, including falcons.

PROFESSIONAL QUIDDITCH TEAMS AND PLAYERS

Britain and Ireland

The British and Irish Quidditch League Headquarters is part of the Ministry's Department of Magical Games and Sports.

Ballycastle Bats: Mentioned in *Flying with the Cannons*. Ballycastle is a seaside town in County Antrim, Northern Ireland.

Chudley Cannons: Ron's bedroom at The Burrow is a shrine to the Cannons, who are ninth in the league during second year. The team colour is orange and their logo is two giant black Cs and a speeding cannonball. There is no place named Chudley in Britain; however, there is a town named Chudleigh in the county of Devon, in southwestern England.

    * **Jenkins, Joey:** Beater.

Kenmare Kestrels: Seamus Finnigan supports them. Kenmare is located in County Kerry, Ireland, and is Gaelic for "the head of the sea."

Pride of Portree: Portree is a town in the Isle of Skye, off northwestern Scotland.

Puddlemere United: Puddlemere is a made-up name (although there is a Puddletown and River Puddle in the county of Dorset, southwestern England). Oliver Wood is signed to their reserve team as Keeper after he leaves Hogwarts.

Tutshill Tornados: *The Quibbler* accuses the Tornados of using a variety of corrupt means to win the League. Cho has supported the team since she was six years old (though Ron seems to doubt this). Their logo is two gold Ts on a background of sky blue. Tutshill is located in the county of Gloucestershire, in southern England.

 Did you know . . . J. K. Rowling's family moved to the village of Tutshill when she was nine years old?

Wimbourne Wasps: The Wasps wear black-and-yellow striped robes with a logo of a giant wasp across the chest. Wimbourne is a town in the county of Dorset, in southwestern England. The Wasps won the league three years running when Ludo Bagman was their Beater.

International

International Association of Quidditch: Global governing body for Quidditch, like FIFA (Federation of International Football Associations) in Muggle football. The International Association of Quidditch oversees the Quidditch World Cup. Hassan Mostafa is the current chair.

★ **Zamojski, Ladislaw:** Best Chaser on the Polish national team.

DIAGON ALLEY

Located in the heart of London, this wizarding shopping district takes its name from the word "diagonally," suggesting the wizarding world exists at an angle to its Muggle counterpart. (Muggles can visit Diagon Alley — Hermione's parents go there with her to buy her school things.)

Diagon Alley is accessed through the walled courtyard at the back of the Leaky Cauldron pub. When wizards tap the third brick from the left above the dustbin with their wands, the bricks rearrange themselves and temporarily create an archway to a long, twisting cobbled street full of shops unique to the wizarding world.

Apothecary: Smells like a mixture of rotten eggs and cabbages. Bundles of feathers, strings of fangs, and snarled claws hang from the ceiling, while jars of herbs, dried roots, and bright powders line the walls. There are barrels full of slimy things (including dragon dung).

(unnamed) cauldron shop: Sells cauldrons that are brass, collapsible, copper, pewter, self-stirring, silver, and solid gold.

Eeylops Owl Emporium: Dimly lit shop (owls are nocturnal creatures) that sells Barn, Brown, Screech, Snowy, and Tawny owls, all with jewel-bright eyes. Hagrid purchased Hedwig here for Harry's eleventh birthday.

    ★ **Owl Treats:** Food substitute for hunting (Pig tends to choke on them).

Florean Fortescue's Ice-Cream Parlour: Harry spends a lot of time doing his homework and eating ice cream outside Florean Fortescue's the summer before third year.

✶ **Florean Fortescue:** Kindly wizard who helps Harry with his essay on medieval witch-burning and gives him free sundaes every half-hour.

Flourish and Blotts: The shelves of this large bookstore are stacked to the ceiling with leather-bound books as large as paving stones, silk-covered books the size of postage stamps, invisible books, biting books, books full of peculiar symbols, and books with nothing in them at all. "Flourish" can mean a sweeping, elaborate style of writing, while "Blotts" calls to mind ink blots.

Much to the delight of numerous middle-aged witches, including Mrs. Weasley, Lockhart does an autograph session at Flourish and Blotts when Harry, Hermione, and the Weasleys are getting their schoolbooks before second year (Mrs. Weasley is not so delighted, however, when a brawl breaks out during the signing).

Wizarding Books

Note to Muggles: *The following list of wizarding books does not include those mentioned in* Quidditch through the Ages *or* Fantastic Beasts and Where to Find Them. *Hogwarts library books are listed in their own section.*

Autobiographies

✶ *Magical Me* — Gilderoy Lockhart
✶ *Who Am I?*: Lockhart's second autobiography, shown only in the *Harry Potter and the Chamber of Secrets* film.

Comics

✶ *The Adventures of Martin Miggs, the Mad Muggle*: Ron's favourite comic.

Cookbooks / Household

* *Charm Your Own Cheese*
* *Enchantments in Baking*
* *Gilderoy Lockhart's Guide to Household Pests*
* *One Minute Feasts — It's Magic!*

Divination

* *Broken Balls: When Fortunes Turn Foul*
* *Death Omens: What to Do When You Know the Worst is Coming*
* *Predicting the Unpredictable: Insulate Yourself Against Shocks*

Defence Against the Dark Arts

* *Practical Defensive Magic and its Use Against the Dark Arts*
* *The Rise and Fall of the Dark Arts*

DA Books (found in the Room of Requirement)

* *A Compendium of Common Curses and their Counter-Actions*
* *The Dark Arts Outsmarted*
* *Jinxes for the Jinxed*
* *Self-Defensive Spellwork*

Genealogy

* *Nature's Nobility: A Wizarding Genealogy*

Herbology

* *Encyclopaedia of Toadstools*
* *Magical Mediterranean Water-Plants and Their Properties*

History

* *Great Wizarding Events of the Twentieth Century*
* *Modern Magical History*
* *Sites of Historical Sorcery*

Literature/Poetry

* *Sonnets of a Sorcerer*: The Ministry confiscates this book because it makes readers speak in limericks for the rest of their lives.

Medical

* *Common Magical Ailments and Afflictions*

Miscellaneous

* *An Appraisal of Magical Education in Europe*
* *The Invisible Book of Invisibility*: Two hundred copies were ordered by Flourish and Blotts, but never found.

Numerology

* *New Theory of Numerology*

Quidditch

* *Flying with the Cannons*
* *Handbook of Do-it-Yourself Broomcare*
* *Quidditch Teams of Britain and Ireland*
* *Quidditch through the Ages* — Kennilworthy Whisp

Spellbooks

* *Curses and Counter-Curses (Bewitch your Friends and Befuddle your Enemies with the Latest Revenges: Hair Toss, Jelly-Legs, Tongue-Tying, and much, much more)* — Professor Vindictus Viridian

Hogwarts Textbooks

First year

* *A Beginner's Guide to Transfiguration* — Emeric Switch
* *The Dark Forces: A Guide to Self-Protection* — Quentin Trimble
* *Fantastic Beasts and Where to Find Them* — Newt Scamander
* *A History of Magic* — Bathilda Bagshot
* *Magical Drafts and Potions* — Arsenius Jigger
* *Magical Theory* — Adalbert Waffling
* *One Thousand Magical Herbs and Fungi* — Phyllida Spore
* *The Standard Book of Spells, Grade 1* — Miranda Goshawk

Second year

* *A Beginner's Guide to Transfiguration* — Emeric Switch
* *Break with a Banshee* — Gilderoy Lockhart
* *Gadding with Ghouls* — Gilderoy Lockhart
* *Holidays with Hags* — Gilderoy Lockhart
* *The Standard Book of Spells, Grade 2* — Miranda Goshawk
* *Travels with Trolls* — Gilderoy Lockhart
* *Voyages with Vampires* — Gilderoy Lockhart
* *Wanderings with Werewolves* — Gilderoy Lockhart
* *Year with the Yeti* — Gilderoy Lockhart

Third year

* *A History of Magic* — Adalbert Waffling
* *Ancient Runes Made Easy*
* *Home Life and Social Habits of British Muggles*
* *Intermediate Transfiguration*
* *Numerology and Grammatica*
* *The Monster Book of Monsters*: Copies are kept in a cage in the shop window, where they viciously tear each other to shreds. The manager has to use gloves and a walking stick to pry the books apart, and they bite him whenever he tries to pick one up. At Hogwarts, Hagrid is dismayed to learn no one figured out that the way to "tame" the books is by stroking a finger down their spines.
* *The Standard Book of Spells, Grade 3* — Miranda Goshawk
* *Unfogging the Future* — Cassandra Vablatsky

 Note to Muggles: *In the American edition of* Harry Potter and the Prisoner of Azkaban, *Bathilda Bagshot is listed as the author of* A History of Magic.

Fourth year

* Rune Dictionary
* *The Standard Book of Spells, Grade 4* — Miranda Goshawk

Fifth year

* *Achievements in Charming*
* *Defensive Magical Theory* — Wilbert Slinkhard
* *Intermediate Transfiguration*
* *Magical Hieroglyphs and Logograms*
* *The Standard Book of Spells, Grade 5* — Miranda Goshawk
* *Dream Oracle* — Inigo Imago (distributed by Trelawney in class)

Sixth year

* *A Guide to Advanced Transfiguration* (Cedric uses this in fourth year, and he is two years ahead of Harry)

 Did you know . . . J. K. Rowling said if she were to have a job in the wizarding world, she would likely write spellbooks?

Gambol and Japes Wizarding Joke Shop: Sells a favourite product of the Weasley twins — Dr. Filibuster's Fabulous Wet-Start, No-Heat Fireworks. "Gambol" means to dance and skip about or frolic playfully, whilst "jape" is an old word meaning to mock, trick, or joke.

Gringotts: The wizards' bank is one of the most secure places to store gold and treasure in the wizarding world, as it is protected by many enchantments and spells. It is a towering, snowy-white stone building with burnished bronze front doors staffed by a uniformed goblin doorman. A second set of silver doors is engraved with a warning to thieves about the dangers of stealing from the vaults.

Inside Gringotts, there is a large marble hall with a long counter. About a hundred goblins sit on high stools behind it, writing in ledgers, weighing coins and jewels in scales, and examining precious stones through eyeglasses. The bank also exchanges wizarding money for Muggle currency, as Mr. Granger was able to do this in order to buy Hermione's school things. Lots of doors lead from the hall to other areas.

Employees

* **Delacour, Fleur:** Takes a job at Gringotts in fifth year to improve her English.

* **Griphook:** Goblin with a rather nasty grin who took Harry and Hagrid down to the vaults before Harry's first day at Hogwarts.

★ **Ragnok:** Bill tries to approach him about the Order, but Ragnok will have none of it — goblins are still upset with wizards in general following the incident with Bagman.

★ **Weasley, Bill:** Works for Gringotts in Egypt as a curse breaker and in London at a desk job.

★ **Vaults:** Regular vaults are opened using tiny golden keys given to the owners. High security vaults have no keyholes — instead, the doors melt away after being stroked. Only Gringotts goblins can do this; if anyone else tried, they would be sucked through the door and trapped inside. (The goblins only check to see if anyone is inside about once a decade.)

The vaults are located hundreds of miles underground. Little carts on tracks take people down to them through a maze of twisting narrow stone passages lit with flaming torches that slope downwards at a steep angle, almost like a subterranean rollercoaster. The carts pass an underground lake, ravines, and bursts of fire (possibly from the dragons who are rumoured to protect the high security vaults).

HARRY'S VAULT

Green smoke filters out of the vault when Griphook unlocks the door. The vault contains a small fortune — evidently James and Lily were fairly well-to-do. (In an AOL online chat in October 2000, J. K. Rowling said James inherited the money, but the source of the riches has yet to be explained. In an early draft of *Harry Potter and the Philosopher's Stone*, J. K. Rowling had the Stone initially appear in the Potters' vault at Gringotts. On her official Web site, the author explains this would have drastically changed the plot of the first book — did Lily and James steal the Stone from Flamel? Were they protecting it for the Order from Voldemort? — so she decided to abandon the story line.)

SIRIUS'S VAULT

Number seven hundred and eleven. Sirius bought a very expensive gift using the gold in his vault, suggesting he has retained some of his family's wealth.

THE WEASLEYS' VAULT

Before second year, it contained a small pile of Sickles and just one Galleon.

VAULT SEVEN HUNDRED AND THIRTEEN

Hagrid produces a letter from Dumbledore authorising him to remove a grubby little package wrapped in brown paper from this high security vault. Afterwards, there is an attempted robbery of the empty vault, but the would-be thief is not caught.

Did you know . . . although the *Harry Potter and the Philosopher's Stone* film states Harry's vault is number six hundred and eighty seven, it is never mentioned by number in the book?

Wizard currency: Comprised of three kinds of coins (and no notes — wizards probably charm their moneybags not to tear). The serial number around the edge of each coin refers to the goblin who cast it.

> ✴ **Galleons:** Gold coins allegedly the size of hubcaps.
> ✴ **Sickles:** Silver coins. There are seventeen Sickles to a Galleon.
> ✴ **Knuts:** Little bronze coins. There are twenty-nine Knuts to a Sickle.

Did you know . . . according to a survey released in May 2004, two out of five people in the UK think the Sickle is real currency?

WHAT THINGS COST IN THE WIZARDING WORLD

assortment of sweets on the Hogwarts Express: eleven Sickles, seven Knuts

bag of Knarl quills: six Sickles

beetle eyes: five Knuts a scoop

bottle of Butterbeer at the Hog's Head: two Sickles

Canary Creams: seven Sickles

dragon livers: seventeen Sickles an ounce

fine for bewitching a Muggle car: fifty Galleons

Harry's wand: seven Galleons

Headless Hats: two Galleons

Hermione's new quill: fifteen Sickles, two Knuts

Knight Bus fare: eleven (basic), thirteen (includes hot chocolate) or fifteen Sickles (includes hot-water bottle and toothbrush)

Omnioculars: ten Galleons

owl delivery of the *Daily Prophet*: five Knuts (but at Hogwarts, Hermione pays one Knut)

pint of Baruffio's Brain Elixir: twelve Galleons

S.P.E.W. membership: two Sickles

reward for information about the escaped Death Eaters: one thousand Galleons

reward for the capture of Sirius Black: ten thousand Galleons

unicorn horns: twenty-one Galleons

Venomous Tentacula seeds: ten Galleons

Weasleys' Wildfire Whiz-bangs: five Galleons (Basic Blaze box) or twenty Galleons (Deflagration Deluxe box)

(unnamed) junk shop: Sells broken wands, stained cloaks, and dodgy scales. Percy finds a book here called *Prefects who Gained Power*, about Hogwarts prefects and their later careers.

The Leaky Cauldron: Tiny, grubby pub and inn on Charing Cross Road, flanked by a book and record shops. Invisible to Muggles, the Leaky Cauldron is dark and shabby inside. A corridor leads from the bar to the private back parlour, which is sometimes used for dining. The small, weed-infested walled courtyard behind the Leaky Cauldron hides the entrance to Diagon Alley.

A narrow staircase leads to the Leaky Cauldron's guest rooms, where Harry stays in room eleven for a fortnight before third year begins. His room is cosy with oak furniture, a crackling fire, and a talking mirror. Other guests during Harry's time include dwarfs, warlocks, and possibly, a hag. Hermione and the Weasleys also stay at the Leaky Cauldron the night before the Hogwarts Express departs. The barman and innkeeper is named Tom. Stooping, bald, and toothless, he resembles a "gummy walnut." Tom is honoured to meet Harry.

Madam Malkin's Robes for All Occasions: Sells Hogwarts uniforms and dress robes. Madam Malkin is a smiling, squat witch dressed in mauve.

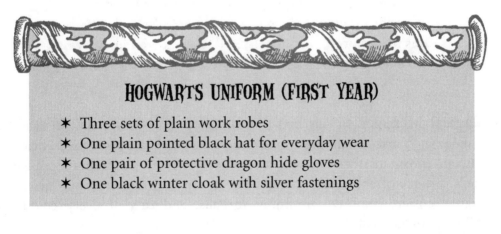

HOGWARTS UNIFORM (FIRST YEAR)

* Three sets of plain work robes
* One plain pointed black hat for everyday wear
* One pair of protective dragon hide gloves
* One black winter cloak with silver fastenings

* **dress robes:** Formal robes for parties and other occasions. The list of Hogwarts students' supplies for fourth year indicates that a set of dress robes is mandatory.

DRESS ROBES

Bagman: bright purple with yellow stars
Crabbe and Goyle: moss green
Fleur: silver-grey satin
Harry: bottle green (Mrs. Weasley chose them to match his eyes)
Hermione: floaty periwinkle-blue
Madame Maxime: lavender silk
Malfoy: black velvet with a high collar that makes him look like a vicar
McGonagall: red tartan
Padma: bright turquoise
Pansy: frilly pale pink
Parvati: shocking pink
Percy: navy-blue
Ron: Ron mistakes a set of second-hand maroon velvet robes for Ginny's dress, and refuses to wear them after Mrs. Weasley explains what they really are. He uses a Severing Charm to remove the mouldy-looking lace from the collar and cuffs, but it leaves them frayed. Fortunately, Ron receives brand new dress robes after fourth year!

Magical Menagerie: This noisy, smelly shop is crammed full of cages, baskets, and tanks containing a range of creatures: giant purple toads, black rats, an enormous tortoise with a jewel-covered shell, poisonous orange snails, ravens, a rabbit that changes into a top hat, double-ended newts, strange custard-coloured humming furballs, and cats of every colour, including Crookshanks.

✷ **Rat Tonic:** Ron buys this for Scabbers after bringing him into the Menagerie to try and find out why he has been so poorly, but it doesn't seem to work.

Obscurus Books: J. K. Rowling wrote *Fantastic Beasts and Where to Find Them* in 2001, as a fundraiser for UK-based charity Comic Relief. The book's publisher is listed as Obscurus Books, located at 18a Diagon Alley.

Ollivander's (**"Makers of Fine Wands since 382 BC"**): A bit on the shabby side, Ollivander's has peeling gold letters over the door and a single wand on a faded purple cushion in the window. It is tiny, dusty, and silent inside and feels like a very strict library, but instead of books thousands of narrow wand boxes are piled neatly up to the ceiling. Ollivander's seems to tingle with some secret magic, and the back of Harry's neck prickled when he entered. Mr. Ollivander is a soft-spoken elderly wizard with wide, pale, silvery eyes and long fingers. He has a slightly creepy air about him, and makes Harry feel somewhat uneasy. Mr. Ollivander knew who Harry was the moment he saw him, and can remember every wand he ever sold. He is called to Hogwarts in fourth year to oversee the Wand Weighing ceremony for the Triwizard Tournament.

✶ **wands:** Made from various woods with a powerful magical substance at the core. There are a few things to remember concerning wands: no two wands are alike, a wizard will never get proper results using another wizard's wand, and, most importantly, the wand chooses the wizard.

Harry tries out several wands before finding his, which emits a stream of red and gold sparks (Gryffindor colours!) when he tests it. Fawkes, whose tail feather is in Harry's wand, only gave one other feather, which was put in Voldemort's wand. Mr. Ollivander expects great things from Harry, as You Know Who did great — terrible, but great — things, too.

THE WAND CHOOSES THE WIZARD

Cedric: Twelve and a quarter inches, ash, and male unicorn hair, pleasantly springy. Ash is a wood of knowledge, purity, and truth (how very Hufflepuff!). Interestingly, it is sometimes called the unicorn tree (because unicorns are meant to be fond of ash), which ties in to Cedric's wand core. Unicorns are a symbol of purity and innocence — this is notable because the centaurs tell Hagrid "always the innocent are the first victims," shortly before a dead unicorn is discovered. Ash wood is also supposed to repel serpents and to protect against their bite.

Fleur: Nine and a half inches, rosewood, and Veela hair (Mr. Ollivander thinks Veela hair makes for temperamental wands — this is interesting as Fleur is part Veela and part temperamental herself), inflexible. How fitting someone named Fleur would have a wand made out of rosewood! Rosewood represents beauty and is known for its power concerning love and matters of the heart.

Hagrid: Sixteen inches, oak, rather bendy (snapped in half when he was expelled from Hogwarts). The oak's energy is masculine in nature — mighty, strong, enduring, and steadfast.

Harry: Eleven inches, holly, and phoenix feather, supple. The properties of holly assure precision, so it was often used in the making of weapons. Because of this, holly is associated with combat, protection, and warding off evil spirits (sounds perfect for Harry!). Holly is also an evergreen, which symbolises endurance. It has a long-standing association with death and rebirth in both Pagan and Christian lore, and is a symbol of Christmas, which represents the birth of the Saviour in Christianity.

James: Eleven inches, mahogany, pliable, excellent for transfiguration. Mahogany is an exceptional protective wood, revered for its strength and durability. (How fitting James's wand was notable for transformations!)

Lily: Ten and a quarter inches, willow, swishy, good for charm work. The willow has long been associated with death and is a symbol of mourning and unlucky love; however, it also represents flexibility and wisdom. Willow wands are used to connect with intuition, dreams, visions, and deep emotions. It is likely no accident Lily's wand is suitable for charm work, given the protective charm she placed on Harry.

Neville: Uses his father's old wand, which is snapped in half at the Department of Mysteries.

Ron: (OLD) Ron inherits Charlie's old, chipped wand, which has a unicorn hair poking out the end. He holds the wand together with Spellotape after nearly breaking it in two, but it malfunctions dreadfully after this, backfiring spells, making strange noises, and emitting objects out the wrong end.

(NEW — THIRD YEAR) Fourteen inches, willow, and unicorn hair. Uh-oh! Given what we know about willow properties and unicorn hair cores (both of Ron's wands have featured them), could this spell trouble for Ron in the future?

Umbridge: Unusually short wand which is snapped in half by a centaur.

Viktor: Ten and a quarter inches, hornbeam, and dragon heartstring, quite rigid. Viktor's wand is made by Gregorovitch and is thicker than most wands. Common to eastern Europe, Hornbeam is also known by the name musclewood. It is associated with toughness and durability.

Voldemort: Thirteen and a half inches, yew, and phoenix feather, very powerful. Yew trees have long been associated with magic and death. However, the yew also represents reincarnation — as the outer tree dies, a new tree grows inside. Celtic priests and priestesses regarded the yew as a symbol of immortality.

Did you know . . . J. K. Rowling said her wand would be mahogany with a phoenix feather core?

Quality Quidditch Supplies: Sells broomsticks as well as robes of professional teams (Ron gazes longingly at the Chudley Cannons uniform hanging in the shop window).

BROOMSTICKS

Only Dark magic can tamper with a broomstick.

Bluebottle: Safe, reliable family broom featuring a built-in Anti-Burglar Buzzer.

Cleansweep Five: Fred and George ride these in second year.

Cleansweep Six: Used by a wizard to fly to the moon, according to *The Quibbler*.

Cleansweep Seven: The Ravenclaw Quidditch team rides these in third year.

Cleansweep Eleven: Ron receives a new one as a gift from his parents in fifth year. It has a Spanish oak handle with built-in vibration control and anti-jinx varnish.

Comet Two Sixty: Malfoy has one at home in first year, while Cho rides one in third year. Tonks rides a Comet Two Sixty as well.

Comet Two Ninety: According to *Which Broomstick?* it can go from zero to sixty miles per hour in ten seconds.

Firebolt: This international standard racing broom (the broom of choice at the Quidditch World Cup) features a streamlined handle made of ash treated with a diamond-hard polish, and a tail of individually selected birch twigs. Aerodynamically crafted, a Firebolt can go from zero to one hundred and fifty miles per hour in ten seconds and includes an unbreakable braking charm. Firebolts are so expensive, their price is only available on request.

Nimbus Two Thousand: Sleek and shiny, with a long tail of neat, straight twigs, and a mahogany handle with the name written in gold near the top. Harry's first broom is a Nimbus Two Thousand, and even after it has seen better days, he cannot bear to throw it out.

Nimbus Two Thousand and One: Lucius Malfoy makes a gift of seven of these to the Slytherin Quidditch team in second year — the same year Malfoy not-so-coincidentally becomes their Seeker.

Shooting Star: Ron's old broom at The Burrow. Harry rides one for a little while in second year.

Silver Arrows: Madam Hooch learned to ride on these brooms, which have been discontinued.

★ **Broomstick Servicing Kit:** Black leather case containing a small brass compass, a pair of silver Tail-Twig Clippers, a large jar of Fleetwood's High-Finish Handle Polish, and the *Handbook of Do-it-Yourself Broomcare.*

second-hand robe shop: Mrs. Weasley buys Ginny's Hogwarts robes and Ron's dress robes here.

Weasleys' Wizard Wheezes: Fred and George's joke shop, located at number ninety three, Diagon Alley.

Opening the shop was the realisation of a long-time dream for the twins. Weasleys' Wizard Wheezes begins the summer before fourth year, when Fred and George create price lists and order forms for their joke items and trick sweets, which they plan to sell at Hogwarts. Mrs. Weasley is furious when she discovers what they are up to and forbids them to continue (but of course, they do anyway).

Weasleys' Wizard Wheezes suffers another setback when Fred and George learn the hard way that all that glitters is not gold. They later receive a gift from an unexpected source and consider not returning to Hogwarts for their final year, but decide it would be a perfect opportunity to conduct "market research" and test their products. The twins spend the year experimenting with ingredients of a dubious nature obtained through questionable means, and testing their new products on themselves and an assortment of unsuspecting volunteers.

Fred and George finally open their shop after leaving Hogwarts, and offer special discounts to students who promise to use their products to get rid of Umbridge.

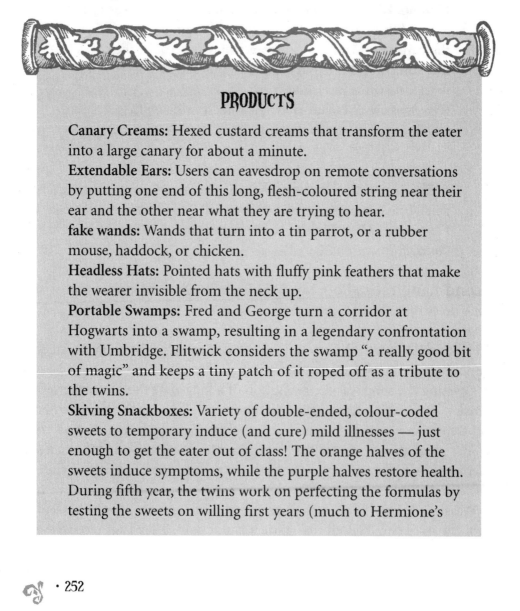

PRODUCTS

Canary Creams: Hexed custard creams that transform the eater into a large canary for about a minute.

Extendable Ears: Users can eavesdrop on remote conversations by putting one end of this long, flesh-coloured string near their ear and the other near what they are trying to hear.

fake wands: Wands that turn into a tin parrot, or a rubber mouse, haddock, or chicken.

Headless Hats: Pointed hats with fluffy pink feathers that make the wearer invisible from the neck up.

Portable Swamps: Fred and George turn a corridor at Hogwarts into a swamp, resulting in a legendary confrontation with Umbridge. Flitwick considers the swamp "a really good bit of magic" and keeps a tiny patch of it roped off as a tribute to the twins.

Skiving Snackboxes: Variety of double-ended, colour-coded sweets to temporary induce (and cure) mild illnesses — just enough to get the eater out of class! The orange halves of the sweets induce symptoms, while the purple halves restore health. During fifth year, the twins work on perfecting the formulas by testing the sweets on willing first years (much to Hermione's exasperation, who threatens to tell their mother). The sweets include Blood Blisterpods, Fainting Fancies, Fever Fudge, Nosebleed Nougat, and Puking Pastilles.

Ton-Tongue Toffee: Innocent-looking sweets that contain an Engorgement Charm to make the eater's tongue swell up to four feet in length.

Weasleys' Wildfire Whiz-bangs: These enchanted, noisy fireworks explode into huge multi-coloured bats, Catherine wheels, flying piglets, rockets, fire-exhaling dragons, and sparklers that create naughty words in midair. Instead of fading away, the fireworks burn brighter as time goes on and multiply by tenfold if someone attempts to Vanish them. Sold in Basic Blaze and Deflagration Deluxe boxes, the fireworks are a huge hit when the twins set them off inside Hogwarts.

Whizz Hard Books: J. K. Rowling wrote *Quidditch through the Ages* in 2001, as a fundraiser for UK-based charity Comic Relief. The book's publisher is listed as Whizz Hard Books, located at 129b Diagon Alley.

KNOCKTURN ALLEY

This dark, dingy, narrow alleyway next to Diagon Alley specialises in Dark Arts shops that sell shrunken heads, giant spiders, poisonous candles, whole fingernails, and Flesh-Eating Slug Repellent, amongst other things. Knockturn Alley is a play on the word "nocturnally," meaning "dark" or "at night."

Borgin and Burkes: The largest shop in Knockturn Alley is full of sinister-looking and illegal wares. It is dimly lit with a stone fireplace. Harry winds up in the shop by accident just before second year. He hides in a wardrobe to escape detection from Malfoy and his father, who is there to do business. The store's owner is Mr. Borgin, a stooped wizard who wears a pince-nez, has oily hair, and a voice to match. Mr. Borgin almost grovels to Lucius Malfoy, and shares his opinion that pure-bloods are superior; however, once Lucius leaves, his admiration turns to contempt.

The name Borgin could be derived from the Borgias — a notorious Renaissance-era Italian crime family whose evildoings spanned several generations. Burke is possibly a reference to William Burke, a nineteenth century murderer and grave-robber in Scotland.

ITEMS SOLD AT BORGIN AND BURKES

* Blood-stained playing cards
* **Cursed opal necklace:** Responsible for the deaths of nineteen Muggle owners. Opals were actually considered lucky for many

centuries. In Roman times, they were good-luck talismans because their colours looked like a rainbow. The modern myth that opals are unlucky can be traced back to one of Sir Arthur Conan Doyle's Sherlock Holmes stories.

* **Glass eye**
* **Hand of Glory:** If a candle is inserted into this withered hand, it will shed light only on the person holding it. Folklore says the Hand of Glory is the severed hand of a hanged man, magically prepared to hold a candle that will put others into a deep sleep for as long as the candle burns. Because of this, it is said to be a useful tool for thieves.
* **Hangman's rope**
* **Human bones and skulls**
* **Masks**
* **Rusty spiked instruments**

HOGSMEADE

The only all-wizard settlement in Britain, the village of Hogsmeade has a lot of interesting shops where strange magical beings can occasionally be found. In winter, it looks like a scene from a Christmas card, featuring snow-covered thatched cottages with wreaths on the doors and trees covered in enchanted candles.

Hogsmeade is located at the foot of a mountain, and is surrounded by wild countryside and winding lanes. The road to Hogsmeade is to the left on the way out of Hogwarts, and curves around the Hogwarts lake.

Hogsmeade Visits

Hogwarts students in third year and up are allowed to visit Hogsmeade on scheduled weekends throughout the year, with consent from their parents or guardians. Filch checks the names of students departing for the village against a list at the front doors of the castle. Harry's arrangement with Uncle Vernon to sign his permission form falls through, so he attempts to get permission from other sources. He takes matters into his own hands for a while, but things work out in the end.

Third year

* **Hallowe'en:** Hermione and Ron bring back loads of sweets for Harry.
* **Last weekend before Christmas holidays:** Some of the Hogwarts teachers and Fudge are overheard discussing Sirius in the Three Broomsticks.

* **February:** Malfoy and his cronies don't know what hit them (at first) when an invisible force hurls mud at them outside the Shrieking Shack.
* **After end-of-year exams:** The trio decide not to go, as they are too exhausted from the events of the previous evening.

Fourth year

* **Saturday before the first task:** Hermione and Harry visit the village but Harry wears his Invisibility Cloak to avoid everyone, including Ron.
* **Saturday in January:** The trio go together, while Parvati arranges to meet up with a Beauxbatons boy she met at the Yule Ball.
* **Two weekends after the second task:** The trio meet up with their favourite black dog, who takes them to a mountain cave on the outskirts of town.

Fifth year

* **First weekend in October:** Students who are interested in Harry teaching them Defence Against the Dark Arts meet at the Hog's Head.
* **Valentine's Day:** Harry goes on a date but winds up at the Three Broomsticks with Hermione and a couple of unexpected guests.
* Umbridge bans Harry from Hogsmeade after his interview runs in *The Quibbler*.

Dervish and Banges: Located at the end of the road out of Hogsmeade, Dervish and Banges sells magical instruments and equipment, including Sneakoscopes. "Dervish" is commonly associated with "whirling dervish" (an order of Muslim ascetics who used to perform frenzied dances as a sign of their devotion), while "Banges" brings to mind explosions, so the items sold inside are likely full of energy, motion, and noise.

Gladrags Wizardwear: Clothing shop that advertises at the Quidditch World Cup, with other branches in London and Paris. The trio buy Dobby the tackiest socks they can find from Gladrags as a thank-you gift in fourth year.

The Hog's Head: Dodgy pub and inn located on a side street, with a tattered wooden sign bearing a picture of a severed, bleeding boar's head. The Hog's Head is small and grubby and smells of goats. It has grime-covered bay windows that don't let in daylight, rough wooden tables, and a stone floor so dirty, it looks as if it is covered with earth. Butterbeer is served in dirty, dusty bottles with rusty tops (though Ron reckons he could have probably ordered Firewhisky without a problem), and students are recommended to bring their own glasses!

The Hog's Head has been around for centuries — it was the headquarters of the 1612 goblin rebellion. A lot of "funny folk" can be found in the Hog's Head according to Hagrid, who won a dragon's egg there from a cloaked stranger in first year. Students do not generally frequent the pub (although there is nothing in the school rules to prevent them from doing so), which is why Hermione chooses it as the location for the first DA meeting. However, many patrons at the Hog's Head disguise themselves, and conversations are never private . . .

Dumbledore first met Trelawney at the Hog's Head when he interviewed her for the Divination post, before Harry was born.

 Did you know . . . a "hogshead" is an old imperial measurement equalling two liquid barrels, or 14,653 cubic inches?

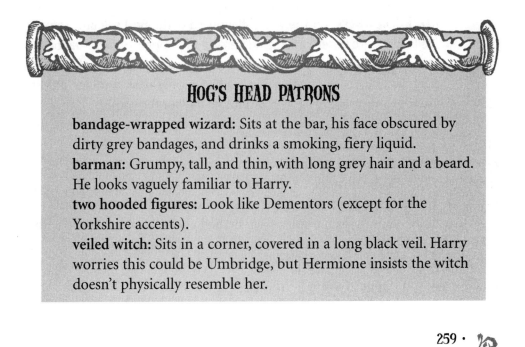

HOG'S HEAD PATRONS

bandage-wrapped wizard: Sits at the bar, his face obscured by dirty grey bandages, and drinks a smoking, fiery liquid.
barman: Grumpy, tall, and thin, with long grey hair and a beard. He looks vaguely familiar to Harry.
two hooded figures: Look like Dementors (except for the Yorkshire accents).
veiled witch: Sits in a corner, covered in a long black veil. Harry worries this could be Umbridge, but Hermione insists the witch doesn't physically resemble her.

Hogsmeade station: Where the Hogwarts Express terminates. The station is adjacent to the Hogwarts lake and a road leading to the castle. Students either travel by boat (first years) or carriages (upper years) from the station to Hogwarts.

Honeydukes: A favourite stop of Hogwarts' students, Honeydukes features barrels and shelves crammed with all manner of sweets, both Muggle (coconut ice, nougat, toffee, and many different kinds of chocolate) and magical (including "Unusual Tastes" and "Special Effects" varieties). A secret passage leads from Hogwarts to the Honeydukes' cellar. The married owners live upstairs from the shop.

Magical Sweets

✶ **Acid Pops:** Ron burnt a hole through his tongue with one when he was seven.
✶ **Bertie Bott's Every Flavour Beans ("a Risk with Every Mouthful!"):** Flavours include baked bean, bogey, chocolate, coconut, coffee, curry, earwax, grass, liver, marmalade, pepper, peppermint, sardine, spinach, sprouts, strawberry, toast, toffee, tripe, and vomit.

Did you know . . . the vomit-flavoured Bertie Bott's Beans, sold by Jelly Belly, are based on a failed version of pepperoni pizza-flavoured beans? Allegedly, the pizza-flavoured beans tasted so vile Jelly Belly decided not to produce them — but it only took a minor adjustment to turn the taste into a suitable flavour for vomit!

✶ blood-flavoured lollipops
✶ Cockroach Clusters
✶ **Chocoballs:** filled with strawberry mousse and clotted cream.
✶ **Chocolate Frogs:** popular frog-shaped chocolates that come with collectible trading cards featuring famous witches and wizards.
✶ **Droobles Best Blowing Gum:** Creates bluebell-coloured bubbles that don't pop for days.

- ✳ exploding bonbons
- ✳ **Fizzing Whizzbees:** Sherbert balls that make the eater levitate.
- ✳ **Fudge Flies:** Favourite of Scabbers
- ✳ **Ice Mice:** Make the eater's teeth squeak and chatter.
- ✳ **Jelly Slugs**
- ✳ **Liquorice Wands**
- ✳ **Pepper Imps:** tiny black sweets that cause the eater to breathe fire and smoke from the mouth.
- ✳ **Sugar Quills:** Students eat these in class while pretending to concentrate.
- ✳ **sugar mice:** Flitwick gives Harry a box after his interview runs in *The Quibbler*.
- ✳ **Peppermint Toads:** Toad-shaped peppermint creams that hop about in the eater's stomach.
- ✳ **Toothflossing Stringmints:** Hermione buys these "splintery" mints for her dentist parents.

✳ **Chocolate Frog cards/Famous Witches and Wizards cards:** Popular amongst Hogwarts students — Ernie, Ginny, Hannah, Harry, Neville, and Ron (who has about 500, but is missing Agrippa and Ptolemy) are all collectors — with requests for trades even appearing on the Gryffindor common room noticeboard.

KNOWN TRADING CARDS

Agrippa: Sixteenth century German alchemist, astrologer and magician

Circe: (pronounced "Sur-see") Legendary Greek witch who could transform men into animals

Cliodna: (pronounced "Cleev-na") Celtic fairy queen, druidess, and goddess of beauty

Dumbledore, Albus: Current Headmaster of Hogwarts (When the Ministry stripped Dumbledore of his various positions and honours, he said he didn't care as long as he was able to keep his Chocolate Frog card.)

Hengist of Woodcroft: British Saxon King (and possible wizard?) circa 450 AD

Grunnion, Alberic: Mythical wizard

Merlin: Considered to be the greatest wizard ever (until Dumbledore!), Merlin was a prophet and advisor, and a central figure in the legend of King Arthur.

Morgana: Priestess and witch who was a key figure in the legend of King Arthur

Paracelsus: Sixteenth century alchemist and physician

Ptolemy: (pronounced "Tole-em-ee") Second century Greek astronomer, cartographer, and mathematician

Note to Muggles: *The* Harry Potter and the Philosopher's Stone *video game (available in Game Boy, Windows, and Macintosh editions) lists over one hundred Famous Witches and Wizard cards, including Harry himself. A trading card game, trading cards of the films, and real Chocolate Frogs with collectible Famous Witches and Wizards cards are also available.*

Madam Puddifoot's: Cramped teashop decorated with lots of bows and frills. On Valentine's Day, golden cherubs throw pink confetti over couples sitting at the teashop's small round tables. Madam Puddifoot is a very stout witch who wears her black hair in a bun.

Owl Post Office: Contains between two and three hundred owls, colour-coded for speed of delivery. (It seems wizards are aware of Muggle post, but don't quite know how to use it — Mrs. Weasley isn't sure how much postage is needed when she writes a letter to the Dursleys, so she covers every square inch of the envelope with stamps!)

✶ **Great Greys:** Large owls used for long distance or heavy postal deliveries.

✶ **Howler:** Marked by a tell-tale red envelope, this angry letter shouts its contents at the recipient in a greatly magnified voice, then bursts into flames and ashes. Howlers explode if not opened immediately.

HOWLERS

Ron: Received one from his mother after the incident with the Ford Anglia.

Neville: Received one from his Gran after he was blamed for a breach of security in Gryffindor Tower.

Percy: Receives multiple Howlers at the Ministry from people putting in claims for damaged property due to the events at the Quidditch World Cup.

Hermione: Receives several Howlers after *Witch Weekly* publishes an unflattering article about her.

Aunt Petunia: Receives a mysterious Howler the summer before fifth year which says *"Remember my last, Petunia."*

✶ **owl-order:** Similar to Muggle mail order. In third year, Harry receives a couple of presents ordered this way because the senders were unable to purchase the gifts in person.

✶ **Scops owls:** So small, they can only manage local postal deliveries.

✶ **Tropical birds:** In warmer climates, brightly coloured birds deliver the post in place of owls.

Scrivenshaft's Quill Shop: Contains a display of pheasant feather quills in the window and other kinds in copper pots inside. "Scrive" is likely a derivative of "scribe," meaning "to write," while "shaft" refers to the shaft of a feather or quill.

Shrieking Shack: Located on a hill on the outskirts of town, the Shrieking Shack has overgrown gardens and boarded-up windows — all the entrances are sealed shut. It is believed to be the most haunted building in Britain (according to Nearly Headless Nick, a very rough crowd lives there), however, the monthly howling once heard from within has long since ceased, and the house has been quiet for many years.

The Shrieking Shack is accessed through a secret passageway underneath the Whomping Willow. The passageway leads to a dusty, run-down room on the ground floor with peeling wallpaper, a stained floor, and broken furniture. Upstairs there is a bedroom with a four-poster bed.

Three Broomsticks: Warm, clean, and popular pub. It has a large bar and very diverse patrons (Hermione thinks she saw an ogre there once). The landlady of the Three Broomsticks is Madam Rosmerta. She is pretty and curvaceous (Ron seems to have a bit of a crush on her) and wears spangly turquoise high heels. Madam Rosmerta has been at the Three Broomsticks for quite some time (at least since James, Sirius, and Lupin were students) and is on a friendly basis with everyone who passes through its doors, from magical beings to Cornelius Fudge.

Rosmerta's name comes from Celtic and Gaul (French) mythology, where she is a goddess of fertility, wealth, fire, warmth, and abundance.

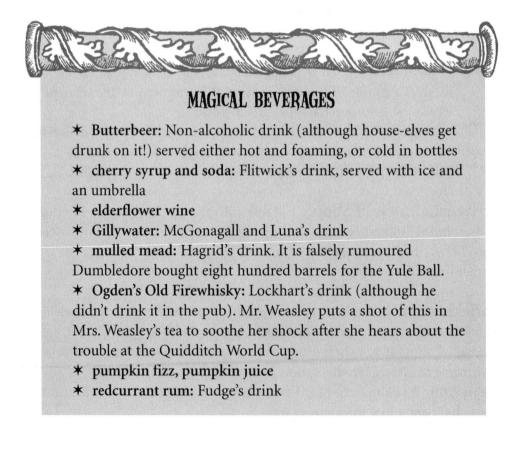

MAGICAL BEVERAGES

* **Butterbeer:** Non-alcoholic drink (although house-elves get drunk on it!) served either hot and foaming, or cold in bottles
* **cherry syrup and soda:** Flitwick's drink, served with ice and an umbrella
* **elderflower wine**
* **Gillywater:** McGonagall and Luna's drink
* **mulled mead:** Hagrid's drink. It is falsely rumoured Dumbledore bought eight hundred barrels for the Yule Ball.
* **Ogden's Old Firewhisky:** Lockhart's drink (although he didn't drink it in the pub). Mr. Weasley puts a shot of this in Mrs. Weasley's tea to soothe her shock after she hears about the trouble at the Quidditch World Cup.
* **pumpkin fizz, pumpkin juice**
* **redcurrant rum:** Fudge's drink

Zonko's Wizarding Joke Shop: Full of joke and trick items, it is a favourite of and inspiration to Fred and George Weasley.

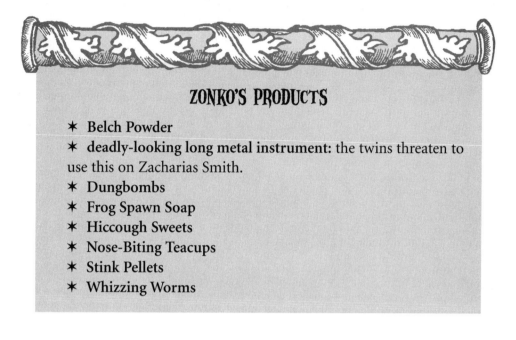

ZONKO'S PRODUCTS

* Belch Powder
* **deadly-looking long metal instrument:** the twins threaten to use this on Zacharias Smith.
* Dungbombs
* Frog Spawn Soap
* Hiccough Sweets
* Nose-Biting Teacups
* Stink Pellets
* Whizzing Worms

ST. MUNGO'S HOSPITAL FOR MAGICAL MALADIES AND INJURIES

Injured in a Quidditch mishap? Bitten by a fanged Geranium? Victim of a Bat Bogey Hex gone awry? Look no further than St. Mungo's to provide the magical cure for most wizarding ailments.

welcomewitch: Irritable plump blonde witch who handles enquiries in the reception area.

Purge & Dowse Ltd.: St. Mungo's is located behind the façade of this permanently-closed-for-refurbishment department store in Muggle London (Diagon Alley wasn't big enough, and it was deemed unhealthy for the hospital to be underground, like the Ministry). The large, red-brick storefront features a glassed-in window display of shabby mannequins wearing outdated fashions. Wizards announce themselves to the mannequins and step through the glass into St. Mungo's reception area.

The bustling reception area contains a number of rickety chairs, where patients wait to be seen, numerous safety posters and notices, and a portrait of Dilys Derwent, a legendary Healer. Portraits of other famous Healers line the corridors, which are lit by candle-filled crystal bubbles that float on the ceilings.

Did you know . . . there really was a St. Mungo? The patron saint of Glasgow, Scotland, he died in 603 AD and is buried in the lower church of Glasgow Cathedral.

Ground floor — Artefact Accidents

Treats accidents involving backfiring wands, broom crashes, and cauldron explosions.

First floor — Creature-Induced Injuries

Treats bites, burns, stings, and embedded spines.

> ✴ **"Dangerous" Dai Llewellyn Ward:** This small, drab ward for serious bite victims has panelled oak walls and one narrow, high window.

 **Note to Muggles:** *While in North America "ground floor" and "first floor" are interchangeable, in Britain they mean two different things. The ground floor is the main floor of a building, while the first floor is the first upper-level floor (the equivalent of the North American second floor).*

Second floor — Magical Bugs

Treats contagious maladies like dragon pox, scrofungulus, and vanishing sickness.

Third floor — Potion and Plant Poisonings

Treats rashes, regurgitation, and uncontrollable giggling.

Fourth floor — Spell Damage

Treats hexes, incorrectly applied charms, and unliftable jinxes.

* **Janus Thickey Ward (Ward 49):** Closed long-term residents' ward for victims of permanent spell damage. Janus was the Roman god of beginnings and endings, and was depicted with a double-faced head showing each face looking in the opposite direction (which was considered to represent a split personality).

Fifth floor — Hospital Shop and Visitors' Tearoom

Patients

* **Agnes:** Has a fur-covered face and barks like a dog.
* **Broderick Bode:** Injured in a workplace accident that seemingly affected his brain, his stay at St. Mungo's turns out to be much more grave than first anticipated.
* **little witch** who sprouts wings
* **Gilderoy Lockhart:** Victim of a misfired Memory Charm, although he has regained some sense of self (he certainly remembers how to sign autographs!).
* **Frank and Alice Longbottom:** Suffer from mental illness and loss of memory.
* **McGonagall:** Transferred to St. Mungo's after being hit with four Stunning Spells.
* **Tonks:** Injured at the Department of Mysteries.
* **two Muggles who lost fingers after buying biting doorknobs:** Undergo bone re-growth and Memory Charms.
* **warlock** whose head clangs like a bell
* **Arthur Weasley:** Bitten by a snake, his wound will not stop bleeding.
* **witch** who refuses to say what bit her leg
* **witch** with a satsuma stuck up her nose
* **wizard** whose shoes eat his feet
* **wizard** who was bitten by a werewolf
* **whistling witch** whose mouth blows out steam

Healers

Wizard physicians who wear lime-green robes with an emblem of a crossed bone and wand.

* **Dilys Derwent:** Healer from 1722 to 1741.

* **Augustus Pye:** Trainee Healer on Mr. Weasley's ward who is interested in Muggle treatments.

* **Hippocrates Smethwyck:** Healer-In-Charge on Mr. Weasley's ward. Hippocrates was a Greek physician born in the fourth century BC who was believed to have descended from the god Apollo. He is the originator of the Hippocratic Oath, which new physicians still take today when they enter medical practice. It pledges to uphold certain morals and principles when practising medicine.

* **Miriam Strout:** Maternal, with a fondness for Lockhart. She is suspended with full pay following an incident on the Janus Thickey Ward, where she works.

THE MINISTRY OF MAGIC

The Ministry's two main functions are to govern the wizarding world and to keep all knowledge of this world from Muggles (except for the Prime Minister). A typical government institution, the Ministry employs hundreds of people in dozens of different organisations.

During Voldemort's reign, the Ministry was in disarray. It tried to exert control over a world where no one knew who was good and who was evil, or who was being controlled and who was thinking for him or herself. Disappearances, tortures, and deaths occurred daily in both the wizarding and Muggle worlds, and it became increasingly difficult to calm the panic and terror.

Since Voldemort's disappearance, things have improved tremendously, and the world the Ministry governs has returned to a peaceful status quo — which the current Minister is determined to maintain at all costs.

The Ministry's visitor's entrance is on a grotty-looking street in the heart of London. Visitors enter a vandalised Muggle telephone box and dial 6-2-4-4-2. After the visitors state their names and business to the female Ministry operator who greets them, they are issued square silver identity badges which shoot out of the phone's coin-return chute. The telephone box then sinks underground like an elevator and a golden beam of light announces its arrival in the Ministry's Atrium about a minute later.

 Did you know . . . on a telephone keypad, 6-2-4-4-2 spells "magic"?

Minister for Magic: The magical equivalent of the Muggle Prime Minister, the Minister for Magic is the head of the Ministry.

✶ **Bagnold, Millicent:** Minister for Magic before Fudge (retired).

✶ **Fudge, Cornelius Oswald:** Current Minister for Magic. In fifth year, *The Quibbler* reveals he was elected five years ago. Fudge is a portly, short man with rumpled grey hair and an anxious, round face. He wears odd, mismatched clothes and can often be seen in a wizarding version of a typical Muggle businessman's outfit — a pinstriped suit and scarlet tie, but with pointed purple boots and a lime-green bowler.

To "fudge" something means to make a mess of it, and true to his name, Fudge is inept and tends to bungle things up. When he first came to power, Fudge relied on Dumbledore heavily for assistance, but he has since become preoccupied with the power of his position and refuses to heed the advice of his former mentor. Harry has always thought of Fudge as kindly, if a little pompous and blustery, but sees his true colours during fifth year.

FUDGE-UPS

✶ Knowingly sends an innocent man to Azkaban as a "precaution" in second year.
✶ Stations Dementors around Hogwarts that disrupt and endanger lives at the castle.
✶ Dismisses Harry and Hermione's story about Sirius in third year.
✶ Believes Madame Maxime would attack someone on account of her heritage.
✶ Does not find anything unusual about Bertha Jorkins's extended absence from work.
✶ Brings a Dementor along for protection when questioning a suspect, but is unable to confirm the suspect's story or use his testimony after the Dementor Kisses him. Instead, Fudge dismisses the suspect's confession as lunacy.

* Refuses to remove the Dementors from Azkaban, even though he is warned they could join Voldemort's side. After a security breach at the prison, Fudge refuses to admit he was wrong and publicly places the blame on a scapegoat.
* Refuses to make peace with the giants, paving the way for them to flock to Voldemort's side.

 Did you know . . . during an online chat for World Book Day in March 2004, J. K. Rowling hinted Fudge's stint as Minister will come to an end in *Harry Potter and the Half Blood Prince*?

* **Umbridge, Dolores:** Senior Undersecretary to the Minister. She sits on the Interrogation panel for disciplinary hearings. Umbridge hates part-humans — she drafts anti-werewolf legislation and lobbies to have all Merpeople tagged. Officially, Umbridge is appointed to the position of Hogwarts High Inquisitor so she can oversee educational reforms at Hogwarts. She has the power to investigate the staff and pupils, and the authority to instate new rules and regulations as she deems fit.

Committees, Departments, and Offices of the Ministry

To help visualise the layout of the Ministry, picture a multi-storey office building completely buried underground. Courtroom Ten and the Department of Mysteries would be in the sub-basement and basement of the building, the Atrium would be the building's "ground floor" and all the other Departments would be located above.

> * **inter-departmental memos:** Violet-coloured paper aeroplanes with "Ministry of Magic" embossed along the wings, that fly between departments via the lifts. (Owls used to provide this service, but were too messy!)

⋆ **Magical Maintenance:** As the Ministry is underground, Magical Maintenance chooses what kind of weather will appear outside the office windows.

Courtroom Ten/Council of Magical Law Courtroom

The lift in the Atrium doesn't even go down as far as this courtroom — it is in the very basement of the building, and is accessed by walking down a flight of stairs from the corridor leading to the Department of Mysteries.

The courtroom hasn't been used in years, but saw a fair amount of activity during the Death Eater trials following the end of Voldemort's reign. It is a large, square dungeon with a high, stone ceiling and no windows. Lit only by torches, it has a bleak, ominous air. There are rising benches for approximately two hundred spectators around the perimeter. Dementors usually lead the accused in and chain him or her to a chair in the centre of the room.

Level Nine – Department of Mysteries

Top-secret department located behind a black door at the end of a plain corridor with no windows or doors. No one knows exactly what takes place in the Department of Mysteries (although Luna insists it is where poisons are made that Fudge secretly administers to his enemies).

black circular room: The door at the end of the corridor leads to a circular room that is completely black, with a marble floor. The walls contain branches of blue-flamed candles and about a dozen identical handleless doors. The walls rotate quickly for a few seconds when all the doors are closed, disorienting occupants so they cannot tell which door is the exit.

Brain Room: One of the doors in the circular room leads to a long rectangular room with more doors around the walls, a few desks and a gigantic tank. The tank is filled with a noxious dark green potion in which numerous pearly-white, cauliflower-like brains drift along. The brains shoot out long ribbons of moving images, like "tentacles of thought," that wrap themselves around people in a suffocating grip.

Death Chamber: Another door in the circular room leads to a large rectangular stone amphitheatre. Benches around the room descend to a twenty-foot deep pit in the centre. A crumbling stone archway hung with a tattered black veil sits on a raised dais in the pit. The veil flutters slightly, as if in a breeze, and whispered voices can be heard from within, but there is nothing visible on the other side. Certain people seem to be drawn to the veil, while others are frightened by it.

locked room: This door in the circular room will not open with magic, weapons, or force. The force and power behind the door is possibly the strongest of all known, and the most mysterious of all things studied in the department.

Time Room: This door in the circular room opens to a room crammed with Time-Turners and clocks of every description that make constant ticking noises. The room is full of a brilliant, diamond-patterned light, coming from a bell jar. During the battle in the Department of Mysteries many of the objects in this room are destroyed, with interesting consequences.

> ✱ **office:** Located off the Time Room, it is cramped and cluttered, with stone walls, a desk, and bookcase.

> ✱ **Hall of Prophecy:** A door in the Time Room leads to this cold, cathedral-sized room lit by blue-flamed candles and lined with rows of dusty glass spheres on labelled shelves.

planet room: Another door in the circular room leads to a dark room filled with the planets from the solar system.

Note to Muggles: *Did you notice the things studied in the Department of Mysteries — the mind, the passage of time, outer space, death and the afterlife, and love — are many of the same mysteries Muggles throughout history have sought a deeper understanding of, too?*

EMPLOYEES/UNSPEAKABLES IN THE DEPARTMENT OF MYSTERIES

Bode, Broderick: Forty-nine years old and sallow-skinned, with a morbid air about him. In fifth year, Bode meets up with an accident at work and winds up in St. Mungo's. "Bode" means to be an omen or to foretell something.

Croaker: "Croak" is a slang expression meaning to die. Both Bode and Croaker are Unspeakables (no one knows exactly what they do).

Rookwood, Augustus: Former employee in the department, although it is not determined if he was an Unspeakable.

Level Eight – Atrium

The Atrium is long and wide, with a gleaming dark wood floor and a blue ceiling full of shimmering golden symbols. The dark wood walls contain numerous gilded fireplaces — employees Floo in from one side and out from the other. At the far end of the Atrium, there are golden gates leading to a smaller hall with about twenty lifts behind grilles.

Fountain of Magical Brethren: A small circular pool in the middle of the Atrium contains five large gilded statues posed idyllically — a foolish-looking wizard and vapid-looking witch, with a centaur, goblin, and house-elf gazing up at them adoringly. Dumbledore thinks the statues tell a lie, and that wizards have mistreated their fellow creatures for far too long (shades of S.P.E.W.!).

Jets of water stream out of the wizard and witch's wands, as well as the centaur's arrow, the goblin's hat, and the house-elf's ears. All coins thrown in the fountain are donated to St. Mungo's (Harry vows to put in ten Galleons if things go well for him, then dumps his entire moneybag in after they do).

EMPLOYEES

Munch, Eric: Unshaven watchwizard in peacock blue robes who manages the security desk in the Atrium. All visitors must check-in at the desk, where they are searched and their wands are inspected and registered. Although the watchwizard seems mostly bored and spends a great deal of time reading the *Daily Prophet*, he encounters some excitement when he arrests someone for trying to break into a high-security area at one o'clock in the morning.

Level Seven – Department of Magical Games and Sports

Includes the British and Irish Quidditch League Headquarters, Ludicrous Patents Office, and the Official Gobstones Club. It has lots of messy-looking corridors with various Quidditch posters on the walls.

⋆ **Quidditch World Cup:** Oversees all aspects, including Muggle-Repelling Charms, Portkeys, Memory Charms, Apparation points, and so on.

⋆ **Triwizard Tournament:** Co-authorises its resurrection with the Department of International Magical Co-operation.

EMPLOYEES/DEPARTMENT HEADS

Bagman, Ludovic (Ludo): Department head (although Percy sniffs he is unsuitable for such an important position). "Ludo" is a kind of British board game. In Latin, it means both to play (a sport) and to deceive. A "bagman" is a slang term for the person who collects money on behalf of loan sharks or gangsters. Bagman walks with a spring in his step, although he has a large belly. He looks a bit like an overgrown schoolboy gone to seed, with his broken nose, short blond hair, blue eyes, and rosy complexion.

Bagman used to be a Beater for the Wimbourne Wasps and even played for England at one time. He was very popular in his day, which helped him get out of at least one particularly dark and knotty situation. Although he now works for the Ministry (thanks to an old friend of his father's, who got him the job), Quidditch has never really left his blood. He is Commentator and one of the judges during the Triwizard Tournament, and seems to have taken a shine to Harry.

Bagman loves to gamble. He has a reputation for being a bit stupid (some reckon he took one too many Bludgers to the head) and gets himself in over his head on more than one occasion. He is also easily excitable — his lack of discretion and booming voice raises a concern about Muggles overhearing him at the Quidditch World Cup, but he doesn't seem to be particularly bothered about potentially breaching security. Unfortunately, Bagman does not always conduct himself in the most sporting way, and when the chips are down, he is nowhere to be found.

Jorkins, Bertha: Dumbledore remembers Bertha as a chubby, sulky sixteen-year-old. A few years ahead of James and Lily, she was also considered a bit dim but had an excellent memory for gossip and scandal, and used to get into a lot of trouble because she couldn't keep her mouth shut.

As an adult, Bertha worked in several departments in the Ministry, including a stint at the Department of International Magical Co-operation, where Crouch apparently thought very highly of her.

The summer before fourth year, Bertha went on holiday to visit family in Albania and never returned. Bagman is not worried, however; Bertha has gone missing lots of times before. He claims she has no sense of direction and a memory like a leaky cauldron.

Level Six – Department of Magical Transportation

Includes the Apparation Test Centre, Broom Regulatory Control, Floo Network Authority, and Portkey Office.

Apparation Test Centre: Oversees Apparating licences for of-age wizards, and issues fines to those who Apparate without a licence.

enchanted cars: Mr. Weasley arranges for his family, Harry, and Hermione to be taken to King's Cross in two old-fashioned dark green Ministry cars, driven by emerald-suited wizards. The cars are able to magically squeeze through narrow gaps and jump ahead in traffic.

Floo Network Authority/Floo Regulation Panel: Mr. Weasley knows someone in this area who was able to connect the Dursleys' fireplace to the Floo Network temporarily, in order for the Weasleys to pick up Harry.

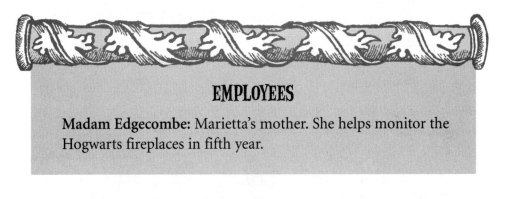

EMPLOYEES

Madam Edgecombe: Marietta's mother. She helps monitor the Hogwarts fireplaces in fifth year.

Level Five – Department of International Magical Co-operation

Includes British Seats of the International Confederation of Wizards, International Magical Office of Law, and the International Magical Trading Standards Body. Sets class designations for Non-Tradeable Substances (such as Venomous Tentacula seeds, which are considered Class C).

Quidditch World Cup: Helped organise certain parts, likely including international Portkey points and so on.

Triwizard Tournament: Co-authorises its resurrection with the Department of Magical Games and Sports.

EMPLOYEES

Crouch Sr., Bartemius (Barty): Department Head. Crouch has had a long and prestigious career at the Ministry — he used to be Head of the Department of Magical Law Enforcement and, at one point, was expected to be the next Minister for Magic. Crouch speaks over two hundred languages, including Gobbledegook and Troll. Stiff and uptight, he follows rules to the letter and is both is power-hungry and powerful. He despises the Dark Arts in any form. Percy thinks very highly of him, even though Crouch usually refers to him as "Weatherby" instead of "Weasley."

Although Crouch is not one to take time off for illness, he is unable to fulfil many of his commitments during fourth year. Officially, his absence is explained as exhaustion due to work overload.

Weasley, Percy (Weatherby): Percy starts his climb up the Ministry's corporate ladder after he leaves Hogwarts, and plans not to stop until he reaches the very top. He tries hard to ingratiate himself with other Ministry employees, particularly Crouch, his boss, who constantly forgets his name and finds him somewhat over-bearing.

One of Percy's first assignments is to write a report about standardising cauldron bottom thickness, which he takes *very* seriously (leakages have been increasing at the alarming rate of almost three per cent per year!). He must have done a good job — he is soon promoted to Crouch's personal assistant and fills in for him at a number of events.

Percy sees less and less of Crouch throughout the year, and continues to take on more of his responsibilities. His instructions are regularly sent by owl post. At the end of the year, Percy receives a promotion to the Junior Assistant to the Minister for Magic. Although Mr. Weasley suggests Fudge has ulterior motives for the promotion, Percy is very pleased about his new role and extremely loyal to his new boss. He sometimes takes on the role of Court Scribe during Wizengamot hearings.

Did you know . . . in an online chat for World Book day in March 2004, J. K. Rowling said Percy's attitude and actions after his promotion were entirely of his own accord? (In other words, his behaviour wasn't the result of an Imperius Curse.)

Level Four – Department for the Regulation and Control of Magical Creatures

Includes Beast, Being, and Spirit Divisions, Goblin Liaison Office, and Pest Advisory Bureau. The department oversees the breeding of new magical species.

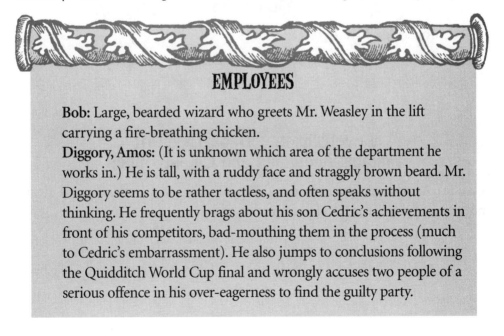

EMPLOYEES

Bob: Large, bearded wizard who greets Mr. Weasley in the lift carrying a fire-breathing chicken.

Diggory, Amos: (It is unknown which area of the department he works in.) He is tall, with a ruddy face and straggly brown beard. Mr. Diggory seems to be rather tactless, and often speaks without thinking. He frequently brags about his son Cedric's achievements in front of his competitors, bad-mouthing them in the process (much to Cedric's embarrassment). He also jumps to conclusions following the Quidditch World Cup final and wrongly accuses two people of a serious offence in his over-eagerness to find the guilty party.

Committee for the Disposal of Dangerous Creatures: Holds hearings and passes judgement on the fate of various magical creatures. It is rumoured some of the committee members are in Lucius Malfoy's pocket.

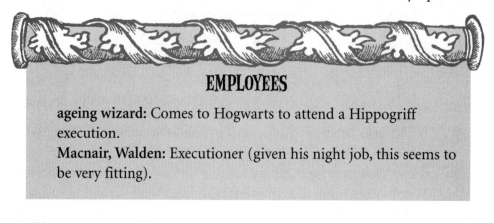

EMPLOYEES

ageing wizard: Comes to Hogwarts to attend a Hippogriff execution.

Macnair, Walden: Executioner (given his night job, this seems to be very fitting).

Goblin Liaison Office: Presumably, this is where the Gringotts' goblins go if they have business with the Ministry.

EMPLOYEES

Mockridge, Cuthbert: Office head.

Level Three – Department of Magical Accidents and Catastrophes

Includes Accidental Magic Reversal Squad, Muggle-Worthy Excuse Committee, and Obliviator Headquarters.

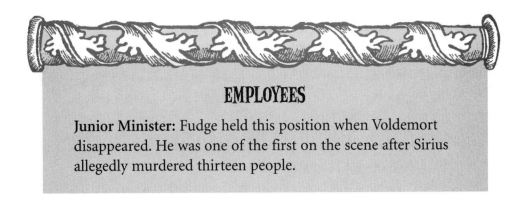

EMPLOYEES

Junior Minister: Fudge held this position when Voldemort disappeared. He was one of the first on the scene after Sirius allegedly murdered thirteen people.

Accidental Magic Reversal Department/Squad: Undoes the effects of magic that has been performed by accident. This group also resolves problems involving splinching (both with the wizard involved, and any Muggles who had the misfortune to see any body parts left behind!).

Committee on Experimental Charms: Presumably, this group regulates new and untried charms and deals with the fallout from any charms gone wrong.

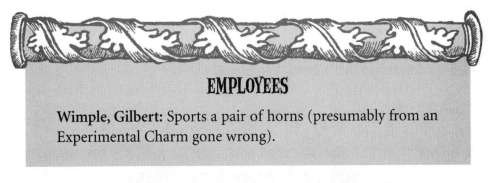

EMPLOYEES

Wimple, Gilbert: Sports a pair of horns (presumably from an Experimental Charm gone wrong).

Note to Muggles: *The exact location for the Committee on Experimental Charms within the Ministry is unconfirmed; however, the Department of Magical Accidents and Catastrophes seemed like the most logical fit for the purpose of this book.*

Obliviator Headquarters: Casts Memory Charms on Muggles who have witnessed magic being performed.

EMPLOYEES/OBLIVIATORS

Peasegood, Arnold (Arnie)

Level Two – Department of Magical Law Enforcement

The largest Department in the Ministry, it includes Auror Headquarters, the Improper Use of Magic Office, and Wizengamot Administration Service. The Department of Magical Law Enforcement also keeps tabs on the residences and locations of witches and wizards throughout Britain.

 Did you know . . . Britain's King George II passed the Witchcraft Act of 1736, making it illegal to prosecute those who practised magic? The Act repealed sixteenth century statutes in England and Scotland that banned witchcraft.

EMPLOYEES/DEPARTMENT HEADS

Crouch, Barty: Department head during Voldemort's reign. Crouch believed in a "fight violence with violence" philosophy. Ruthless and cruel, he ordered tough measures against Voldemort's supporters, including the use of the Unforgivable Curses on suspects and sentencing suspects to Azkaban without holding trials.

Bones, Madam Amelia Susan: Current Department head. Broad and square-jawed, she has short grey hair, thick eyebrows, and wears a monocle. Although Madam Bones speaks in a booming voice and gives the impression of being a bit brisk, she is considered to be fair (she is impressed that Harry can produce a corporeal Patronus at his age). She is Susan Bones's auntie and the sister of Edgar Bones, who was killed with his family during Voldemort's reign.

Council of Magical Law: Crouch oversaw this council, which deals with wizarding trials and hearings.

Auror Headquarters: Double oak doors lead to a messy, chatter-filled area divided into cubicles. Aurors are dark wizard catchers. In Voldemort's time, Crouch gave them the power to kill instead of capture. It takes three years of training to become an Auror. Areas of study covered include Concealment and Disguise, and Stealth and Tracking.

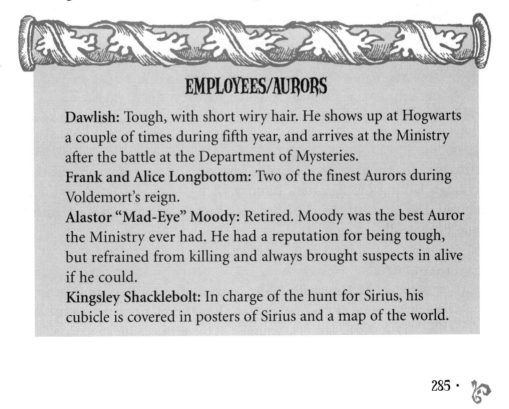

EMPLOYEES/AURORS

Dawlish: Tough, with short wiry hair. He shows up at Hogwarts a couple of times during fifth year, and arrives at the Ministry after the battle at the Department of Mysteries.

Frank and Alice Longbottom: Two of the finest Aurors during Voldemort's reign.

Alastor "Mad-Eye" Moody: Retired. Moody was the best Auror the Ministry ever had. He had a reputation for being tough, but refrained from killing and always brought suspects in alive if he could.

Kingsley Shacklebolt: In charge of the hunt for Sirius, his cubicle is covered in posters of Sirius and a map of the world.

Nymphadora Tonks: Novice Auror who is also a Metamorph-magus (which must come in handy!).

Williamson: Scarlet-robed wizard with long ponytail. He arrives at the Ministry after the battle at the Department of Mysteries.

a witch who wears an eye-patch

Scrimgeour: (It is unconfirmed he is an Auror.) He asks Tonks and Kingsley a lot of questions, and possibly suspects something is up with them. Scrimgeour is a Scottish surname, derived from the French "escrimeur," or swordsman.

Improper Use of Magic Office: Monitors the use of magic in inappropriate circumstances, such as by underage wizards, or in the Muggle world. (Mrs. Weasley despairs that Fred and George will turn up in front of this office one day.) The Improper Use of Magic Office is also responsible for registering Animagi.

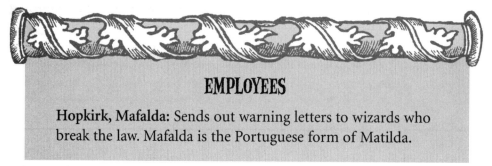

EMPLOYEES

Hopkirk, Mafalda: Sends out warning letters to wizards who break the law. Mafalda is the Portuguese form of Matilda.

Animagi: All Animagi must register what animal they become and their markings. During the twentieth century, there were only seven registered Animagi. The Ministry can also offer assistance to an Animagi if a transformation goes badly.

Registered

✶ **Minerva McGonagall:** Tabby cat. Her square glasses are exactly the same shape as the markings she has around her eyes as a cat. Just like McGonagall, cats are symbolic of cleverness, independence, wisdom, and agility. And, of course, cats have a long-standing association as a symbol of magic!

Unregistered

* **Sirius Black:** (Black) dog. Appropriately, Sirius is the "dog star." Dogs represent loyalty, friendship, trust, devotion, and protection — all very fitting for Sirius.
* **Peter Pettigrew:** Rat. Rats generally have negative connotations in symbolism, such as deviousness, betrayal, and filth. However, rats can also represent devotion to a cause.
* **James Potter:** Stag. The stag represents nobility, pride, boldness, independence, strength, and bravery.
* **Rita Skeeter:** Beetle. Rita the beetle has markings around her antennae that match the glasses she wears as a witch. Beetles represent change and endurance — and in ancient Egypt, scarab beetles were known for laying their eggs in dung.

Magical Law Enforcement Patrol/Squad: Seem to be the wizarding equivalent of the police. They deal with everything from regurgitating public toilets to subduing and arresting criminals — it took twenty members to take Sirius away after he was charged with murdering a street full of Muggles.

* **Hit Wizards:** Deal with high-level crimes and criminals.

Misuse of Muggle Artefacts Office: Located at the end of a dim corridor across from a broom cupboard. It has no windows and is very cramped, with lots of overflowing filing cabinets. There are a few Muggle posters on the walls and bewitched items on the two desks. Considered by Ron to be the most boring part of the Ministry, the Misuse of Muggle Artefacts Office handles the fallout when wizards bewitch Muggle-made items that accidentally end up back in the Muggle world. The office also deals with anti-Muggle wizarding pranksters and occasionally conducts raids of wizarding homes in search of Dark Arts objects.

Confiscated items

✳ Malfoy Manor was raided for Dark Arts objects, but Lucius Malfoy managed to sell or hide most of his questionable items beforehand.

✳ Wizarding books, including one that burnt out readers' eyes, one the owner could never stop reading, and *Sonnets of a Sorcerer* which made readers speak in limericks for the rest of their lives.

EMPLOYEES

Bonao, Lasuris: First office head.

Weasley, Arthur: Current office head. He is the only one who can get Moody out of trouble when he is under investigation by the Improper use of Magic Office. Mr. Weasley wrote a loophole in the law permitting the enchantment of Muggle objects (such as cars) as long as wizards didn't actually intend to use them. Ironically, he finds himself subject to a hefty fine when this very law backfires in his face.

Ron is testy about his father's position after Malfoy mocks it as a "junior" role — Ron claims his father could get a promotion whenever he wants, but is happy where he is. Mr. Weasley's love of Muggles is, in fact, what has likely held him back from advancement, as Fudge thinks he lacks "proper wizarding pride."

Perkins: Timid-looking warlock with fluffy white hair. He is stooped and has lumbago. Mr. Weasley borrows two tents from Perkins for the Quidditch World Cup.

Wizengamot: Wizard High Court. About fifty members attend hearings. They wear plum-coloured robes with a silver "W" on the left breast. During hearings, the Wizengamot act as jury whilst three Ministry officials serve as Interrogators. There is also a Court Scribe.

MEMBERS OF THE WIZENGAMOT

frizzy-haired witch: Voted to find the accused guilty during a hearing prior to the beginning of fifth year.

Dumbledore: Demoted from Chief Warlock in fifth year after he made some controversial remarks.

dumpy, thick-moustached wizard: Voted to find the accused guilty during a hearing prior to the beginning of fifth year.

Marchbanks, Griselda: Head of the Wizarding Examinations Authority for many years — she remembers examining Dumbledore during his NEWTs! Griselda resigned in protest because of the introduction of the Hogwarts High Inquisitor position, although the *Daily Prophet* tried to discredit her for speaking out. She is a friend of Neville's Gran (and a bit like her in temperament).

Ogden, Tiberius: Resigned in protest because of the introduction of the Hogwarts High Inquisitor position. He is good friends with Professor Tofty of the Wizarding Examinations Authority.

Acts, Bans, Codes, Decrees, Laws, and Statutes

Just like the Muggle government, the Ministry implements a variety of laws and legislations to make the wizarding world run more smoothly.

Anti-werewolf legislation: Drafted by Umbridge, this legislation makes it very difficult for werewolves to find employment.

Ban on Experimental Breeding: Outlaws cross-breeding between certain species, such as fire-breathing chickens.

changing time: One of the most important laws in the wizarding world. No wizard is supposed to alter the course of time, as it can lead to dangerous consequences — often, a person's past and future selves will attack or kill each other on sight, out of confusion. Because of this, the Ministry keeps tight control over the use of Time-Turners and other time-manipulating devices.

Code of Wand Use: The third clause states that no non-human creature is permitted to carry or use a wand.

Decree for the Reasonable Restriction of Underage Sorcery, 1875:

Paragraph C states that underage wizards are not allowed to perform magic outside of school. First-time offenders receive an official letter of warning, while repeat offenders face expulsion from Hogwarts and the destruction of their wands.

Dumbledore thinks these punishments are unrealistic, and reminds the Ministry they have no jurisdiction to expel students, nor can they confiscate a wand until a charge against a wizard has been proven.

Clause Seven states that magic can be used in front of Muggles in exceptional circumstances. There is also a provision in the decree permitting the use of underage magic in life-threatening situations.

Note to Muggles: *In third year, this decree is referred to as the Decree for the Restriction of Underage Wizardry.*

Educational Decrees: The Ministry gives the Hogwarts High Inquisitor complete authority to create and implement new laws relating to educational standards at Hogwarts. These include:

✴ **Number Twenty-Two:** Passed on the thirtieth of August, just before fifth year begins. In the event the current Head of Hogwarts is unable to find a candidate to fill a teaching post, the Ministry will choose an appropriate person instead.

✴ **Number Twenty-Three:** Creation of the Hogwarts High Inquisitor position.

✴ **Number Twenty-Four:** Disbands all student clubs, organisations, societies, and groups until the High Inquisitor grants permission for them to be reformed. Any student forming or belonging to a non-approved activity will be expelled.

∗ **Number Twenty-Five:** The High Inquisitor has complete authority over all student punishments and removal of privileges, including the power to alter those administered by other staff members.

∗ **Number Twenty-Six:** Teachers are forbidden from giving students any information unrelated to the subjects they teach.

∗ **Number Twenty-Seven:** Any student caught with a copy of *The Quibbler* will be expelled.

∗ **Number Twenty-Eight:** Umbridge is instated as the Head of Hogwarts.

∗ **Number Twenty-Nine (pending):** Filch has the authority to punish students as he sees fit, including stringing them up by the ankles from chains and whipping them.

Guidelines for the Treatment of Non-Wizard Part-Humans:
Paragraph Twelve deals with vampires.

home and self-defence guides:
The Ministry distributes these free to all wizarding homes at the end of fifth year, after acknowledging Dumbledore and Harry's claims were true.

International Ban on Duelling:
Various wizarding nations are urged to sign this treaty, which presumably prohibits duelling.

International Confederation of Warlocks' Statute of Secrecy, Section 13:
Deals with performing magic in front of Muggles, which is a serious offence. First-time offenders receive an official letter of warning, while repeat offenders face disciplinary hearings before the Wizengamot.

Note to Muggles: *In fourth year, Hermione refers to the International Code of Wizarding Secrecy, which seems to cover the exact same concept. Whether this is a mistake on J. K. Rowling's part or an intentionally separate law is not known.*

Law Fifteen "B" from the Department for the Regulation and Control of Magical Creatures: Pertains to attacks by "half-breeds" and magical creatures possessing "near-human intelligence."

Ministry decrees: The Ministry posts notices throughout Hogsmeade advising people to avoid the streets at night, as Dementors will be on patrol looking for Sirius.

Muggle Protection Act: Lucius Malfoy is vehemently opposed to this proposed legislation, founded by Mr. Weasley. He does everything in his power to throw the book at Mr. Weasley and derail the act.

Order of Merlin: Prestigious medal awarded to witches and wizards who display great feats of bravery or valour (although judging by some of the recipients, it is a somewhat dubious distinction).

ORDER OF MERLIN RECIPIENTS

Dumbledore: Order of Merlin, First Class (reason not given — possibly his defeat of Grindelwald?). There was talk of taking this honour away from him in fifth year after he made some controversial remarks.

Cornelius Fudge: Order of Merlin, First Class (reason not given). Fudge signs an Educational Degree with this designation after his name.

Gilderoy Lockhart: Order of Merlin, Third Class (reason not given, but it was probably bestowed for all the "heroic deeds" he performed).

Peter Pettigrew: Order of Merlin, First Class. Awarded after his "murder."

Snape: Fudge reckons Snape deserves an Order of Merlin, Second Class (or even First Class if he can arrange it), for "rescuing" Harry, Hermione, and Ron in third year. To Snape's chagrin, Fudge changes his mind after Dumbledore convinces him someone else was actually responsible.

Sirius's grandfather: Order of Merlin, First Class. Given for "services to the Ministry," but it was likely a reward for giving the Ministry a lot of gold.

Registry of Proscribed Charmable Objects: List of objects that are prohibited from being Charmed, including many items that are classified as Muggle Artefacts (such as carpets).

residency records: Registers the locations where witches and wizards live (Squibs are not included). According to the Ministry's records, Harry is the only magical person living in Little Whinging.

Trade Restrictions: Certain magical materials, substances, and goods are subject to various degrees of control over their possession, handling, buying, and selling. Some items can be bought or sold under certain conditions, whilst others are banned outright.

Veritaserum guidelines: The use of this powerful truth serum is controlled by very stringent regulations.

Wizengamot Charter of Rights: States the accused in a trial has the right to present witnesses.

Other Wizarding Government Organisations and Officials

Andorran Minister for Magic: Communicates with Crouch during fourth year.

Bulgarian Minister for Magic: Mr. Oblansk (or, as Fudge says, Obalonsk) attends the Quidditch World Cup final.

Dark Force Defence League: Little is known about this group. Lockhart claimed to be an honourary member, while Rita Skeeter quoted the organisation in an article criticising Harry — but that's not saying much!

International Confederation of Wizards: Hold conferences over the summer. Dumbledore is Chairman (Supreme Mugwump) of the Confederation, but faced disciplinary action in fifth year after making some controversial remarks.

Did you know . . . there are a few different political meanings for the word Mugwump? Over the years, a Mugwump has come to be known as any independent voter, an egotistical or self-important politician, or a neutral voter who takes no side and votes for no party. Mugwump is originally derived from the Algonquian (Native American) word *mogkionzp*, meaning "great man" ("mogki" meaning great, and "omp" meaning man).

International Federation of Warlocks: Criticised Fudge for telling the Muggle Prime Minister about Sirius's escape from Azkaban.

Transylvanian Head of Magical Co-operation: Refuses to sign the International Ban on Duelling.

THE ORDER OF THE PHOENIX

"What's comin' will come, an' we'll meet it when it does."
— Hagrid, *Harry Potter and the Goblet of Fire*

Founded by Dumbledore, the Order of the Phoenix is a secret society of magical people who fought Voldemort and his supporters during his reign. At the end of fourth year, Dumbledore decides to resurrect the Order to continue the fight. The Order has its hands full waging a war on two fronts — against Voldemort's supporters, and also against the Ministry, which is in denial about the severity of the situation. In addition, most of the wizarding world is unaware or misinformed about what has happened, leaving it vulnerable to attack.

To join the Order, witches and wizards must be out of school. Currently, there are more than twenty members. Some work on recruitment, some monitor known Death Eaters, and others are assigned to various kinds of guard duty. Members of the Order have secure, stealthy methods of communicating with each other.

Note to Muggles: *Warning! Descriptions of certain members of the Order of the Phoenix may include some information about the double lives they lead — read at your own risk!*

The Original Order (1970s)

Lupin tells Mrs. Weasley the original Order was outnumbered twenty to one by Death Eaters. (It seems a little strange Mr. and Mrs. Weasley weren't in the original Order themselves.)

Black, Sirius

Bones, Edgar: Brother of Amelia and uncle of Susan, he and his family were murdered by Death Eaters. Edgar was the name of an old Saxon king who was also a saint, which is fitting, as Edgar Bones was considered to be a great wizard.

Dearborn, Caradoc: Vanished; his body was never found. According to the legend of King Arthur, Caradoc was an evil lord who relished capturing and imprisoning the Knights of the Round Table. He was eventually killed by Lancelot.

Diggle, Dedalus

Doge, Elphias

Dumbledore, Aberforth: Dumbledore's brother. He is described as strange and seems to keep to himself. Aberforth once caused a scandal when he was prosecuted for practising inappropriate charms on a goat. (Dumbledore reckons the reason his brother was able to hold his head high afterwards was because he was unable to read, so he didn't see what the papers wrote about him.)

Did you know . . . many fans have speculated Aberforth could be the barman at the Hog's Head? The Hog's Head "smelled strongly of something that might have been goats," a possible nod to Aberforth's earlier mistake. The man behind the bar looks "vaguely familiar" to Harry — possibly because he saw Aberforth's picture during the summer in a photo of the original Order, and also possibly because the barman is tall and thin, with long grey hair and a beard . . . which, other than the hair being white instead of grey, is the same description as Dumbledore.

Dumbledore, Albus: Founder and leader.

Fenwick, Benjy: Only parts of him were ever found.

Hagrid, Rubeus

Longbottom, Frank and Alice: Tortured into insanity from the Cruciatus Curse by the Lestranges. Their attack came after Voldemort disappeared, and was met with widespread outrage through the magical world. The Ministry was under tremendous pressure to catch those responsible, but given their state of mind, the Longbottoms' evidence wasn't very reliable.

Lupin, Remus

Meadowes, Dorcas: Murdered by Voldemort. The name *Dorcas* is of Greek origin, and means gazelle.

McKinnon, Marlene: She and her family were murdered by Travers, a Death Eater.

Moody, Alastor "Mad-Eye"

Pettigrew, Peter

Podmore, Sturgis

Potter, James and Lily: Murdered by Voldemort, who was trying to kill Harry.

Prewett, Fabian and Gideon: Brothers who fought heroically against the Death Eaters who murdered them. Both Fabian and Gideon are names of historical heroes — Fabian is derived from Fabius, a Roman general who stopped the invasion of Hannibal, while Gideon led the Israelites against the Midianites in the Old Testament of the Bible. The Prewetts are related to Molly Weasley, who was a Prewett before she got married.

Vance, Emmeline

The New Order (1990s)

At the end of fourth year, Dumbledore gives instructions to gather "the old crowd" and lie low. The Black family's house (see page 41) has been offered as Headquarters for the Order (meetings are held in the kitchen). Dumbledore has also added his own protective measures — he is the Secret-Keeper for the Order, so no one can find Headquarters unless he personally tells them where it is.

Black, Sirius: For his own safety, Dumbledore wants to keep Sirius hidden as much as possible. This limits Sirius's involvement in the Order, which makes him feel frustrated and useless (although he does manage to accompany Harry to King's Cross). Sirius gets into a heated argument over what Harry should be told about the Order's business — he feels Harry has the right to know at least part of what is going on. Sirius defies orders and fights in the battle at the Department of Mysteries, where he encounters a veiled threat.

Diggle, Dedalus: Before Harry knew he was a wizard, this tiny man in a violet top hat once bowed to him when he was shopping. Squeaky-voiced and excitable, he is suspected to be the cause of the shooting stars that are seen the day after Voldemort disappeared. McGonagall thinks he has no sense, and she may be right — his name comes from the Greek myth of Daedalus, who flew too close to the sun with his son, Icarus, on wings made from wax and feathers. Diggle is part of the Advance Guard that escorts Harry to Headquarters.

Doge, Elphias: Wheezy-voiced with silver hair, he is part of the Advance Guard that escorts Harry to Headquarters.

Dumbledore, Albus: Oversees all Order business, but seems to be keeping his distance from certain members — especially Harry. Dumbledore suffers a series of reprimands by the Ministry for his speeches, statements, and beliefs. He fights in the battle at the Department of Mysteries.

Figg, Arabella Doreen (Figgy): Mad old lady who lives in the same neighbourhood as the Dursleys. Mrs. Figg has looked after Harry since he was a baby whenever his relatives go on holiday, but he dreads going to her house because it smells of cabbage and cats. The summer before fifth year, she takes to inviting Harry round for tea whenever she sees him.

Mrs. Figg has frizzy grey hair and seems somewhat eccentric — she talks to herself and often wears her carpet slippers outdoors. A cat lover, she used to show Harry photos of all the cats she ever owned. Currently, she has four cats and once broke her leg tripping over one of them.

In Biblical times fig leaves were used to conceal things, and true to her name, Mrs. Figg has secrets of her own. Her involvement with the Order is limited, and she sometimes relies on her beloved cats for help.

Fletcher, Mundungus (Dung): With his unshaven face, clothing that resembles a pile of rags, and ever-present odour of stale tobacco and alcohol, Mundungus looks like the last kind of wizard who would belong in the Order. He is short, squat, and bandy-legged, with stringy ginger hair and droopy bloodshot eyes like a basset hound. His manner, language, and jokes can often be as coarse and noxious as the billowing green clouds of smoke emanating from his ever-present pipe. ("Mundungus" is an old word meaning a particularly smelly kind of tobacco, so this is very fitting!)

Mundungus's seedy appearance is only matched by his reputation. He was barred from the Hog's Head twenty years earlier — which, considering the notoriety of the pub, is really saying something! Mundungus is always involved in some kind of shady undertaking, from trying to defraud the Ministry in a claim for damaged property after the Quidditch World Cup to storing ill-begotten goods at Grimmauld Place. Nor is he the most trustworthy of wizards — he once tried to hex Mr. Weasley during a raid when his back was turned, and eagerly admits to having stolen items from a friend only to resell them to him later at a higher price.

Despite this, Mundungus is loyal to Dumbledore, who once got him out of a tight spot. His purpose in the Order is to keep an eye on all crooks — being one himself, he hears things the other Order members don't. He is also quite skilled at disguises and skulking around without being detected (naturally). Beyond this, however, Mundungus is fairly hopeless at keeping up with his responsibilities as a member of the Order. He is scatterbrained, falls asleep during meetings, and has been known to skive off from guard duty to pursue a "business opportunity" involving a batch of stolen cauldrons.

Much to Mrs. Weasley's disapproval, Mundungus seems to have become chummy with Fred and George.

Hagrid, Rubeus: Goes on an extended mission with Madame Maxime to gain the trust and ear of a Gurg, and tell him what Dumbledore has to say. It goes well in the beginning, but subsequent attempts prove extremely unsuccessful on all fronts.

Jones, Hestia: Pink-cheeked and black-haired, she is part of the Advance Guard that escorts Harry to Headquarters. In Greek mythology, Hestia was goddess of the home and hearth.

Lupin, Remus: Part of the Advance Guard that escorts Harry to Headquarters. He also escorts Ginny and the twins to King's Cross in fifth year, and the children back to Hogwarts after Christmas holidays. Lupin stays at Grimmauld Place throughout the year, but leaves for extended periods of time on secret missions. He fights in the battle at the Department of Mysteries.

Maxime, Madame Olympe: Goes with Hagrid on his mission, but they separate on the return trip. Though Madame Maxime is elegant and well-dressed, Hagrid is impressed she does not complain about the roughness of their voyage.

Moody, Alastor "Mad-Eye": Part of the Advance Guard that escorts Harry to Headquarters, he also fights in the battle at the Department of Mysteries.

Podmore, Sturgis: Podmore is thirty-eight years old and has a square jaw with thick, fair hair. He is part of the Advance Guard that escorts Harry to Headquarters, although he doesn't turn up for guard duty to escort Harry to King's Cross. He also forgets to return Moody's best Invisibility Cloak. Other members of the Order start to question his reliability and threaten to report him to Dumbledore — but this turns out to be the least of his worries. Inexplicably, Podmore finds himself in the wrong place at the wrong time, and must suffer the consequences of his actions.

It is unknown if Podmore is related to Sir Patrick Delaney-Podmore, one of Nearly Headless Nick's ghostly acquaintances.

Shacklebolt, Kingsley: Tall, bald, and black, with a single gold hoop earring and a deep, slow voice, Kingsley is the epitome of cool. At the Ministry he is the Auror in charge of the hunt for Sirius, whom he says was last seen in Tibet. Part of the Advance Guard that escorts Harry to Headquarters, Kingsley also fights in the battle at the Department of Mysteries and has been known to perform covert Memory Charms. Abbreviating his name results in "king bolt," or kingpin, implying he has a lot of authority and power. Another interpretation of his name is that he is the king of shackling and bolting criminals!

Snape, Severus: Assigned to a top-secret mission, he reports about his activities at Order meetings. Snape later tells Harry it is his "job" to discover what Voldemort is saying to Death Eaters, giving weight to the idea that he is a spy for Dumbledore.

Did you know . . . although Snape seems like he may not be so bad, J. K. Rowling warned readers not to think he was "too nice"? At London's Royal Albert Hall in June 2003, she cryptically remarked it was "worth keeping an eye on old Severus Snape, definitely."

Tonks, Nymphadora: Tonks, as she prefers to be called, is one of the youngest members of the Order. She has a pale, heart-shaped face and dark twinkling eyes. She is also a Metamorphmagus, and frequently comes up with new disguises, which include unusual hairstyles (and noses). Tonks wears colourful clothes and is enthusiastic and slightly mischievous — she was never a prefect at school because her head of house said she lacked the ability to behave herself. Her father is Muggle-born and very messy, something Tonks seems to inherited as she hasn't quite got the knack of most household spells.

Tonks is an Auror, although she is very accident-prone and nearly failed Stealth and Tracking during Auror training. Part of the Advance Guard that escorts Harry to Headquarters, she also escorts him to King's Cross at the beginning of fifth year and back to Hogwarts after the Christmas holidays. Tonks fights in the battle at the Department of Mysteries.

Vance, Emmeline: Stately looking witch with an emerald shawl. She is part of the Advance Guard that escorts Harry to Headquarters.

Weasley, Arthur: Tries to discreetly persuade people at the Ministry about the Order's work, and escorts Hermione and Ron to King's Cross in fifth year. Mr. Weasley suffers an injury whilst on duty for the Order.

Weasley, Bill: Transferred to a desk job in London at Gringotts so he could work for the Order. He has approached the goblins about the Order's work, but they are suspicious of all wizards following a negative experience with one the year before. Bill does not know where the goblins stand on the subjects of Voldemort and the Order. It is possible their allegiance will depend on what freedoms they are offered.

Weasley, Charlie: Works for the Order from Romania, where he tries to recruit as many foreign wizards as possible.

Weasley, Molly: Supervises the cleaning and decontamination of Grimmauld Place, and escorts Harry to King's Cross in fifth year. The trio learn she also goes on "duty" for the Order, but no further explanation is given when they ask. Mrs. Weasley gets into a heated argument over what Harry should be told about the Order's business — she feels he should only hear what Dumbledore thinks he needs to know. She is deathly afraid one of her family members or Harry will be killed by Voldemort's hand.

Did you know . . . *Harry Potter and the Order of the Phoenix* sold 1,777,541 copies in Britain in just one day, making it the fastest-selling book of all time?

DARK ARTS

"There is no good and evil, there is only power, and those too weak to seek it."
— Professor Quirrell, *Harry Potter and the Philosopher's Stone*

Like the Muggle world, the wizarding world has its share of crime, criminals, terrorism, and unspeakable evil. It is the intent to do evil that is at the root of the Dark Arts.

As Professor Binns says, just because a wizard doesn't use Dark Magic doesn't mean he can't. The majority of magic can be used for either constructive or destructive purposes (for example, the Incendio spell can light a simple fire in a fireplace, or burn down a house); however, most wizards choose to use it benignly. Dark Arts magic is used purely for destructive purposes (for example, the Unforgivable Curses), and those who practise it must have a conscious and deliberate intent to do harm.

The Dark Arts encompasses more than just magic, however. It also includes potions, objects, beings, creatures, and, perhaps most evil of all, people.

Grindelwald: A Dark wizard Dumbledore was famous for defeating in 1945. Coincidentally (or maybe not), 1945 also marked the end of World War II — is it possible Grindelwald could have had ties to Hitler?

 Did you know . . . Grindelwald can be broken down into the Middle English *grindel*, meaning angry, and the Germanic *wald*, meaning forest? (Could there be a connection between Grindelwald's defeat and the Forbidden Forest?)

Lord Voldemort (The Dark Lord, You Know Who, He Who Must Not Be Named): Voldemort is the most feared and powerful Dark wizard in over a century. In fact, most wizards are so frightened of him, they cannot bring themselves to say his name and refer to him only as "You Know Who." His knowledge of magic is more extensive than any wizard alive.

A descendent of Salazar Slytherin himself, Voldemort is a diabolical psychopath, who sees himself as godlike and omnipotent (he describes himself as the "greatest sorcerer in the world"). He does not forgive mistakes easily, and is as ruthless and cruel to his supporters as he is his enemies. He also has a razor-sharp ability to discern when someone is lying to him. Like Slytherin, Voldemort is a Parseltongue. Also like Slytherin, Voldemort wants to purge the wizarding world of Muggle-borns and Muggles, whom he calls filthy and common (though he is a half-blood). He speaks of murder in a detached, almost amused manner and has a high, cold, cruel laugh.

The only wizard Voldemort has ever feared is Dumbledore, who has seen through him from the very beginning. Voldemort's one weakness — the one thing he does not understand and always underestimates — is love.

Voldemort's Rise and First Reign

Voldemort planned his rise to power for many years. As a young man, he travelled extensively throughout the world, where he associated with the most evil kinds of wizards and became increasingly involved with the Dark Arts. After undergoing numerous magical transformations that made him almost unrecognisable, he re-emerged, using a name he had created for himself during his school days — Voldemort. *Vol de mort* is French for both "thief of death" and "flight from death" — appropriate, as Voldemort's chief goal is to become immortal.

As Voldemort accumulated more skills and knowledge of the Dark Arts, he also began to accumulate supporters (who became known as Death Eaters). In addition, he took advantage of the bad relationship that giants had with wizards and he harnessed them to do his bidding. After many years, he had enough power to take over the wizarding world, and began a reign of terror that lasted eleven years. An atmosphere of fear, chaos, and violence prevailed, where atrocities, mind control, disappearances, torture, and murder in both the wizarding and Muggle worlds were commonplace. No one was safe, nor did anyone trust anyone else, as it was impossible to determine which side people were really on. It seemed like Voldemort truly had become invincible.

Voldemort's Fall and Disappearance

During the height of Voldemort's reign, he received some information about the circumstances that would possibly bring about his eventual defeat. He set out to neutralise the threat, based on his interpretation of the information combined with intelligence from a well-placed spy.

On Hallowe'en, Voldemort appeared at the home of the Potters. He killed James first, who fought valiantly. Inexplicably, Voldemort gave Lily the opportunity to stand aside, but she refused and was killed trying to protect her one-year-old son, Harry. Voldemort turned on Harry next, but when he cast the Killing Curse something happened that had never happened before — the curse backfired. Harry was unharmed, except for a scar on his forehead in the shape of a lightning bolt. He survived because his mother's sacrifice formed an ancient magic inside his blood, creating a power Voldemort did not know about or possess.

The rebounded curse destroyed Voldemort's powers and tore his essence from his body. He disappeared. Some thought he was just biding his time to return, although most believed he was still alive and just too weak to carry on. Others thought he had died, but Dumbledore knew this was not the case. He knew Voldemort would return one day.

First Year

After disappearing, Voldemort exists in a disembodied, near-death state in a forest in Albania, where he hides from Aurors and hopes to be rescued by Death Eaters. His (unknown) experiments on achieving immortality were the only thing that saved him from actual death when the curse struck. He becomes shadow and vapour, only able to take form by possessing another person or creature's body.

Ten years after he disappeared, Voldemort meets an impressionable wizard whom he uses like a parasite to try to restore his body and power. He uses the blood of magical creatures to sustain his life, although his plan to use alchemy to become immortal is not set in stone.

Second Year

Voldemort continues to cling to his weak existence in the forests of Albania, a mere echo of the person he used to be. Elsewhere, a hidden memory from his past resurfaces and seems determined to ensure history repeats itself.

Third Year

Weak, alone, and fearful he will never regain his power, Voldemort considers this his darkest hour until a long-lost servant finds him in the forest.

Fourth Year

When Wormtail encounters Voldemort in the Albanian forest, he brings along a gift, which Voldemort finds very useful. Wormtail nurses Voldemort to a weak, almost-human state on a diet of unicorn blood and snake venom. They return to the wizarding world, where Voldemort develops an elaborate plan involving an undercover servant, some complex Dark Magic, and Harry.

The pieces of the plan fall into place over the coming year and except for one spare part, which is quickly disposed of, it is executed flawlessly. When Voldemort summons the Death Eaters, about thirty Apparate to his side, but he is not happy to see them. He accuses them of disloyalty — all lied about their allegiance to evade capture after he vanished thirteen years earlier.

When Voldemort gives Harry a chance to defend himself, a very rare event unfolds unexpectedly. The results are extremely emotional for Harry to watch, but help to save his life.

Did you know . . . there was an error in the first edition of *Harry Potter and the Goblet of Fire*, concerning the order of James and Lily's deaths? At the end of first year, Voldemort tells Harry he killed James first, then Lily. Yet during Priori Incantatem, James's echo was the first of the pair's to emerge from the wand. (In Priori Incantatem, echo spells emerge from a wand in the reverse order in which they were cast — this means Lily's echo should have emerged first, because she was killed after James.)

J. K. Rowling discovered the mistake after the first edition of the book had been printed, and subsequent editions have the Potters emerging in the correct order — Lily first, then James.

Fifth Year

At the end of fourth year, Voldemort transforms from a grotesque, hairless, hunched-over creature with scaly, raw, reddish-black skin into a tall, thin, pale being. His legs and arms are spindly, with long, spider-like fingers. His snakelike face has a flat nose with slits for nostrils, a lipless mouth, and wide, glowing scarlet eyes with slitted pupils. Voldemort specifically wanted Harry's blood for the spell that resurrected him — he figured the ancient magic in Harry's blood that Lily put there when he was a baby would now flow through his own veins as well.

Voldemort's return does not go quite the way he anticipated. He had planned to amass a powerful army and the critical information he needed in secret before making his presence known. But when Harry survived their duel, Voldemort lost the element of surprise because Harry was able to alert Dumbledore to his return almost immediately.

Regardless, Voldemort goes ahead with his plans. He convinces two groups of creatures to join forces with him and the Death Eaters, and spends a great deal of effort trying to obtain a secret weapon from the past containing important information about the future. This leads to a showdown with his two biggest foes.

Did you know . . . the only people to have called You Know Who by his proper name so far are Dumbledore, Lupin, Sirius, Harry, and Hermione? (Hagrid and McGonagall have also said his name, but only once and after much trepidation.)

Azkaban: Azkaban is the wizard fortress prison, located on a tiny island far out at sea. It is run by the Ministry and guarded by Dementors. Most prisoners lose their minds and sit muttering to themselves in the dark because the Dementors render them incapable of any happy thoughts. Instead, prisoners relive the bleakest, most terrible memories and moments of their lives. Many eventually lose the will to live — they go quiet, stop eating, and die.

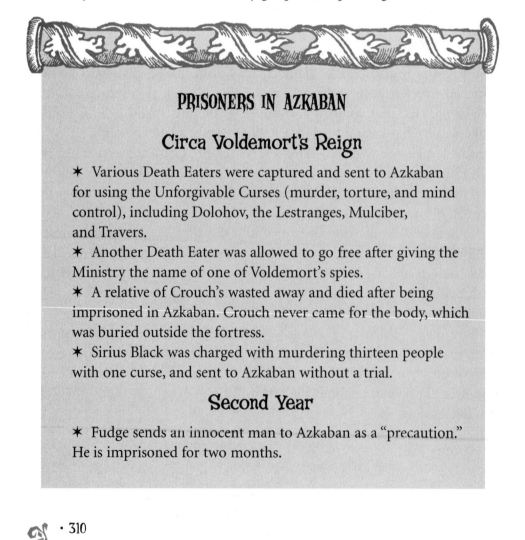

PRISONERS IN AZKABAN

Circa Voldemort's Reign

✴ Various Death Eaters were captured and sent to Azkaban for using the Unforgivable Curses (murder, torture, and mind control), including Dolohov, the Lestranges, Mulciber, and Travers.
✴ Another Death Eater was allowed to go free after giving the Ministry the name of one of Voldemort's spies.
✴ A relative of Crouch's wasted away and died after being imprisoned in Azkaban. Crouch never came for the body, which was buried outside the fortress.
✴ Sirius Black was charged with murdering thirteen people with one curse, and sent to Azkaban without a trial.

Second Year

✴ Fudge sends an innocent man to Azkaban as a "precaution." He is imprisoned for two months.

Third Year

✱ Considered the most infamous and insane of Azkaban's prisoners, Sirius is the only inmate ever to escape. All Ministry employees are pulled from their normal work to join in the hunt to recapture him.

Fifth Year

✱ Sturgis Podmore receives a six-month sentence after being convicted of trespassing and attempted robbery.
✱ Ten Death Eaters escape, including Dolohov, the Lestranges, Mulciber, and Rookwood.
✱ After the battle at the Department of Mysteries, several Death Eaters are caught and sent to Azkaban, including a father of a Hogwarts student.

Dementors: Prison guards at Azkaban. Dementors are tall, sinister, cloaked figures whose faces are hidden by their hoods. Underneath, they are blind, with grey scabbed skin stretched over hollow eye sockets. Their mouths are shapeless holes, and their breath is cold and putrid. Dementors have slimy grey-skinned hands that look like they are decaying.

Dementors are like depression personified. They inhabit the darkest of places and drain all hope, peace, and happiness from their surroundings through deep long breaths, which sound like a death-rattle. Dementors turn the air around them icy and cast a chill deep inside anyone in their presence. They sense people by their emotions. and get very excited when they can sense death is coming. People who get too close to Dementors will have every good memory and thought sucked out of them. If they can, Dementors will feed on people long enough to reduce them to something with no soul, leaving only the worst memories and experiences of their lives. Even Muggles feel their presence, although they cannot see them. The more Dementors there are, the harder it becomes to fight them.

Harry has a number of encounters with Dementors, and is particularly affected by their presence. When he sees them, he shivers and breaks out in a cold, clammy sweat. He feels nauseated, weak, and dizzy, as if he is drowning in ice and being dragged down through a thick, white fog. His eyes roll back in his head and he starts twitching, then he goes rigid and faints.

The only way to repel Dementors is by casting the Patronus Charm. This produces a silvery white animal form that projects what Dementors feed upon and diverts their attention from the caster.

Dementors are under the Ministry's control at Azkaban. As prison guards, they do not care about guilt or innocence as long as they have a steady supply of humans to feed on. Dementors can see through almost all manner of tricks and guises, including Invisibility Cloaks, and have no compassion or tolerance for excuses. They are loyal to no one.

In third year, Dementors patrol Hogsmeade at night looking for an escaped convict. Although Dumbledore doesn't like them, he agrees to allow Dementors to be positioned around all the entrances to Hogwarts, but refuses to let them inside the grounds. However, after the Dementors become overzealous, Dumbledore demands they be sent back to Azkaban.

Dementor's Kiss: Nickname given to a Dementor's most dangerous weapon — so sinister and destructive, the Ministry has to grant permission for it to be used. A Dementor "kisses" its victim by removing its hood and clamping its jaws on its victim's mouth, then sucking out his soul (in a way, the opposite of mouth-to-mouth resuscitation). Although this will not physically kill the victim, it is a fate worse than death. The victim will be left like an empty shell, without any memories or sense of self, for the rest of his life.

SEALED WITH A KISS

★ In third year, Fudge authorises the Kiss to be performed on Sirius.

★ In fourth year, Fudge brings a Dementor for protection when he arrives to question a suspect, but the Dementor immediately Kisses the suspect on sight.

★ In fifth year, a Muggle is almost Kissed when two Dementors appear in an alleyway in his neighbourhood.

Death Eaters: The Death Eaters are Voldemort's loyal servants and supporters. They have masked faces and wear hooded robes, and have his mark branded into their left inner forearms.

Death Eaters willingly do Voldemort's bidding, no matter what the task may be. They are deeply sadistic by nature and thrive on destruction and pandemonium. Death Eaters particularly enjoy terrorising, torturing, and killing Muggles for sport — half the Muggle murders during Voldemort's reign were just for fun. Their crimes during this time were notorious, and as a result, their names are known and feared almost as much as Voldemort's. While some Death Eaters were sent to Azkaban after Voldemort disappeared, others were able to escape by lying about their involvement with him, but live in fear of his eventual wrath and punishment.

Because Voldemort operated in the utmost secrecy, he was the only one who knew the identities of all the Death Eaters. Death Eaters were prohibited from having this information so they would not be in a position to turn others in if they were captured.

Did you know . . . the Death Eaters were once called the Knights of Walpurgis, according to the history J. K. Rowling wrote for them? In an interview with the BBC in June 2003, the author explained she had outlined the rise of the Death Eaters in her notes, and they were formerly known by this name. The actual "night of Walpurgis" is the evening before May Day (April 30), which falls directly opposite Hallowe'en on the calendar. The name comes from Walburga, Abbess of Heidenheim near Eichstätt, Germany. Ironically, she was a Catholic saint who protected against witchcraft — so it would seem strange to call the Death Eaters her "knights," as she was anti-sorcery!

Known Death Eaters

Note to Muggles: *Warning! Descriptions of certain Death Eaters may include some information about the double lives they lead — read at your own risk!*

★ **Avery:** Cleared when Voldemort disappeared — he avoided Azkaban by saying he had been under the Imperius Curse. Avery was a friend of Snape's at Hogwarts. Avery has displeased Voldemort on more than one occasion, and is punished for his mistakes by means of the Cruciatus Curse. He is involved in the battle at the Department of Mysteries.

★ **Black, Regulus:** Dead. Sirius's younger brother became a Death Eater without fully understanding the extent of their activities. When Regulus realised what he was expected to do, he panicked and tried to leave but was killed on Voldemort's orders.

★ **Crabbe:** Cleared when Voldemort disappeared. Crabbe's son Vincent is a Slytherin in Harry's year. Like his son, Crabbe is heavy-set. He is involved in the battle at the Department of Mysteries.

★ **Crouch Jr., Bartemius** (Barty): When Crouch was first caught by the Ministry just after Voldemort disappeared, he was a pale, freckle-skinned, and fair-haired young man of about nineteen. He was considered an all-around nice boy, who came from a respectable pure-blood home. He received twelve OWLs and loved Quidditch.

At the time of his capture, it seemed Crouch may have just been in the wrong place at the wrong time — he was caught with the Lestranges after the Cruciatus Curse had been performed. Yet despite his insistence he was innocent throughout his trial, he was found guilty and sent to Azkaban.

Crouch had a strange and estranged relationship with his father, who was Head of the Department of Magical Law Enforcement at the time of his capture. Crouch Sr. was so disgusted and ashamed of what happened, he disowned his son. Fortunately for Crouch, he had a much better relationship with his mother (not to mention his long-time bond with the family house-elf).

In some ways, Crouch is a paradox. He is controlling, yet controlled by others. He is a prisoner, yet imprisons others. Crouch is moody and obsessed with keeping up appearances. He feels he has a lot in common with Voldemort when it comes to fathers — both were named after and felt betrayed by theirs, among other things. Crouch is extremely loyal and will go to great lengths to prove it. Though he leads a charmed life, it is one full of subterfuge and secrets, and the fate that eventually awaits him is one worse than death.

✳ **Dolohov, Antonin:** Captured and sent to Azkaban during Voldemort's reign. Dolohov has a long, pale face. He is a torturer of Muggles, as well as wizards who do not support Voldemort, and was convicted of the murders of Gideon and Fabian Prewett. Dolohov escapes during fifth year and is involved in the battle at the Department of Mysteries.

✳ **Goyle:** Cleared when Voldemort disappeared. Goyle's son Gregory is a Slytherin in Harry's year. (Interestingly, Goyle is not mentioned during the battle at the Department of Mysteries, nor is his son mentioned as a member of the Inquisitorial Squad. Could the Goyles be turning over a new leaf, or are they simply not considered important enough by the evil powers that be? Hmmm . . .)

✳ **Jugson:** Involved in the battle at the Department of Mysteries.

✳ **Karkaroff:** Captured and sent to Azkaban after Voldemort disappeared, following a six-month manhunt during the end of his reign. Karkaroff is desperate to save himself. He renounces his allegiance and anxiously offers the Ministry (mostly useless) information in exchange for his freedom. However, when his past later rises to meet him, Karkaroff knows his betrayals will cost him dearly and flees in fear to an unknown location.

✳ **Lestrange, Bellatrix Black** (Bella): Captured and sent to Azkaban for using the Cruciatus Curse after Voldemort disappeared. Bellatrix is Sirius's cousin, and the sister of Andromeda Tonks and Narcissa Malfoy. She was a friend of Snape's at Hogwarts and is married to Rodolphus. Bellatrix is tall, with hooded eyes and a thin mouth with an arrogant smile. During her years in prison, her face has become drawn and skeletal and her once thick, gleaming dark hair has gone straggly.

Bellatrix is the name of a star in the constellation Orion (the Great Hunter). Her name means "warrioress," which is all too accurate — Bellatrix learned the Dark Arts directly from Voldemort and is possibly his most fervent supporter and loyal servant. Vicious and sadistic, she has no qualms about torturing children or even killing a member of her own family. She mocks her opponents by adopting an annoying baby voice. Bellatrix defiantly proclaims Voldemort will return after she is sentenced to Azkaban. For his part, Voldemort sees Bellatrix's time in prison as a symbol of devotion to him, and vows to free her. Bellatrix escapes during fifth year and is involved in the battle at the Department of Mysteries.

★ **Lestrange, Rabastan:** Captured and sent to Azkaban after Voldemort disappeared for using the Cruciatus Curse. Rabastan is the brother of Rodolphus. He escapes during fifth year and is involved in the battle at the Department of Mysteries.

★ **Lestrange, Rodolphus:** Captured and sent to Azkaban after Voldemort disappeared for using the Cruciatus Curse. Rodolphus is married to Bellatrix. He was a friend of Snape's at Hogwarts. Rodolphus escapes during fifth year and is involved in the battle at the Department of Mysteries.

★ **Macnair, Walden:** Cleared when Voldemort disappeared, Macnair now works for the Ministry. He is tall and broad, with a thin black moustache. During fifth year, he is dispatched to the giants' camp to try and sway them to Voldemort's side. Macnair is involved in the battle at the Department of Mysteries.

★ **Malfoy, Lucius:** Cleared when Voldemort disappeared. Lucius Malfoy was amongst the first to renounce Voldemort in the public eye, claiming to have been bewitched. Below the surface, however, his allegiance has never wavered. Despite this, he is reprimanded for his past behaviour and told better loyalty is expected of him in the future. During fifth year, Lucius Malfoy uses the Imperius Curse to try and steal a weapon for Voldemort. He is involved in the battle at the Department of Mysteries, where his double life finally catches up with him.

★ **Mulciber:** Captured and sent to Azkaban during Voldemort's reign. Mulciber is an expert in the Imperius Curse. He escapes during fifth year and is involved in the battle at the Department of Mysteries.

★ **Nott, Theodore:** Cleared when Voldemort disappeared. Nott's son, also named Theodore, is a Slytherin in Harry's year. Nott is a very elderly widower with a stooped posture, and is involved in the battle at the Department of Mysteries.

★ **Rookwood, Algernon/Augustus:** Captured and sent to Azkaban after Voldemort disappeared, when another Death Eater gave his name to the Ministry. Prior to this Rookwood worked in the Department of Mysteries. He was a spy for Voldemort and obtained information from a number of people throughout the Ministry, sometimes without their knowledge.

An old friend of Ludo Bagman's father, Rookwood has a stooped posture, pockmarked skin, and greasy hair. The word "rook" has two different but equally appropriate meanings, as far as a Death Eater is concerned. To "rook" means to deceive or swindle, while a rook is a powerful piece in the game of chess.

Rookwood escapes during fifth year and is involved in the battle at the Department of Mysteries.

Note to Muggles: *In all editions of* Harry Potter and the Goblet of Fire, *Rookwood's name is given as Augustus (meaning "great" or "venerable" — fitting, from a Death Eater's perspective!). However, in the British edition of* Harry Potter and the Order of the Phoenix, *Rookwood's first name appears as Algernon (which, oddly, is derived from the French* aux gernon, *meaning "having a moustache"). The American edition still lists his name as Augustus.*

★ Rosier, Evan: Killed by Aurors the year before Voldemort disappeared. Rosier gouged out a piece of Moody's nose when he fought being captured. Rosier is a Welsh derivative of the surname Rogers, which comes from the German *hrod* (fame) and *gar* (spear) — fitting for a person who is remembered for his carving skills!

★ Snape, Severus: Reformed. Few details are known about Snape's involvement with Voldemort, or the circumstances of his defection.

Snape was fascinated with the Dark Arts at Hogwarts, where he was part of a gang whose members almost all became Death Eaters. However, Snape later turned against Voldemort before he disappeared, at great risk to himself. He has never been accused of any Dark Arts activity since.

Dumbledore trusts Snape and gave him a second chance, although he will not say why. Snape may have re-established his connection to Voldemort on Dumbledore's orders, but some wonder where his real loyalty lies.

★ Travers: Captured and sent to Azkaban during Voldemort's reign. Travers helped murder the McKinnons.

★ Wilkes: Killed by Aurors the year before Voldemort disappeared. Wilkes was a friend of Snape's at Hogwarts. Wilkes's name may possibly come from John Wilkes Booth, who assassinated Abraham Lincoln.

★ Wormtail: It is a mystery how and why Wormtail, also known as Peter Pettigrew, first came to be involved with Voldemort, though it is likely he was just easy prey.

Wormtail speaks in a squeaky voice. Short and shrunken-looking, he has thinning, mousy hair and a pasty face, with a pointy nose and small, watery eyes. His skin is grimy except for one hand, which is made of gleaming silver. Although he is weak, meek, and cowardly, Wormtail seems to have had luck and circumstance on his side for many years. He is two-faced (in more ways than one), but it is this trait that saves his life on more than one occasion.

Wormtail took advantage of a situation to betray those close to him to Voldemort. However, there were serious, unforeseen repercussions for Voldemort based on Wormtail's information. This earned Wormtail the wrath of not only Voldemort, but his fellow Death Eaters, who thought he was a traitor. For twelve years, he lived in isolation and secrecy, biding his time until he could prove himself and clear his name.

Eventually, two of the people who felt betrayed by Wormtail confront him, but his life is spared by a last-minute intervention from the most unlikely of people. For Wormtail, this is a curse as well as a blessing — when one wizard saves another's life it creates a deep, impenetrable magical bond between them. Wormtail now owes a debt to the one person he cannot afford to become indebted to.

After a narrow escape, Wormtail scurries as far away as he possibly can. In doing so, he stumbles across a memorable opportunity to redeem himself and is later rewarded for his efforts. While Voldemort does not regard him as the most trusted or faithful of servants, Wormtail certainly gives his pound of flesh to prove his loyalty. Even when the ghosts of past deeds come back to haunt him, he remains by his master's side. By finding ways to ingratiate himself, Wormtail establishes himself as Voldemort's right hand man.

Note to Muggles: *At his "rebirthing party" Voldemort makes an enigmatic reference to six missing Death Eaters — three who have died in his service (Rosier and Wilkes; the third is unclear), one "too cowardly to return" (possibly Karkaroff), one who has left forever (possibly Snape), and one who remains Voldemort's most faithful servant and is already in his employ (possibly Crouch).*

Dark Mark: Voldemort's symbol — an enormous serpent-tongued skull composed of glittering emerald stars, that floats high into the sky and burns in a haze of green smoke. Voldemort and the Death Eaters conjured it as a sign whenever they killed.

The Dark Mark is also branded into the left inner forearm of all Death Eaters as a means for them to identify each other and a way for Voldemort to communicate with them. The Dark Mark of any Death Eater is vivid red, and when Voldemort touches it, it turns jet-black and acts as a signal to all other Death Eaters to Apparate to his side immediately. The Death Eaters' Dark Marks have faded in the years since Voldemort's disappearance.

Prior to the beginning of fourth year, the Dark Mark is conjured for the first time in thirteen years. The wizards and witches who see it are terrified, because they think Voldemort has returned and wants to kill innocent people. Some of the Death Eaters who see it are also afraid, because they think Voldemort is seeking revenge on those he felt betrayed him, while others interpret it as a symbol of support for their actions.

MAGICAL BEINGS AND CREATURES

Chimaeras and Kneazles and Bugbears — oh my! Like its Muggle counterpart, the magical animal kingdom is full of diverse creatures, from docile to dangerous, and part-being to full beast.

Note to Muggles: *This list of the beings and creatures mentioned in the Harry Potter book series is comprehensive, but not complete. To learn about other magical creatures in the Harry Potter universe, see* Fantastic Beasts & Where To Find Them *by Newt Scamander (Obscurus Books, 18a Diagon Alley). J. K. Rowling wrote this book in 2001 as a fundraiser for Comic Relief, a UK-based charity that helps underprivileged children in some of the poorest countries in the world. Rather than reproduce the contents here, I urge Muggles to purchase this marvellous book for themselves.*

Abraxan horses: Madame Maxime breeds these giant winged palomino horses, a dozen of which pull the Beauxbatons carriage. They have red eyes and enormous hooves, and drink only single-malt whisky.

Aquavirus Maggots: Luna thinks the brains in the Department of Mysteries are Aquavirus Maggots, which her father told her the Ministry was breeding.

Aragog: This giant spider has a long history with Hagrid. When a web of lies was spun about spiders many years ago, Aragog took refuge in the Forbidden Forest. He has lived there ever since, in an enormous domed web.

Over the years, Aragog's black, elephant-sized body has become streaked with grey and his formerly gleaming eyes have turned milky-white with blindness. He has fathered a huge colony of spiders with his mate, Mosag, and considers any humans who enter his lair "fresh meat" for his children.

Although giant spiders do not fear humans (it is their instinct to attack them), there is one creature they are so terrified of, they won't even call it by name — an interesting parallel to wizardkind and Voldemort.

banshee: Rooted in Irish folklore, the banshee, from the Gaelic *Bean Sidhe* meaning "woman of the faerie," is a ghostly, long-haired woman who makes unearthly wailing noises and is a harbinger of disaster. Seamus's Boggart is a banshee with floor-length black hair and a green skeletal face. Lockhart claims to have banished the Bandon Banshee.

Basilisk: Also known as the King of Serpents, the Basilisk is an enormous bright green snake capable of very advanced Dark Magic. Born from a chicken's egg hatched beneath a toad, a Basilisk can live for hundreds of years, although it finds a rooster's crow deadly. The Basilisk can kill with its poisonous, sabre-like fangs or its yellow eyes — those who meet its stare directly will die instantly.

Basilisks have been mentioned in myth and legend throughout the ages. Also called a cockatrice, it is a creature born from an egg laid by a seven-year-old rooster during the last days of Sirius (the Dog Star) and hatched by a toad. Interestingly, one of the basilisk's natural enemies is the weasel, who is immune to its deadly gaze. If a weasel is bitten by a basilisk, it will retreat to eat a rue plant (the only vegetation that will not wilt under a basilisk's eye) and return to fight with renewed stamina.

 Did you know . . . according to legend, basilisk carcasses were hung in homes to keep spiders away?

Blast-Ended Skrewts: Hagrid bred these (illegally) from Manticores and fire crabs. Pale and slimy, Skrewts look like shell-less lobsters with legs that stick out in strange places. Their diet is unknown, as they have no heads (or eyes), and they smell like rotting fish. Just six inches long at birth, Skrewts grow very fast, eventually reaching a length of over ten feet.

Mature Skrewts produce a thick grey protective armour. Their ends emit sparks and explosive noises which blast them forward several inches at a time (and burn anyone nearby!). Male Skrewts have stingers at one end, while females have suckers on their stomachs, possibly to suck blood. Skrewts are vicious, destructive, and very hard to control, and Hagrid is secretly relieved when they begin killing each other off.

Blibbering Humdinger: Luna believes in the existence of this mythical (or is it?) creature. A "humdinger" is something that is quite remarkable or spectacular, whilst "blibbering" sounds like a possible cross between "gibberish" and "blubbering." This suggests a Blibbering Humdinger is a spectacular creature that speaks nonsense and cries!

Blood-Sucking Bugbear: Hagrid reckons this creature killed the school roosters in second year. Bugbears are imaginary creatures (like Bogeymen) that cause needless fright, especially in children.

Boggart: This malevolent spirit occupies dark enclosed spaces and shape-shifts into whatever a person most fears. Boggarts become confused in the presence of more than one person, because they don't know what form to assume.

Did you know . . . tales of Boggarts go back hundreds of years throughout British history? Thought to be related to brownies (faeries that can be both helpful and mischievous), Boggarts were mischievous poltergeists that dwelled in houses. Of Scottish origin, Boggarts have also been known as hobgoblins and the Bogeyman. There are several places in Britain named after Boggarts, including Boggart Clough, near Manchester, and Boggart's Hole, in Lancashire.

Bowtruckles: Tiny brown "stick-men" that look like living twigs. Bowtruckles have a flat, bark-like face with brown eyes, and knobbly wooden legs and arms featuring two twig-like fingers on each hand. They guard trees that produce wood for wands and can be dangerous when angry. It is advisable to distract Bowtruckles with a gift of food — faerie eggs or woodlice — if attempting to take wood from a tree they are protecting.

Centaur: With the body of a horse and the chest, arms, and head of a man, centaurs represent both power and intelligence. Mythologically, they have been depicted as being friendly and on good terms with humans; however, the centaurs in the Forbidden Forest keep to themselves and are mistrustful of wizards. They are a proud, ancient race who refuse to submit to wizarding rule, control, or notions of superiority. Although the centaurs will speak to Hagrid if he asks, they will not tolerate outside interference in their matters. They are not especially friendly and keep to themselves.

As stargazers, centaurs impartially observe the heavens and are sworn not to go against what the heavens have in store. It is considered a great betrayal for a centaur to share his secret knowledge with humans. Although centaurs know things, they don't say much, and tell the future in an exceedingly slow and cryptic manner. In first year, the centaurs tell Hagrid that "Mars is bright tonight." Mars is the Roman god of war — could this be prophesising Voldemort's return and the subsequent war? The centaurs also state, "always the innocent are the first victims." The first person to fall is, indeed, an innocent bystander.

The ninth sign of the zodiac, Sagittarius, is represented by a centaur.

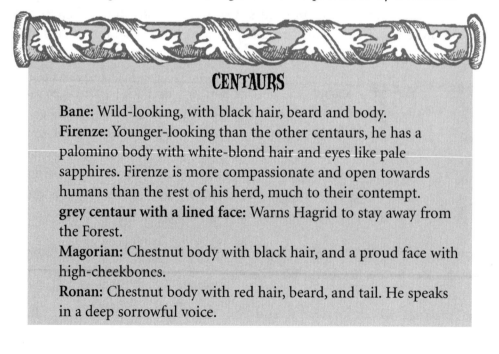

CENTAURS

Bane: Wild-looking, with black hair, beard and body.
Firenze: Younger-looking than the other centaurs, he has a palomino body with white-blond hair and eyes like pale sapphires. Firenze is more compassionate and open towards humans than the rest of his herd, much to their contempt.
grey centaur with a lined face: Warns Hagrid to stay away from the Forest.
Magorian: Chestnut body with black hair, and a proud face with high-cheekbones.
Ronan: Chestnut body with red hair, beard, and tail. He speaks in a deep sorrowful voice.

Chimaera: This sibling of the Sphinx has a lion's head, goat's body, and a dragon's tail. Chimaeras are extremely dangerous, and their eggs are very hard to come by.

Cornish pixies: Native to Cornwall, these mischievous faeries are eight inches tall and blue, with pointed faces and very shrill voices. Although Seamus mocks their lack of ferocity, the pixies wreak havoc when unleashed in Defence Against the Dark Arts class.

Crumple-Horned Snorkack (Kacky Snorgle): Luna believes in the existence of this supposedly mythical non-flying creature. It is possibly located in Sweden.

Crup: Similar to a Jack Russell terrier, but with a forked tail.

Doxys: Insect-like creatures with bodies covered in thick black hair, shiny wings like beetles, and needle-sharp poisonous teeth. Doxys lay black eggs and emit venom, with which Fred and George experiment for their Skiving Snackboxes.

dragons: These winged scaly beasts are about fifty feet tall and can shoot fire up to twenty feet. Their eyes are their weakest point. Dragons cannot be tamed and it is dangerous to attempt to do so (not that this has ever stopped Hagrid!). They are very difficult to kill — only the most powerful spells can penetrate the magic stored in their thick hides. Although dragon breeding has been outlawed since the 1709 Warlocks' Convention, species of wild dragons still exist in Britain.

DRAGON SPECIES

Chinese Fireball: Red, with a fringe of gold spikes around its face.
Common Welsh Green: Green, smaller, and smooth-scaled.

> **Hebridean Blacks:** Black dragons native to islands just west of Scotland.
>
> **Hungarian Horntail:** Black, with long bronze spikes along its tail. It is enormous and especially vicious, and can shoot fire up to forty feet.
>
> **Norwegian Ridgebacks:** Black, with spiny wings, a long snout and stubby horns.
>
> **Swedish Short-Snout:** Blue-grey, with long pointed horns.

ferrets: Although these small furry mammals from the weasel family are not particularly magical, it is worth noting Malfoy is turned into a bouncing white ferret after trying to attack Harry. "Unusual" ferrets were also turned up in a wizard's home after a Ministry raid. Buckbeak feasts on dead ferrets.

Flesh-eating slugs: Diet consists of cabbages — amongst other things!

Flobberworms: Slimy, toothless brown worms, ten inches long. They function best when left alone, and eat mainly lettuce.

fire crabs: Hagrid illegally breeds fire crabs with Manticores to create Blast-Ended Skrewts. Native to Fiji, fire crabs resemble enormous tortoises. They have a protective jewelled shell and shoot flames from their ends when attacked.

giants (and half-giants): Much like trolls, giants are vicious, bloodthirsty, and dangerous. Twenty to twenty-five feet tall, they destroy everything they encounter, including each other.

At one time, there were about one hundred giant tribes globally but they have become almost extinct due to infighting. There are only about seventy to eighty giants left in the world, living inside an inaccessible mountain range in eastern Europe. (Muggles have seen giants, but never live to tell the tale — their deaths are explained as "mountaineering accidents.") Though the remaining giants stick together for their own protection, they are not meant to live in such close proximity so their numbers are ever-dwindling.

There are no giants left in Britain — wizards forced most of them into exile and Aurors killed the remaining few who had joined Voldemort's side and were responsible for some of the worst mass-Muggle killings during his reign. It is difficult to Stun giants due to their size and toughness.

★ **Fridwulfa:** Hagrid's giantess mother was "not very maternal" and left when he was three years old. He did not know what happened to her, but later discovered she met another giant, had a child, and has been dead for many years.

★ **Golgomath:** One of the largest giants, with black hair and teeth to match. Golgomath wears a necklace made from bones and becomes the new Gurg after decapitating Karkus.

Did you know . . . Golgomath's name may be a play on the word "googol"? A googol is a "math" term for a one with a hundred zeroes after it — in other words, one of the largest numbers known.

★ **Grawp** (Grawpy): At "only" sixteen feet tall, Hagrid's half-brother is considered "runty" for a giant, and gets picked on by the others at the giant camp. Grawp doesn't fare much better in his new home; he is considered an unwelcome addition to the Forbidden Forest by some of its other residents.

Grawp looks like a deformed person, with a grey, round head that is much larger than his body. He has tightly-curled hair, small sludge-coloured eyes, a stubby nose, and misshapen yellow teeth. His hands are as big as umbrellas and his feet are the size of sledges. Grawp destroys everything in his path because he doesn't know any better. He doesn't speak much English or have many manners but Hagrid is desperate to teach him.

★ **Karkus:** The biggest, ugliest, and laziest giant of all, his name is a play on the word "carcass," which is appropriate as he doesn't live very long. Karkus is about twenty-three feet tall, with skin like rhinoceros hide. He does not speak English. As the old Gurg, he is waited on by the other giants.

giant squid: Resides in the Hogwarts lake. The giant squid is fairly domesticated as it permits Fred, George, and Lee to tickle its tentacles and gives Dennis Creevey a helpful boost back into his boat after he falls in the lake.

gnomes: Completely unlike the Muggle garden variety, magical gnomes are about ten inches tall and potato-like in appearance, with large knobbly bald heads, leathery skin, sharp teeth, and horny feet. Gnomes live in gnomeholes and are not very bright. They are considered a household pest and must be purged frequently from the garden by swinging them in circles by their feet and flinging them into the air, which disorients them. Mr. Weasley finds gnomes amusing and is accused of being too soft with them.

goblins: Goblins have swarthy, clever faces, with dark, slanting eyes and pointed beards. They are about a head shorter than Harry, and have very long fingers and feet. Goblins speak in Gobbledegook and are highly intelligent creatures. Unlike house-elves, they are quite capable of sticking up for themselves and dealing with wizards (hence the goblin rebellions Professor Binns talks about in History of Magic class). Goblins run Gringotts with an iron fist, and have little tolerance for would-be thieves.

Grim: Black, bear-sized dog that haunts churchyards and is an omen of death (like an animal version of the Grim Reaper). Harry is repeatedly haunted by the sight of a large black dog throughout third year. (It doesn't help matters when Trelawney keeps seeing a Grim in his tea leaves and crystal ball, either.)

Mysterious black dogs are prominent in British folklore. One of these, the Kirk (Scottish for church) Grim, was a black dog that guarded graveyards and protected the dead against evil spirits and creatures.

 Did you know . . . in the Yorkshire region there was a legendary black calf-sized dog that haunted desolate roads, named Padfoot?

Grindylows: Small, green, water-dwelling demons with sharp horns, pointed fangs, and long spindly fingers. Merpeople keep Grindylows as pets. British folklore tells of a Yorkshire water spirit called the "Gindylow" that dragged people beneath the water.

Heliopaths: Luna claims the Ministry has a private army of these tall fire spirits that gallop and burn everything in their path.

Hinkypunks: Frail-looking one-legged creatures that seem to be made from smoke and lure people into bogs with their lanterns.

"Hinky Punk" is a regional name for a will o' the wisp — a low-rising smoky light found in dangerous areas, thought to be a malevolent spirit of the dead. Travellers follow the "will" of this "wisp" of light to their doom.

 Did you know ... the name "Hinky Punk" is local to southwestern England? Other regional names include the Pinket, the Ellylldan, and Spunkies.

Hippogriff: Very rare mythical Greek creature. Half horse and half griffin, Hippogriffs symbolise both love and impossibility — horses and griffins were adversaries, so the likelihood of them mating was impossible. However, the product of their union, the Hippogriff, is a symbol of love so strong it overcomes impossibility.

The Hippogriffs Hagrid brings to class are a cross between horses (bodies, tails, and hind legs) and eagles (heads, front legs, and wings), with steel-coloured beaks, sharp talons, and orange eyes. Hippogriffs are proud and easily offended creatures, and will lash out if insulted. Humans must maintain eye contact (preferably without blinking) and bow, then wait for them to bow back before approaching.

house-elves: Bony, bald, and brown, these small creatures look like large, ugly dolls. As servants, they carry out menial tasks without pay for their masters, who are usually old, wealthy wizarding families like the Blacks, Crouches, and Malfoys (although Mrs. Weasley wishes she had one to do the ironing). The mark of a good house-elf is that it is neither seen nor heard. House-elves speak of themselves in the third person, as if to underscore their inferiority.

House-elves must always uphold their family's honour and keep their secrets. They cannot speak ill of their masters and must punish themselves if they do (although Dumbledore gives one permission to call him a "barmy old codger" if he likes!). Bound to serve their family and house for a lifetime, house-elves can only be set free if presented with a piece of clothing by their masters.

House-elves Disapparate and Apparate (even inside Hogwarts's grounds, which wizards cannot do) with a loud whip-like crack. They have powerful wandless magic of their own, but cannot use it without their masters' permission. During Voldemort's reign house-elves were treated horribly, but their situation has improved somewhat since his disappearance.

* **Dobby**: Dobby has a pencil-shaped nose, large bat-like ears, enormous bulging green eyes like tennis balls and a toothy grin. He has long fingers and toes. Shrill-voiced and emotional, Dobby is prone to fits of self-punishment for breaking rules and bursts into tears when shown kindness. He has great respect for Dumbledore and is very taken with Harry — he fawns over him with constant praise and compliments, which makes Harry rather uncomfortable and embarrassed.

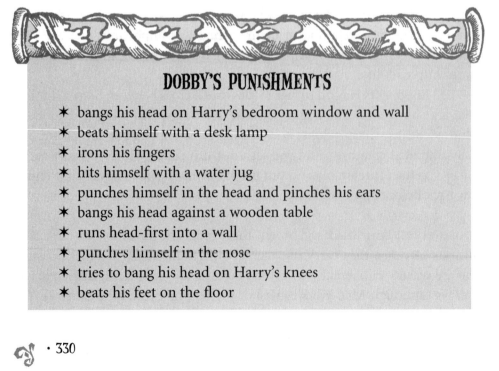

DOBBY'S PUNISHMENTS

* bangs his head on Harry's bedroom window and wall
* beats himself with a desk lamp
* irons his fingers
* hits himself with a water jug
* punches himself in the head and pinches his ears
* bangs his head against a wooden table
* runs head-first into a wall
* punches himself in the nose
* tries to bang his head on Harry's knees
* beats his feet on the floor

Second year

Dobby receives several death threats a day at his masters' house, where he wears a dirty old pillowcase. Throughout the year, he tries to warn Harry about the "terrible things" conspiring at Hogwarts, but his "help" is a hindrance. Eventually the truth comes out, and Dobby is inadvertently rewarded for his role in saving Harry's life.

Fourth and Fifth years

After gaining his freedom from the Malfoys, Dobby decides he wants to earn a wage and searches in vain for paid work for two years. Eventually, he finds a dream job at Hogwarts, where he earns a Galleon a week, with a day off each month (Dobby talked Dumbledore down from ten Galleons a week and weekends off.) One of the things Dobby likes best about his freedom is the ability to wear proper clothes, although his taste leaves much to be desired! He has been seen sporting a tea-cosy hat, loud ties, and numerous odd socks (his favourite piece of clothing). Dobby's loyalty to Harry never wavers over the years.

Did you know . . . a Dobby is a kind of hobgoblin, or good-natured household sprite, found in the Lancashire and Yorkshire regions of England? Dobby stones were special stones where gifts for faeries were placed.

✶ **Hogwarts house-elves:** To Hermione's horror, Hogwarts has over one hundred house-elves, the most in any building in Britain. They wear tea-towels, tied like togas, with the Hogwarts crest. The house-elves are offended by the idea of being paid for their work, which includes cleaning the castle and preparing meals.

✶ **Kreacher:** The Black family's ancient house-elf is a nasty little "creature" indeed. Kreacher has white hair growing out of his ears, a snout-like nose, and bloodshot, watery grey eyes. He walks slowly, with a hunched back. His skin seems to be too big for his body and he wears a dirty rag as a loincloth.

Kreacher's family has served the Blacks for generations (he aspires to have his head mounted on a plaque in the hallway after his death, like his mother). Unlike other house-elves, Kreacher doesn't do much cleaning — he spends his days sulking and reclaiming various Dark objects thrown out during the decontamination of Grimmauld Place.

Like Harry during his early years at the Dursleys, Kreacher sleeps in a cramped cupboard. Also like Harry, he does not feel much loyalty towards those he lives with — he is regarded with indifference at best and open hostility at worst. Unlike Harry, however, Kreacher's miserable existence and the way he has been treated have resulted in a spiteful, mean attitude.

True to the prevailing mentality of the Blacks, Kreacher believes in the superiority of pure-bloods. He glares hatefully at the "beasts, brats, and blood-traitors" that pass through Grimmauld Place, muttering horrible things in their presence. Hermione thinks Kreacher is out of his mind and insists on treating him kindly. She even suggests setting him free but Kreacher knows too much about the goings-on at Grimmauld Place, even though he is forbidden to reveal any of it.

Although Kreacher is fondest of the "blackest" members of the Black family, he must obey the direct orders of all their relations, even those whom he holds in contempt. However, he has no trouble lying to those whom he does not serve.

★ **Winky:** A friend of Dobby's, Winky has enormous bulging brown eyes, long bat-like ears, and a nose like a large squashed tomato. Her family has served the Crouches for three generations, and she wears a tea-towel as a toga. Winky is a model house-elf and always does as she is told, even if she doesn't like it. She takes great pride in having kept her master's most important secret.

Winky is accused of a serious offence by members of the Ministry but insists she is innocent. Although her master believes her, she still suffers serious consequences for disobeying him and shaming his reputation. Winky comes to Hogwarts, where she spends most of her time in a drunken, dirty, dishevelled mess. Almost as dramatic as Dobby, she is ashamed of herself and sobs constantly, pining for Crouch.

Kappas: Water-dwelling demons that have webbed hands and look like monkeys covered in scales. Kappas strangle people who unknowingly wade into their waters. Snape states Kappas are commonly found in Mongolia (he is incorrect — according to *Fantastic Beasts and Where to Find Them*, Kappas are Japanese). Japanese mythology depicts the Kappa as a highly intelligent creature that is part ape, part tortoise, and feeds on blood and cucumbers.

kelpies: Lockhart gives Hagrid unwanted advice about how to get these water demons out of a well. According to Scottish legend, the kelpie is a shape-shifter that usually takes the form of a horse and haunts bodies of water. (Of course, Hagrid already knew the only way to tame and defeat a kelpie is through its bridle, where its shape-shifting power resides. Bridling a kelpie renders it docile.)

Knarls: Similar to hedgehogs, but their quills are magical. Knarls are highly distrustful by nature.

Kneazles: These cat-like creatures have spotted fur, large ears, and a tail like a lion.

Manticore: Extremely dangerous Greek monster, with a man's head, lion's body, and scorpion's tail filled with poisonous darts. Manticores shoot darts at their victims, killing them instantly, then swallow them whole. Bred with fire crabs to create Blast-Ended Skrewts, Manticores were likely responsible for the vicious nature of the Skrewts (although it seems unlikely a creature as fierce as a Manticore could ever have been bred with a kind of crab!).

The trio read up on a Manticore attack dating back to 1296 — the beast in question wasn't punished because no one was brave enough to approach it.

Mosag: Giant female spider and Aragog's mate, whom Hagrid found for him.

Nargles: According to Luna, these creatures often infest mistletoe.

Nifflers: Cuddly, fluffy black creatures with long hairy snouts and flat, spade-like front paws (all the better to dig with). Nifflers are like little treasure detectors. They are attracted to shiny objects and are commonly found down mines.

owls: Postal delivery in the wizarding world is provided by these wise, nocturnal birds, who courier packages and letters, often across great distances, in exchange for money or food. Owl communication is usually very secure, although it has been known to be intercepted.

During the school year, owls drop their deliveries into recipients' laps during breakfast in the Great Hall. There are a number of owls kept at Hogwarts for general use, and an Owl Post Office in Hogsmeade.

phoenix: Legendary bird that bursts into flames when it dies, only to be reborn from the ashes. Appropriately, the phoenix's majestic plumage is the colour of fire, with scarlet body feathers and golden tail feathers.

Ancient Greeks and Egyptians associated the phoenix with Apollo (god of sun and light) and Ra (sun god), respectively. Only one phoenix could exist at a time, living for up to hundreds of years before burning itself on a pyre of flames and making way for the new phoenix to rise. Because of this, the phoenix represents resurrection and immortality.

Phoenixes have numerous magical abilities — they are capable of carrying incredibly heavy loads and their tears can heal wounds. Phoenix song revitalises those who hear it (Harry associates it with Dumbledore).

Did you know . . . of all the fantastic beasts in the Harry Potter series, J. K. Rowling said her favourite is the phoenix? In an interview with Comic Relief, the author said she liked phoenixes best because they were very beautiful and had all sorts of interesting properties.

Did you know . . . the Cornish name for faerie is "piskie"? (They are known as pixies in other southern English counties.)

Porlocks: Found in Dorset (southwestern England) and parts of Ireland, Porlocks somewhat resemble the herds of horses they keep guard over — they are two feet tall with shaggy fur, and have two small arms and two legs with cloven feet.

 Did you know . . . Porlocks were likely named after the village of Porlock in the county of Somerset, which is just above Dorset?

Red Caps: Short, goblin-like creatures that lurk wherever blood has been spilt, such as dungeons or battlefields. Scottish mythology describes Red Caps as small, wiry bearded spirits with steel claws, who haunted castles where violence or evil had occurred. They kill by bludgeoning their victims with boulders or tearing at them with their claws. Red Caps were named after the bonnets they wore, which were dipped in the blood of their victims.

salamanders: Small lizards that live in fires. Hagrid treats a few salamanders with scale rot by rubbing chilli powder on them.

sphinx: Mythical creature with the body of a lion and the head of a human. The Greek sphinx represents bad luck and death. It has a female head and is known for asking travellers a riddle that must be answered correctly in order to pass by. The most famous Greek sphinx comes from Sophocles's play *Oedipus Rex*. Conversely, the Egyptian sphinx represents nobility and wisdom. It has the head of a king or god, and is known for protecting treasure (Bill Weasley likely encountered a few sphinxes on the job!). The most famous Egyptian sphinx can be found at the Pyramids of Giza.

 Did you know . . . the word sphinx comes from the Greek "sphingo," to strangle, which is how the sphinx would kill its victims?

spiders: Ron has a lifelong phobia of these eight-legged arachnids, dating back to childhood, when Fred turned his teddy bear into a spider after Ron broke Fred's toy broomstick. The spiders at Hogwarts like the dark and quiet, and live in fear of their one monstrous enemy. The spiders in the Forbidden Forest, on the other hand, also like the dark and quiet but are quite fearless.

Thestrals: Eerie-looking, leathery-winged creatures that have the dragon-like head of a reptile and the black silky coat and long tail of a horse. Thestrals have fleshless, skeletal frames, with blank white eyes and pointed fangs. They are attracted to the scent of blood and raw meat. Only those who have seen death can see Thestrals — to everyone else, they are invisible. They can fly very fast and have an excellent sense of direction.

Thestrals are classified as dangerous by the Ministry. They are meant to bring bad luck to those who see them, but Hagrid insists this is not true. He has the only domesticated herd in Britain (which began with one male and five females), and trained the Thestrals not to touch the school owls, as they sometimes attack birds. Tenebrus, Hagrid's favourite, was the first Thestral born in the Forbidden Forest. *Tenebrus* means gloomy or dark in Latin.

Did you know . . . there was a reason why Harry didn't see Thestrals at the end of fourth year? At London's Royal Albert Hall in June 2003, J. K. Rowling said she felt there wasn't the space at the end of *Harry Potter and the Goblet of Fire* to properly explain what Thestrals were or why Harry was suddenly seeing them. Instead, she decided wizards would have a delayed reaction to seeing them after seeing death. "If Harry had seen them then and we hadn't explained them then, I thought that would be rather a cheat on the reader in that Harry suddenly sees these monsters but we don't go anywhere with them. So, to explain to myself, I said that you had to have seen the death and allowed it to sink in a little bit before slowly these creatures became solid in front of you." (On her official Web site, J. K. Rowling said Harry didn't see Thestrals starting in his first year as he was in his cot when his parents died and he didn't actually see them being killed. She added that Harry passed out just before the death at the end of the end of the first year, and didn't see it, either.)

trolls: Strong, slow, and incredibly smelly ("a mixture of old socks and the kind of public toilet no one seems to clean"), trolls make good security guards. Although they communicate by grunting, they carry wooden clubs and use brute force to get their point across!

Trolls are about twelve feet tall, with long arms that drag on the floor and feet that shuffle when they walk. They have short, thick legs and flat, horny feet. Their bodies are lumpy and boulder-like, with dull grey skin and coconut-sized heads.

unicorns: Powerful magical creatures with a pearly-white mane, golden hooves, and a horned head. Unicorn foals are gold-coloured, turn silver around age two, grow horns at age four, and turn a luminous white when fully-grown (around age seven). Unicorns are very hard to catch, and it is a great crime to kill one. In first year, the unicorns in the Forbidden Forest are targeted for their blood, which will keep a person alive. However, anyone who drinks a unicorn's blood will have a cursed life for slaughtering such a pure and innocent creature. Adult unicorns prefer a female's touch, although foals are more trusting of either sex.

vampires: Pale undead creatures that maintain their immortality by biting humans and feasting on their blood. Vampire lore is common the world over, but largely associated with eastern Europe. Lockhart claims to have turned a vampire into a vegetarian after doing battle with him.

werewolves: People (usually male) who are bitten by werewolves transform into them during the full moon. Deeply mistrusted by most wizards, these vicious creatures have long jaws, hunched shoulders, clawed paws, and furry faces. Defence Against the Dark Arts professors seem to be prone to experiences with werewolves. Malfoy and Ron have heard these creatures live in the Forbidden Forest, although it has never been proven.

yeti: Giant troll-like creature with thick white fur that lives in the Himalaya mountains, bordering Tibet and Nepal. The Nepalese know the yeti as *rakshasa* (Sanskrit for demon), but throughout the world, it is also called Bigfoot, Sasquatch, and the Abominable Snowman. Although yetis are notorious for savagely attacking anything they encounter, Lockhart claims to have cured one that had a head-cold.

Did you know . . . the yeti became the national symbol of Nepal after the Nepalese government (despite no solid proof) officially declared its existence in 1961?

PETS

Binky: Lavender's baby rabbit, which is killed by a fox (Lavender believes Trelawney correctly predicted this).

Buckbeak (Beaky): Hagrid takes a shine to this great grey Hippogriff with the large orange eyes. Like all Hippogriffs, Buckbeak must be treated with respect, and there are grave consequences when this doesn't happen, reaching as far as the Hogwarts board of governors and the Ministry. Buckbeak becomes a victim of corruption, despite the trio's help. However, in due time, he meets up with a kindred spirit and begins a new life.

(unnamed) cat: If the hair found on Hermione's robe is anything to go by, Millicent Bulstrode's cat is likely black with yellow eyes and long, pointy ears.

Crookshanks: Hermione bought her cat in third year from the Magical Menagerie, where he had been residing for quite a long time. Crookshanks is the size of a small orange tiger, with thick, fluffy fur and a bushy tail. He looks perpetually grumpy, and has a squashed face with yellow eyes and bow-legs (of course, Hermione thinks he is beautiful). Crookshanks's name is a play on his bandy legs — "crook" is an abbreviation of "crooked" and a "shank" is commonly known as an animal's leg.

Crookshanks frequently imitates his mistress's behaviour and has been known to give Harry and Ron a withering look when they don't finish their homework. An excellent judge of character, he seems to know instinctively when things are not as they appear — although his natural feline reactions sometimes lead to suspicions and accusations from others.

Half-Kneazle, Crookshanks is called "the most intelligent cat of his kind," which is not unlike Lupin referring to Hermione as the cleverest witch of her age . . . perhaps it is not so much of a coincidence that they wound up together?

Did you know . . . Crookshanks is based on a cat J. K. Rowling frequently used to see on her lunch hour when she worked in London in the late 1980s? The large ginger cat had a face that looked like it ran into a wall, and used to prowl haughtily among the people eating lunch in an outdoor square, refusing to be stroked!

eagle owl: Malfoy's owl, which regularly delivers treats from home.

Errol: The Weasley family's owl resembles a grey, moulting feather duster. Large, feeble, and old, he collapses frequently from the strain of delivering the post.

Fang: Hagrid's enormous black boarhound. Though he looks fierce, like Hagrid, Fang's bark is worse than his bite — he drools, licks people, and is a general coward.

Fawkes: Dumbledore's phoenix. The size of a swan, Fawkes is a beautiful bird when young, with brilliant red plumage and a tail as long as a peacock full of "strangely hot" golden feathers. He has a long sharp golden beak and talons, and beady black eyes. As Fawkes ages, his eyes become dull, his feathers fall out, and he makes strange sounds. Harry first meets Fawkes on a Burning Day, when the phoenix catches fire and is reborn from the ashes, wrinkled and ugly.

Fawkes has a gentle, calming disposition. He is very loyal to Dumbledore, but seems to have a special connection to Harry as well. He has saved Harry's life before, and his pearly tears have healed Harry's wounds on numerous occasions. His song comforts and fortifies Harry in times of need.

Fawkes is an extremely magical bird. He can transport great weights with his tail and performs a kind of Apparation and Disapparation amid a burst of flame. Like owls, Fawkes can also deliver messages. However, he does not need to fly — he sends messages in a burst of flames, out of which falls a parchment scroll and a golden tail feather. Fawkes's tail feathers are also highly magical. Dumbledore uses one as a quill, while Harry and Voldemort's wands contain the only two feathers Fawkes ever gave for wands.

Fawkes likely gets his name from Guy Fawkes, a British historical figure who is burned in effigy every Bonfire Night (see page 396).

Fluffy: Enormous three-headed dog Hagrid bought from a "Greek chappie" in the pub. Fluffy has mad eyes, yellow fangs, and foul breath. The dog's thunderous growl and fierce nature makes it a perfect guard dog. Greek mythology tells of a three-headed dog named Cerberus who guarded the entrance to the underworld (Hades), and was lulled to sleep by the sound of Orpheus's lyre.

Hedwig: Harry's owl, a gift for his eleventh birthday from Hagrid. Hedwig is a snowy owl with large amber eyes. A perceptive and clever owl, she seems to understand Harry when he speaks to her. She is loyal and affectionate, often nipping Harry gently, but can be moody, too — she clicks her beak when annoyed and has even been known to cuff Harry about the head when she is cross with him for not showing enough appreciation for her efforts.

Hedwig takes great pride in delivering the post (but is rather disdainful towards Pigwidgeon's style of delivery). She suffers an injury to her wing during a delivery in fifth year.

 Did you know . . . although Harry found Hedwig's name in his *History of Magic* book, J. K. Rowling likely took the owl's name from a twelfth century saint? A former duchess, St. Hedwig was noted for her great benevolence and comforting and compassionate nature.

Hermes: Percy's screech owl, a gift from his parents for being made prefect. Hermes is the Greek god of commerce — an apt name, considering Percy's career ambitions!

Mr. Paws, Snowy, Mr. Tibbles, and Tufty: Mrs. Figg's cats.

Mrs. Norris: Filch's scrawny, dusty-grey coloured cat. Mrs. Norris seems to have a sixth sense for seeking out things that do not belong. She is likely named after the character of Mrs. Norris in Jane Austen's *Mansfield Park* — a (human) busybody! She has bulging yellow lamp-like eyes and prowls the Hogwarts corridors late at night looking for rule-breakers. In second year, Mrs. Norris encounters something truly petrifying on one of her nightly patrols.

Nagini: Voldemort's snake, whose venom is milked to make a life-sustaining potion. She is twelve feet long and has a diamond-pattern tail. Nagini warns Voldemort of eavesdroppers and carries out attacks for him.

Norbert: Hagrid won a huge, black Norwegian Ridgeback dragon's egg in a card game at the Hog's Head. The baby dragon looks like a crumpled black umbrella when it emerges, with spiny wings and a skinny body. It has stubby horns, bulging orange eyes, pointed poisonous fangs, and a long snout with wide nostrils. It also has a nasty temperament and bites and snaps at people, although Hagrid is completely blind to this undesirable behaviour. He names the baby dragon Norbert and dotes on him like a surrogate "Mummy" — feeding him every half hour on a diet of chicken blood mixed with brandy, and even singing him lullabies.

Like all "children," Norbert goes through a growth spurt (three times his length in a week). The damage done by his increasing size, plus the fear of his discovery (dragon breeding is illegal) soon poses a big problem, but the trio finally convince Hagrid to send Norbert to Charlie in Romania.

Pigwidgeon (**Pig**): Ginny named Ron's neurotic little owl, which was a gift as a replacement for Scabbers (Ron verifies with Crookshanks that Pig is a real owl before accepting him as a pet). The owl equivalent of Colin Creevey, Pig is highly excitable and constantly flutters around twittering shrilly. He is so tiny, he resembles a fluffy grey Snitch. All the other animals Pig encounters regard him as a useless nuisance; however, Luna, Ginny, and most other female students think he is rather sweet.

 Did you know . . . Pigwidgeon (Pigwiggen) was the name of a dwarf faerie knight who fell in love with the tiny flower faerie Queen

Mab? The name has come to be associated with any faerie of a small stature, or anything very small.

Ripper: Aunt Marge's favourite bulldog. He is old and bad-tempered, and once chased Harry up a tree after Harry accidentally trod on his paw.

Scabbers: Ron's fat grey rat, a hand-me-down from Percy. Scabbers has been in the Weasley family for twelve years, well beyond the average lifespan for a rat. He has a tattered left ear, a missing toe on his front paw, and seems to have no magical ability (although he did have the good sense to bite Goyle). Ron frequently complains Scabbers is boring and useless, as all he does is sleep and eat. Literally and figuratively, Scabbers is a dirty old rat.

Throughout third year, Scabbers seems to take a turn for the worse. His whiskers begin to droop, he moults in patches, and he wastes away to skin and bone. Ron blames this on stress due to constant attacks by Crookshanks, and when the worst is feared, he insists the cat (and by extension, Hermione) is at fault.

(unnamed) tarantula: Lee Jordan owns one of these large furry spiders, which he shows off on the Hogwarts Express.

Trevor: Neville's toad, a gift from his Great Uncle Algie (according to Hagrid, toads are unfashionable pets). Trevor occasionally goes missing, but this could be from Neville's forgetfulness as much as Trevor's ability to leap away! After Neville botches a Shrinking Solution, Snape decides to teach him a lesson by feeding a few drops to Trevor at the end of class. Fortunately, Hermione helps Neville correct the potion and Trevor safely shrinks to tadpole size instead of being poisoned (much to Snape's disappointment).

 Did you know . . . in the Spanish translation of the series, Trevor the toad has been replaced by a turtle?

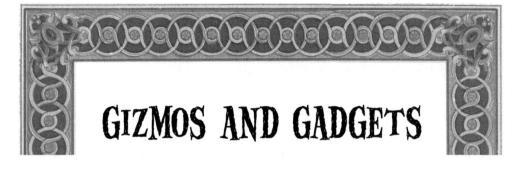

GIZMOS AND GADGETS

"Never trust anything that can think for itself if you can't see where it keeps its brain."
— Mr. Weasley, *Harry Potter and the Chamber of Secrets*

From teapots to Time-Turners, the wizarding world is full of magical and sometimes mysterious objects. Many are designed to simplify life, others are dangerous, while some are purely whimsical in nature.

animated clothing: Ron finds a set of robes that tries to choke him during the decontamination of Grimmauld Place, while his father has a pair of gloves that twiddle their thumbs on his desk at the Ministry.

Auto-Answer Quills: Banned from the examination hall during OWLs and NEWTs.

battle helmet: An indestructible goblin-made helmet was given to the Gurg of the giants as a gift.

bell jar: The Time Room in the Department of Mysteries contains a tall bell jar filled with a glittering current. Inside the jar is a hummingbird egg, which hatches as it rises, but the tiny bird inside falls to the bottom of the jar and becomes sealed inside the egg once again. The process is repeated continually, and may pertain to that age-old mystery: which came first, the [bird] or the egg?

bewitched snowballs: Fred and George enchant snowballs to knock on the Gryffindor common room window, then pelt Ron in the face after he opens it.

biting doorknobs: Willy Widdershins was arrested for selling these to Muggles.

biting kettle: Found by Mr. Weasley during a raid.

Cribbages Wizarding Crackers: Unlike Muggle Christmas crackers, wizard crackers go off with a loud cannon-like blast when pulled and emit a cloud of blue smoke. Cribbage is a type of two-player (Muggle) card game. However, its name fits in the wizarding world too, as the crackers are pulled between two people and their contents are playful in nature.

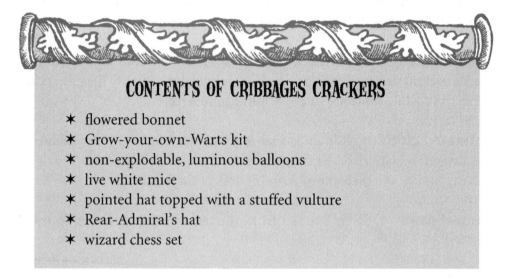

CONTENTS OF CRIBBAGES CRACKERS

* flowered bonnet
* Grow-your-own-Warts kit
* non-explodable, luminous balloons
* live white mice
* pointed hat topped with a stuffed vulture
* Rear-Admiral's hat
* wizard chess set

Detachable Cribbing Cuffs: Banned from the examination hall during OWLS and NEWTS.

Doxycide: Noxious black liquid that immobilises Doxys.

dragon skin: Powerfully magical substance — only the strongest spells can penetrate the magic stored in dragon hides. An enormous roll of dragon skin was given to the Gurg of the giants as a gift.

Dr. Filibuster's Fabulous Wet-Start, No-Heat Fireworks: A favourite of Fred and George's, who use them for a variety of celebratory and prank-related purposes. After the twins feed a Filibuster Firework to an orange salamander, it whizzes around making exploding noises and emitting tangerine stars from its mouth.

Dumbledore's watch: Gold-coloured pocketwatch that has no numbers and twelve hands, with tiny planets revolving around the face.

enchanted dustbins: Moody owns dustbins that make a racket and shoot out rubbish if anyone trespasses on his property.

enchanted lawnmower: Mr. Weasley helped Otto Bagman out of a sticky situation involving a lawnmower with unnatural powers.

Ever-Bashing Boomerangs: On Filch's list of forbidden objects in fourth year.

Exploding Snap: Similar to the Muggle card game, only with more volatile results. Ron builds a castle out of Exploding Snap cards which singes his eyebrows when it blows up.

Fanged Frisbees: On Filch's list of forbidden objects in fourth year.

Floo Network: This group of magically connected fireplaces is one of the key methods of transportation and communication in the wizarding world. Controlled by the Ministry, the Floo Network enables wizards to travel to or talk with people in different locations. Muggle fireplaces are not meant to be connected to the Floo Network unless special permission is granted.

To travel, wizards throw a pinch of Floo powder into a fireplace and state where they want to go (making sure to speak clearly!), then step into the flames and are transported to their destination. The same process is followed to make a "call" through the flames, but the wizard only places his head in the flames (it will appear in the other person's fireplace). Fireplaces are not a completely secure method of communication and can be subject to interference from third parties.

Harry doesn't particularly care for travel by Floo as it involves spinning around at a dizzying speed, like being sucked down a drain.

Floo powder: Glittering powder which, when thrown into a fire, turns the flames bright green and makes them feel like warm air. "Floo" is a play on "flue," a pipe that conveys smoke from a fireplace to a chimney.

Foe-Glass: Mirror with dark, shadowy shapes moving around inside. When the figures' faces come into focus, they reveal any enemies who are nearby. Traditionally, Foe-Glasses are considered Dark Magic detectors (but this is not always the case). There is a Foe-Glass in the Defence Against the Dark Arts office in fourth year, and another in the Room of Requirements during DA lessons.

Ford Anglia: Launched in 1959, over one million of these classic British cars were made until production ended nine years later. Mr. Weasley took apart his turquoise Ford Anglia to see how it worked, then reassembled it with some "modifications." The interior and trunk are bewitched to accommodate far more than they would ordinarily fit, and the dashboard has a compass and a tiny silver Invisibility Booster button that is supposed to make the car unseen to Muggles when it takes flight. (Although Mr. Weasley enchanted the car to fly, he had no intention of actually flying it himself, so he was technically acting within the bounds of magical law.) After an impromptu flight and crash, the Ford Anglia develops a mind of its own. Covered in mud and scratches, it seems to have been turned wild by its new home.

 Did you know . . . J. K. Rowling had a friend in secondary school named Séan, who drove a turquoise Ford Anglia? *Harry Potter and the Chamber of Secrets* is dedicated to him, and he is also the person whom the character of Ron Weasley was modelled after.

flying carpets: Considered a Muggle Artefact, flying carpets are on the Registry of Proscribed Charmable Objects and currently under embargo (although Crouch's grandfather had one that could seat twelve before they were banned). Despite this, Ali Bashir is keen to export them to Britain as a means of family transportation for wizards.

flying motorbike: One of Sirius's prized possessions, which he gave to Hagrid to fly baby Harry to safety the day after Voldemort disappeared.

Garrotting Gas: Allegedly lethal colourless gas that strangles those who breathe it in (a garrotte is a device used for execution by strangulation). Fred and George planned to tell students a load of Garrotting Gas had been released in the Hogwarts corridors!

Gobstones: Similar to marbles, except these stones squirt a foul-smelling liquid into the other player's face when points are lost. Harry is tempted to buy a set of solid gold Gobstones in Diagon Alley.

grandfather clock: Found during the decontamination of Grimmauld Place, it spits bolts out at anyone passing by.

Gubraithian fire: Everlasting fire — *gu brath* is Scottish Gaelic for "forever." A branch of Gubraithian fire was given to the Gurg of the giants as a gift.

Hagrid's overcoat: The pockets of Hagrid's black moleskin coat can store many items simultaneously, including balls of string, a bottle of amber liquid (likely alcohol), Harry's birthday cake, a handkerchief, a kettle and teapot, keys, letters, mice, mint humbugs, mouldy dog biscuits, mugs, an owl, a poker, a quill, a roll of parchment, sausages, slug pellets, tea-bags, an umbrella, and wizarding money!

Hagrid's umbrella: Though Hagrid's wand was snapped in half when he was a teenager, he is still able to perform some magic — such as giving Dudley a pig's tail, opening the entrance to Diagon Alley, and growing enormous pumpkins — with the help of his battered flowery pink umbrella (which contains the pieces of his wand).

hiccoughing toaster: Sits on Mr. Weasley's desk at the Ministry (one wonders if it really hiccoughs, or if the toast popping up simply makes the toaster look like it is hiccoughing to wizards).

homework planners: Hermione gives these to Harry and Ron to help them keep track of their studies. In addition to the usual diary and calendar, the planners shout encouragement and reminders to do homework whenever they are opened.

Invisibility Cloak: Very rare and valuable silvery grey robe that makes the wearer invisible. It is as light as air and feels fluid and silky, as if water has been woven into the material. An Invisibility Cloak does not give total protection against detection — the wearer will still show up on the Marauder's Map and can be seen by Dementors and Moody's magical eye.

Harry inherits an Invisibility Cloak from his father, who left it in Dumbledore's hands before he died. (Curiously, Dumbledore later says he doesn't need a cloak to become invisible.) Moody has at least two Invisibility Cloaks of his own, one of which goes missing during fifth year.

INCIDENTS WITH INVISIBILITY CLOAKS

According to Dumbledore, James Potter used his Invisibility Cloak chiefly for sneaking into the school kitchens for a midnight snack! James, Sirius, and Pettigrew also used to sneak out under the Cloak each month to join Lupin for a nightly prowl around the Hogwarts grounds.

First year

✦ Harry dons his Cloak for a midnight journey to the library's Restricted Section.
✦ Harry and Ron wear the Cloak to visit the Mirror of Erised.
✦ Harry and Hermione transport Norbert up to the Astronomy Tower under the Cloak. After Harry forgets the Cloak there, it mysteriously reappears on his bed with a note reading "Just in case."

Second year

* Harry and Ron wear the Cloak to visit Hagrid and ask about the Chamber of Secrets, then hide under it again when Dumbledore, Fudge, and Lucius Malfoy arrive.

Third year

* Harry uses his Cloak to sneak into Hogsmeade where he has a little fun at the expense of Malfoy and his cronies, until things go awry. To avoid being caught, he stashes the Cloak away in a secret passageway, where it remains for months.
* After Hermione rescues the Cloak, the trio use it to visit Hagrid.
* Snape discovers the Cloak near the Whomping Willow and uses it to eavesdrop at the Shrieking Shack.

Fourth year

* Harry wears the Cloak to visit Hogsmeade with Hermione.
* After Hagrid asks Harry to pay him a midnight visit under the Cloak, Harry learns some valuable information about the Triwizard Tournament.
* Harry and Hermione sneak out under his Cloak to an empty classroom to practise the Summoning Charm.
* Harry wears his Cloak on his way to the Prefects' bathroom. When he is caught in a trick stair on the way back, even his Invisibility Cloak cannot protect him from being discovered — or can it?
* Harry sneaks out under his Cloak to spend a night in the library before the second task.

Fifth year

* Moody's best Cloak is misplaced when members of the Order take turns using his Cloaks when on duty.

Did you know . . . J. K. Rowling said if she could have a magical power, she would choose invisibility? (She also said she'd like to be able to fly, and sometimes turn off other peoples' voices!)

Knight Bus: Invisible to Muggles, this triple-decker purple bus provides emergency transportation for stranded wizards to any above-ground location. Wizards summon the Knight Bus by sticking out their wand arm.

The Knight Bus's interior is wood-panelled, with a narrow wooden staircase leading to the upper levels. The driver and conductor sit in large armchairs. If ridden in the evening, the bus has six brass beds on the ground level instead of seats. During the day, the beds are replaced by a variety of chairs.

The Knight bus is able to cover the length and width of Britain in a single evening by jumping from place to place with a loud bang. Passengers are in for a bumpy ride because of the bus's speed and jerky motions, not to mention the driver's questionable skills.

✶ **Shunpike, Stan:** Purple-uniformed bus conductor. Only a few years older than Harry, Stan is skinny with bad skin and prominent ears. Stan attends the Quidditch World Cup, where he tries to chat up a few Veela by bragging that he is about to become the youngest-ever Minister for Magic.

✶ **Madam Marsh:** Regular passenger who perpetually suffers from motion sickness.

✶ **Prang, Ernie:** Elderly bus driver, who wears very thick glasses that make him look like an owl. Ernie is not the best driver, but fortunately trees, lamp posts, and all other objects have the good sense to jump out of his way whenever he veers off the road. Ernie is well named — a "prang" is British slang for a fender-bender!

★ **tiny wizard in nightcap**: Talks in his sleep about pickling slugs.

KNIGHT BUS TRIPS

Third year

★ Harry takes the Knight Bus to the Leaky Cauldron after he accidentally summons it when he trips.
★ Hagrid and Buckbeak ride the Knight Bus to the Ministry.

Fifth year

★ Hermione takes the Knight Bus to Grimmauld Place for Christmas holidays.
★ The Weasley children, Harry, Hermione, Tonks, and Lupin travel back to Hogwarts on the Knight Bus after Christmas.

 Did you know . . . the Knight Bus takes its name from "night bus" — the network of buses that travel throughout London in the early hours of the morning, after the Underground and trains have stopped for the night?

knitting needles: Hermione makes clothing for house-elves using needles she bewitches to knit in midair.

lunascope: Sold in Diagon Alley, a lunascope is a silver instrument used by astronomers as a replacement for moon charts. Dumbledore has one in his office.

Luna's hats: To show her support for the Gryffindor Quidditch team against Slytherin, Luna wears a giant hat that looks like a lion's head and roars realistically. However, when Gryffindor play Ravenclaw, her hat has changed, and seems to be made from a live eagle!

Marauder's Map: Tapping this worn square of blank parchment with a wand and repeating *"I solemnly swear I am up to no good"* reveals a map of Hogwarts — including seven secret passageways — that shows the exact location of every person inside the grounds at that moment. The Marauder's Map never lies: it even shows people under Invisibility Cloaks. Tapping the map with a wand again and repeating *"Mischief managed"* will return it to a blank state.

The map was created by Messrs. Moony, Wormtail, Padfoot, and Prongs — the Marauders — during their Hogwarts days, when they roamed the castle grounds freely as Animagi. Filch confiscated the map from them (although it is unlikely he knew how to use it himself), but Fred and George stole it from him in their first year. They "bequeath" the map to Harry in third year because they feel sorry for him.

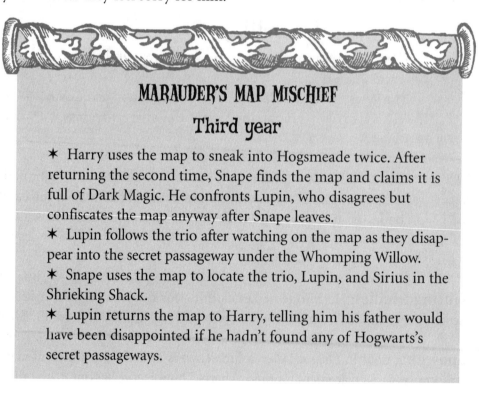

MARAUDER'S MAP MISCHIEF

Third year

★ Harry uses the map to sneak into Hogsmeade twice. After returning the second time, Snape finds the map and claims it is full of Dark Magic. He confronts Lupin, who disagrees but confiscates the map anyway after Snape leaves.

★ Lupin follows the trio after watching on the map as they disappear into the secret passageway under the Whomping Willow.

★ Snape uses the map to locate the trio, Lupin, and Sirius in the Shrieking Shack.

★ Lupin returns the map to Harry, telling him his father would have been disappointed if he hadn't found any of Hogwarts's secret passageways.

Fourth year

✱ Harry notices a strange name on the map on his way back from the Prefects' bathroom. He is almost caught when he drops the map on his way to investigate, but his rescuer asks to borrow it instead.

✱ Moody uses the map to try and locate Crouch on the Hogwarts grounds.

Fifth year

✱ Harry uses the map on the way to the first DA lesson to locate Umbridge, Filch, and Mrs. Norris. He also consults the map to ensure the DA members get back to their dormitories safely after practice ends.

✱ Harry uses the map when the trio visit Hagrid after he returns from his excursion.

Did you know . . . it was never explained how Harry got the map back after Moody "borrowed" it in fourth year? However, in an online chat for World Book Day in March 2004, J. K. Rowling explained Harry simply nipped into Moody's empty office at some point and took it back!

Mirror of Erised: This enchanted mirror stands on two clawed feet and is as tall as the ceiling. It has an ornate gold frame with a carved inscription at the top that reads, *"Erised stra ehru oyt ube cafru oyt on wohsi."* Instead of seeing their reflections, those who look into the mirror see the deepest desires of their heart.

When Harry looks in the mirror, he sees his parents for the first time, as well as a group of other relatives who smile and wave at him. Ron sees himself as Head Boy and Quidditch Captain, holding both the House and Quidditch Cups. It is interesting that the deepest desires of Harry's heart are family and security, which Ron has, and the deepest desires of Ron's heart are recognition and fame, which Harry has.

Dumbledore (who sees himself holding a pair of woollen socks!) cautions Harry that the mirror gives the viewer neither knowledge nor truth, and that people have been driven mad or wasted away from staring into it.

Did you know . . . J. K. Rowling said if she could see herself in the Mirror of Erised, she would probably see herself very much as she is now, with her family. "I always say I would see what Harry sees, which is my mother alive again and a scientist over my shoulders inventing a cigarette that would be healthy, and I can think of a particular journalist I'd like to see being boiled in oil over my other shoulder." (Ouch!)

Moody's trunk: Each of the seven locks on the trunk has its own key and opens to reveal different contents. Unlocking the first lock reveals a pile of spellbooks. Unlocking the second shows the trunk full of parchment and quills, broken Sneakoscopes, and an Invisibility Cloak. When the seventh lock is opened, the inside of the trunk has become a ten-foot deep chamber like a prison cell — and it is not empty.

Mrs. Skower's All-Purpose Magical Mess-Remover: "Skower" is a play on "scour," meaning to remove dirt by scrubbing vigorously — which is exactly what a mess-remover does! While it might be advertised as all-purpose, it wasn't able to get rid of the message on the wall about the Chamber of Secrets.

Mundungus's car: Mundungus "borrows" a car whose insides are magically proportioned to accommodate ten people, much like the Ford Anglia.

music box: Found during the decontamination of Grimmauld Place, its sinister-sounding song induces drowsiness in listeners.

Omnioculars: Similar to binoculars but covered in knobs and dials that can slow down or replay action, or show a play-by-play breakdown.

penknife: Harry receives a magical penknife containing attachments to unlock any lock and undo any knot. Its blade melts when he tries to use the knife to open a locked door in the Department of Mysteries.

Pensieve: Thoughts and memories can be extracted from a wizard's mind by touching his wand tip to his temple. The long, silvery-white, cloud-like strands are placed in a Pensieve — a shallow, round stone bowl with carved runes and symbols around the rim. The strands continually swirl around the Pensieve, and can be examined or retrieved at any time. Touching the strands makes them move faster and become transparent, like glass, allowing the wizard touching them to see their contents projected through the bottom of the bowl. For further insight, the wizard can put his face against the strands, which will pull him forwards through a cold, dark whirlpool and into the memory being shown as an invisible observer.

Pensieves can be used to store happy or important memories completely intact, to clear the mind when there are too many thoughts, or to examine thoughts for patterns and links. During the practice of Occlumency, private thoughts and memories can be stored in a Pensieve to avoid being accessed by the person breaking into the mind.

 Did you know . . . the word "Pensive" comes from the French *penser* (to think) and the English "sieve" (a strainer used to separate solids from liquids)? So a pensive is . . . a thought strainer!

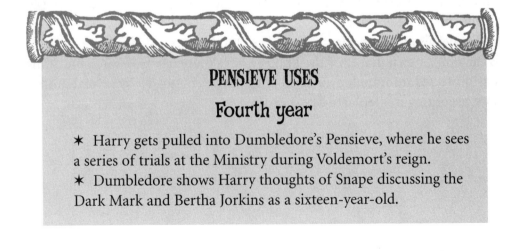

PENSIEVE USES
Fourth year

★ Harry gets pulled into Dumbledore's Pensieve, where he sees a series of trials at the Ministry during Voldemort's reign.
★ Dumbledore shows Harry thoughts of Snape discussing the Dark Mark and Bertha Jorkins as a sixteen-year-old.

* During his conversation with Harry about Voldemort, Dumbledore pauses occasionally to remove thoughts from his mind and put them in the Pensieve.

Fifth year

* Snape uses Dumbledore's Pensieve to extract memories from his mind before commencing Occlumency training with Harry.
* After Snape leaves the Pensieve unattended, a curious Harry sees Snape during his Hogwarts days, and another side of his parents, Lupin, and Sirius.
* Dumbledore uses the Pensieve to show Harry what Trelawney said the night he first met her.

Philosopher's Stone: The legend of the Philosopher's Stone dates back to the real Nicolas Flamel, a fourteenth century French alchemist (a medieval "pseudoscience" combining chemistry and philosophy). Flamel came across a mystical book full of ancient writings, and consulted with scholars all over the world to decipher it. The book was said to hold the secrets of the Philosopher's Stone — a blood-red stone that had the ability to transform any metal into gold and produces the Elixir of Life, which made the drinker immortal. Flamel became a very skilled alchemist and was able to successfully produce the Stone. Flamel is said to have died in 1410 — but according to legend, his grave is empty!

Flamel also inhabits Harry's world as Dumbledore's alchemy partner, and is the only known maker of the Philosopher's Stone. At Hogwarts, the Stone was protected from theft by a number of devices bestowed by several professors, according to their area of expertise.

PROFESSORS, PROTECTIONS, AND SOLUTIONS

Here are the creators of the obstacles guarding the Philosopher's Stone, the obstacles, and how they were overcome.

Hagrid: Three-headed dog named Fluffy — lulled to sleep by music.

Sprout: Devil's Snare — killed by Bluebell Flames.

Flitwick: Enchanted winged keys — Harry flies to catch the right one.

McGonagall: Wizard's chess game — Harry (bishop), Hermione (castle), and Ron (knight) play their way across under Ron's direction.

Quirrell: Troll — already knocked out.

Snape: Potions riddle — solved by Hermione.

Dumbledore: Mirror of Erised — used by Harry to locate the Stone.

Did you know . . . "Philosopher's Stone" was changed to "Sorcerer's Stone" in America by J. K. Rowling's editors because it was felt "sorcerer" was easier for children to understand, and that they might not have heard of the legend of the Philosopher's Stone? The wording was also changed for the film's title in the U.S.

Portkey: An inconspicuous object, often disregarded as litter by Muggles, that is enchanted to transport any wizard who touches it from one location to another at a set time. Travelling by Portkey feels like being pulled forward by the navel and speeding through a swirling wind of sound and colour, until coming to an abrupt stop. All Portkeys must be authorised by the Ministry.

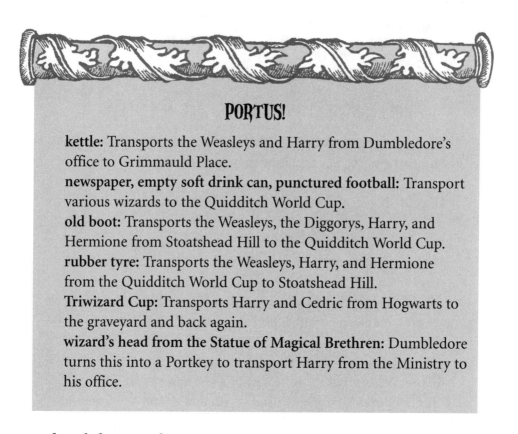

PORTUS!

kettle: Transports the Weasleys and Harry from Dumbledore's office to Grimmauld Place.

newspaper, empty soft drink can, punctured football: Transport various wizards to the Quidditch World Cup.

old boot: Transports the Weasleys, the Diggorys, Harry, and Hermione from Stoatshead Hill to the Quidditch World Cup.

rubber tyre: Transports the Weasleys, Harry, and Hermione from the Quidditch World Cup to Stoatshead Hill.

Triwizard Cup: Transports Harry and Cedric from Hogwarts to the graveyard and back again.

wizard's head from the Statue of Magical Brethren: Dumbledore turns this into a Portkey to transport Harry from the Ministry to his office.

powdered dragon claw: Alleged brain stimulant sold to OWL and NEWT students during exams.

prophecies: Records of prophecies are kept in small, dusty glass orbs found in the Hall of Prophecy in the Department of Mysteries. The prophecies are heavily protected — only the person about whom a prophecy was made can remove it from the Hall. Some of the orbs glow softly, whilst others look like burnt-out lightbulbs. Little yellowing labels underneath indicate what they are about. When an orb is broken, a pearly-white figure emerges and speaks the prophecy, then evaporates. The person to whom the prophecy was made can recall it verbatim.

> ★ **Harry's prophecy:** Located in row ninety-seven, it reads: "S.P.T. to A.P.W.B.D., Dark Lord and (?) Harry Potter." Trelawney originally told the prophecy to Dumbledore before Harry was born. It explained how a child would come to be Voldemort's nemesis and what the future held for them both. It was originally unclear whom

the prophecy referred to, as there were two children who would fit the description. When the prophecy was first told, one of Voldemort's spies overheard the beginning. Voldemort later realised there was more to it, and made numerous attempts to hear the prophecy in its entirety.

★ **old bearded man:** He emerges from a smashed orb, saying, ". . . at the solstice will come a new . . ."

★ **young woman:** She emerges from a smashed orb, saying, ". . . and none will come after . . ."

Do you know . . . some fans think these two snippets are "prophecies" from J. K. Rowling about the Harry Potter series? "At the solstice will come a new" is believed to mean the June 21, 2003, release date of the "new" Harry Potter book, *The Order of the Phoenix* — June 21 is the summer solstice. "And none will come after" is believed to refer to J. K. Rowling affirming there will only be seven books in the series . . . and none will come after.

protective devices: Secret sales of amulets and talismans, including a purple pointed crystal, a rotting newt-tail, and a foul-smelling green onion, flourish throughout Hogwarts in second year because of the Chamber of Secrets.

Put-Outer: Looks like a silver cigarette lighter, but with the opposite effect. A Put-Outer extinguishes streetlamps with a small pop when it is held open towards them and clicked. Clicking the Put-Outer once more sends balls of light back to the streetlamps.

plates: The plates in the Great Hall at Hogwarts are enchanted to magically fill with food at the beginning of each course, refill as many times as necessary, then clean themselves after the meal is over.

Quick-Quotes Quill: Rita Skeeter's acid green quill automatically takes dictation during her interviews, turning facts into melodramatic exaggerations. To activate the quill, she sucks on the tip then places the quill in front of a sheet of parchment.

regurgitating toilets: Jinxed to vomit their contents whenever Muggles flush them.

Remembrall: Glass ball the size of a large marble. It is full of white smoke that turns red if the person holding it has forgotten to do something.

Revealer: The opposite of an eraser, a Revealer is rubbed on a blank piece of paper to uncover what was written before it was erased. They are bright red.

self-dictating quill: Similar to a Quick-Quotes Quill, it writes as a person speaks, except without the embellishments!

scales: At the Ministry, all visitors' wands are examined by a brass instrument resembling a set of scales with only one dish. When a wand is placed on the dish, the instrument vibrates and analyses the wand's make-up, then spits out a strip of parchment with this information which the Ministry keeps as a record.

Screaming Yo-yos: On Filch's list of forbidden objects in fourth year.

Secrecy Sensor: Squiggly, golden-coloured aerial that hums and vibrates when it detects lies or concealment. Moody has one in his office at Hogwarts, although he reckons it is useless as it has hummed constantly since his arrival. He claims it does so because students are constantly lying about why their homework isn't finished.

Self-Correcting Ink: Banned from the examination hall during OWLS and NEWTS.

Self-Shuffling playing cards: Ron has a pack of these in his room at The Burrow.

shrinking door-keys: Found by Mr. Weasley during a raid. He thinks wizards sell these to Muggles to bait them, because Muggles don't realise the keys are shrinking — they just think they've lost them.

silver instruments: Dumbledore's office contains a number of fragile-looking silver instruments that whirr and emit puffs of smoke. Their exact functions are unknown. Dumbledore seems to be able to communicate with one, which makes clinking noises and creates a serpent's head out of green smoke.

silver snuffboxes: Found during the decontamination of Grimmauld Place, these tarnished silver boxes bear inscriptions in strange languages and bite those who touch them. One contains Wartcap powder, which covers the skin in a tough brown crust.

Sneakoscope: Similar to a small spinning top made of glass, it glows, spins, and whistles shrilly if someone dishonest is nearby. Ron gives Harry a pocket Sneakoscope that goes off Christmas morning in third year. Moody has a larger Sneakoscope in his office in fourth year, but disables it because he claims it is too sensitive and picks up vibrations from over a mile around. A Sneakoscope is also in the Room of Requirement during DA lessons.

Spellotape: Magical tape that binds things together. "Spellotape" gets its name from Sellotape, a British brand of sticky tape.

spider-like instrument: Found during the decontamination of Grimmauld Place, this silver device looks like a multi-legged pair of tweezers. It scuttles about and tries to puncture the skin.

talking mirrors: The mirror in the kitchen at The Burrow and in Harry's room at the Leaky Cauldron both pass comment on those who look into them.

tape measure: In order to determine which wand might be suitable for a wizard, Mr. Ollivander's tape measure performs a series of intricate measurements, controlled by his voice.

tea set: Bought by a Muggle in an antiques shop after its owner (a witch) died, with disastrous results. The teapot spurted scalding tea everywhere and the sugar tongs attached themselves to the nose of a man who had to go to hospital to have them removed.

Time-Turner: Small, sparkling hourglass used for time travel. A wizard can go back in time one hour for each turn of the hourglass; however, he must not be seen by anyone in the past — especially himself, as this could result in the future and past selves attacking or killing each other out of confusion. Using a Time-Turner feels like flying backwards at high speed. Although Time-Turners can be real life-savers, they can also take their toll if used excessively. The use of Time-Turners is strictly controlled by the Ministry.

Tom Riddle's diary: Discovered in Moaning Myrtle's flooded bathroom (Myrtle claims someone threw the diary down her toilet), this small, thin black book has a shabby cover bearing a fifty-year-old date on the front and the address of a London newsagent's on the back. Inside, the name T. M. Riddle is written in smudged ink on the first page. All the other pages are seemingly blank and are also dated from fifty years earlier.

Harry is intrigued by the mysterious diary and cannot bring himself to throw it away. The name T. M. Riddle seems vaguely familiar to him, like some sort of old, half-forgotten friend from early childhood, but he cannot understand why. He thinks the diary may be concealing hidden information, and tries a number of things in vain to make it reveal its contents. Strangely, the diary remains clean and dry when Harry accidentally breaks a bottle of ink over it. When he tries to write in the diary, his ink disappears into the page. It reappears a moment later, forming different words and identifying the writer as Tom Riddle.

Riddle tells Harry his diary holds memories of things recorded in a way more lasting than ink. It is able to take readers physically inside memories, where they can invisibly observe events from the past (similar to a Pensieve). Conversely, memories can also physically come out of the diary and interact with readers in the present. One thing is for certain — this is one book that should definitely not be judged by its cover.

two-way mirrors: Sirius and James used these two old, small square mirrors to communicate when they were in separate detentions, like visual walkie talkies. Harry is given one of the mirrors in fifth year, but smashes it in a fit of rage.

Umbridge's quill: Used during detentions to write lines. The words written with this long, thin black instrument of torture are simultaneously carved into the back of the writer's hand as they appear on the parchment — in blood. The cut magically heals and reappears with every line, leaving the skin a little more raw with every word written.

Umgubular Slashkilter: No one seems to know quite what this is except for Luna, who swears Fudge has one at the Ministry for his own sinister purposes!

Vanishing Cabinet: Items put in this cabinet often disappear to unknown destinations for several weeks at a time.

Weasleys' clocks: A clock in the kitchen at The Burrow has one hand with things like "Time to make tea," "Time to feed the chickens," and "You're late" written around the edges instead of numbers. The grandfather clock in the living-room has nine golden hands, each engraved with a family member's name, with descriptions where the numbers should be, including "home," "hospital," "lost," "prison," "school," "travelling," "work," and "mortal peril" (at twelve o'clock).

wizard chess: Similar to Muggle chess except the pieces are instructed to move by the players, like troops being directed in a battle. At the end of each move, the piece that is taken is smashed by the other piece. Like wands, the pieces do not seem to work as well when used by someone other than their owner — when Harry borrows Seamus's pieces, they distrust him and shout different bits of advice. Ron's battered chess set was formerly his grandfather's, but for once he doesn't mind owning a hand-me-down because he knows the pieces so well, they obey his commands without question. Wizard chess is the only thing Hermione ever loses at (which the boys think is good for her!).

Wizarding Wireless Network (WWN): Magical radio station that broadcasts popular wizarding music.

WIZARDING MUSIC

The Hobgoblins: Popular band which Sirius (using the alias Stubby Boardman) was allegedly the lead singer of, according to *The Quibbler*.

Warbeck, Celestina: Well-known singing sorceress heard during the "Witching Hour" on the WWN. "Celestina" sounds like celestial, meaning heavenly.

Weird Sisters: Tonks is a fan of this famous group Dumbledore books to play the Yule Ball, consisting of drums, guitars, lute, cello, and bagpipes. The members of the Weird Sisters are hairy and dress in tastefully ripped and torn black robes. They are likely named after the three witches in Shakespeare's *Macbeth*.

wizard paintings: People in wizard paintings are fully animated — they can speak back to the person looking at them, and even leave to visit other paintings. If a wizard's painting is hung in more than one building, he can move between his own paintings freely and pass messages or information back and forth.

Hogwarts Paintings

✴ **Clagg, Elfrida:** A painting of this former Chief of the Wizards' Council hangs at the Ministry.

✴ **Derwent, Dilys:** Former Hogwarts Head whose paintings are in Dumbledore's office and at St. Mungo's. "Derwent" comes from the Celtic name for the river *Deru wen*, meaning "the place of the white oak."

★ **Dippet, Armando:** Dumbledore's predecessor. His painting is in Dumbledore's office.

★ **Everard:** Former Hogwarts Head whose paintings are in Dumbledore's office and at the Ministry.

★ **The Fat Lady:** Her painting guards the entrance to the Gryffindor common room.

★ **Fortescue:** Former Hogwarts Head whose painting is in Dumbledore's office.

★ **group of women in crinolines:** Their painting hangs on the wall of the spiral staircase leading to the Divination classroom.

★ **mermaid:** Her painting is in the Prefects' bathroom, where she sometimes peeks at people taking baths!

★ **Nigellus, Phineas:** Former Hogwarts Head whose paintings are in Dumbledore's office and at Grimmauld Place.

★ **sinister-looking monks:** Their painting is near the top of the spiral staircase leading to the Divination classroom.

★ **Sir Cadogan:** Hapless knight-in-armour who takes over for the Fat Lady for a while during third year.

★ **soppy-looking witch:** Runs for cover when one of the twins' enchanted fireworks hits her painting.

★ **Rackharrow, Urquhart** (1612 to 1697): Inventor of the Entrail-expelling Curse, his painting is in Mr. Weasley's ward at St. Mungo's.

★ **Violet** (Vi): A friend of the Fat Lady, Vi is a pale, wrinkled witch whose painting is in the antechamber behind the Great Hall. She spends most of her time gossiping with the Fat Lady and getting tipsy on liqueur-filled chocolates at Christmastime.

★ **walrus-moustached wizard:** His painting hangs next to Violet's.

wizard photographs: People in wizard photographs can move about freely and even leave. They can also acknowledge the people looking at them. At the end of first year, Hagrid gives Harry a leather-bound album full of photographs he collected from Lily and James's old school friends.

 Did you know . . . in the Harry Potter films, crew members were used to portray some of the moving pictures of the witches and wizards in the portraits on the walls at Hogwarts?

WIZARDING PUBLICATIONS

Like its Muggle counterpart, there is a variety of newspapers and magazines available in the wizarding world, covering everything from broomsticks to witches' issues. Also similar to the Muggle world, some publications in the wizarding world are not always the best examples of journalistic objectivity or impartiality, with contents that are influenced by pressure from external sources.

Daily Prophet: Prominent wizarding newspaper. The *Prophet* also publishes evening and Sunday editions, and features a zoological column every Wednesday. Hermione takes out a subscription to keep up with events in the wizarding world.

Daily Prophet Articles

First year

✶ Ron tells Harry the *Prophet* has been covering an attempted high security vault break-in at Gringotts.

✶ "Gringotts Break-In Latest" Further details about the attempted vault robbery.

Second year

✶ Article about Lockhart's autograph session at Flourish and Blotts, with a photo of Lockhart and Harry.

✶ "Ford Anglia Mystifies Muggles" — Article about sightings of the car flying over London.

* "Enquiry at the Ministry of Magic" — Article about Mr. Weasley's fine for bewitching a Muggle car, and a call for his resignation from Lucius Malfoy.
* At the end of the year, Dumbledore places an advertisement for a new Defence Against the Dark Arts teacher.

Third year

* "Ministry of Magic Employee Scoops Grand Prize" — Article about Mr. Weasley's win of seven hundred Galleons in the paper's annual draw, accompanied by a photo of the Weasleys on holiday in Egypt.
* Advertisement for a Broomstick Servicing Kit.
* "Black Still at Large" — Photo and article about Sirius's escape from Azkaban.
* Article about a Muggle sighting of Sirius not far from Hogwarts.
* Article stating the Ministry has given the Dementors permission to Kiss Sirius when they catch him.

Fourth year

* Article by Rita Skeeter criticising the Ministry's focus and priorities.
* "Scenes of Terror at the Quidditch World Cup" — Photo of the Dark Mark with an article by Rita Skeeter criticising the Ministry for failing to catch the Death Eaters.
* "Further Mistakes at the Ministry of Magic" — Photo of Mr. and Mrs. Weasley at the Burrow with an article by Rita Skeeter blaming "Arnold" Weasley for the skirmish with Muggle police at Moody's home.
* There was meant to be a photo and article about the four Triwizard Tournament champions, but after Rita Skeeter corners Harry for an "exclusive," the article contains a photo of only him and is a four-page exaggerated profile of his life. It neglects to mention Cedric and only briefly mentions the other champions (with their names spelled incorrectly).
* "Dumbledore's Giant Mistake" — Very negative article about Hagrid by Rita Skeeter, exposing his heritage and suggesting he is an irresponsible, unfit teacher.
* "Ministry Witch Still Missing — Minister for Magic Now Personally Involved" — Article about Bertha Jorkins's disappearance.
* "Mystery Illness of Bartemius Crouch" — Article about Crouch's sudden disappearance and rumoured serious illness.

✶ "Harry Potter 'Disturbed and Dangerous'" — Another hatchet job from Rita Skeeter, this time about Harry's supposed mental instability following his collapse in Divination class.

✶ Small article the day after the third task, stating who won the Triwizard Tournament. The more sordid aspects of the event are not mentioned, and Hermione thinks the paper was forced to keep quiet.

Did you know . . . there may be more truth to Rita's tabloid tales than meets the eye? Her first article quotes Harry as saying he knows nothing will hurt him during the Triwizard Tournament because his parents are watching over him. It sounds like one of her usual exaggerations — except James and Lily do play a role in ensuring Harry's safety following the third task! Perhaps there is more foreshadowing and other facts cleverly disguised as fiction inside Rita's stories?

Fifth year

✶ Not only does the *Prophet* ignore any mention of Voldemort, it continually discredits Harry's story by slipping nasty comments about him into their articles.

✶ Untrue article about Dumbledore being voted out of the International Confederation of Wizards because he is too old and losing touch.

✶ Fred and George take out mail-order advertisements for Weasley's Wizard Wheezes.

✶ Mention of the Weird Sisters's bass player getting married.

✶ Article stating the Ministry has received a tip about Sirius hiding in London.

✶ Advertisement for a sale at Madam Malkin's Robes for All Occasions.

✶ "Trespass at Ministry" — Short blurb about Sturgis Podmore's arrest, conviction, and sentencing.

✶ "Ministry Seeks Educational Reform: Dolores Umbridge Appointed First Ever High Inquisitor" — Photo and article about Umbridge's appointment, after the Ministry passed new legislation giving more control at Hogwarts.

The article is highly critical of Dumbledore and the "falling standards" at the school.

✶ Article alleging Griselda Marchbanks has ties to "subversive" goblin groups, because she spoke out in support of Dumbledore.

✶ Article about Willy Widdershins's arrests for anti-Muggle pranks.

✶ "Mass Breakout From Azkaban: Ministry Feels Black Is 'Rallying Point' For Old Death Eaters" — Front page article and photos announcing the escape of ten Death Eaters, allegedly with Sirius's help.

✶ "Tragic Demise of Ministry of Magic Worker" — Article about Broderick Bode's death.

✶ "He Who Must Not Be Named Returns" — Article restoring credibility to Dumbledore and Harry, and quoting Fudge as confirming Voldemort's return. Other headlines in the issue include "You Know Who's Last Attempt to Take Over," "What the Ministry Should Have Told Us," "Why Nobody Listened to Albus Dumbledore," and "Exclusive Interview with Harry Potter" (a reprint of *The Quibbler*'s interview).

✶ Articles about hunting down Death Eaters, Voldemort sightings, and how to repel Dementors.

The Quibbler: Although it is widely considered a tabloid full of rubbish, Luna's father, the editor, insists he publishes important stories the public needs to know. He does not care about making money, nor does he pay contributors (Luna says people write for the magazine because it is an honour). Hermione is very dismissive of *The Quibbler*, but attempts to be more supportive after Luna arranges for Harry's interview to be printed.

Quibbler Articles

Fifth year

✶ Article about a wizard who flew his broom to the moon and brought back a bag of moon frogs.

✶ "Corruption in the Quidditch League: How the Tornados are Taking Control" — Suggests the Tutshill Tornados are using torture, blackmail, and broom-tampering to win.

✷ "How Far Will Fudge Go to Gain Gringotts?" — Cover story featuring a caricature of Fudge clutching a bag of gold and strangling a goblin. The article implies "Goblin-Crusher" Fudge will use force, if necessary, to take control of Gringotts and paints him as having ordered the murders of numerous goblins.

✷ "Secrets of the Ancient Runes Revealed" — Turning the runes upside-down apparently reveals a spell to turn an enemy's ears into kumquats.

✷ "Sirius Black: Villain or Victim?" — Features a cartoon of Sirius standing on a pile of bones, with the caption "Sirius — Black as He's Painted?" The article claims Sirius is really Stubby Boardman, reclusive lead singer of the Hobgoblins, and quotes a witch who says she was with him the night he was accused of the murders. Kingsley Shacklebolt passes a copy of the article along to Sirius, thinking he will find it amusing.

✷ "Very important" article about sightings of Crumple-Horned Snorkacks.

✷ "Harry Potter Speaks Out at Last: The Truth about He Who Must Not Be Named and the Night I Saw Him Return" — Harry's interview with Rita makes the front page of the March issue. He receives a mixed, but mostly positive, reaction from readers and the issue sells out in record time, causing the need for additional print runs.

Transfiguration Today: Two wizards in the Leaky Cauldron argue over an article in this publication.

Which Broomstick: Reviews and profiles broomsticks, with an order form in the back.

Witch Weekly: Women's magazine featuring a Most-Charming-Smile contest, which Lockhart won for five consecutive years. Mrs. Weasley buys it "for the recipes," but snubs Hermione after reading what Rita Skeeter wrote about her.

Witch Weekly Articles

Fourth year

✷ "Harry Potter's Secret Heartache" Article by Rita Skeeter about Harry, Hermione, and Krum. Poor Hermione receives Howlers and hate mail (not to mention an extra-small Easter egg!) from readers who think she is behaving like a "scarlet woman."

Skeeter, Rita: A Special Correspondent to the *Prophet*, Rita is every inch the obnoxious, ruthless reporter, whose appearance is as tacky and offensive as her articles. She is in her mid-forties, with a heavy jaw and three gold teeth. She has elaborately curled blonde hair, talon-like painted nails, and is always heavily made up. Rita wears jewel-framed glasses and owns a multitude of brightly-coloured robes. Her trusty acid green (all the better to burn people with!) Quick-Quotes Quill is never far from her side.

Pushy, tactless, and unethical, her reporting style consists of putting words in the mouths of whomever she is interviewing. Rita appeals to peoples' egos and uses false sympathy to try to make them spill their secrets, but when it doesn't work she simply makes things up instead. Her vicious exposés are full of speculation, half-truths, rumours, and insults (she once called Bill Weasley a "long-haired pillock" and Dumbledore an "obsolete dingbat"). Dumbledore bans Rita from Hogwarts, but this doesn't seem to keep her from getting scoops.

Hermione in particular is driven buggy by Rita's unscrupulous manner of reporting and her damaging articles. After clashing with Rita, Hermione finds herself the target of a sordid story but she doesn't care — in fact, it seems to make her more determined to squash Rita's troublemaking ways once and for all. In doing so, Hermione uncovers a secret about Rita that enables her to keep the reporter under her thumb. They make a deal ensuring each other's silence — Hermione will not reveal what she knows on the condition Rita doesn't write anything nasty for a period of one year.

In fifth year, Hermione uses this deal as leverage to blackmail Rita into telling Harry's story. After being unemployed for so long, Rita's appearance is unkempt and tattered but her nose for gossip and scandal is still as sharp as ever. She wastes no time delving into Harry's love life and suggesting he may be delusional, but Hermione will have none of it and forces her to write an honest, truthful account of what he has to say.

Appropriately, "skeeter" is slang for mosquito, another kind of irritating, bloodsucking pest.

Bozo: Paunchy photographer who accompanies Rita Skeeter on most of her interviews. He covertly watches Fleur during the Wand Weighing ceremony and keeps trying to put her front-and-centre in the pictures. "Bozo" is, of course, a common name for a clown.

OTHER LOCATIONS IN THE WIZARDING WORLD

The wizarding world is as diverse as its inhabitants. From Aberdeen to Albania and Yorkshire to Wagga Wagga, it seems there's magic to be found in the four corners of the globe.

Places that don't actually exist and were created for the Harry Potter series are indicated with an asterisk (*).

Britain

Aberdeen: The Knight Bus passed through this city in northeastern Scotland.

Abergavenny: Madam Marsh got off the Knight Bus at this Welsh town, located near Pontypool.

Anglesea: The Knight Bus passed through this island in northwestern Wales.

Argyllshire: The Fat Lady hid in a map of this western region of Scotland after she was attacked.

Bath: City in western England, near the Welsh border. A witch from Bath owned an enchanted book she couldn't stop reading, forcing her to do everything with one hand.

Birmingham: The Knight Bus travelled on a motorway near this city in the English midlands.

Bristol: City in western England, near the Welsh border. Baby Harry fell asleep over Bristol when Hagrid flew him to Privet Drive.

Blackpool: Popular seaside resort in Lancashire (northwestern England). Neville was pushed off the end of Blackpool pier as a child to see if he had any magical ability.

Clapham: There are multiple Claphams in England, including one just south of London. Sturgis Podmore lives in Laburnum Gardens, Clapham.

Devon: County in southwestern England, and home of Nicolas and Perenelle Flamel.

Didsbury: Kwikspell student D. J. Prod lives in this area of Manchester in England.

Dundee: Shooting stars were seen in this eastern Scottish town immediately after Voldemort disappeared.

Godric's Hollow (*): Village where Harry lived with his parents until Voldemort killed them and demolished their home. The village's name is likely tied to Godric Gryffindor, one of the Hogwarts founders.

Hebrides: The Hebridean Black dragon is from this group of islands to the west of Scotland.

Kent: This county southeast of London is home to Dedalus Diggle. Kent is also the home of the Wailing Widow, a friend of Nearly Headless Nick's.

Little Norton: Doris Purkiss, a witch from Acanthia Way, Little Norton, came up with a rather unusual alibi for Sirius. There are multiple locations named Little Norton in England, including places in Staffordshire and South Yorkshire.

London: England's capital is located in the southeastern part of the country. Among the magical locations in London are King's Cross station (platform nine and three quarters), Diagon Alley, the Ministry, St. Mungo's, and Grimmauld Place.

> ★ **Charing Cross Road:** The front entrance to the Leaky Cauldron is located on this busy street in the heart of London, nestled in between a book shop and record shop.

Nottingham: Voldemort murdered a goblin family in this city in the English midlands.

Ottery St. Catchpole (*): There is an Ottery (no St. Catchpole, though) in the county of Cornwall, in southwestern England. The Diggorys, Fawcetts, Lovegoods, and Weasleys live in the vicinity of Ottery St. Catchpole, which has a post office with a Muggle telephone. They are the only wizarding families in the area.

> ★ **The Burrow:** The Weasleys' cosy, cluttered home is bursting with life, energy, and magic. It is several storeys high, and has undergone numerous additions over the years that teeter crookedly and seem to defy gravity. Chickens roam in the front garden, while the overgrown, weed-filled back garden contains old trees, unusual plants, and flowerbeds (not to mention gnomes), and a frog-filled pond. The tumbledown shed is crammed full of Mr. Weasley's disassembled Muggle gadgets. The Weasleys also own a small orchard at the top of a nearby hill where the boys play Quidditch (using apples for balls) during holidays.
>
> Inside, The Burrow has a cramped kitchen, multiple fireplaces, and all sorts of magical household devices. A rickety staircase leads up to the bedrooms (Percy's is on the second floor, Ginny's is on the third) and attic, where a noisy ghoul resides. Ron's perpetually messy room is beneath the attic, on the fifth floor. It has a sloping ceiling and is decorated in bright orange (a tribute to his beloved Chudley Cannons). How appropriate that a family whose name brings to mind small, furry animals would name their home after the warm, snug, safe refuge where these creatures live!

★ **Stoatshead Hill** (*): A Portkey point for the Quidditch World Cup was set up on top of this hill near Ottery St. Catchpole.

 Did you know . . . a stoat is an animal from the same family as the weasel?

Paisley: A witch from this town near Glasgow, Scotland, writes Harry a letter of support.

Topsham: Kwikspell student Madam Z Nettles lives in this town, which is part of Exeter, in Devon.

Wales: Home to the Common Welsh Green dragon species, the principality of Wales is located to the west of England.

Wiltshire: County in south central England where the Malfoys live. Wiltshire has long been associated with magic through crop-circle sightings and the ancient mystical formation of Stonehenge.

★ **Malfoy Manor:** The Malfoys live in an old stately mansion, and for many years, kept a house-elf to run the household. Lucius Malfoy hides Dark Magic artefacts in a secret chamber under the drawing room.

Yorkshire: Shooting stars were seen in this northern English county immediately after Voldemort disappeared.

The Rest of the World

"It was only just dawning on Harry how many witches and wizards there must be in the world; he had never really thought much about those in other countries."
— *Harry Potter and the Goblet of Fire*

Albania: Bertha Jorkins was last seen in this small southeastern European nation, where she went to visit her family.

Andorra: Very small European principality located between France and Spain. The Andorran Minister for Magic is mentioned in *Harry Potter and the Goblet of Fire*.

Assyria: Ancient kingdom in northern Mesopotamia (modern-day Iraq), where Neville's Mimbulus mimbletonia plant is from.

Bandon: Small town in County Cork, Ireland, where the Bandon Banshee (whom Lockhart allegedly banished) hails from.

Black Forest: Located in the southwestern part of Germany, Quirrell allegedly met vampires here before coming to teach at Hogwarts. A party also Portkeys in from the Black Forest for the Quidditch World Cup.

Brazil: Bill Weasley had a Brazilian pen-pal when he was at Hogwarts.

Bulgaria: The national Quidditch team for this eastern European nation plays in the Quidditch World Cup final.

Egypt: Bill Weasley worked in Egypt as a curse breaker for Gringotts. He took his family on a tour of the pyramids and old tombs, which Egyptian wizards cursed against Muggle trespassers.

France: Hermione marvels at the local wizarding history whist on vacation in France before third year. Hagrid and Madame Maxime also travel through France on their mission for Dumbledore, but realise they are being followed and detour towards Beauxbatons instead.

Liechtenstein: This tiny European nation had trouble with mountain trolls, leading to their refusal to join the International Confederation of Wizards.

Minsk: Hagrid argued with a vampire in the capital of Belarus, a country in eastern Europe.

Norway: Home of the rare Norwegian Ridgebacks dragon species.

Ouagadogou: Capital city of Burkina Faso, a small African nation. Lockhart claimed to have saved the townspeople from a curse by giving them amulets.

Poland: Hagrid and Madame Maxime encountered a pair of mad trolls at the Polish border whilst on their mission for Dumbledore.

Romania: Charlie Weasley studies wild dragons in this eastern European nation. Romania is also where Quirrell says he encountered a vampire before coming to teach at Hogwarts.

> ★ **Transylvania:** Count Dracula is probably the most famous name associated with this province in northwestern Romania, although Lockhart may beg to differ (he allegedly cured a Transylvanian of a Babbling Curse). Transylvania refuses to sign the International Ban on Duelling.

Salem: Town in Massachusetts, America, historically associated with witchcraft. Members of the Salem Witches' Institute attend the Quidditch World Cup.

 Did you know . . . a five-day symposium for Harry Potter fans is planned for October 2005, in Salem? Details can be found at www.witchinghour.org.

Sweden: The Lovegoods visit Sweden the summer after fifth year, in search of a Crumple-Horned Snorkack.

Tibet: Kingsley Shacklebolt tells the Ministry Sirius was spotted in Tibet.

Wagga Wagga: Wagga Wagga is an actual city in New South Wales, Australia, and home of a legendary werewolf Lockhart claims to have defeated. Its unusual name means "the place of many crows" in the local aboriginal language.

LOCATIONS IN THE MUGGLE WORLD

Though both Muggle and magical people live in the same countries, cities, and streets, the split between them is so wide it still seems like two different worlds. Just as there are magical places that Muggles cannot see or hear, there are Muggle places magical people would likely never frequent.

Places that don't actually exist and were created for the Harry Potter series are indicated with an asterisk (*).

Barnsley: The home of Bungy, the water-skiing budgerigar. There are places named Barnsley in the English counties of Gloucestershire and South Yorkshire.

Cokeworth (*): Uncle Vernon takes his family and Harry here to escape the constant influx of Hogwarts letters.

> ✶ **Room 17, Railview Hotel:** Gloomy-looking hotel in Cokeworth where the Dursleys and Harry stayed.

Eton: Extremely prestigious boys' boarding school just west of London, founded in the fifteenth century by King Henry VI. Applications to attend are generally submitted several years in advance. Justin Finch-Fletchley's name was down for Eton until he got his Hogwarts letter.

Great Hangleton (*): Frank Bryce is questioned at the Great Hangleton police station after being accused of murder. Although there is a Hangleton in the county of Sussex, in southern England, no Great or Little Hangleton exists.

Grunnings (*): Uncle Vernon is a director of this drillmaking firm, and has an office on the ninth floor.

Hut-on-the-rock (*): Uncle Vernon takes his family and Harry here to escape the constant influx of Hogwarts letters.

Isle of Wight: Aunt Marge holidayed on this small island off the coast of southern England.

Little Hangleton (*): Little Hangleton is about two hundred miles from Little Whinging. Although there is a Hangleton in the county of Sussex, in southern England, no Great or Little Hangleton exists.

    ✶ **The Hanged Man:** Local pub that was very busy the night of the murders.

    ✶ **graveyard:** This dark, run-down cemetery is located at the bottom of a hill, adjacent to a large yew tree and a small church.

    ✶ **Riddle House:** Located atop a hill, the home of Mr. and Mrs. Riddle and their adult son was the grandest house around, until tragedy struck. The families that later moved in complained of a "nasty" feeling and didn't stay long. Over the years, the vacant house became run-down and creepy-looking, with boarded-up windows and ivy growing wildly over the walls. The village children often broke in or vandalised the grounds. A wealthy man finally bought the house for tax purposes, but did not move in.

    ✶ **gardener's cottage:** Frank Bryce lived in this neglected cottage on the Riddle estate for over fifty years.

London: England's capital is located in the southeastern part of the country.

    ✶ **Bethnal Green, Elephant and Castle, Wimbledon:** Areas around London where public toilets have been mysteriously regurgitating.

✱ **London Zoo:** Harry communicated with a boa constrictor in the Reptile House when the Dursleys took him, Dudley, and Piers to the zoo for Dudley's birthday.

✱ **Paddington station:** Harry takes a train back to the Dursleys from here after his first trip to Diagon Alley.

✱ **Post Office Tower:** Two Muggles saw the Ford Anglia fly over this building, which was the tallest in England (six hundred and twenty feet) when it opened in 1965.

✱ **Vauxhall Road:** Tom Riddle bought his diary from a newsagent's in Vauxhall Road. Vauxhall Tube station is located in the south end of London.

✱ **West Ham:** The football club Dean Thomas supports (he even has pyjamas in their colours, claret and sky blue).

Majorca: The Dursleys had hoped to buy a holiday home on this Spanish island.

Norfolk: The Ford Anglia was seen flying over this eastern England county.

Peebles: The Ford Anglia was seen flying over this Scottish Borders town near Edinburgh.

Smeltings (*): Uncle Vernon's alma mater and Dudley and Piers's secondary school. The uniform consists of a maroon tailcoat, orange knickerbockers, a flat straw boater hat, and a knobbly stick to hit people with.

St. Brutus's Secure Centre for Incurably Criminal Boys (*): The Dursleys told Aunt Marge Harry attends this "first-rate institution for hopeless cases." (She is delighted to think the school is strict and severe in dispensing punishments.) There is no St. Brutus, but if there were, he would likely be the patron saint of "brutal" or savage behaviour.

Stonewall High (*): The local secondary school Harry was meant to go to. Not surprisingly, a "stone wall" is commonly used to symbolise alienation or a dead end.

Surrey: One of the British home counties, located southwest of London.

> ★ **Little Whinging** (*): The town in Surrey where the Dursleys live.

> ★ **number four, Privet Drive** (*): The Dursleys and Harry live in this large, square house which is identical to all the others in the area. It has a tidy garden surrounded by a low wall. The house is equipped with all the modern conveniences. The living room features an electric fire in front of a boarded-up fireplace, and there are four bedrooms (Dudley had so many possessions, he was given two rooms). Aunt Petunia keeps the house immaculate.

> ★ **cupboard under the stairs** (*): Many two-storey British houses have a very small storage space underneath the staircase. Harry slept here for many years before he was allowed to move into Dudley's second bedroom.

> ★ **Magnolia Crescent** (*): Located in the same subdivision as Privet Drive. Harry summons the Knight Bus from here after seeing a large black dog in the alleyway beside number two.

> ★ **Magnolia Road** (*): It has a play park and is located off Magnolia Crescent.

> ★ **Wisteria Walk** (*): Mrs. Figg's street, in the same subdivision as Privet Drive.

WIZARDING LANGUAGE

While English is chiefly spoken in the wizarding world and variations of Latin are used for spells, there are certain words and expressions that are purely magical in nature.

Animagi: Wizards who have learnt how to transform into animals. Becoming an Animagus is extremely difficult and takes many years to master.

 Did you know . . . wizards cannot choose their Animagi form? In an online chat for World Book Day in March 2004, J. K. Rowling explained that wizards become the animal that suits them best.

blood traitors: Pure-bloods who are considered a disgrace to their heritage because of their association with Muggles, Muggle-borns, and half-breeds.

Draco dormiens nunquam titillandus: The Hogwarts motto translates to "Never tickle a sleeping dragon" — the wizarding equivalent of "let sleeping dogs lie."

Erised stra ehru oyt ube cafru oyt on wohsi: The inscription on the Mirror of Erised is written backwards, like a reflection. It reads, "I show not your face but your heart's desire."

Gallopin' Gorgons: Holy smoke!

Gobbledegook: Language spoken by goblins.

✶ **Bladvak:** Gobbledegook for "pickaxe."

God Rest Ye, Merry Hippogriffs: A familiar wizarding Christmas carol.

gormless gargoyle: A stupid or slow-witted person.

Gulping gargoyles: Good grief!

Gurg: The title given to the chief of the giants.

half-blood: Someone with both magical and Muggle heritage. Half-bloods are common in the wizarding world, as wizards would have likely become extinct if they hadn't married Muggles. Harry, Tom Riddle, and Seamus are known half-bloods.

Note to Muggles: *Arguably, Harry could be considered pure-blood because his parents were a wizard and a witch. However, Lily was Muggle-born (although her ancestry is unknown) so Harry's background is not entirely magical.*

Hold your Hippogriffs!: Hold your horses!

I don't have two Galleons to rub together: I don't have two pennies to rub together.

It's no good crying over spilt potion: It's no good crying over spilt milk.

Kwikspell: This "all-new, fail-safe, quick-result, easy-learn" correspondence course teaches remedial magic to witches and wizards who are having difficulties using their wands.

Merlin's beard: Oh, my goodness!

Mermish: Dumbledore knows this language, spoken by Merpeople. Out of water, it sounds like screeching noises.

Metamorphmagi: Wizards born with the very rare ability to change their physical appearance at will. A wizard cannot be taught how to become a Metamorphmagus.

might as well be hanged for a dragon as an egg: Might as well be hanged for a sheep as a lamb. (The penalty for stealing any kind of livestock in old Britain was hanging, so would-be thieves figured if they were going risk this punishment, it might as well be for the biggest animal. In other words, if you're going to do something, do it in full and not by halves.)

Mudblood: Very rude, serious insult meaning dirty blood, directed towards Muggle-borns because of their background.

Muggle-born: Witch or wizard who comes from a non-magical family. Many Hogwarts students are Muggle-borns, including Hermione, Justin Finch-Fletchley, Dean Thomas, Penelope Clearwater, and the Creeveys.

Muggles: Non-magical people, such as the Dursleys. Wizards are not allowed to use magic in the Muggle world, except in very special circumstances.

MUGGLE WORDS WIZARDS MISPRONOUNCE

* ecklectic/eckeltricity (electric/electricity)
* fellytone (telephone)
* firelegs (firearms)
* please-men (policemen)
* pumbles (plumbers)

WIZARDING WORDS MUGGLES MISPRONOUNCE

* Dementy-whatsits, Dementoids, Demenders, Dismembers, Demembers
* Lord Voldything

Nitwit! Blubber! Oddment! Tweak!: The "few words" Dumbledore wanted to say at the first year start-of-term feast, prompting Harry to ask if the Headmaster was perhaps a bit mad.

Node iddum eentup sechew: Ron's "apology" to Nearly Headless Nick after unintentionally insulting him. Without a mouth full of food, it probably sounded like, "No, I didn't mean to upset you."

Parselmouth: A wizard who possesses the rare ability to communicate with snakes. It is considered a dark wizard's trait — Voldemort is a Parselmouth, as was Salazar "Serpent-tongue" Slytherin (which is why he chose a serpent to represent his house). Before he knows he is a wizard, Harry shows signs of being a Parselmouth when he "speaks" to a boa constrictor at the zoo, although it is a couple of years before he understands what this means and how it came to be. At London's Royal Albert Hall in June 2003, J. K. Rowling said Parselmouth is an old word for "someone who has a problem with their mouth, like a hairlip."

Parseltongue: Hissing language spoken by snakes. When speaking Parseltongue, some wizards enter a sort of trance — they are unaware they are speaking another language, and cannot speak in Parseltongue if they consciously try.

 Did you know . . . a linguistic expert from the University of Oxford created a Parseltongue alphabet specifically for the *Harry Potter and the Chamber of Secrets* film, so English words could be "translated"?

Peskipiksi Pesternomi: The "spell" Lockhart uses to try and bring the Cornish pixies under control: "Pesky pixie, pester no(t) me!" (Needless to say, it doesn't work.)

poisonous toadstools don't change their spots: A leopard doesn't change its spots.

pure-blood: Someone whose heritage is exclusively magical. Some pure-blood families, such as the Malfoys and most of the Blacks, consider themselves superior because they do not have any Muggle ancestry. There are not many pure-blood families left, and most are related because they will only marry other pure-bloods. The Crouches, Longbottoms, Macmillans, and Weasleys are also pure-bloods.

son of a Bludger: A mildly rude expression referring to an unsavoury person.

spattergroit: Medieval skin disease that leaves the victim pockmarked (sounds suspiciously like spots!). It is allegedly cured by standing naked in a barrel of eels' eyes during the full moon, with a toad's liver tied around the throat. Ron's freckles are mistaken for spattergroit at St. Mungo's.

splinching: This occurs when body parts are left behind as a result of Apparating incorrectly. A splinched wizard will be stuck in both places until he can be restored by the Ministry.

Squib: The opposite of a Muggle-born wizard, a Squib is someone from a magical family who has no magical ability (although they can still see Dementors). Squibs are not registered with the Ministry, and are fairly unusual in the wizarding world. There are two known Squibs in the Harry Potter series so far — although poor Neville sometimes wonders if he's almost one himself! The word "squib" has several meanings, but perhaps the most fitting is a firecracker that is broken, or burns but does not explode.

The cat's among the pixies now: The cat's among the canaries now.

There isn't room to swing a Kneazle!: There isn't room to swing a cat!

Time is Galleons: Time is money.

to "do a Weasley": To unexpectedly jump on your broom and leave, in the manner of Fred and George.

Toujours pur: The Black family motto, French for "always pure."

Troll: Language spoken by Trolls, which Fred reckons anyone can speak as it is just pointing and grunting.

Umbridge-itis: Students complain of this mysterious illness after fainting, vomiting, and bleeding in Umbridge's classes (little does she know their symptoms come straight from the contents of Skiving Snackboxes!).

Unplottable: A building that has been enchanted so it will not appear on a map.

working like house-elves: Much to Hermione's displeasure, this expression implies someone is working very hard.

Weasley is our King: The Slytherins make up this taunting rhyme to affect Ron's confidence and concentration. However, the Gryffindors later create a revised version that literally sings his praises.

PART FOUR:

The Muggle Reader's World

BRITISH TRANSLATION GUIDE

Many of the words and phrases used in the Harry Potter series are British in nature, and not readily understood in other parts of the world. Below, you'll find most of the British words used throughout the books and brief explanations for what they mean.

 Did you know . . . one of the biggest differences between the American and British editions of the Harry Potter series is the capitalisation of certain words? For example, "Dementors," "Boggart," and "Hippogriff" all take capitals in the British editions, but use lower case letters in the American editions.

aerial: antenna

airing cupboard: linen cupboard

Alice band: thick hairband (like the style worn in *Alice in Wonderland*)

all right for some: similar to "it must be nice"

aqualung: scuba diving equipment

balaclava: knitted hat that covers the entire face with holes for eyes and mouth

banging on: harping on, talking about something non-stop

bank note: paper money (bills)

barking: crazy, insane

berk: person who is easily taken advantage of

bilge: foolish talk, nonsense

(dust)bin: garbage can

(to) bin: to throw away

blasted (thing): expression of frustration, similar to "darned"

blighter: annoying person

blimey: indicates amazement or astonishment, similar to "wow" (slang, abbreviated from "God blind me")

bloke: guy

board dusters: blackboard erasers

bobble hat: knitted hat typically worn by children, with a pompom on top

bogey: booger

bog-standard: run of the mill

bold as brass: without shame

bollards: garbage cans

Bonfire Night: The fifth of November marks Guy Fawkes' failed attempt to blow up the parliament of King James I in 1605. Traditionally, people burn effigies of Guy Fawkes on bonfires and set off fireworks to mark the occasion.

bonnet: (1) hood of a car (2) women's hat

boot: trunk of a car

bowler: thin-brimmed round hat, traditionally worn by businessmen

braces: suspenders (the kind that hold up a man's trousers, not the kind women fasten to their lacy stockings)

bracken: large, coarse fern that grows in dense thickets

brilliant: excellent

budge up: move over, make room

budgerigar (budgie): parakeet

builder: home construction worker or handyperson

bullclips: paper clamps or butterfly clips

bully for you: good for you (sarcastic)

bungler: someone who makes a lot of mistakes or is inept

cadge: to scrounge or freeload

car park: parking lot

caretaker: janitor

carriage: car on a train

chap(pie): fellow, guy

cheek: sauciness or insolence

cheers: (1) popular drinking toast (2) expression of thanks

chest of drawers: dresser drawers

chivvy: to hurry or rush someone along

chucked out: thrown out

chuffed: pleased

chunter: to grumble

cine-camera: camcorder

cinema: movie theatre

clear off!: get lost!

cock and bull story: unbelievable tale

cock-crow: dawn (when the rooster crows)

codger: old person (mildly derogatory)

codswallop: foolish talk, nonsense

collywobbles: severe nausea

common: someone who is uncouth or lacking class or manners

conk: nose (slang)

conker: chestnut

constable: police officer

cooker: stove

(to) cop it: to get into trouble

corking: splendid

cot: crib

cotton on: to understand or catch on

council: local government

cracking: really good, fantastic

crikey: exclamation of surprise

cross: angry

cuppa: cup of tea

dead: very (e.g. dead useful, dead easy) (slang)

doddery: senile

(a bit) dodgy: something suspicious, uncertain, or risky

do me a brew: to make a cup of tea

do a runner: to run away or escape

do someone in: to kill someone

dotty: scatter-brained

do your nut: to throw a fit

dozy: dim-witted

draughts: (1) checkers (2) draft (breeze)

draw (with): to tie (in a match, race, or game)

drawing-pin: thumbtack

dressing-gown: housecoat

dry rot: fungus that attacks wood in a house

duffer: useless, bumbling, slow person

earth: dirt (pathway)

effing: politer way of saying a certain four-letter word!

end-of-year report: report card

engagement: appointment

faerie lights: Christmas lights

fancy: (1) to be attracted to someone (2) to want something

flutter: to place a bet or gamble

Father Christmas: Santa Claus

film: movie

flagon: flask

(to be in a) flap: to get overly excited, worked up, or flustered

flat: apartment

football: soccer

fortnight: two weeks

fringe: bangs (hair)

galumph: to run clumsily

gaol (pronounced "jail"): prison

garden: yard or lawn

gawp: to stare with the mouth hanging open

Gerroff: contraction of "get off" (slang)

get out of it: cut it out

ginger: orange-coloured (hair)

git: stupid person, moron, idiot

gormless: stupid, moronic, or slow-witted

grass (on): to tattle-tale

grotto: cave

guff: foolish talk, nonsense

hacked off: annoyed or upset

have a go: (1) to try (2) to pick on

haversack: large bag soldiers use on excursions

hearing trumpet: old-fashioned, cone-shaped hearing aid

hiccough: hiccup

High Street: main street in a town, usually where all the shops are

hoover: vacuum (Hoover is a name-brand, like Kleenex, that has become interchangeable with the product it makes)

hosepipe: garden hose

ickle: little, usually referring to toddlers or babies

in a right state: in a bad way, or very agitated

jam jar: Mason jar

jumper: sweater

keen: eager

keep your pecker up: keep your chin up

kerfuffle: commotion

kip: nap or sleep

knickerbockers: knee-length baggy trousers with a buckle or button at the cuff (not to be confused with knickers, which are women's underwear!)

lad: young boy

lassie: young girl

leg it: make a run for it

lessons: classes

letter box: traditional red mail box, usually shaped like a cylinder

lift: (1) ride (in a car) (2) elevator

loggerheads: to strongly disagree or be at odds with someone

loo: toilet

(that's your) lookout: responsibility or problem (slang)

looks a treat: to look fantastic

lorry: truck

lounge: living room

lumbago: lower back pain usually brought on by arthritis or rheumatism

mackintosh: waterproof raincoat

mad: crazy or insane (not angry)

manky: dirty or grungy

mate: friend (usually a male's way of referring to another male)

maths: mathematics

matron: head nurse

mean: stingy

mess someone about: to give someone a hard time

mess about: to play around or waste time

mind: to watch out for

midges: tiny mosquitoes that travel in swarms

motorbike: motorcycle

motorway: freeway or highway

milkman: person who delivers milk and/or eggs to the door

multi-storey car park: parking garage

mum/mam (Irish): mom

nancy boy: an effeminate male

nappy: diaper

newsagents: a convenience store that also sells a wide variety of newspapers and magazines

newsreader: television news anchor-person

nick: to steal

nip (off): to hurry somewhere

nobble: to tamper with something

nosh: meal or food

not a dicky bird: nothing

nought: zero

nutter: mentally unbalanced person

off his rocker: crazy, insane

oi! (sometimes spelt oy!): hey!

out of order: to behave inappropriately

pants: men's underwear

pavement: sidewalk

pay rise: raise in salary

peaky: wan or pale

pebble-dash: exterior house wall covering resembling gravel mixed with plaster

petrol: gasoline

philosopher: sorcerer

pillock: stupid person, moron, idiot

pitch: field

plait: braid

plonking: to drop or set something down heavily

plughole: drain of a sink or tub

plus-fours: old-style men's knicker-bockers, usually worn for golf

popinjay: (1) parrot (2) person who chatters incessantly

popkin: term of endearment for a child, like sweetheart or darling

pop my clogs: to die (slang, like kick the bucket)

post: mail delivery

pouffe: footstool

prat: someone who behaves like the part of the body you sit on; a jerk

pub: a cornerstone of British culture — establishments where locals gather to drink, eat, socialise, and often watch a football game on the television (if they're Muggles, or Dean Thomas).

pudding: dessert

pudding-basin haircut: bowl cut (hair-style that looks like a bowl has been turned upside-down on a person's head)

(to be) put out: upset

put paid to: killed, exterminated

quailing: cowering

queue: line-up

quits: to make things even with someone, to settle a debt

rabbit (on): to blabber or chatter incessantly

reckon: to think

red card: card shown by football referee to eject a player from the game

revisions: studies

romper suit: track suit

rounders: sport similar to baseball

round on (someone): to tell someone off

row (pronounced like "now"): argument

rubbish: garbage

rucksack: backpack

ruddy: milder version of "bloody"

sack: to fire (from a job)

satsuma: similar to a mandarin orange

scallywag: mischief-maker, imp, or rascal

scarper: to scurry away

Sellotape: scotch tape

set: to give, as in homework or an exam

shan't: contraction of "shall not"

(have a) shifty: take a look

shirty: huffy

skip: dumpster

skirting board: baseboard

skive: to dodge classes or work

sledge: toboggan

slog: to work at something doggedly

smarmy: overbearingly suave or smug

snog: to kiss

snuff it: to die

sorted: to get something straightened out or taken care of

spangles: sequins

(go) spare: to become agitated or distraught

spots: acne

starkers: naked

(to be in a) state: to be worked up about something

stile: set of steps over a low wall or fence

stoat: an ermine (small mammal), when it has its brown summer coat

summat: something (regional dialect)

surname: last name

swot: someone who studies excessively (derogatory)

(to) take the mickey: mock or make fun of someone

tarradiddles: tall tales

term: semester

telephone box: traditional red payphone booth

tetchy: irritable

thick: stupid

ticked off: (1) to check off (a list) (2) to be annoyed

tinned: canned (fruits or vegetables)

titchy: tiny

toerag: slimy, untrustworthy person

torch: flashlight

tosh: foolish talk, nonsense

trainers: running shoes

trials: try-outs

trod: to step on something

trolley: cart

trousers: pants

the Tube (Underground): London subway

tuck in: to dig in or start eating

tyre: tire

vole: mouse-like rodent with a thick head, small ears, and hairy, short tail

waffle: vague but verbose speech

wardrobe: closet

washing-powder: laundry detergent

waste-paper basket: garbage bin

wee: (1) little (2) early (as in "wee hours of the morning")

weedy: scrawny and pale, wimpy

wellington boots (wellies): rubber boots

what are you like?: expression of exasperation used to mock someone's behaviour

what are you on about?: what are you talking about?

what are you playing at?: what do you think you're doing?

windscreen: windshield

(to) wind someone up: to deliberately annoy someone or to take advantage of someone's gullibility

woolly: confusing or vague

wonky: something that is broken or malfunctioning in an amusing or perverse way

wotcher: casual greeting; abbreviation of "what cheer" (slang)

DIFFERENCES BETWEEN THE BOOKS AND FILMS

Harry Potter and the Philosopher's Stone

✴ In the book, the boa constrictor at the London Zoo is from Brazil. In the film, the snake is from Burma.

✴ In the book, Hagrid recognised Harry straight away. In the film, Hagrid mistook Dudley for Harry initially.

✴ In the film, there is a flashback scene that shows Voldemort attacking Lily Potter and baby Harry. In the book, the events of that night are only recounted by third parties (Dumbledore, Hagrid, etc.) and we never see what happened first-hand.

✴ In the film, Mrs. Weasley instructs Ron to go through to platform nine and three quarters first, to show Harry how it's done. In the book, she tells Harry to go before Ron.

✴ In the film, a Chocolate Frog is shown hopping out the window of the Hogwarts Express. In the book, Chocolate Frogs do not move.

✴ The character of Peeves the poltergeist does not appear in any of the films.

✴ The book says first-year Gryffindors and Slytherins only have Potions together, but in the film they also take Transfiguration together.

✴ In the book, McGonagall pulls Oliver Wood out of Charms class to tell him about Harry's potential as a Seeker. In the film, she interrupts his Defence Against the Dark Arts class.

★ In the film, Hermione points out a school trophy indicating that James Potter was a Seeker. This was never confirmed in the books (it was only stated that James was an excellent Quidditch player). Moreover, in an interview with Scholastic Books, J. K. Rowling said that James was a Chaser.

★ In the film, Harry unwraps his Nimbus Two Thousand in the Great Hall, with Ron and Hermione's help. In the book, he and Ron open the parcel in their dormitory (Hermione is not their friend yet).

★ In the book, spectators at Quidditch matches can sit anywhere (hence Malfoy, Crabbe, and Goyle's fight with Ron and Neville, who are sitting in front of them), but in the film, the stands are separated by house.

★ In the book, Harry, Hermione, Malfoy, and Neville serve detention with Hagrid in the Forbidden Forest after they are all caught out after curfew the night Norbert the dragon is sent to Romania. In the film, Neville is replaced by Ron, and they are all given detention after being caught out after curfew the night Norbert hatches.

★ Seamus is depicted as accident-prone in the film, which is not at all the case in the book.

★ The Potions riddle Snape created (and Hermione solved) to protect the Philosopher's Stone was omitted from the film.

 Did you know . . . *Harry Potter and the Philosopher's Stone* earned almost $969 million USD (£517 million) at the box office, making it the third-most successful film of all time?

Harry Potter and the Chamber of Secrets

✳ In the book, Dobby causes Aunt Petunia's pudding to crash down on Harry, and an owl drops a letter on Mrs. Mason's head. In the film there is no owl, and Mrs. Mason gets covered in the pudding instead.

✳ In the film, Ron rescues Harry from the Dursleys on Harry's birthday. In the book, he saves him three days later.

✳ In the book, Mr. Weasley repairs Harry's broken glasses. In the film, it is Hermione who casts an "Occulus Reparo" spell to fix them.

✳ In the book, Lockhart's special announcement at Flourish and Blotts is that he has been appointed Defence Against the Dark Arts teacher. In the film, the students don't find out he is their teacher until the first class at Hogwarts. Mr. Weasley and Lucius Malfoy's brawl at Flourish and Blotts is also omitted from the film. Also in the film, Lucius Malfoy mentions seeing Mr. Weasley "at work," but in the books Malfoy does not work for the Ministry.

✳ When Harry and Ron arrive at Hogwarts, it is Snape who greets them in the book; in the film, it is Filch.

✳ In the book, the Gryffindors and Hufflepuffs have Herbology together. This is still the case in the film, but the Slytherins seem to be in the class, too. All three houses have Transfiguration and Defence Against the Dark Arts together in the film, as well.

✳ When Ron explains what a Mudblood is in the book, Hermione is unfamiliar with the term. In the film, Hermione provides the explanation.

✳ In the book, Lockhart calls upon Justin Finch-Fletchley and Neville to volunteer during Duelling Club. Snape dismisses the idea, claiming Neville causes devastation with the simplest of spells. In the film, Lockhart asks Harry and Ron to volunteer, and Snape makes the comment about Ron's broken wand instead.

✳ In the book, Professor Binns provides the explanation about the Chamber of Secrets. In the film, the explanation is given by McGonagall.

✳ Harry has a confrontation with Ernie Macmillan in the book that does not happen in the film.

✳ In the book, Harry and Ron hide in a wardrobe in the staff room and over-hear McGonagall telling the teachers about Ginny being taken into the Chamber. In the film, the staff is told in the second floor corridor, and Harry and Ron hide around the corner.

✳ In the film, Hermione says the message on the wall about the Chamber of Secrets is written in blood. In the book, Ginny says it was written using red paint.

✳ In the film, Lucius Malfoy begins to use Avada Kedavra on Harry after Dobby is freed, until Dobby magically stops him. In the book, he merely "lunges" at Harry, and no spells are cast. (This is fairly significant as Avada Kedavra is the worst curse known to wizardkind, so to have Lucius use it — at Hogwarts, no less — for merely losing a house-elf seems a bit over the top.)

✳ In the book, the end-of-year feast is held late at night, and the students attend wearing pyjamas. In the film, it is held earlier and they are in uniform.

✳ At the end of the film, Harry and Hermione hug, Ron and Hermione share an awkward moment, and Hagrid enters the Great Hall after his name is cleared. None of these things happens in the book.

✳ At the very end of the film, after Lockhart is hit with the backfiring Memory Charm, he writes another autobiography called *Who Am I?*, which is shown in the window of Flourish and Blotts. This scene was created exclusively for the film and does not appear in the book.

 Did you know . . . Repton School in Staffordshire, England made a ballet out of *Harry Potter and the Chamber of Secrets*? There were one hundred and seventy children in the cast — and Harry was played by a girl!

Harry Potter and the Prisoner of Azkaban

✶ In the film, a shrunken head hung from the rear-view mirror of the Knight Bus acts as another set of eyes for near-sighted Ernie, the driver. This does not happen in the book.

✶ In the film, a chambermaid at the Leaky Cauldron knocks on a bedroom door and announces herself to clean the room. The door flies open and a blast of wind, noise, and white light almost blows her over, prompting her to say she will come back later. This scene is not in the book.

✶ In the book, Harry meets Hermione and Ron outside of Florean Fortescue's and they later go to the Magical Menagerie, where Hermione buys Crookshanks. In the film, Harry meets Hermione and Ron at the Leaky Cauldron, and Hermione has already bought the cat.

✶ In the book, the conversation where Mr. Weasley makes Harry promise he won't go looking for Sirius takes place at platform nine and three-quarters. In the film, it occurs at the Leaky Cauldron.

✶ Both the Dementors in the book and the film make people feel cold on the inside, but the film Dementors also literally freeze the area around them as they glide past. Also, Harry hears his mother begging for her life to Voldemort whenever he encounters Dementors in the book, but in the film, he only hears her screaming.

✶ In the book, Dementors are repelled by casting the Patronus Charm, which takes the silvery, corporeal form of an animal. In the film, Dementors seem to be repelled by a bright white circular force shield (although a corporeal Patronus is also produced at one point).

✶ In the film, a group of Hogwarts students sing in a choir in the Great Hall, carrying enormous frogs (which, according to director Alfonso Cuarón, were meant to be used as instruments!). This does not happen in the book. The Slytherin and Gryffindor tables are also side-by-side in the film, which is not the case in the book.

✳ In the film, Harry, Neville, Seamus, Dean, and Ron are seen in their dormitory the first night of school, eating sweets and clowning around. This scene is not in the book.

✳ While both the book and the film reveal Ron's Boggart in Defence Against the Dark Arts class to be a giant spider, only the film shows Ron repelling the spider by forcing it to wear roller skates. In the film, Parvati's Boggart is shown to be a giant cobra, which is turned into a grotesque jack-in-the-box, but in the book, her Boggart is a mummy, which becomes unwrapped.

✳ In the book, Sir Cadogan plays a role in protecting Gryffindor Tower after the Fat Lady is attacked. Although Sir Cadogan's part was filmed, it was cut from the final edit of the film. However, he can still be seen in the background when the Fat Lady is trying to shatter a glass with the sound of her voice (a scene not in the book!).

✳ In the book, Neville loses his list of passwords, allowing Sirius access to Gryffindor Tower. Ron wakes to find his bed curtains slashed by Sirius. In the film, none of this happens . . . but Ron does have a nightmare where spiders want him to tap-dance (which is not in the book)!

✳ In the film, Malfoy draws a caricature of Harry being struck by lightning during a Quidditch match, folds it into an origami crane, and magically flies it over to Harry during a Defence Against the Dark Arts class. This does not happen in the book.

✳ During the Quidditch scenes, the characters of Oliver Wood and Cho Chang appear in the book, but not in the film. Also, during the book's Gryffindor v Hufflepuff match, Hermione casts an Impervius charm on Harry's glasses so he can see in the torrential rain. In the film, Harry wears goggles instead.

✳ Arguably the biggest difference between the book and film is that the book explains who Moony, Wormtail, Padfoot, and Prongs are and why they created the Marauder's Map. In the film, the origins of the Marauder's Map are not explained at all (and "Moony" is spelt as "Mooney," an inside joke referring to the film's visual effects supervisor, Karl Mooney). Director Alfonso Cuarón suggested this will be explained in a future Harry Potter film.

✷ In the book, Snape finds Harry in possession of the Marauder's Map when Harry sneaks back into Hogwarts from Hogsmeade. In the film, Snape finds Harry with the Marauder's Map in the middle of the night, after Harry spots Peter Pettigrew on it. In the book, Peter is not seen on the map by Harry, and his existence is alluded to in other ways.

✷ In the book, Harry flings mud at Malfoy and his cronies from beneath his Invisibility Cloak. In the film, the mud has been replaced with snow, and the scene takes place earlier in the year.

✷ In the book, Harry, Hermione, and Ron are in the Leaky Cauldron pub when they accidentally overhear Fudge, Hagrid, Professor Flitwick, Professor McGonagall, and Madam Rosmerta discussing Sirius's betrayal of James and Lily. In the film, Harry enters the Leaky Cauldron alone under his Invisibility Cloak, and deliberately eavesdrops on Fudge and Professor McGonagall telling Madam Rosmerta the story in a private chamber.

✷ Harry hears Trelawney's prophecy during his final exam in the book. In the film, he hears it when he returns a crystal ball to her that Hermione knocked off the table in class.

✷ In the book, Hermione slaps Draco when he insults Hagrid. In the film, Hermione threatens him at wandpoint, then punches him instead.

✷ When Hermione time-travels in the film, she throws rocks into Hagrid's hut to get the attention of her past self. This does not happen in the books.

✷ In the film, Hermione makes a werewolf call to lure Lupin away from Harry. In the book, this does not happen. Hermione and Harry hide from Lupin the werewolf in Hagrid's hut in the book, but in the film they run into the Forbidden Forest.

✷ In the book, the Whomping Willow is frozen by pressing a knot on its trunk. In the film, Lupin freezes it with an "Immobilus!" command. The film also shows Harry and Hermione being taken for a terrifying ride by the Whomping Willow, which does not happen in the book.

✳ In the film, Hermione tells Sirius in the Shrieking Shack, "If you want to kill Harry, you'll have to kill us, too!" In the book, this is Ron's line.

✳ In the film, there is no reason given for the white stag Patronus Harry sees across the shore of the Hogwarts lake. In the book, the stag and its connection to Harry are explained in much more detail.

✳ In the film, Sirius is imprisoned in the topmost cell of the Dark Tower; in the book, he is held captive in Professor Flitwick's office (thirteenth window from the right of the West Tower, on the seventh floor).

✳ In the book, Harry is given a Firebolt for Christmas, which is confiscated for inspection. In the film, he doesn't receive it until the end of the year and is able to use it immediately.

 Did you know . . . British Prime Minister Tony Blair's son Euan had a summer job as a gofer on the *Harry Potter and the Prisoner of Azkaban* film set?

WIZARDING TOUR OF BRITAIN

To the delight of fans, the distinctly British nature of the Harry Potter series has been preserved in perfect detail onscreen. In addition to an almost-exclusively British cast featuring some of the nation's most esteemed names in acting, the films use unmistakably British scenery and settings as a back-drop. From the Scottish Highlands to southern England, the Harry Potter films have captured some of the most beautiful landscapes and historical locations Britain has to offer.

Alnwick Castle, Northumberland (England): Situated near the Scottish border, eleventh century Alnwick Castle (pronounced "An-ick") is the second largest inhabited castle in England. The home to the Duke of Northumberland for many centuries, Alnwick Castle's grounds provided the backdrop for the Hogwarts' exteriors in the first two films.

Australia House, London: Located in the heart of London on the Strand, Australia House, home of the Australian High Commission (embassy), was opened in 1918 by King George V. English Heritage designated Australia House as a Grade II building on account of its majestic architecture, modelled after Roman and French styles. Some of the Gringotts interior scenes were shot here, although the exteriors were filmed at the nearby silver vaults.

Black Park, Buckinghamshire (England): West of London lies the county of Buckinghamshire, which contains some England's most pictur-esque countryside and woodlands. A popular recreational centre, the 530-acre Black Park provided the setting for the Forbidden Forest and Hagrid's hut in the first two films.

Borough Market, London: This busy eclectic food market in southeast London was once a medieval market held on London Bridge, moving to Borough High Street in 1276. It served as the exterior for the Leaky Cauldron in *Prisoner of Azkaban* (the Leaky Cauldron used in the *Philosopher's Stone* was filmed at a different location).

Durham Cathedral, Durham (England): This Norman cathedral, founded in 1093, is located on the bank of the river Wear in northeastern England. The cloisters, corridors, and rooms of Durham Cathedral were used for some of the interior Hogwarts settings, including the Transfiguration classroom and Moaning Myrtle's bathroom.

Exmoor, Devon (England): Many of the location scenes for *Goblet of Fire* are being filmed in this picturesque county in southwestern England.

Fort William, Western Highlands (Scotland): Two areas near Fort William have played a role in the films. The dramatic scenery of Glen Nevis provided the backdrop for the Quidditch match in *Philosopher's Stone* as well as the first task of the Triwizard Tournament in the upcoming *Goblet of Fire*, while picturesque Torlundy recreated parts of Hogsmeade and the Hogwarts grounds in *Prisoner of Azkaban*.

Gloucester Cathedral, Gloucestershire (England): Gloucester Cathedral (pronounced "Gloss-ter") is one of Britain's most beautiful places of worship. Founded over 1300 years ago, its Gothic architecture and cloisters have been seen in several interior Hogwarts scenes. However, in order to disguise the nature of the cathedral, tombstones embedded in the floor were covered with painted felt, haloes were hidden in stained glass windows — and Adam and Eve were clothed!

Did you know . . . there was a local controversy surrounding the use of the cathedral in a film about witchcraft? Protesters wrote the local paper, claiming it was blasphemy and threatening to block the film crew's access. Although protesters did show up to the shoot, the filming went ahead without incident.

Glencoe, Western Highlands (Scotland): The rugged mountainside beauty of Torren, near the village of Glencoe, was featured in *Prisoner of Azkaban* for scenes involving Hagrid's hut — but unfortunately, the cast and crew had to battle swarms of midges, endless rain, and removal of some props by souvenir-seekers (part of the set was built on a popular hiking trail) during the shoot.

Glenfinnan Viaduct, West Highlands (Scotland): Completed in 1894, the 1,248-foot long Glenfinnan Viaduct crosses the River Finnan valley. The curved concrete structure is comprised of twenty-one arches, the tallest being one hundred feet high. The Hogwarts Express can be seen travelling across the viaduct's impressive arches in all three films.

 Did you know . . . during the filming for *Prisoner of Azkaban*, sparks from the Hogwarts Express caused a brushfire in the dry Glenfinnan countryside? Luckily, no one was hurt but dozens of acres of hillside were burnt in the blaze.

Goathland Station, North Yorkshire (England): Several hours north of London, the North Yorkshire Moors Railway operates steam engines along an eighteen-mile route from Pickering to Goathland. In operation since 1865, the tiny station of Goathland doubled as Hogsmeade station in the films.

Harrow School, Middlesex (England): Founded in 1572, the Harrow School in northwest London is one of Britain's foremost independent schools, boasting alumni such as Lord Byron and Winston Churchill. A well-preserved seventeenth century classroom at the school was used as the Charms classroom in the first film.

Hunton Bridge, Hertfordshire (England): Located a Galleon's toss west of Leavesden Studios, a plot of private land in Hunton Bridge, north of London, provided the location for The Burrow. A sixty-foot tall set was constructed for the façade of the house.

King's Cross station, London: Opened in 1852, King's Cross station was built as the terminus for the Great Northern Railway. Of course, it is more famous now as the terminus for the Hogwarts Express, and appears in the first two films.

J. K. Rowling came up with the idea of platform nine and three quarters when she was not living in London, and accidentally mixed up King's Cross with Euston station. Platforms nine and ten at King's Cross are for suburban trains. They are in a different area and do not look anything like the inter-city platforms that go to points north (including Scotland). As a result, the Hogwarts Express scenes at King's Cross were filmed on platform four, which bears more of a resemblance to the platforms nine and ten described in the books.

The King's School Gloucester, Gloucestershire (England): Affiliated with Gloucester Cathedral, this prestigious school is one of seven in the country refounded by Henry VIII in 1541. Many of the students were used as extras in the first two films.

Lacock Abbey, Wiltshire (England): Part of the quaint southeastern village of Lacock, Lacock Abbey was founded in 1232 and converted to a manor home in the sixteenth century. Over the years, the abbey has incorporated a variety of styles including medieval cloisters, Tudor, Gothic arches and gargoyles, and Victorian gardens. Its rooms and corridors were used for some of the Hogwarts interiors.

Leadenhall Market, London: Originally a meat, poultry, and fish market dating back to the fourteenth century, the first Leadenhall Market was destroyed in the Great Fire of London in 1666. It has been rebuilt numerous times — the current architecture is from the Victorian era — and now hosts a variety of cafés, shops, and merchants. A market pub was the setting for the Leaky Cauldron in the *Philosopher's Stone*.

Leavesden Studios, Hertfordshire (England): This former airfield north of London contains enormous soundstages (converted from aeroplane hangars) which house many of the films' long-term interior sets, including Diagon Alley, Hogsmeade, Gringotts, and numerous areas within Hogwarts.

The London Zoo, London: Set on the edge of Regent's Park in north London, the zoo existed as a place of scientific study before opening its doors to the public in 1847. The Reptile House seen in the first film was designed in 1927, and is home to the largest collection of reptiles in Britain.

Did you know . . . Harry's boa constrictor isn't the only famous resident of the zoo? A black bear named Winnie was given to the London Zoo in 1914, where she was visited by A. A. Milne and his son, Christopher. The tales of Winnie the Pooh and Christopher Robin are as classic and endearing as the Harry Potter series.

Martins Heron, Berkshire (England): Martins Heron was built up in the late 1980s as part of the town of Bracknell, in southern England. An ordinary house in the suburb was transformed into the Dursleys' home for the first two films. For *Prisoner of Azkaban*, a new location around the corner from Leavesden Studios was used for the Durlseys' neighbourhood.

Did you know . . . the house used for number four, Privet Drive in the first two films was put up for sale by auction in the spring of 2003? The owners failed to receive their asking price of £250,000 ($450,000 USD)!

Nicolson's, Edinburgh (Scotland): Possibly, the most important "location" of all, although nothing was filmed there — this popular two-storey southside café was where J. K. Rowling spent many hours writing *Harry Potter and the Philosopher's Stone*. In 1999, the ground floor was turned into a Black Medicine Coffee Company café, while the upstairs became more of a restaurant. Sadly for Potterphiles, the upstairs was sold and reopened as a Chinese buffet in 2003.

University of Oxford, Oxfordshire (England): Naturally, one of the oldest and grandest academic institutions in the world would be a perfect double for Hogwarts. Steeped in history, the University of Oxford is so old there is no definitive date for its foundation, although teaching has existed in some form at Oxford since 1096. The fifteenth century Divinity School, with its stunning vaulted Gothic ceiling, was used as the Hogwarts hospital wing in the first two films. Hogwarts's Great Hall was modelled after the sixteenth century dining hall at Christ Church college, while the college's magnificent marble staircase is featured in the castle's Entrance Hall. Duke Humfrey's Library in the Bodleian Library, the university's main research centre, played its Hogwarts counterpart in the films.

 Did you know . . . J. K. Rowling was thrilled with the set for the Great Hall in the films? In an online chat for World Book Day in March 2004, she remarked, "It really was like walking into my own brain!"

Palmers Green, Middlesex (England): This north London suburb was specially chosen because of its Edwardian-style homes and shops. The Knight Bus can be seen weaving precariously down its roads in *Prisoner of Azkaban.*

Shepperton Studios, Middlesex (England): Located west of London, near Heathrow Airport, Shepperton Studios houses the set for the Hogwarts lake, used at the end of *Prisoner of Azkaban.*

St. Pancras station, London: With its red-bricked walls, soaring clock-tower, and enormous iron and glass roof — St. Pancras station was a spectacular addition to the cityscape when it opened in 1868. Adjacent to the more functional King's Cross station, the ornate façade of St. Pancras was thought to be a better fit for the exterior station shots.

Virginia Water, Surrey (England): This 130-acre man-made lake near Windsor Great Park, south of London, was created by the Duke of Cumberland in the eighteenth century. Virginia Water was used as the backdrop for the Care of Magical Creatures class scenes during *Prisoner of Azkaban.*

HOW TO HOST YOUR OWN HARRY POTTER PARTY

Whether you're planning a Hallowe'en Feast, a birthday bash, or a celebration for the release of the latest book or film, Harry Potter makes a great theme for an event. Here's all you need to know about costuming, food, decorations, games, and more to plan the perfect Potter party, including some creative and unique suggestions from mega-fan Britta Peterson, who has thrown two Hogwarts-themed extravaganzas — check out her Web site at www.britta.com/hogwarts.

Invitations

✶ Although you might have trouble finding an owl to deliver them, parchment-style paper and ivory envelopes (available at most stationery shops) will make your invitations look as aged as Dumbledore himself.

✶ Send your guests individually addressed, Hogwarts-style "letters" (be sure to use green ink!) with all the party details on them — be creative! Trim the invitations using deckle-edged scissors (available at most craft shops).

✶ A letter "H" seal (available at some craft and stationery shops) in purple sealing wax on the back of your envelopes is the perfect finishing touch, but be sure to practise making seals first — they can be tricky! Tip: As real sealing wax doesn't hold up very well in Muggle post, consider a more flexible alternative from www.FauxWax.com.

Decorations

★ A wide variety of official Harry Potter merchandise is available from most party supply shops, including cups, plates, tablecloths, napkins, streamers, stickers, and House banners.

★ Official Harry Potter fabric (available at some fabric shops) is perfect for throwing over furniture to give it a Hogwarts feel. Even novice sewers can create simple pillows out of the fabric stuffed with bunting, which can later be given away as prizes.

★ Hallowe'en is a great time to stock up on supplies, no matter what time of year your party is. In addition to witches' hats and cloaks, you'll also find rats, swords, spiders, broomsticks, cauldrons, pumpkins, small trophies, skulls, plastic insects, gargoyles, candles, treasure chests, coins, goblets, and much more!

★ Stencil signs for your front garden welcoming guests to Hogwarts and reminding them to beware of the Whomping Willow! Hang a giant spider in a nest of gauze cobwebbing from a tree in your garden, along with a sign announcing the Forbidden Forest. A small angled spotlight or strobe light creates added drama.

★ Inside your home, stencil signs for the entrance of each room, mapping out the party. For example, people can sit and chat in the "Gryffindor

Common Room," food can be served in the "Great Hall" . . . and the doors of any off-limit areas can become the "dungeons."

★ Fill a small flowerpot with sparkly glitter, and have guests "Floo" from your front door into your home by throwing a pinch and announcing "Hogwarts!" as they cross the threshold.

Note to Muggles: *As Muggles cannot use Vanishing Spells, you may need to vacuum thoroughly the next day!*

★ Candles of all shapes and sizes will add plenty of atmosphere, but be sure never to leave them unattended!

★ Transfigure pens into quills by taping feathers to the end. A giant peacock feather on the end of a felt-tip marker is perfect for guests to sign a guest book.

★ You can find lots of specialty Hallowe'en designs at your local fabric shop. Adhere black fabric (preferably with a star pattern) to your dining room ceiling with double-sided foam tape to turn it into the night sky, just like the Great Hall. Alternatively, you can use black garbage bags covered in stick-on glow-in-the-dark stars.

★ Tape small plastic spiders up a wall and along a windowsill to recreate the spiders fleeing from Hogwarts in *Harry Potter and the Chamber of Secrets*.

★ Cover empty cereal or frozen food boxes in broadcloth or faux vinyl (available at most craft or fabric shops), then use a gold or silver pen to write in the names of Hogwarts textbooks or library books.

★ Small fishbowls turned up-side down and set on candle-holders make great crystal balls. Add a tea cup containing tea leaves, a deck of cards and some candles or incense, to recreate Trelawney's Divination classroom.

★ Create a display of different-sized jars and bottles (available at most thrift or craft shops, or use empty spice or sauce bottles, jam jars, bottles of bath salts, etc.) filled with different Potions "ingredients" (dried herbs and fruit slices, flakes of chocolate, water with food colouring added, strings of liquorice, concentrated fruit juice, sugar, etc.). Label the bottles with the ingredient name on the front, and the Muggle name on the back.

✶ Create labels for household plants, renaming them after their counterparts in Professor Sprout's greenhouse.

✶ Get parental help to carve out faces on the sides of large turnips (with the foliage attached). Glue on googly-eyes and colour the "lips" with a red marker, then half-bury the turnips on a bed of shredded paper in a large flowerpot or planter, and voilà . . . instant Mandrakes!

MAKE YOUR OWN MOANING MYRTLE

1. From a craft shop, buy a large unfinished rag doll, iron-on face transfers, miniature glasses, black yarn, black broadcloth, and two pieces of grey felt (approximately twelve inches by twelve inches).
2. Gently iron the transfer to the doll's face (be sure to follow the instructions!). After it cools, glue the glasses to the doll's face.
3. Cut the yarn in one foot lengths. Braid it into two plaits and glue the tops to the doll's head. Cut and glue shorter lengths for the fringe (bangs).

4. Sew or glue one edge of the two pieces of felt vertically. Cut a U-shape out of the top, so the felt resembles the front of a pinafore-style dress, and glue or pin it to the doll.

5. Staple a wire coat hanger to the doll's back, ensuring it is level with the back of the doll's head so the "shoulders" of the coat hanger correspond with the doll's shoulders. Cut the broadcloth into a large square and drape over the coat hanger, like a cloak. Dust the cloak with baby powder to give it an aged look.

6. Tie fishing wire securely around the coat hanger, then hang "Myrtle" from a bathroom ceiling using a hook. Or, pull the fishing wire through the hook and tie the other end to the bathroom door handle, so it operates as a pulley and "Myrtle" moves every time someone opens the door!

Costuming

✳ No Potter party is complete without a cast of characters! If you're a stickler for detail, there are numerous Web sites which can help you create an authentic Hogwarts look. Here's just a sampling:

> ✳ **Alivans Wands:** www.alivans.com
>
> ✳ **atypically.knit:** http://knit.atypically.net (hand-knitted scarves and socks plus handy instructions for how to knit your own)
>
> ✳ **Frank Bee School Uniforms:** www.schoolunif.com (their uniforms appeared in the films)
>
> ✳ **French Toast:** www.frenchtoast.com (skirts and trousers)
>
> ✳ **Hobbie's House of Wizard Wear:** www.wizardknits.com (scarves and jumpers)
>
> ✳ **The Kids Window:** www.thekidswindow.co.uk (stocks the Weasley jumpers seen in the films)
>
> ✳ **Patch Palace:** www.patchpalace.com (Hogwarts, House, and Quidditch patches)
>
> ✳ **TCE Badges:** www.tcebadges.co.uk (prefect badges)
>
> ✳ **Whirlwood Wands:** www.whirlwood.com
>
> ✳ **Wizard Uniforms:** www.wizarduniforms.com (jumpers in all four House colours)
>
> ✳ **The Wizards Wear Shoppe:** http://geocities.com/thewizardswearshoppe/thewizardswearshoppe (jumpers, ties, and scarves)

✳ Second-hand clothing shops are excellent resources for quirky items to put the finishing touches on your costume, including ear muffs (Sprout), shabby trousers and threadbare jumpers (Lupin), frilly or floral clothing (Umbridge), glasses, jewellery, and scarves (Trelawney), whistles and goggles (Madam Hooch), hand mirrors (Lockhart), and possibly even a pink umbrella (Hagrid)!

✳ Craft shops can also help add detail to your costume. For example, a round glass ornament filled with red tissue paper makes an excellent Remembrall, while red faux jewels can turn an ordinary sword into a true Gryffindor's. Craft shops are also great places to find stencils for lettering signs.

Sorting the Students

✷ Record short descriptions for each House on a tape recorder spaced five seconds apart (e.g. "Brave . . . daring . . . must be GRYFFINDOR!"). As guests arrive, place the Sorting Hat on each person's head and play one message per person to "sort" them for the party. Make small ribbons in the four House colours for sorted guests to wear.

BRITTA'S INSTRUCTIONS FOR MAKING YOUR OWN SORTING HAT

1. Cut the arms off an old brown leather jacket, then cut each along the seam so both pieces lay flat. (If you don't have an old jacket, check second-hand clothing shops. The more distressed the jacket, the better — remember, the Sorting Hat is a thousand years old!)

2. Put the arms together, right side in, and cut your Sorting Hat shape, with a bit of a curve towards the pointed top.

3. Carefully machine-sew together, and be sure to have extra needles handy since you might break one or two!

4. Use pieces from the rest of the jacket (a hood is ideal) to make a wide circular brim. If you want, you can line the brim with interfacing to make it stiff.

5. Once your hat is completely assembled, arrange the folds into a face shape (pin in place if necessary). Stand the hat over a bottle or upturned vase to hold it steady, then spray the hat with fabric stiffener until the folds hold their shape. The fabric stiffener will stain the leather, but that just adds to the distressed effect. To help the hat retain its shape, stuff the peak with newspaper.

6. If you have any leather left, you can make the hatband tie around the crown and hang down in back, just like the Hat in the film.

Food

Acid Pops: Roll round lollipops (Chupa Chups super sour apple or lemon-lime flavours are ideal) lightly in honey, then coat them in Pop Rocks for a taste that's both sour and explosive!

Aragog's children: Bake sugar cookies using a snowman cookie cutter. Cover the tops with black icing (available at most baking supply shops, or make your own by mixing food colouring into vanilla icing). Place eight silver balls (cake decorations) in a cluster at the smallest end to create the spider's eyes, and use eight short lengths of black liquorice around the edges of the "body" to create the spider's legs. Creepy!

Butterbeer: Make your own by adding butterscotch extract to ginger ale, to taste. Delicious!

Cauldron Cakes: Bake a batch of chocolate cupcakes without using liners. Turn them upside down and hollow out the centres. Inset a thin piece of black liquorice into either side, like a handle, then fill each centre with a piece of candy floss.

Cockroach Clusters: Melt chocolate until smooth, then stir in broken pretzels pieces and dry chow mein noodles. Drop by the tablespoonful on to a sheet of wax paper, then freeze until hardened.

Devilled Dragons' Eggs: Prepared just like Muggle devilled eggs, but with a few drops of green food colouring added to the egg yolk mixture.

Edible wands: Decorate thick liquorice sticks or rod pretzels with coloured frosting and sprinkles.

Sweets: Jelly Belly (www.jellybelly.com) carries Bertie Bott's Beans, whilst other official Harry Potter sweets can be found at some specialty shops, or ordered online from Tiggywig (www.tiggywig.com) and numerous other Web sites.

Wand Skewers: Spear a "wand" (bamboo barbecue skewers, available at most kitchen supply shops) with chunks of fruit, cheese, or vegetables for a healthy magical treat.

Activities and Games

Bertie Bott's Beans Guess: Similar to the Muggle version, except in addition to the regular jelly beans a few packages of Bertie Bott's Beans are added — make sure to count them first! Instead of guessing the number of jelly beans in total, guests must only guess the number of Bertie Bott's Beans contained in the jar.

Catch the Snitch: Make your own Snitch from a small Styrofoam ball and feathers (available at most craft shops) spray-painted gold (sphere) and silver (wings). The first person to find the hidden Snitch at the party wins.

House Trivia: Separate players into House teams. Compile a list of trivia questions from the books, with five House points awarded for correct answers and deducted for wrong answers — the first House to reach two hundred points wins the House Cup!

Mirror of Erised: Buy an inexpensive mirror with a wide frame from a second-hand shop or discount department store. Spray-paint the frame gold, then carefully stencil the inscription from the Mirror of Erised around the edge. Have guests look in the mirror and record what they "see" (their heart's desire) on a piece of parchment, with a prize awarded for the most creative description.

Potions Class: Using the various Potions ingredients, have guests create their own concotions, explaining the name of their potion, its purpose, and the ingredients on a piece of parchment. Read out the descriptions and have guests vote on the most creative and original.

Spot the Spell: Prepare for your OWL in Charms with this game designed to test your knowledge of spells, jinxes, and hexes. In random order, write the names of spells on one side of a sheet of paper, and their functions on the other (for example, "Wingardium Leviosa" — Spell that levitates objects). Give each guest a photocopy and have them match the spells with their functions, with prizes awarded for the most correct answers.

Whirled Words: Like Tom Riddle in the Chamber of Secrets, create jumbles out of some common Harry Potter words (for example, "Prof Fig Hip" is a whirled word for "Hippogriff"). House teams compete to decipher the most whirled words.

Wizard Hat Decorating: Pre-cut and form sheets of black construction paper into cones, using double-sided tape along the seam. Add elastic thread for under the chin. Elementary-age Hogwarts students can use gel pens, stickers, and glitter to design their own hats.

Britta's Quidditch

PLAYERS

One Keeper: The Keeper guards the goals as usual. If a goal is made, the Keeper throws the Quaffle back to the referee who puts the ball back into play.

Two Chasers: The Chasers try to throw the Quaffle through the goals.

One Bludger: The Bludger stands on the sidelines, throwing the Bludger balls at the opposing team.

One Beater: The Beater tries to prevent the Bludger balls from injuring any of their own team.

One Seeker: The Seeker tries to capture the Golden Snitch.

One Referee: Just in case Madam Hooch isn't available!

EQUIPMENT

Bats for the Bludgers can be taken from cheap caveman costume bats, sold at Hallowe'en, or bought from party supply or toy shops. Goalpost hoops can easily be made from lengths of white PVC pipe cut to four-, five-, and six-foot increments. PVC T-joints are glued to the top of each post, then flexible ribbed tubing is shaped into a circle and glued to the joints. (All supplies are available at most hardware shops.)

Foam balls of various sizes painted red and black with fabric paint make an excellent Quaffle and Bludgers, respectively, whilst a Golden Snitch can be made from a golf ball painted gold, with feathers attached.

SCORING

The same as regular Quidditch — ten points for each goal and one hundred and fifty points for capturing the Snitch.

RULES

Regular Quidditch rules apply (Quaffle scoring continues until the Golden Snitch is captured), except without broomsticks, and with the following substitutions for adherence to the Wizard Council Decree of 1419, which states "Quidditch should not be played anywhere near any place where there is the slightest chance that a Muggle might be watching or we'll see how well you can play whilst chained to a dungeon wall."

The Bludgers: Bludger balls are thrown at players by human Bludgers on the sidelines of the pitch. Once hit by a Bludger ball, a player must remain stationary and out of play for a count of five seconds. The Beaters on the pitch are responsible for throwing the Bludger balls back to the Bludger players on the sidelines.

The Golden Snitch: The Golden Snitch is attached to a string on a pole. One person on the sidelines is in charge of the Snitch, pulling it out of play and throwing it back in at random.

THE WORLD WIDE (WIZARDING) WEB:
SELECTED HARRY POTTER WEB SITES

A recent Google search for "Harry Potter" turned up over 8.2 million entries — that's an awful lot of magic! Here's a selection of the best the 'Net has to offer on our favourite bespectacled boy wizard.

Note to Muggles: *The following list does not include Web sites dedicated to the cast members of the Harry Potter films, as the focus of* A Muggle's Guide to the Wizarding World *is on the Harry Potter books.*

News and Information

BBC Newsround's Harry Potter section:
news.bbc.co.uk/cbbcnews/hi/static/find_out/specials/harry_potter
The BBC's Web site has a special section dedicated to the nation's favourite wizard, which includes interviews with the cast and J. K. Rowling, plus loads of pictures, games, quizzes, reader reports, and polls.

Bloomsbury: www.bloomsbury.com/harrypotter
Harry's British publishers have two terrific versions of their site available — one for "Muggles" and one for "witches and wizards." The Muggle version offers information about J. K. Rowling, as well as reviews and awards the series has won. On the magical version, you'll find screensavers, answers to frequently asked questions, and more. You can even send someone a Howler!

DarkMark: www.darkmark.com

The owners of DarkMark.com have gone to great lengths to ensure their site is as family-friendly as possible — even including a parent's guide to Potter. You'll find news and information about the books, as well as editorials, opinion pieces, theories, and rumours as to what might happen in the rest of the series.

Harry Potter Automatic News Aggregator: www.hpana.com

This fantastic site compiles Harry Potter news and information from numerous other resources around the Web into one convenient location. There's also an extensive gallery of sounds, videos, art, and photos, categorised by character and actor.

HP4U.CO.UK: www.hp4u.co.uk

This terrific news site features a number of behind-the-scenes photos and exclusive reports from the sets of the Harry Potter films.

J. K. Rowling: www.jkrowling.com

An imaginative site featuring exclusive content written by J. K. Rowling herself, including never-revealed-before information about the series. Search the author's interactive desktop to find FAQs, rumours, links, and, if you're lucky, several hidden pages featuring sketches, discarded drafts of scenes from early manuscripts, and much, much more!

The Leaky Cauldron: www.the-leaky-cauldron.org

A fan favourite, the Leaky Cauldron features daily news updates, exclusive interviews, and spirited discussion about all things Potter.

Mugglenet: www.mugglenet.com

Mugglenet covers all things Potter, from the serious to the sublime. In addition to the usual news, reviews, movie, and book information, there are essays and editorials ("Cornelius Fudge: Death Eater or Dimwit?"), recipes, trivia, puzzles, a weekly screen caption contest, and much more.

Official Harry Potter Web site: www.harrypotter.com

The official site sports a darker and spookier makeover, in light of the recent *Prisoner of Azkaban* film. Use the Marauder's Map to navigate through various places in Hogwarts and Diagon Alley, each of which features various activities and objects seen in the film.

Quick Quotes: www.quick-quote-quill.org
An incredible archive of interviews with J. K. Rowling, dating back to 1997.

Scholastic Books: www.scholastic.com/harrypotter/home.asp
Harry's American publishers have designed a site with interesting things to do for younger readers, including a Discussion Chamber where little witches and wizards come up with answers to creative questions that put them inside Harry's world.

The Snitch: www.thesnitch.co.uk
Founded in 2001, The Snitch is a great resource for fans, especially for those of the Harry Potter films. News, trailers, photo galleries, cast information, release dates . . . you'll find it all here!

Fan Fiction

Fiction Alley: www.fictionalley.org
You're guaranteed to find something you like in Fiction Alley's extensive archive, featuring stories of all genres, pairings, and ratings. There are also dozens of helpful essays, links, and resources for writers.

Harry Potter Fan Fiction: www.harrypotterfanfiction.com
With thousands of stories to choose from, there's something for everyone here. To assist budding authors, the site also features a glossary of commonly used fan fiction terminology and a writer's school for help with grammar, structure, and characterisation.

Portkey: www.portkey.org
Stories of all genres and ratings for fans of Harry/Hermione, Ron/Luna, Draco/Ginny, and James/Lily. You'll also find fan art, message boards, and a collection of essays and theories related to the Harry Potter series.

Checkmated: www.checkmated.com
This site hosts Ron/Hermione stories of all ratings. It offers a beta reading service and occasionally issues story challenges to authors to keep them on their toes.

Miscellaneous

The Floo Network: www.floo-network.org
Updated weekly, the Floo Network is a wonderful source of trivia, links, and information that features real-time weather forecasts for Hogwarts and Diagon Alley as well a unique "This Week in History" section that relates events in the timelines of the books to the current calendar week. The Floo Network is also the homepage to a portal of outstanding Harry Potter Web sites, including The Harry Potter Lexicon, Quick Quotes, and The Leaky Cauldron.

The Harry Potter Lexicon: www.hp-lexicon.org
A meticulously-compiled treasure trove of information and details about the Harry Potter series, including a bestiary, maps, atlases, timelines, and a handbook of Quidditch, as well as numerous essays providing additional insight into how the wizarding world works.

Harry & The Potters: www.eskimolabs.com/hp/index.htm
This Harry Potter–inspired band features a pair of Harry-lookalike brothers, who rock out to songs such as "The Dark Lord Lament," "Gryffindor Rocks," and "Follow the Spiders." There are even downloadable tracks — "Saving Ginny Weasley" must be heard to be believed.

Virtual Hogwarts: www.hol.org.uk/new/index.php
The next best thing to going to Hogwarts! Students must pass a mock entry exam to attend this simulated wizarding school, where they can collect points for their house, enrol in "classes," and compete for the Quidditch Cup.

What's in a Name?: www.theninemuses.net/hp
This excellent site provides a comprehensive look at the origins and meanings of the names used in the Harry Potter series.

Did you know . . . according to J. K. Rowling's official Web site, the author once visited the Mugglenet chat room using a different name? Rowling said she tried to impart some information and theories about her seventh book — but none of her fellow chatters were interested in what she had to say!

APARECIUM SOURCES!

Some of the information in *A Muggle's Guide to the Wizarding World* came from the following sources:

All Refer Reference & Encyclopedia Resource. Online. reference.allrefer.com

Alnwick Castle. Online. www.alnwickcastle.com

"Animal Guides," *PathWalkers.net*. Online. www.pathwalkers.net/animal-guides/index.html

"Animal Symbolism," *Princeton Online*. Online. www.princetonol.com/groups/iad/Files/animals.htm

Association of British Counties. Online. www.abcounties.co.uk

Astro Chat with June. Online. astrochat-with-june.com/signs.htm

"Australia House," *Australian High Commission UK*. Online. www.australia.org.uk

Baby Name Network. Online. www.babynamenetwork.com

Behind the Name. Online. www.behindthename.com

Bethune, Brian. "The Rowling Connection: How a young Toronto girl's story touched an author's heart." *Maclean's*. November 2000.

"Black Park," *Visit Buckinghamshire*. Online. www.visitbuckinghamshire.org

"The Borgias," *Crime Library*. Online. www.crimelibrary.com

British Tourist Authority. Online. www.visitbritain.com

Burdick Harmon, Melissa. "J. K. Rowling: The Real-Life Wizard Behind Harry Potter." *Biography*. September 2003.

Burdick Harmon, Melissa. "The Magic of England: Following in Harry Potter's Footsteps." *Biography*. September 2003.

Carter, Larry. "Pagan Magick & the Rowan Tree," *Rowan*. Online. www.angelfire.com/ks/larrycarter/Rowan/Tree.html

Celtic Tree Lore. Online. www.dutchie.org/Tracy/tree.html

Columbus, Chris. *AOL Chat*. Online. November 2002.

"The Constellations," *CosmoBrain Astronomy and Astrophysics*. Online. www.cosmobrain.com

DarkMark. Online. www.darkmark.com

Dragons of the British Isles. Online. www.wyrm.org.uk/ukdracs/index.html

"Dream Dictionary," *DreamMoods*. Online. www.dreammoods.com

Early British Kingdoms. Online. www.earlybritishkingdoms.com

Encyclopedia Mythica. Online. www.pantheon.org

"Fairy Lore," *eFairies*. Online. www.efairies.com/fairy_lore.htm

"Fictional cash fools Potter fans." *BBC News*. Online. news.bbc.co.uk. April 2004.

"Fort William and Area," *Internet Guide to Scotland*. Online. www.scotland-inverness.co.uk/fortwill.htm

Fraser, Lindsay. "Harry Potter - Harry and me," *The Scotsman*. news.scotsman.com/. November 2002.

Fraser, Stephen. "Harry Potter and the fields of fire," *The Scotsman*. Online. news.scotsman.com/movies.cfm?id=228402003. February 2003.

Freesearch British English Dictionary. Online. www.freesearch.co.uk/dictionary

"Gloucester Cathedral Harry Potter," *Gloucester Cathedral*. Online. www.gloucestercathedral.uk.com

"Gloucester's Harry Potter trail in detail," *BBC*. Online. bbc.co.uk.

Gods, Heroes, and Myth. Online. www.gods-heros-myth.com

Greek Mythology Today. Online. mythman.com

"Hand of Glory," *House Shadow Drake*. Online. www.shadowdrake.com/folklore/hand.html

"Harry Potter and the Chamber of Secrets," *Internet Movie Database*. Online. www.imdb.com/title/tt0295297/

"Harry Potter and the Chamber of Secrets," *Movie Mistakes*. Online. www.moviemistakes.com/film2434

"Harry Potter and the Philosopher's Stone," *Movie Mistakes*. Online. www.moviemistakes.com/film1654

"Harry Potter and the Philosopher's Stone," *The Worldwide Guide to Movie Locations*. Online. www.movie-locations.com/movies/h/harry_potter1.html.

"Harry Potter and the Sorcerer's Stone," *Internet Movie Database*. Online. www.imdb.com/title/tt0241527/

"Harry Potter ballet?" *CBBC Newsround*. Online.

"Harry Potter Books from Bloomsbury," *Bloomsbury.com*. Online. www.bloomsbury.com/harrypotter/muggles_index.html

"Harry Potter in Glencoe," *Glencoe Scotland*. Online. www.glencoescotland.com

"Harry Potter in Lochaber," *Visit Scotland*. Online. www.visitscotland.com

"Harry Potter magic at Lacock," *BBC*. Online. bbc.co.uk. August 2003.

Harry Potter Lexicon. Online. www.hp-lexicon.org

Harry Potter News Review More. Online. www.kewlplaces.net/movienews

"Harry Potter Tours," *British Tours.* Online.
www.britishtours.com/harry_potter.html

"Harry Potter: The Scottish Dimension," *Visit Scotland.* Online. www.visitscot-land.com

"Harry's Privet Drive house fails to sell," CBBC *Newsround.* Online.
news.bbc.co.uk/cbbcnews/. July 2003.

Hartland, Edwin Sidney. "English Faerie and other Folk Tales," *Internet Sacred Text Archive.* Online. www.sacred-texts.com/neu/eng/efft

HPANA *(Harry Potter Automatic News Aggregator).* Online. www.hpana.com

"Inquisition," *Catholic Encyclopedia.* Online.
www.newadvent.org/cathen/08026a.htm

"The Islands of St Kilda," *Film Hebrides.* Online.
www.filmhebrides.com/islands/kilda

"J Spray Rowling," *Daily Record.* Online. www.dailyrecord.co.uk/. September 2003.

J. K. Rowling. Online. www.jkrowling.com

"J. K. Rowling's notebook," *The Crusaders.* Online. www.crusaders.no/~afhp/note-book

Jerome, Helen M. "Welcome Back, Potter," *Book Magazine.* Online. www.book-magazine.com/may2000/potter.shtml. May/June 2000. Kennedy, Maev. "New broom for Harry Potter's old home," *Guardian Unlimited Film.* Online. film.guardian.co.uk/harrypotter. July 2003.

Kloves, Steven (writer) and Columbus, Chris (director). *Harry Potter and the Sorcerer's Stone.* Motion picture. Warner Brothers. November 2001.

Kloves, Steven (writer) and Columbus, Chris (director). *Harry Potter and the Chamber of Secrets.* Motion picture. Warner Brothers. November 2002.

Kloves, Steven (writer) and Cuarón, Alfonso (director). *Harry Potter and the Prisoner of Azkaban.* Motion picture. Warner Brothers. June 2004.

"Lacock Abbey, Fox Talbot Museum & Village," *The National Trust.* Online.
www.nationaltrust.co.uk

Last Name Meanings. Online. www.last-names.net

Latin Vocabulary to Catullus and Cicero. Online.
www.personal.umich.edu/~markusdd/301Voc.htm

London Underground. Online. tube.tfl.gov.uk

London Zoo. Online. www.londonzoo.co.uk

"Magikal Trees and Flowers," *Mystickblue*. Online.
   mystickblue.homestead.com/MagikalTreesandFlowers.html

"May Day / Maifest / Walpurgis," *German Customs, Traditions, Origins of Holidays*.
   Online. www.serve.com/shea/germusa/walpurgi.htm

"Mini," *GB Classic Cars*. Online. www.gbclassiccars.co.uk/mini.html

Mugglenet. Online. www.mugglenet.com

"Mugwump," *LoveToKnow Encyclopedia*. Online.
   19.1911encyclopedia.org/M/MU/MUGWUMP.htm

Multimap. Online. www.multimap.com

Mysterious Britain. Online. www.mysteriousbritain.co.uk

Mzimba, Lizo. "JK Rowling Talks About Book Four," *CBBC Newsround*. Online.
   news.bbc.co.uk/cbbcnews/. July 2000.

Naysmith, Stephen. "VisitScotland seek ways to use Harry Potter's magic," *The
   Herald*. Online. www.theherald.co.uk. August 2003.

"The Origins of the Runes," *Oswald the Runemaker*. Online.
   www.runemaker.com/histhome.htm

Paralumun New Age Women's Village. Online. www.paralumun.com

"Potts Of Magic As Fan Buys Harry Book For £35,000," *Daily Record*. Online.
   www.dailyrecord.co.uk/. November 2003.

Prisoner of Azkaban Movie News Site. Online. www.zanzaro.com/azkaban

Probert Encylopaedia of Mythology. Online.
   www.probertencyclopaedia.com/mythology.htm

Quick Quotes. Online. www.quick-quote-quill.org

Quinion, Michael. "Weird Words: Dumbledore," *World Wide Words*. Online.
   www.quinion.com/words/weirdwords/ww-dum1.htm

Raincoast Books. Online. www.raincoast.com/harrypotter/index.html

"Revelations 9:11," *The Bible Gateway*. Online. bible.gospelcom.net

Robinson, David. "Potter's magical effect on UK book sales," *The Scotsman*.
   news.scotsman.com/archive.cfm?id=19292004

Rowling, J. K. (as Kenilworthy Whisp). *Quidditch through the Ages*. Vancouver:
   Raincoast Books, 2001.

Rowling, J. K. (as Newt Scamander). *Fantastic Beasts & Where To Find Them*.
   Vancouver: Raincoast Books, 2001.

Rowling, J. K. *AOL Chat*. Online. October 2000.

Rowling, J. K. *Barnes & Noble Chat*. Online. October 2000.

Rowling, J. K. *Comic Relief Chat*. Online.

www.scholastic.com/harrypotter/author/transcript3.htm. March 2001.

Rowling, J. K. *Harry Potter and Me*. BBC1 TV special. December 2001.

Rowling, J. K. *Harry Potter and the Chamber of Secrets*. Vancouver: Raincoast Books, 1998.

Rowling, J. K. *Harry Potter and the Goblet of Fire*. Vancouver: Raincoast Books, 2000.

Rowling, J. K. *Harry Potter and the Order of the Phoenix*. London: Bloomsbury Publishing Plc, 2003.

Rowling, J. K. *Harry Potter and the Order of the Phoenix*. New York: Scholastic Books, 2003.

Rowling, J. K. *Harry Potter and the Philosopher's Stone*. Vancouver: Raincoast Books, 1997.

Rowling, J. K. *Harry Potter and the Prisoner of Azkaban*. Vancouver: Raincoast Books, 1999.

Rowling, J. K. *Interview with Evan Soloman on CBC*. July 2000.

Rowling, J. K. *Interview with Jeremy Paxman on Newsnight*. June 2003.

Rowling, J. K. *Interview with Stephen Fry at Royal Albert Hall*. June 2003.

Rowling, J. K. Online. www.jkrowling.com

Rowling, J. K. *National Press Club Interview*. www.quick-quote-quill.org/articles/1999/1099-pressclubtransc.html. October 1999.

Rowling, J. K. *Scholastic.com Chat (number 1)*. Online. www.scholastic.com/harrypotter/author/transcript1.htm. February 2000.

Rowling, J. K. *Scholastic.com Chat (number 2)*. Online. www.scholastic.com/harrypotter/author/transcript2.htm. October 2000.

Rowling, J. K. *World Book Day Chat*. Online. March 2004.

Rowling, J. K. *Yahooligans! Chat*. Online. October 2000.

Scholastic Books. Online. www.scholastic.com/harrypotter

Seaton, Matt. "Interview with J. K. Rowling," *Guardian Unlimited Film*. Online. film.guardian.co.uk/harrypotter. April 2001.

Snape Homepage. Online. www.snapevillage.org.uk

Sphinx's Page. Online. www.nmia.com/~sphinx

The Leaky Cauldron. Online. www.the-leaky-cauldron.org

The Mystica and Mythical-Folk. Online. www.themystica.com

The Realm of the Fae. Online. thefae.freeservers.com/forestfaeries.html

Todd, Ben. "Harry It Up, Euan," *Sunday Mirror*. Online. www.sundaymirror.co.uk. August 2003.

Topham, Gwyn. "Harry Potter is wizard for tourism," *Guardian Unlimited Film.* Online. film.guardian.co.uk/harrypotter. April 2003.

Tour UK. Online. www.touruk.co.uk

Undiscovered Scotland. Online. www.undiscoveredscotland.co.uk

University of Oxford. Online. www.ox.ac.uk

"Viktor Krum Looming as Bulgaria's Tourism Face," *Sofia News Agency.* Online. www.novinite.com/view_news.php?id=32055. March 2004.

Welsh Names and Meanings. Online. www.amlwchdata.co.uk/welsh_surnames.htm

What's In A Name? Online. www.theninemuses.net

White Dragon. Online. www.whitedragon.org.uk

"William Burke and William Hare," *Crime Library.* Online. www.crimelibrary.com

"Winter 2002," *Edinburgh Restaurant Index.* Online. www.edinburghrestaurant-index.co.uk

"Witchcraft," *Catholic Encyclopedia.* Online. www.newadvent.org/cathen/15674a.htm

Wikipedia. Online. en.wikipedia.org

Wizard News. Online. www.wizardnews.com/story.20031124.html

"XV World Cup — USA '94," *World Cup History Page.* Online. www.worldcup.isn.pl/en/cups/1994.htm

APARECIUM ENDNOTES!

While not directly mentioned in the Harry Potter series, the following information has been confirmed by J. K. Rowling through a variety of other sources.

The Grangers

J. K. Rowling verified Hermione's middle name and birthday in two separate online chats.

The Weasleys

Rowling verified Ron's middle name in an online chat for World Book Day in March 2004, and his birthday in an online chat in October 2000.

Rowling confirmed Arthur Weasley is one of three brothers on her Web site.

Rowling states on her official Web site that Mrs. Weasley's maiden name is Prewett and that some of her family members were killed by Death Eaters.

Rowling verified Bill Weasley's age in an online chat for World Book Day in March 2004.

Rowling verified Charlie's age in an online chat for World Book Day in March 2004; however, this doesn't seem to be consistent with the series — if Charlie were two years older than Percy, he would have still been at Hogwarts during Ron's first year, when Percy was fifteen.

Rowling states on her official Web site that Fred and George Weasley's birthday is April Fool's Day.

Rowling confirms Ginny's full name on her official Web site, and verified her middle name in an online chat for World Book Day in March 2004. She also confirms on her Web site that Ginny is the first girl born into the Weasley clan in several generations.

The Blacks

Rowling confirms Sirius Black's eye colour on her official Web site.

Hogwarts Staff

In an online chat with Scholastic Books in October 2000, Rowling said that Dumbledore was 150 years old.

Rowling verified that Flitwick was the head of Ravenclaw in an online chat with Barnes & Noble in October 2000.

Rowling verified Lupin's middle name and heritage in an online chat for World Book Day in March 2004.

In an online chat with Scholastic Books in October 2000, Rowling said McGonagall was seventy years old.

Rowling verified Trelawney's middle name in an online chat for World Book Day in March 2004.

Houses

Rowling confirms prefects can deduct points on her official Web site.

Rowling verified Hagrid and Lily were Gryffindors in online chats with Barnes & Noble and Scholastic Books respectively, in October 2000. She confirmed Sirius, Lupin, and James were all Gryffindors in an online chat for World Book Day in March 2004 (though Pettigrew's house was not confirmed, it is assumed it was Gryffindor as he was such close friends with the others).

Death Eaters

Rowling states on her Web site that Theodore Nott is an elderly widower with a stooped posture.

Pets

Rowling confirms Crookshanks is half-Kneazle on her Web site.

INDEX